BATWOMAN
elegy
THE DELUXE EDITION

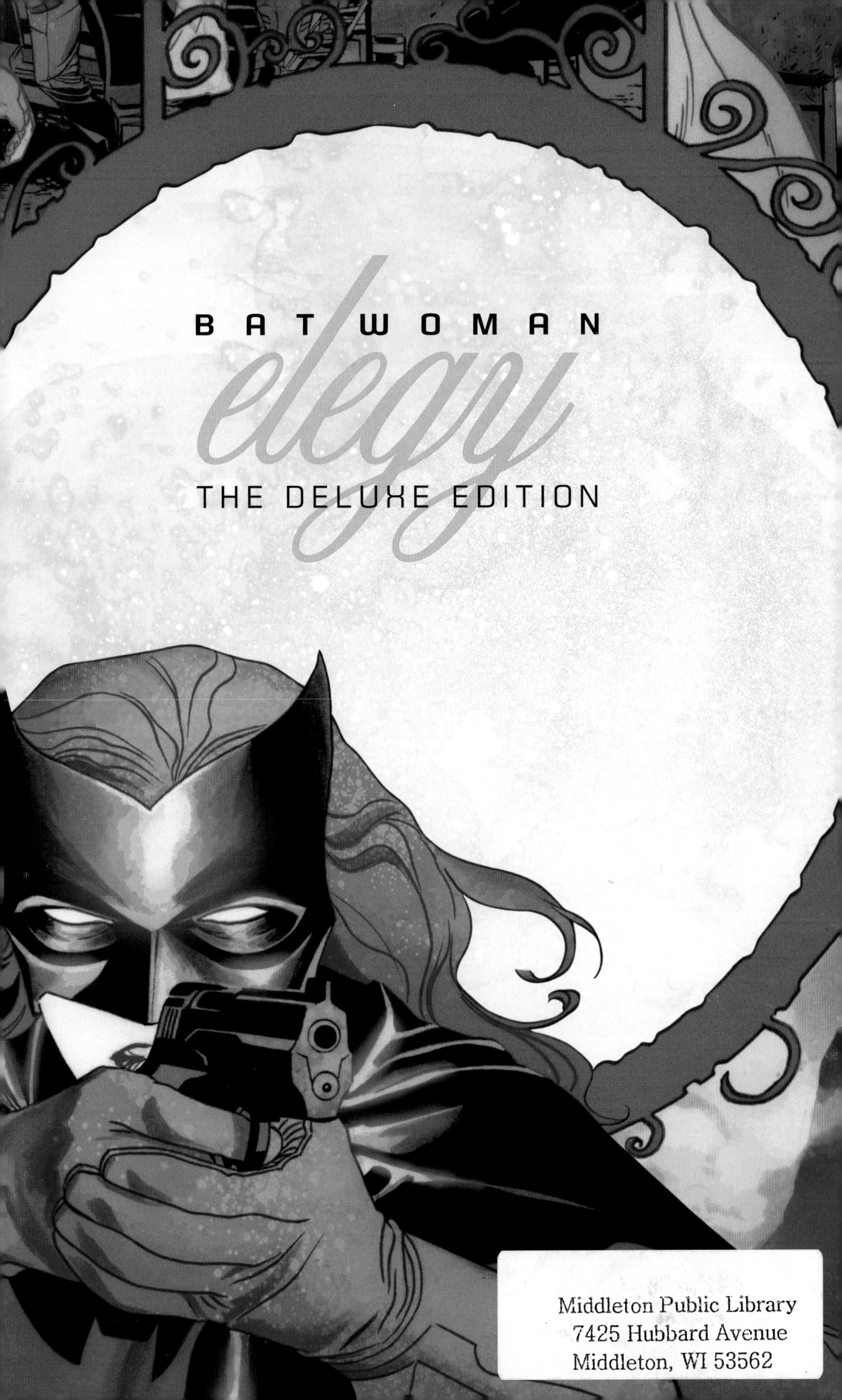

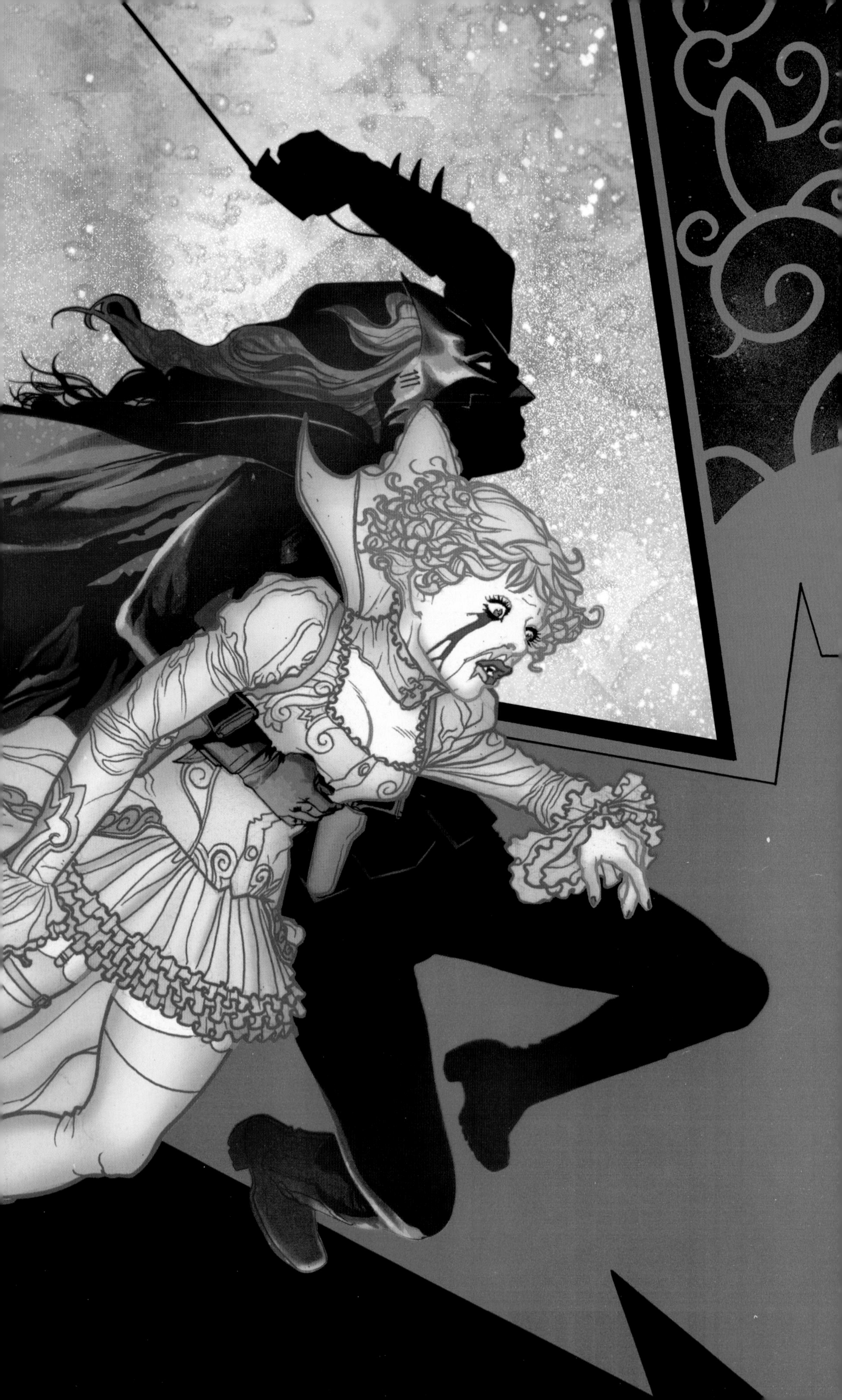

BATWOMAN

elegy

THE DELUXE EDITION

GREG RUCKA WRITER

J.H WILLIAMS III ARTIST

DAVE STEWART COLORIST

TODD KLEIN LETTERS

BATMAN CREATED BY **BOB KANE**

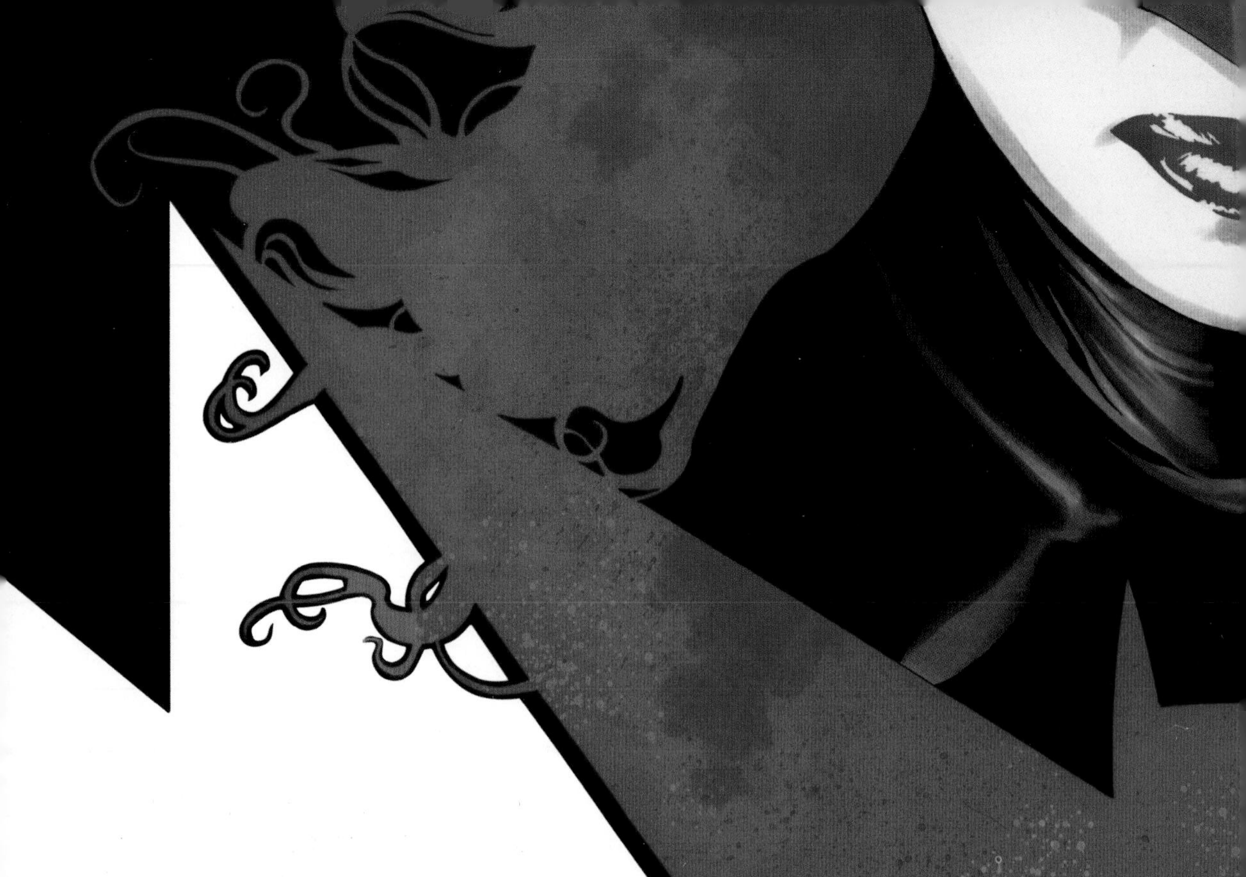

MICHAEL SIGLAIN EDITOR-ORIGINAL SERIES
HARVEY RICHARDS ASSISTANT EDITOR-ORIGINAL SERIES
BOB HARRAS GROUP EDITOR-COLLECTED EDITIONS
ANTON KAWASAKI EDITOR
ROBBIN BROSTERMAN DESIGN DIRECTOR-BOOKS

DC COMICS
DIANE NELSON PRESIDENT
DAN DIDIO AND **JIM LEE** CO-PUBLISHERS
GEOFF JOHNS CHIEF CREATIVE OFFICER
PATRICK CALDON EVP-FINANCE AND ADMINISTRATION
JOHN ROOD EVP-SALES, MARKETING AND BUSINESS DEVELOPMENT
AMY GENKINS SVP-BUSINESS AND LEGAL AFFAIRS
STEVE ROTTERDAM SVP-SALES AND MARKETING
JOHN CUNNINGHAM VP-MARKETING
TERRI CUNNINGHAM VP-MANAGING EDITOR
ALISON GILL VP-MANUFACTURING
DAVID HYDE VP-PUBLICITY
SUE POHJA VP-BOOK TRADE SALES
ALYSSE SOLL VP-ADVERTISING AND CUSTOM PUBLISHING
BOB WAYNE VP-SALES
MARK CHIARELLO ART DIRECTOR

Cover by J.H. Williams III
Publication design by Robbie Biederman

BATWOMAN: ELEGY
THE DELUXE EDITION

DC Comics, 1700 Broadway, New York, NY 10019
A Warner Bros. Entertainment Company
Printed by RR Donnelley, Salem, VA, USA. 6/2/10.
First Printing. ISBN: 978-1-4012-2692-3

SUSTAINABLE FORESTRY INITIATIVE
Certified Fiber Sourcing
www.sfiprogram.org
Fiber used in this product line meets the sourcing requirements of the SFI program.
www.sfiprogram.org NFS-SPICOC-C0001801

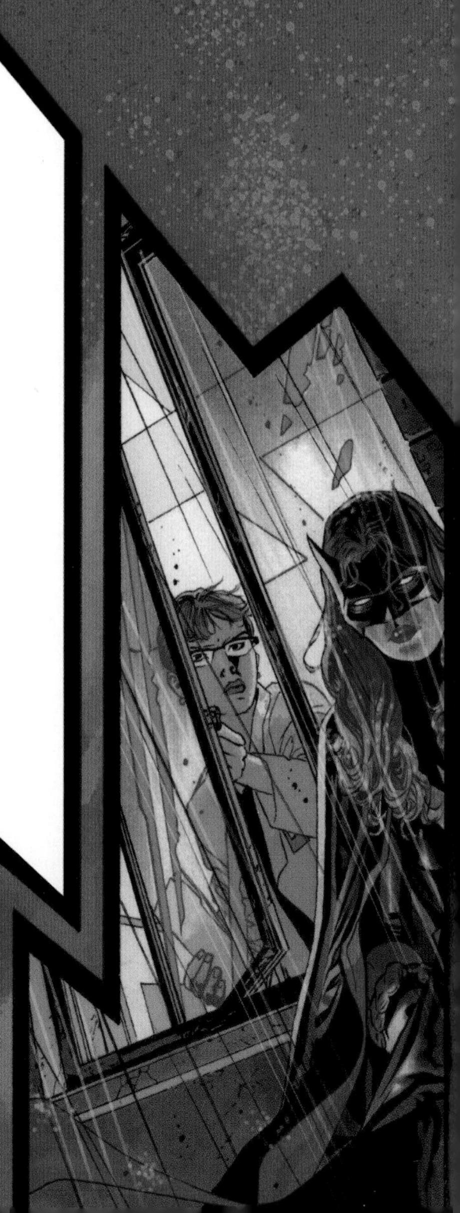

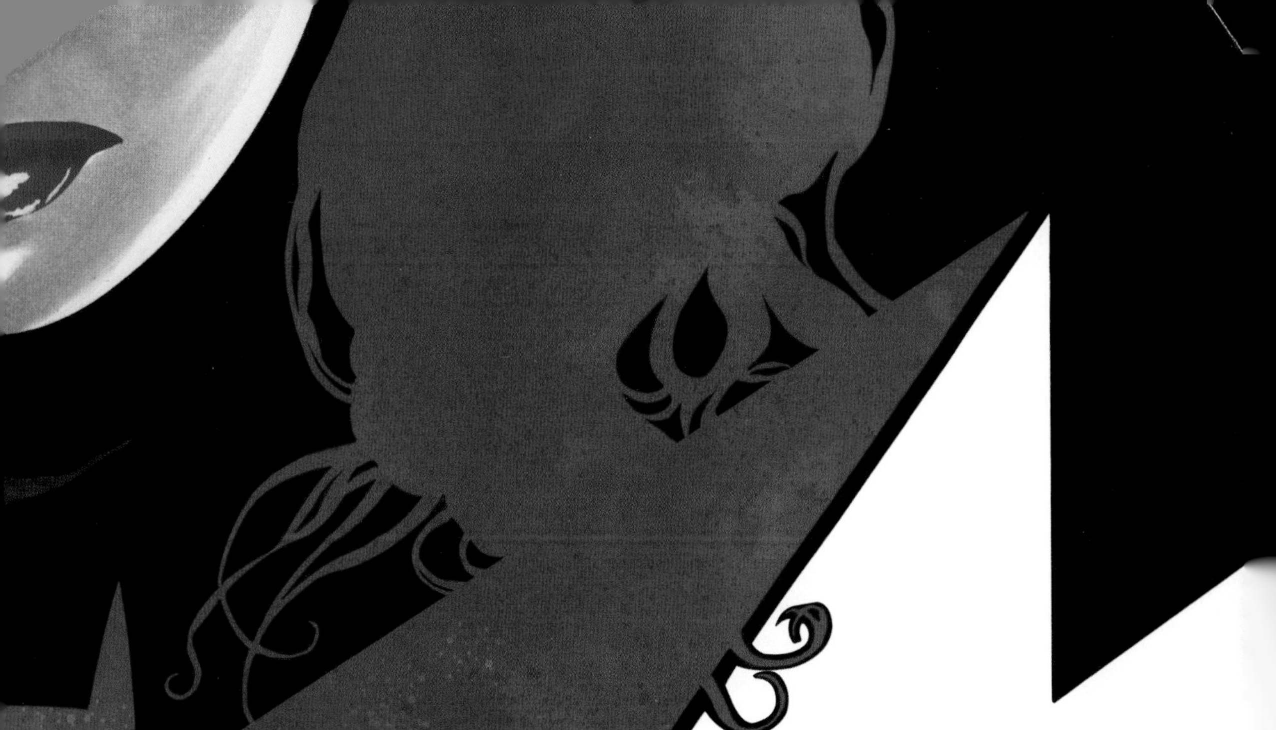

Introduction

BY RACHEL **MADDOW**

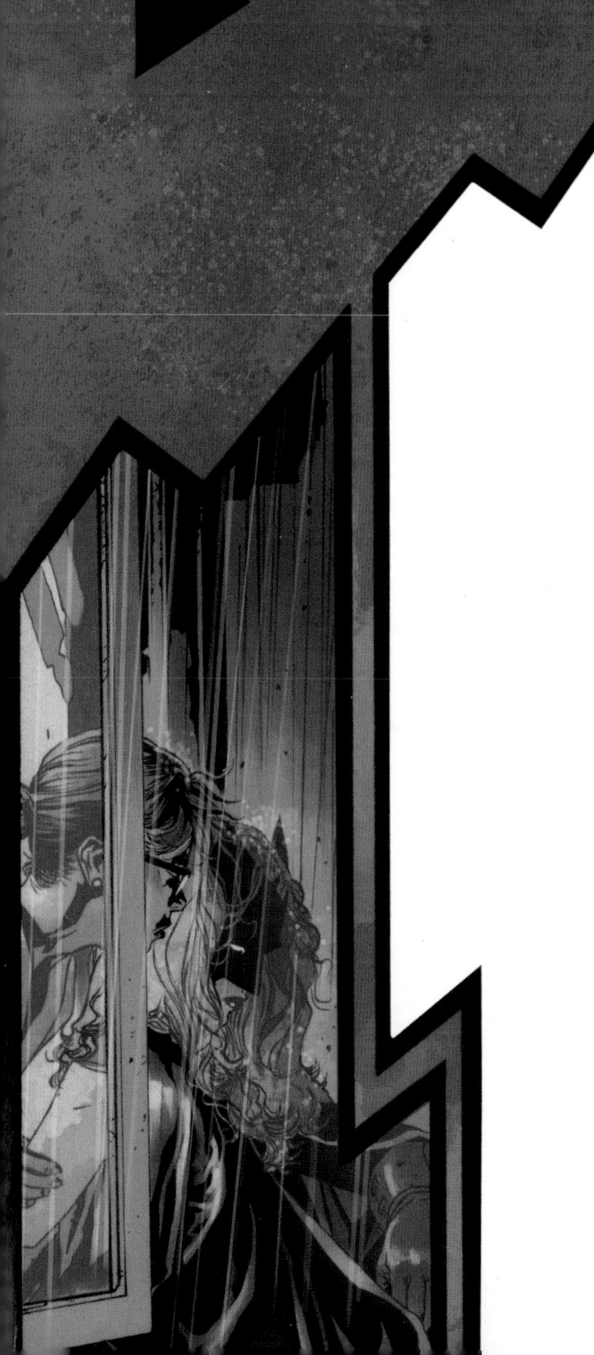

I confess to once giving a copy of Greg Rucka's *Queen and Country: Operation Broken Ground* to a member of the Senate Intelligence Committee, because I thought it might be helpful to the Senator. It's not as crazy as it sounds: get to know Rucka's character Tara Chase and then Google the real modern American spook Dusty Foggo, and see which one you find more edifying.

In Batwoman, Katherine Rebecca Kane is another character written by Rucka that you can't quite believe doesn't exist in the real world. Her recitation of West Point's honor code — "A cadet shall not lie, cheat or steal, nor suffer others to do so" — rings in my ears like Lieutenant Dan Choi reciting the same code to me on television in March 2009, proving that the "Don't Ask, Don't Tell" policy forced him to lie as a condition of his military service.

In Kate Kane's quiet but life-defining drive to serve, there's the veterans of my generation who in the absence of a draft but through nine straight years of war, have done three, four, five combat tours, to come home to a nation that doesn't always quite remember we're at war.

"When you act wrongly, you have to answer for it. Without hiding, without complaint.... That's integrity, and it is the foundation of honor." That's the moral spine on which Kate Kane's battered frame is hung. She is brave and surly and hurt and strong and always on the Batman rule. For all the brilliant literary allusion, mystery, and trademark Rucka attention to detail, what you won't be able to shake when you're done here is that damn compelling lead character.

Well, maybe that and the art.

In a single, wordless panel showing Kate's father's reaction after she tells him why she's been separated from the Army, artist J.H. Williams III captures both a turning point between characters, and a nation's point of decision. It actually feels, right now, in America, the way Colonel Kane looks in that panel, hurt by the plain open ask of his daughter's green eyes.

Yes, cyanogen chloride is a real thing. No, "Southern Misunderstandistan" is not a real place, but you can bet I'll steal it for commenting on our wars, if I haven't done so already by the time you read this. Yes, some of the baddies in the true religion of crime are super genderqueer and yes, guns mix with magic. Get over it. It's all true, it's all gutwrenching, and you love it.

I won't lie to you: I would read anything Greg Rucka wrote. I would read Greg Rucka's grocery lists. I would read Greg Rucka's discarded edits. I would read a Greg Rucka forty-volume soft-hearted navel-gazer about characters I couldn't care less about, if he was capable of writing such a thing, and if he did I'd probably read it out loud to my friends and exclaim and swear about how he made me care.

Batwoman's in good hands here. You'll see.

Rachel Maddow
March, 2010

Rachel Maddow is a political commentator and television host. She has been the anchorwoman of several syndicated talk radio programs and is currently the host of the nightly television program The Rachel Maddow Show on MSNBC.

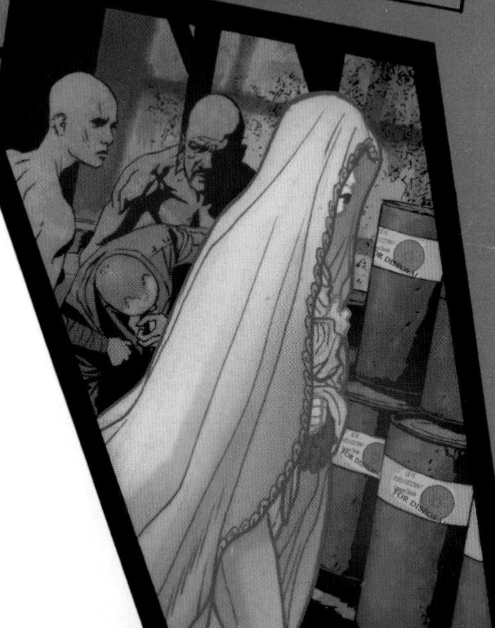

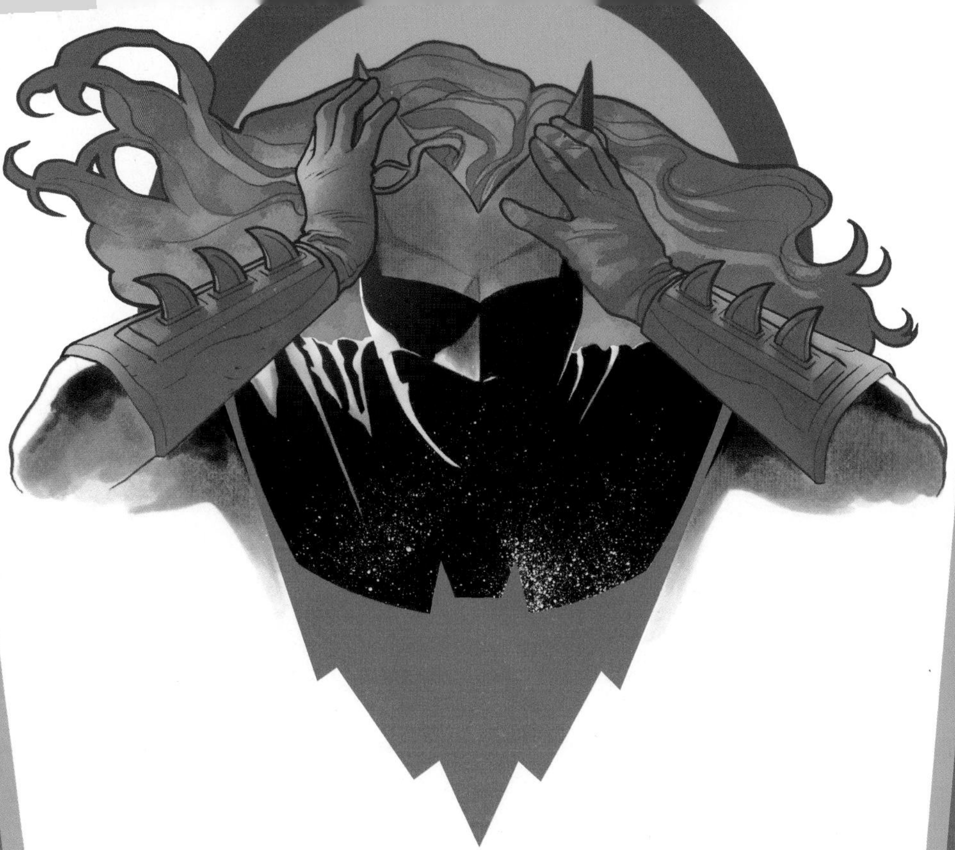

There was a year, not so very long past, where the world turned without the eyes of its three greatest heroes looking upon it, when Batman, Superman, and Wonder Woman stepped back from their roles.

It was in Gotham City, then, that the symbol of the red bat was first truly noted, though some have speculated that both it and its wearer had been there for quite some time already, watching and waiting. But it was not until the Dark Knight's absence that this new presence became truly known.

This new hero was, in many ways, a reflection of the Batman — the same ruthless pursuit of justice; the same savage need to defend the innocent. But this was not some Robin all-grown-up, nor was it some boy raised to fit boots he had no hope of being able to fill.

This was a woman, the Batwoman, and while there was, indeed, a reflection, it was clear to all who saw her that this was something different. This was not another devotee of the Dark Knight. This woman went her own way.

At the end of this year, the Batwoman fell, captured by a cult devoted to evil, a cult that saw in her the fulfillment of its dark destiny. It was the hand of the cult's leader, the High Madame of the Religion of Crime, that drove a knife into the heart of Batwoman.

She should have died. She nearly did. Instead, it was the High Madame who fell, and the Batwoman who survived. But a wound to the heart is not one easily healed.

It has been a long road back, and now the Batwoman hears whispers in the night: a new High Madame is coming to Gotham.

The Batwoman is looking forward to meeting her....

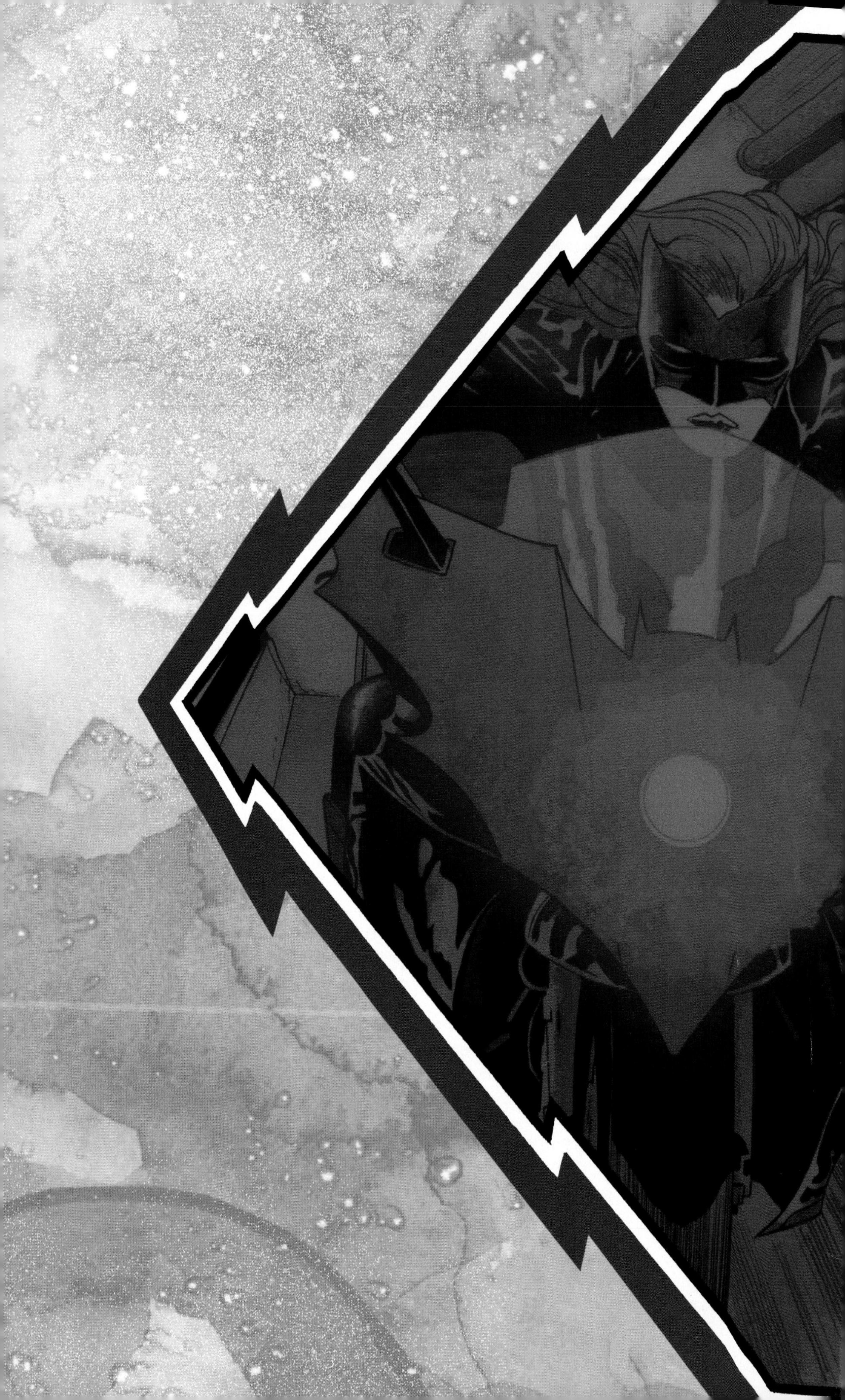

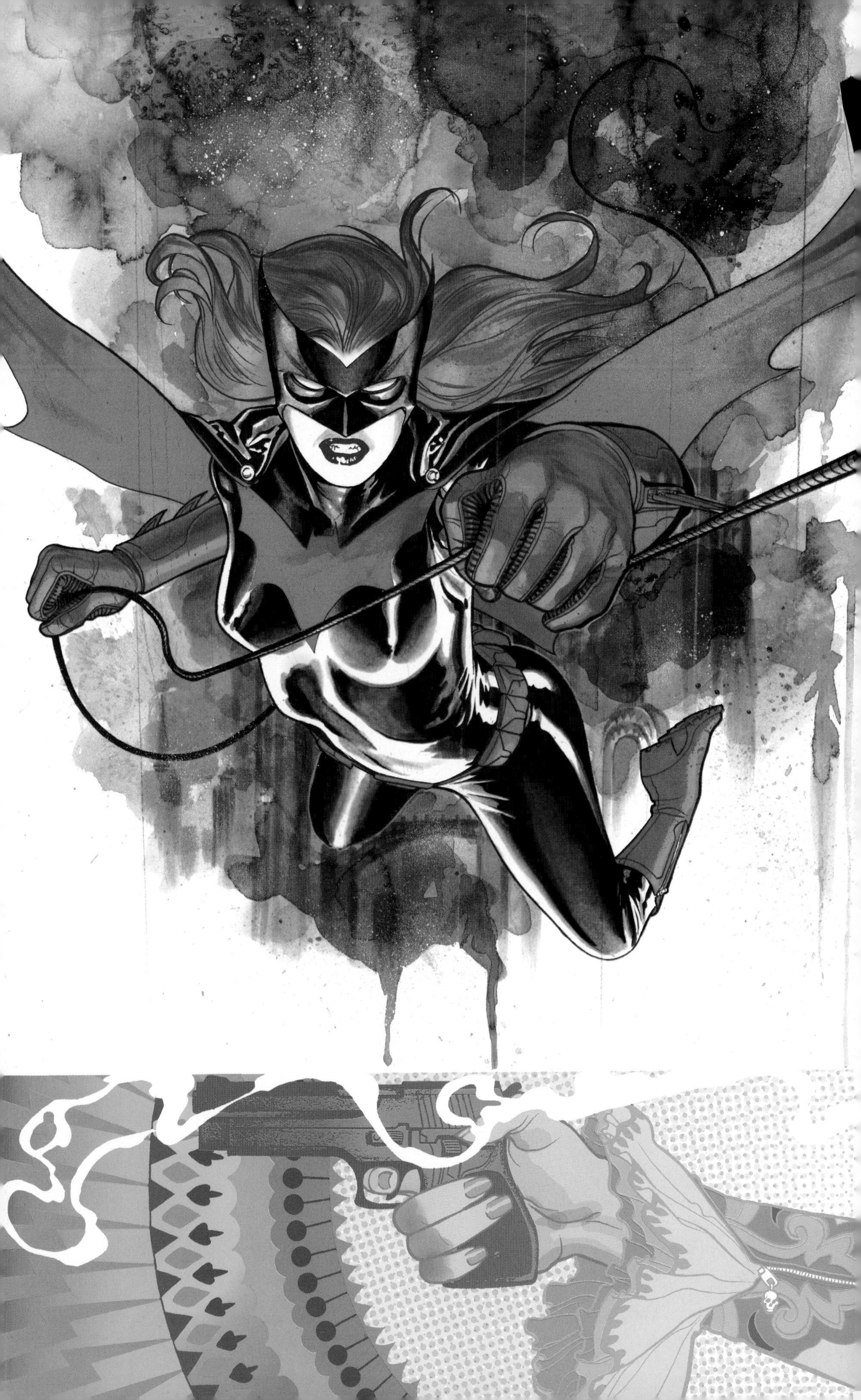

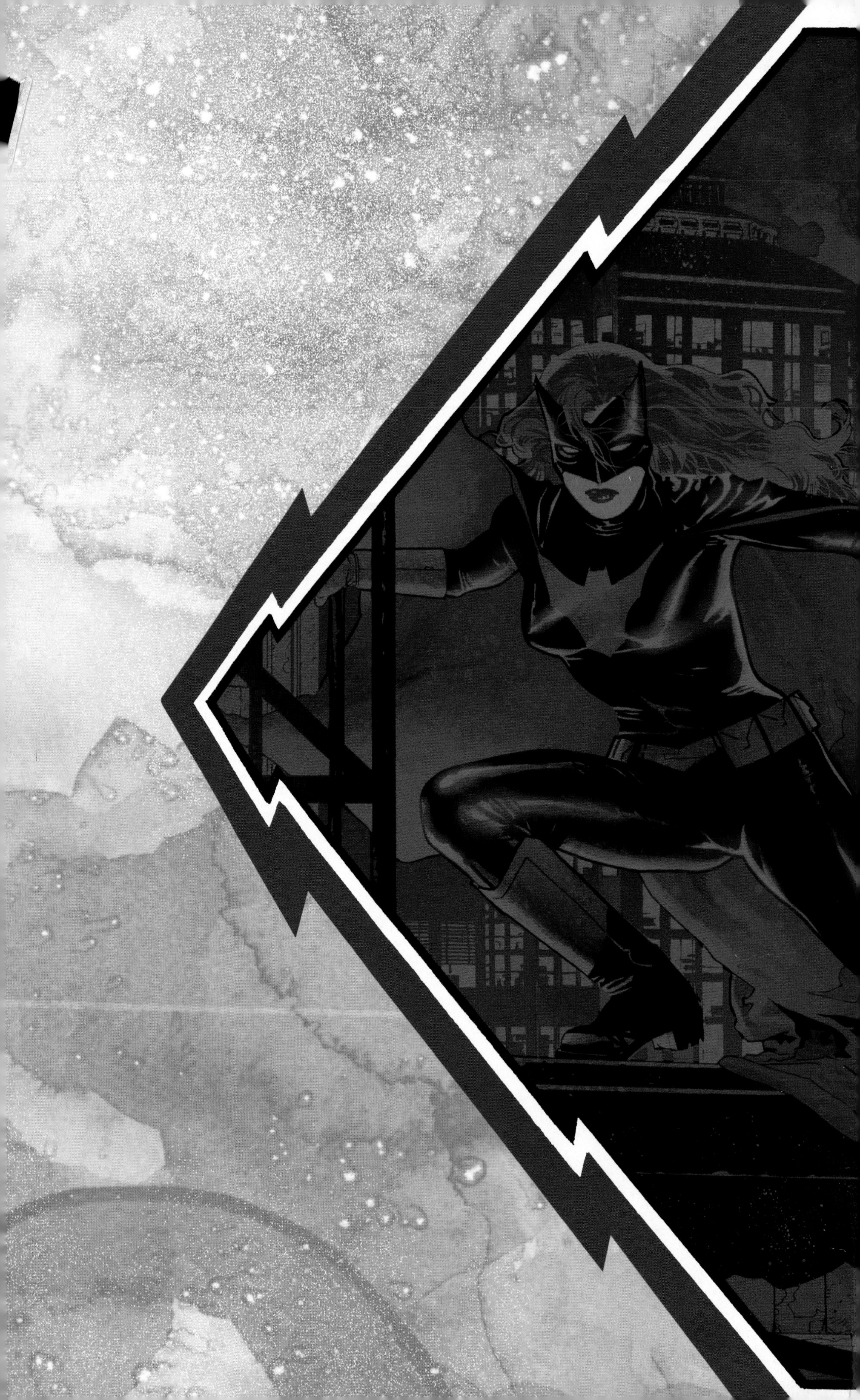

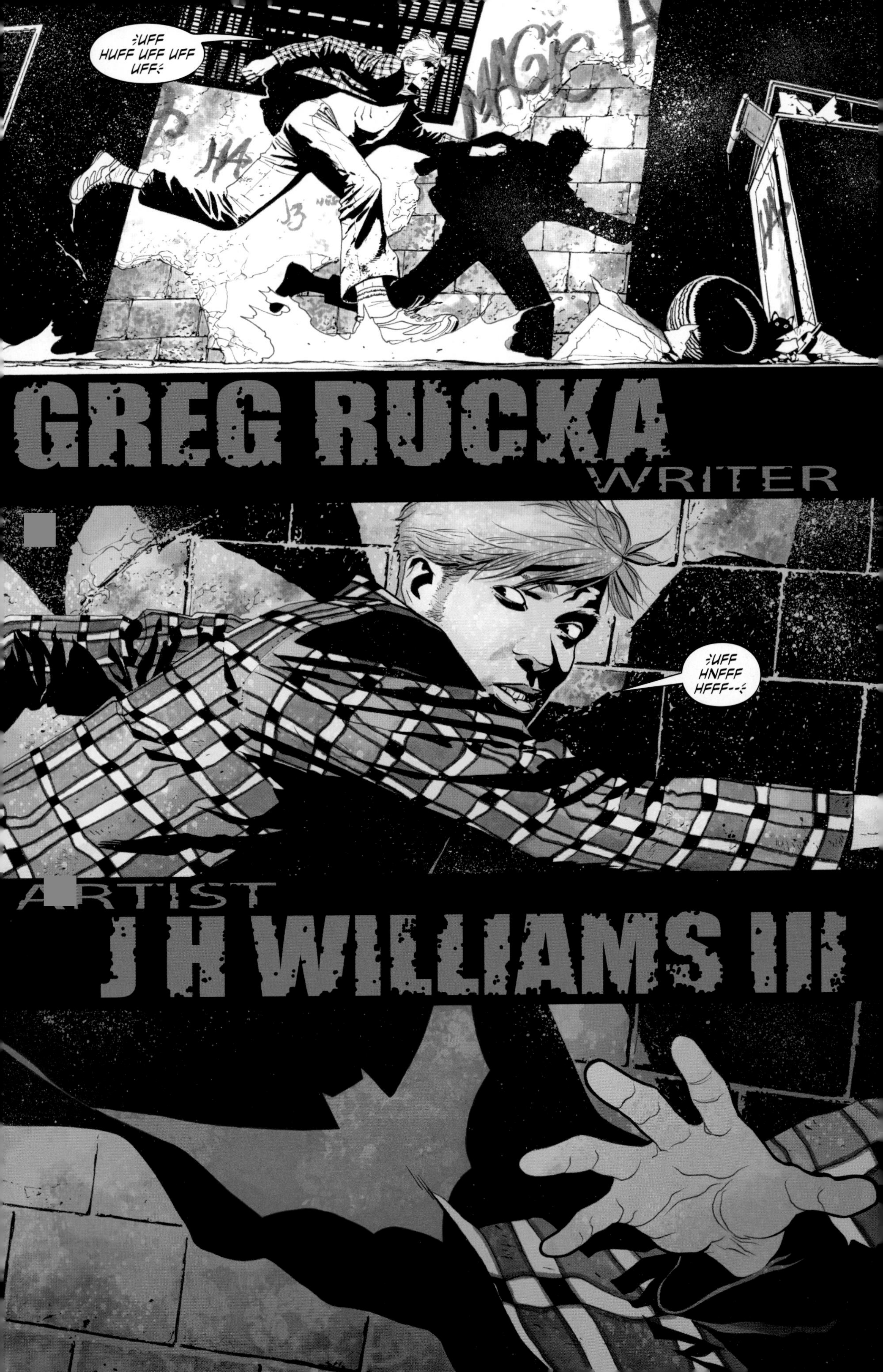
UFF HUFF UFF UFF UFF
GREG RUCKA
WRITER
UFF HNFFF HFFF--
ARTIST
J H WILLIAMS III

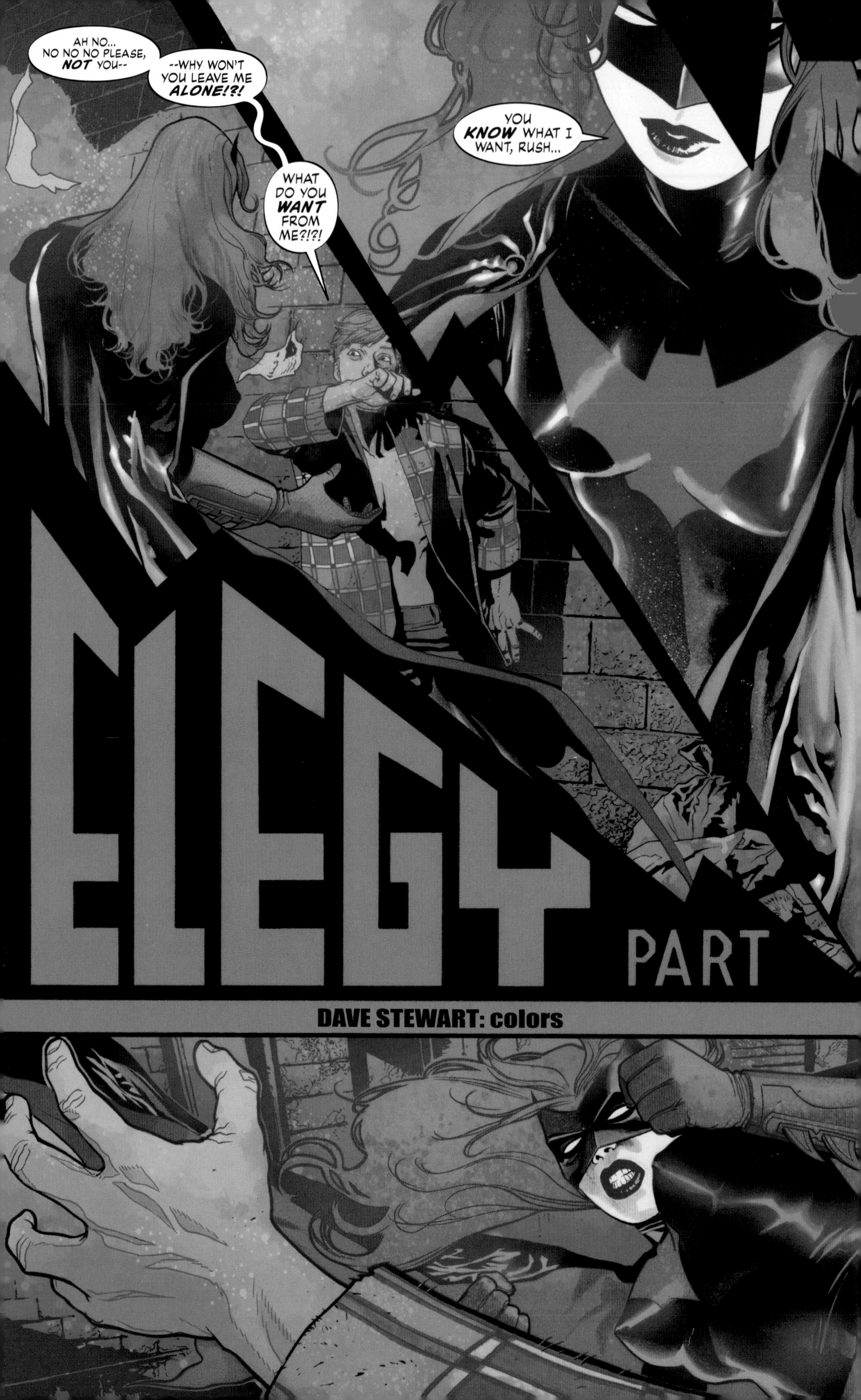

AH NO... NO NO NO PLEASE, NOT YOU--
--WHY WON'T YOU LEAVE ME ALONE!?!
WHAT DO YOU WANT FROM ME?!?!
YOU KNOW WHAT I WANT, RUSH...
ELEGY PART
DAVE STEWART: colors

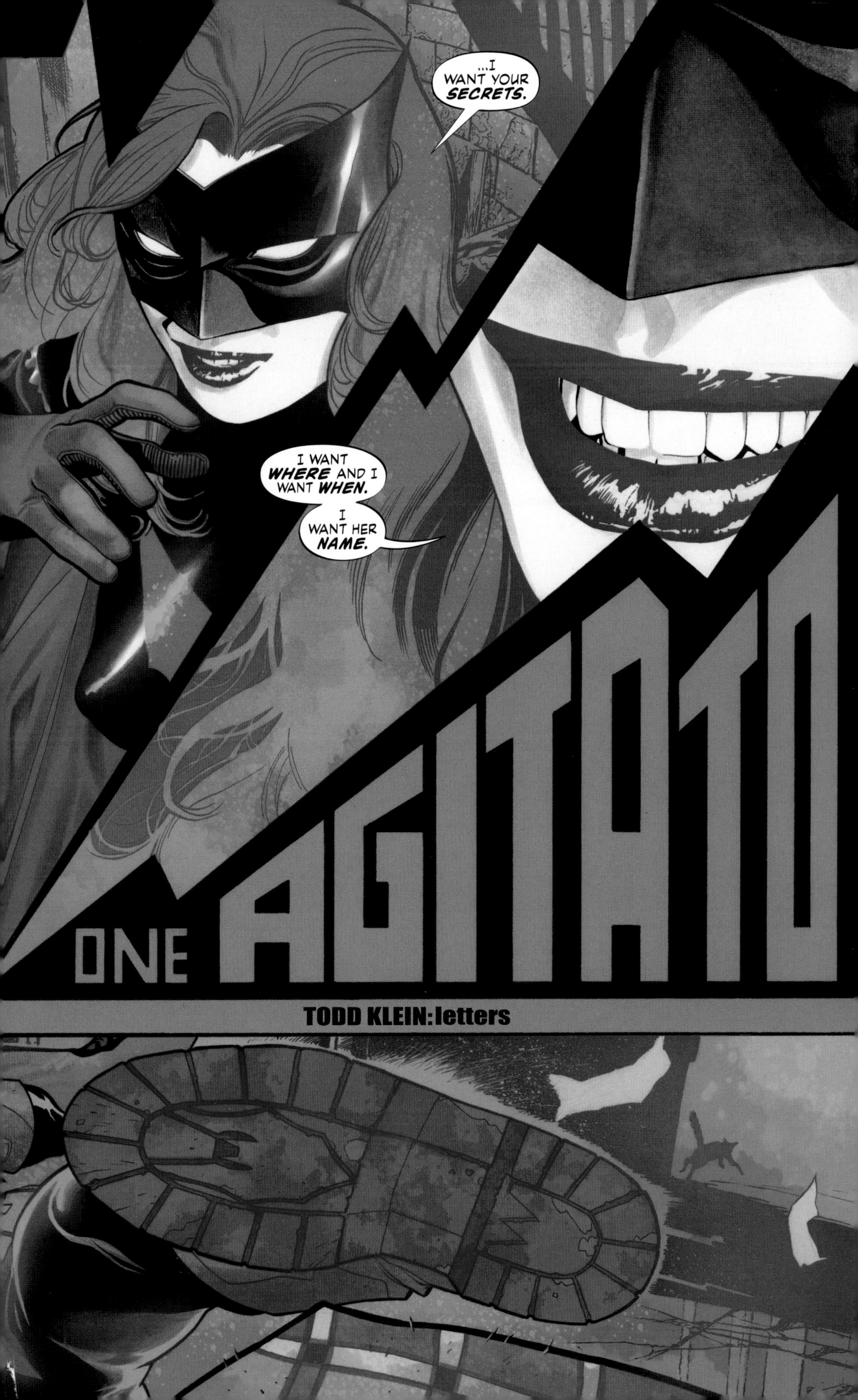
...I WANT YOUR SECRETS.
I WANT WHERE AND I WANT WHEN.
I WANT HER NAME.
ONE AGITATO
TODD KLEIN: letters

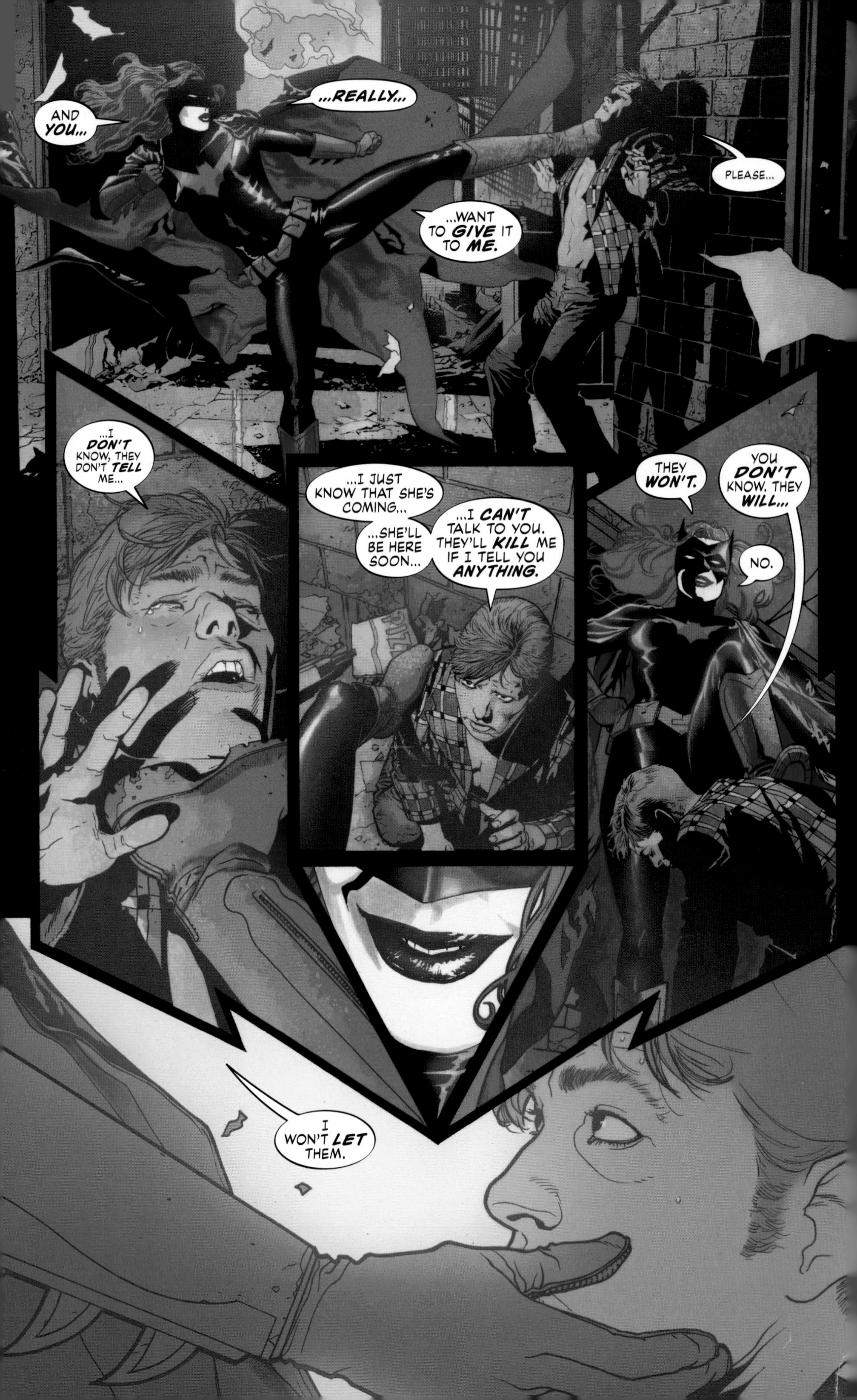

AND YOU...
...REALLY...
...WANT TO GIVE IT TO ME.
PLEASE...
...I DON'T KNOW, THEY DON'T TELL ME...
...I JUST KNOW THAT SHE'S COMING...
...SHE'LL BE HERE SOON...
...I CAN'T TALK TO YOU. THEY'LL KILL ME IF I TELL YOU ANYTHING.
THEY WON'T.
YOU DON'T KNOW. THEY WILL...
NO.
I WON'T LET THEM.

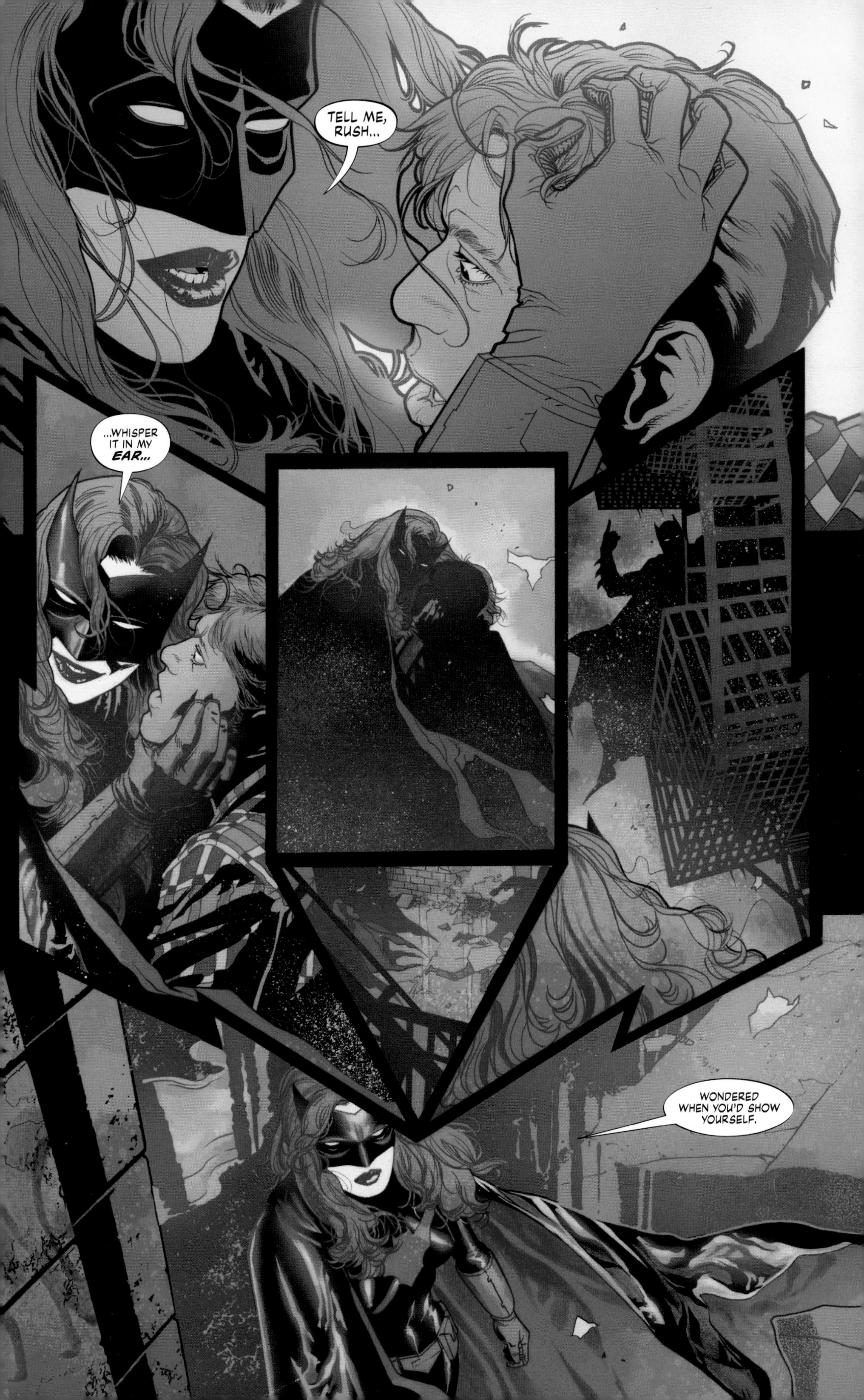
TELL ME, RUSH...
...WHISPER IT IN MY EAR...
WONDERED WHEN YOU'D SHOW YOURSELF.

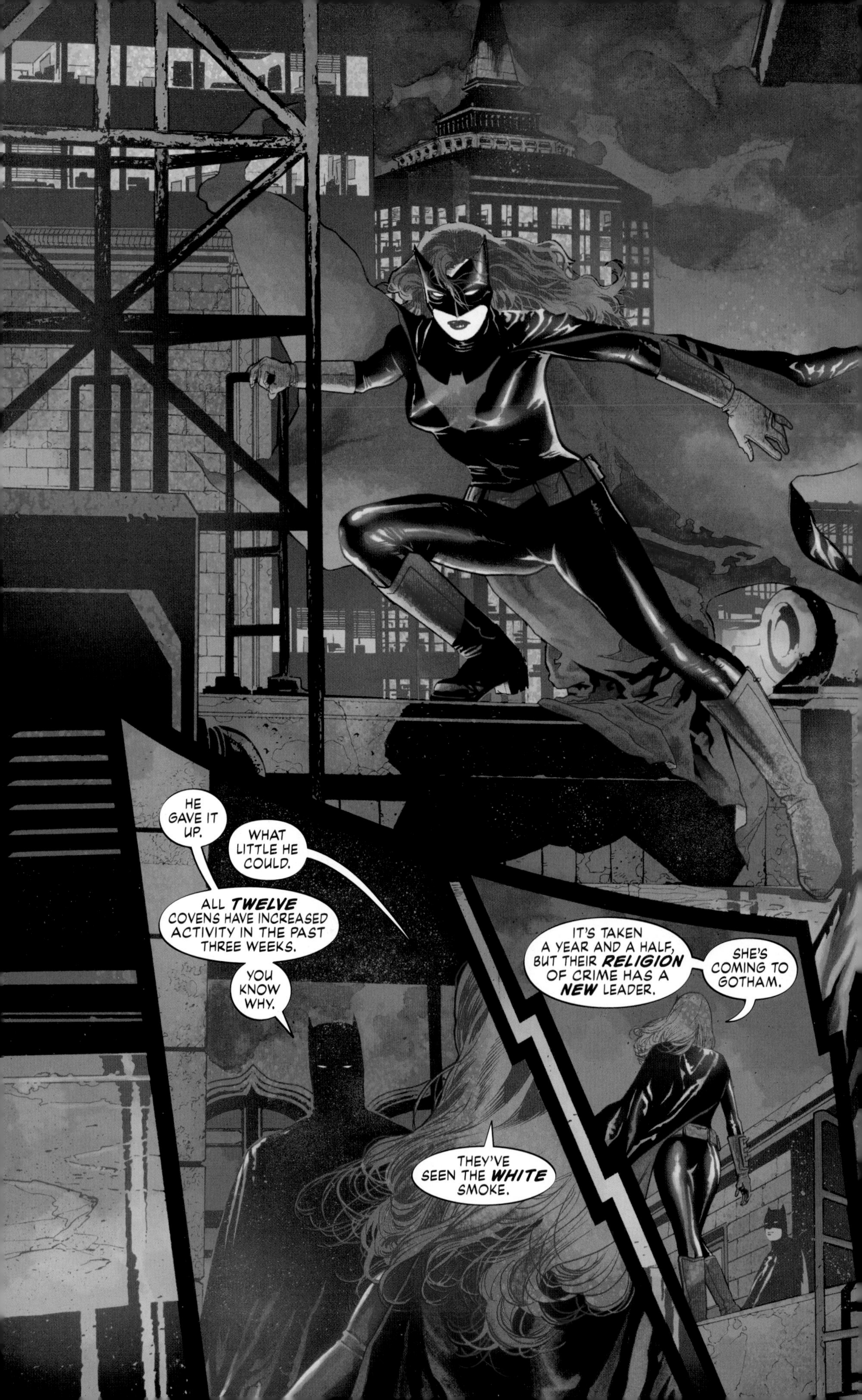
HE GAVE IT UP.
WHAT LITTLE HE COULD.
ALL TWELVE COVENS HAVE INCREASED ACTIVITY IN THE PAST THREE WEEKS.
YOU KNOW WHY.
THEY'VE SEEN THE WHITE SMOKE.
IT'S TAKEN A YEAR AND A HALF, BUT THEIR RELIGION OF CRIME HAS A NEW LEADER.
SHE'S COMING TO GOTHAM.

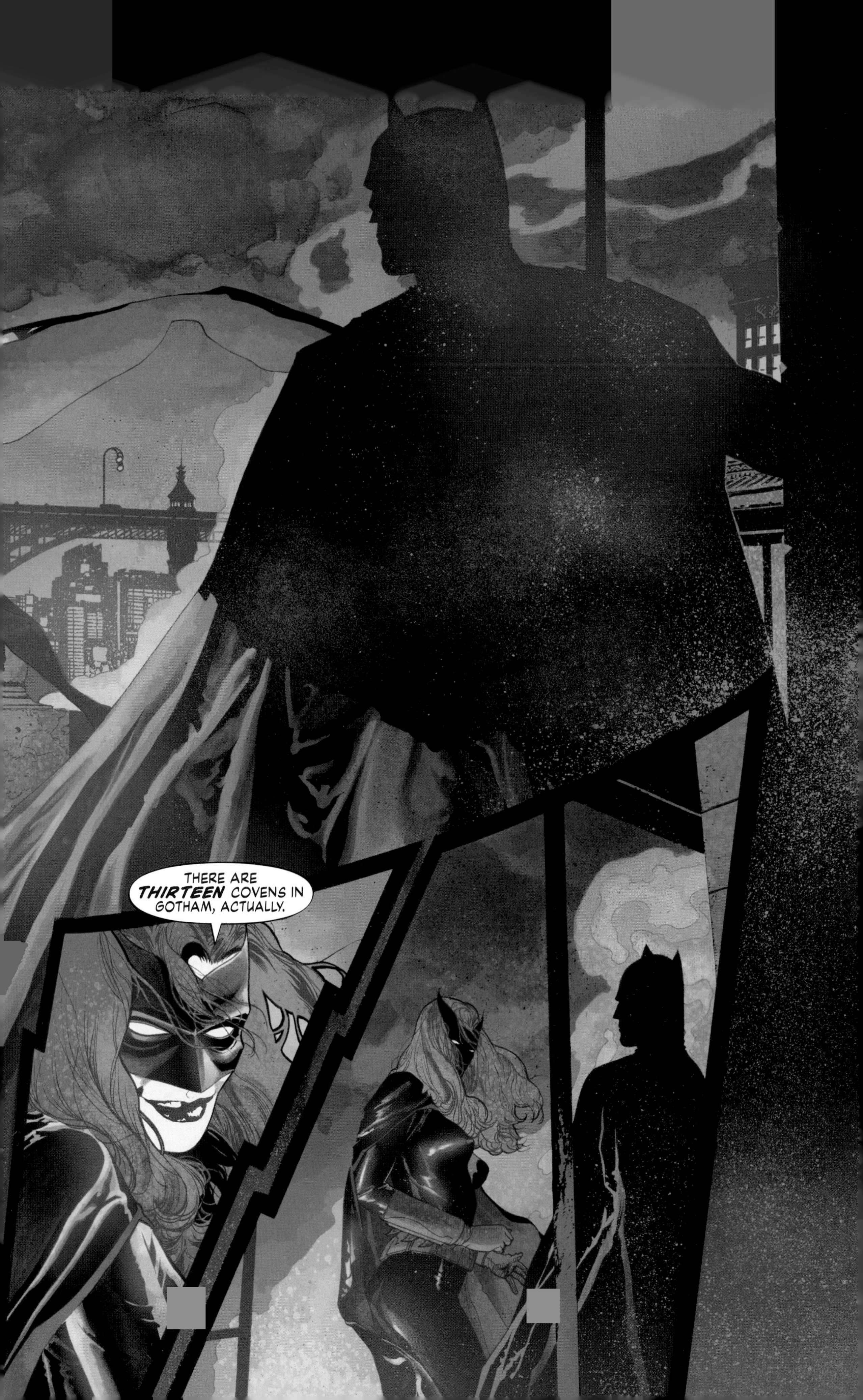
THERE ARE THIRTEEN COVENS IN GOTHAM, ACTUALLY.

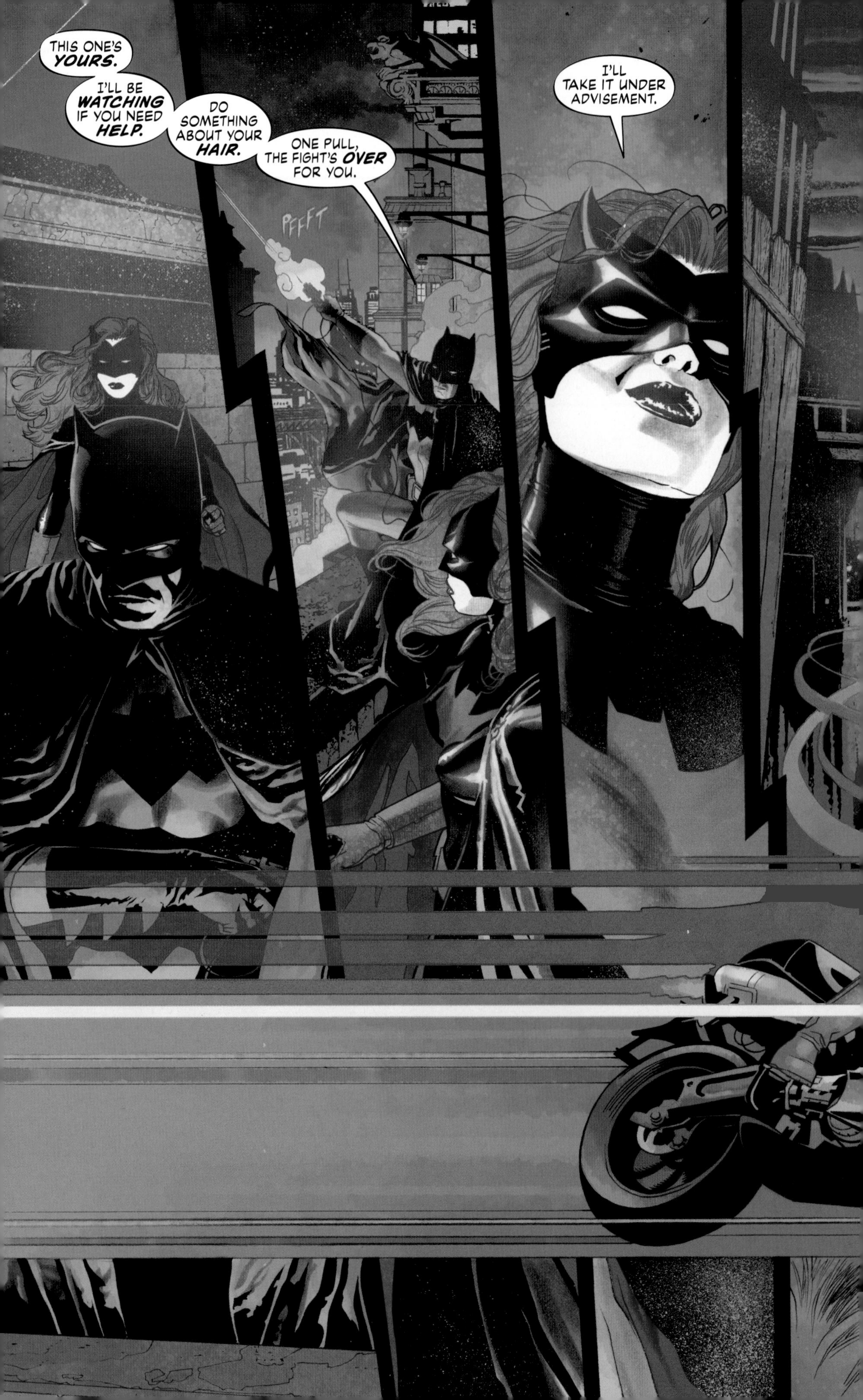
THIS ONE'S YOURS.
I'LL BE WATCHING IF YOU NEED HELP.
DO SOMETHING ABOUT YOUR HAIR.
ONE PULL, THE FIGHT'S OVER FOR YOU.
PFFFT
I'LL TAKE IT UNDER ADVISEMENT.

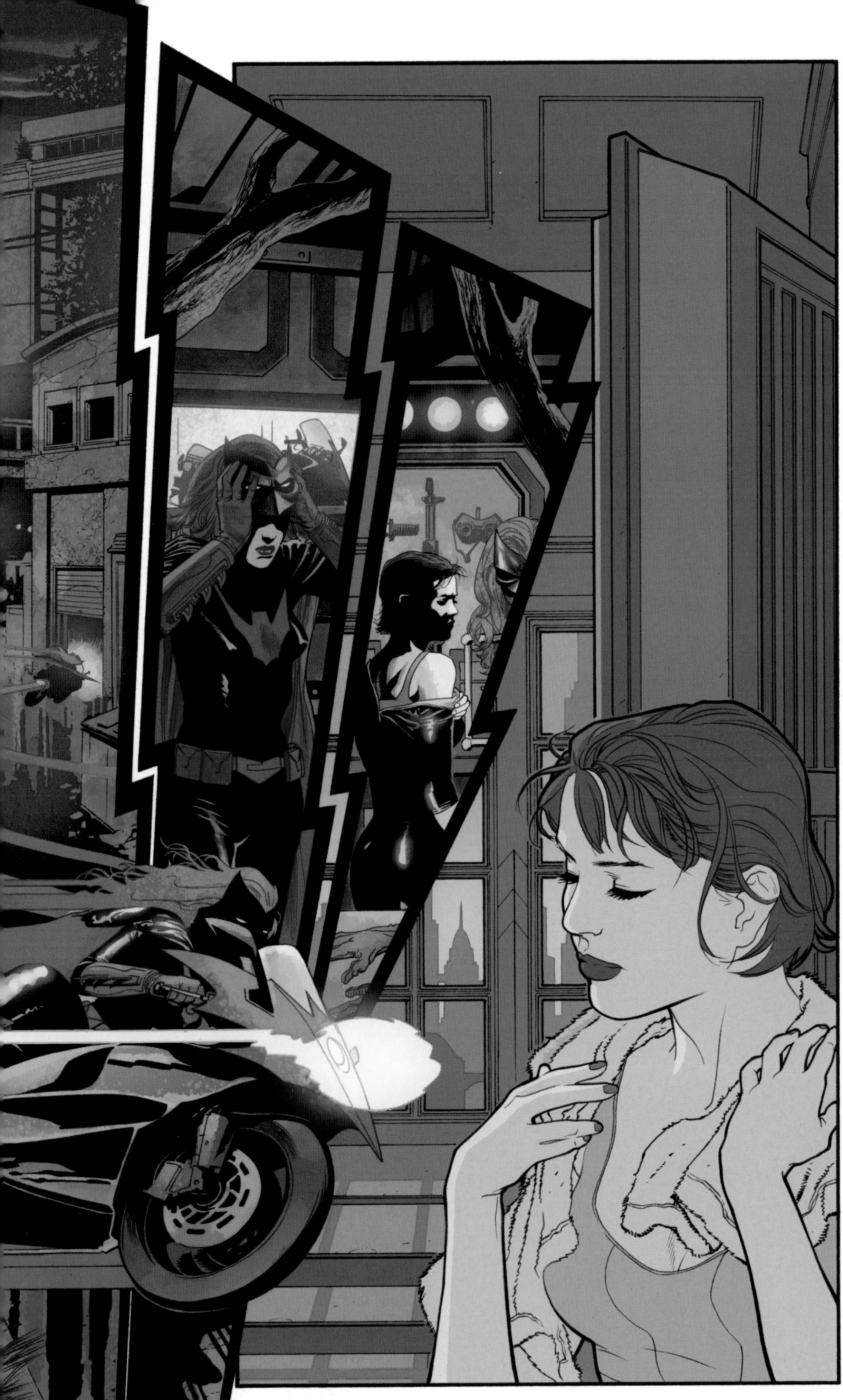

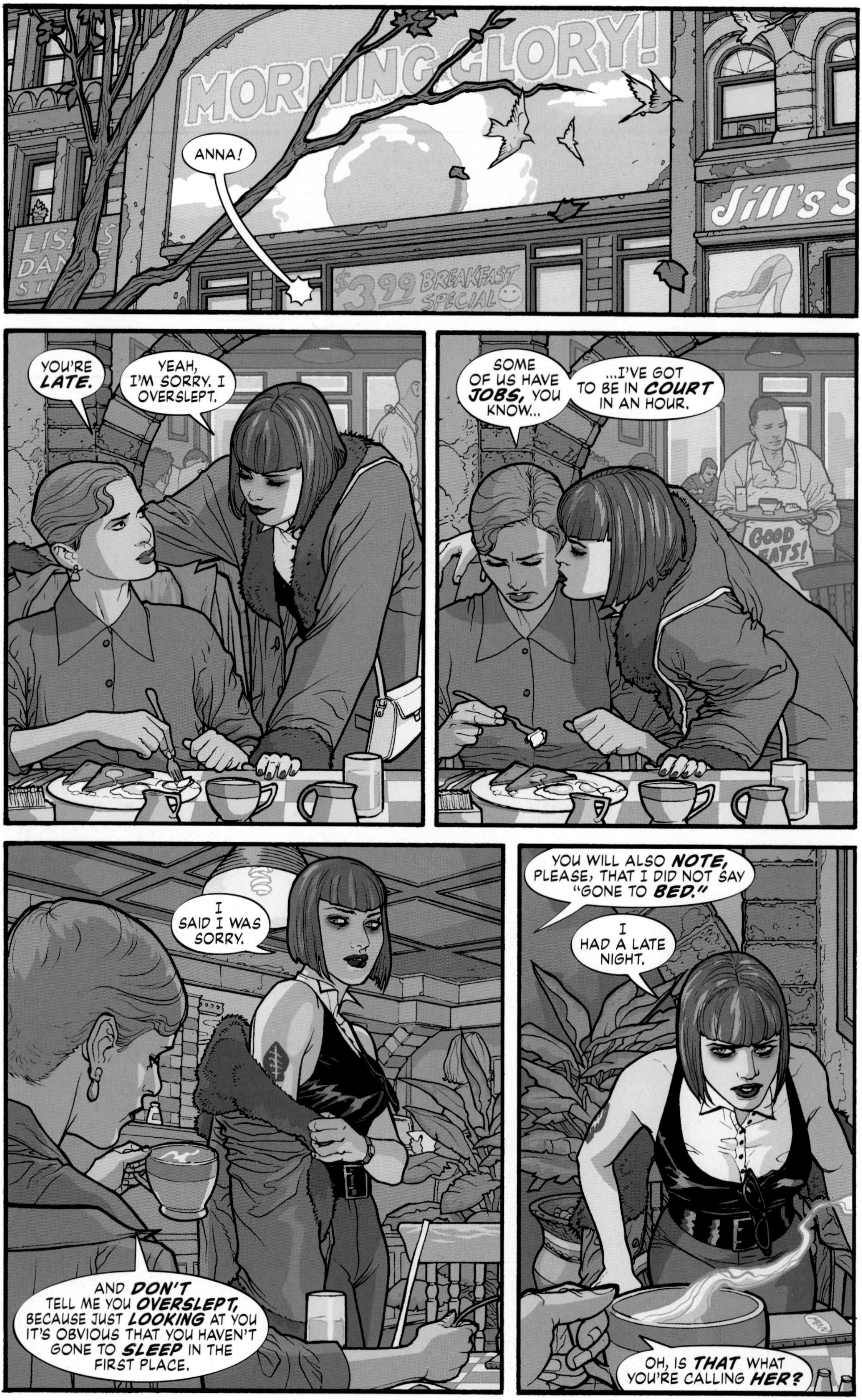
MORNING GLORY!
ANNA!
$3.99 BREAKFAST SPECIAL
YOU'RE LATE.
YEAH, I'M SORRY. I OVERSLEPT.
SOME OF US HAVE JOBS, YOU KNOW...
...I'VE GOT TO BE IN COURT IN AN HOUR.
I SAID I WAS SORRY.
AND DON'T TELL ME YOU OVERSLEPT, BECAUSE JUST LOOKING AT YOU IT'S OBVIOUS THAT YOU HAVEN'T GONE TO SLEEP IN THE FIRST PLACE.
YOU WILL ALSO NOTE, PLEASE, THAT I DID NOT SAY "GONE TO BED."
I HAD A LATE NIGHT.
OH, IS THAT WHAT YOU'RE CALLING HER?

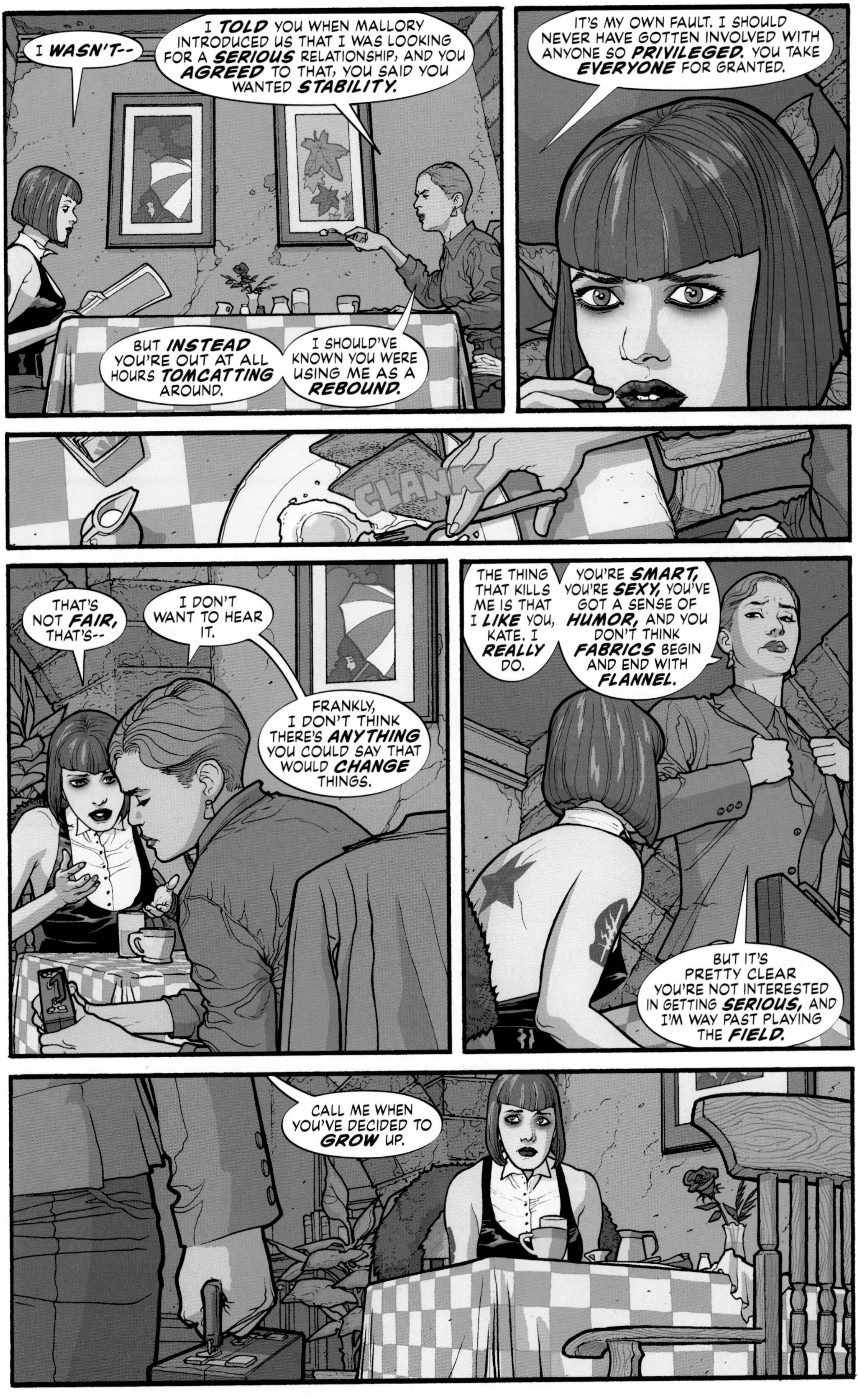
I WASN'T--
I TOLD YOU WHEN MALLORY INTRODUCED US THAT I WAS LOOKING FOR A SERIOUS RELATIONSHIP, AND YOU AGREED TO THAT, YOU SAID YOU WANTED STABILITY.
BUT INSTEAD YOU'RE OUT AT ALL HOURS TOMCATTING AROUND.
I SHOULD'VE KNOWN YOU WERE USING ME AS A REBOUND.
IT'S MY OWN FAULT. I SHOULD NEVER HAVE GOTTEN INVOLVED WITH ANYONE SO PRIVILEGED. YOU TAKE EVERYONE FOR GRANTED.
CLANK
THAT'S NOT FAIR, THAT'S--
I DON'T WANT TO HEAR IT.
FRANKLY, I DON'T THINK THERE'S ANYTHING YOU COULD SAY THAT WOULD CHANGE THINGS.
THE THING THAT KILLS ME IS THAT I LIKE YOU, KATE. I REALLY DO.
YOU'RE SMART, YOU'RE SEXY, YOU'VE GOT A SENSE OF HUMOR, AND YOU DON'T THINK FABRICS BEGIN AND END WITH FLANNEL.
BUT IT'S PRETTY CLEAR YOU'RE NOT INTERESTED IN GETTING SERIOUS, AND I'M WAY PAST PLAYING THE FIELD.
CALL ME WHEN YOU'VE DECIDED TO GROW UP.

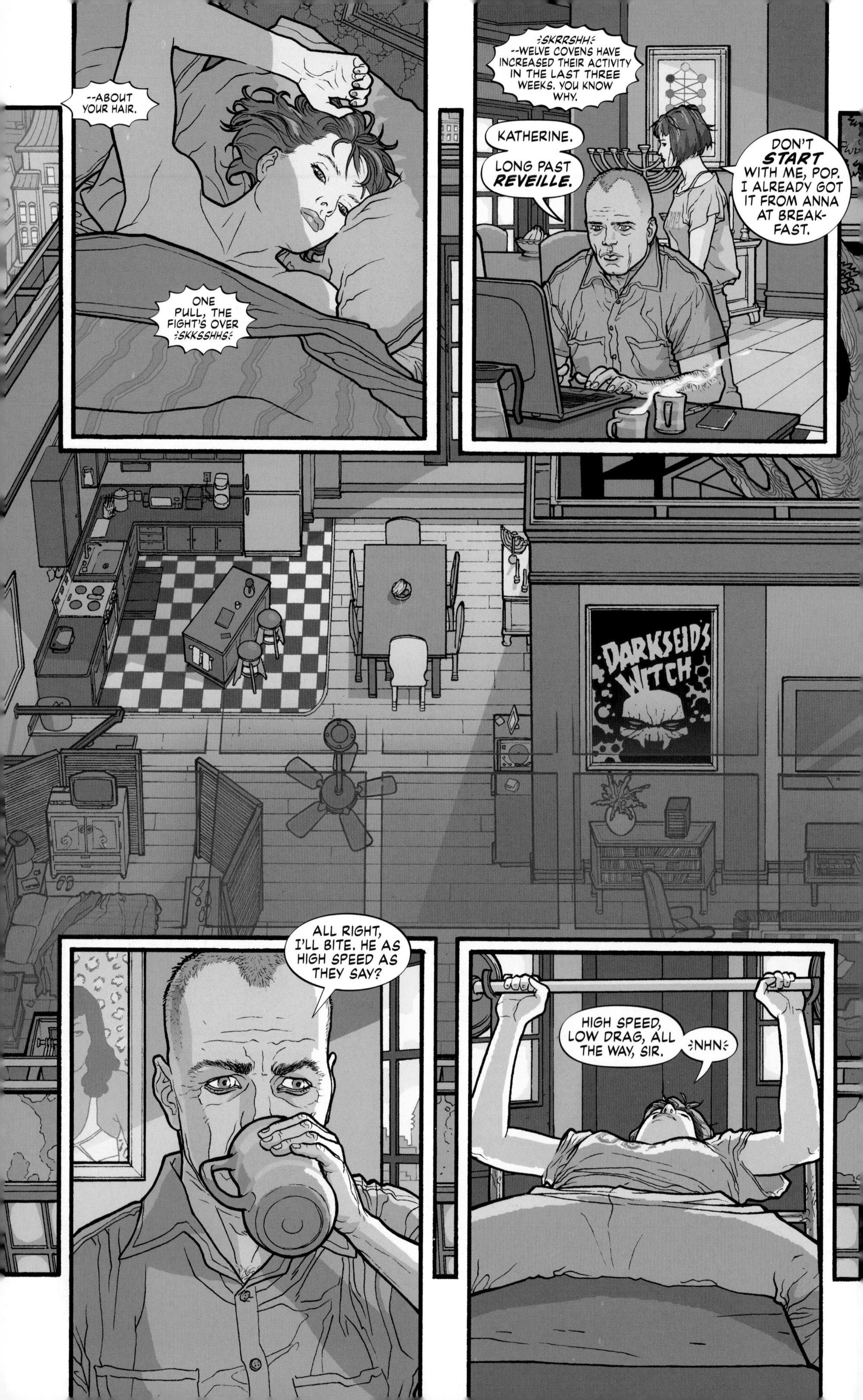
--ABOUT YOUR HAIR.
ONE PULL, THE FIGHT'S OVER *SKKSSHHS*
SKRRSHH --WELVE COVENS HAVE INCREASED THEIR ACTIVITY IN THE LAST THREE WEEKS. YOU KNOW WHY.
KATHERINE.
LONG PAST **REVEILLE.**
DON'T **START** WITH ME, POP. I ALREADY GOT IT FROM ANNA AT BREAK-FAST.
DARKSEID'S WITCH
ALL RIGHT, I'LL BITE. HE AS HIGH SPEED AS THEY SAY?
HIGH SPEED, LOW DRAG, ALL THE WAY, SIR.
NHN

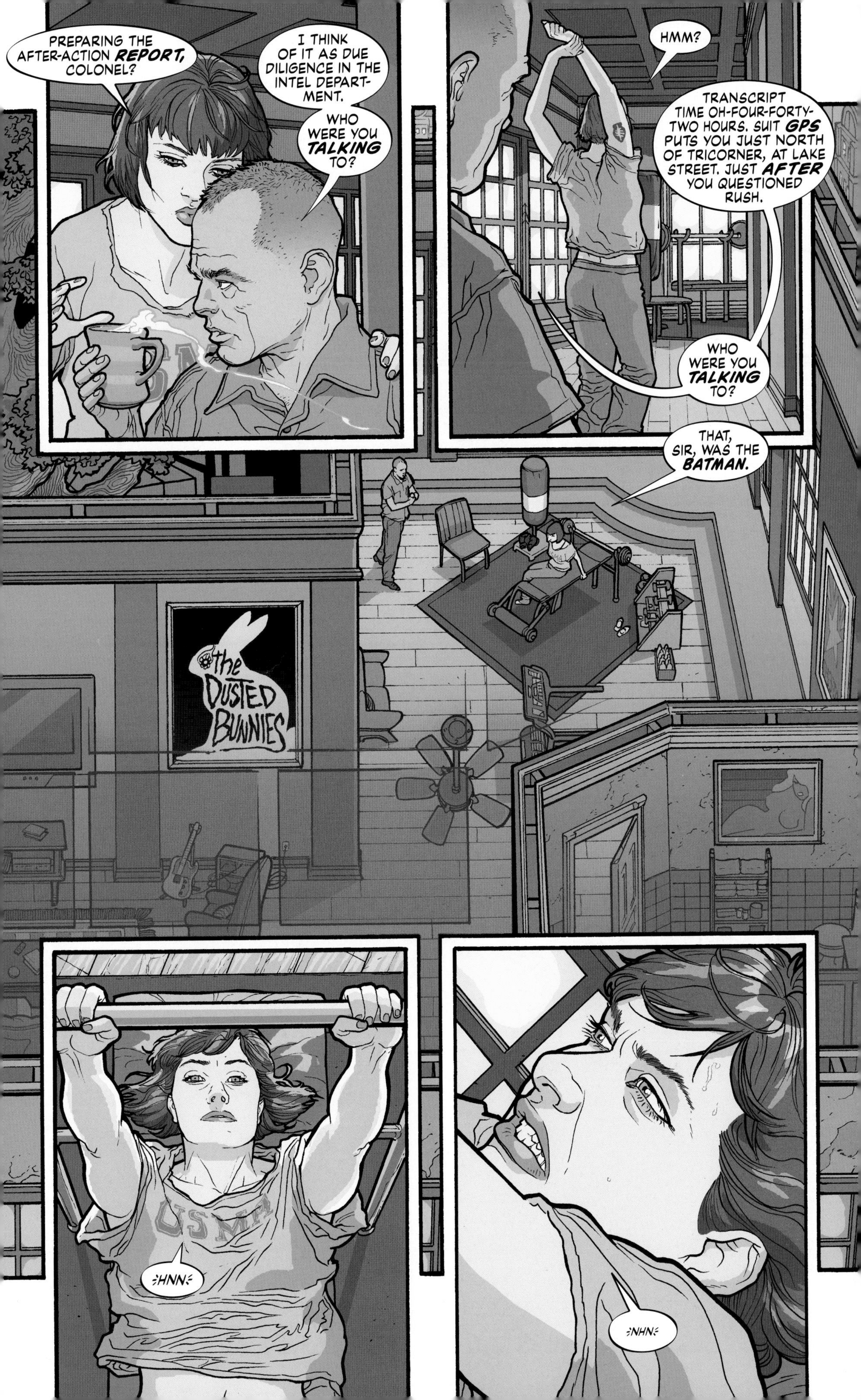
PREPARING THE AFTER-ACTION REPORT, COLONEL?
I THINK OF IT AS DUE DILIGENCE IN THE INTEL DEPARTMENT.
WHO WERE YOU TALKING TO?
HMM?
TRANSCRIPT TIME OH-FOUR-FORTY-TWO HOURS. SUIT GPS PUTS YOU JUST NORTH OF TRICORNER, AT LAKE STREET. JUST AFTER YOU QUESTIONED RUSH.
WHO WERE YOU TALKING TO?
THAT, SIR, WAS THE BATMAN.
the DUSTED BUNNIES
USMA
HNN
NHN

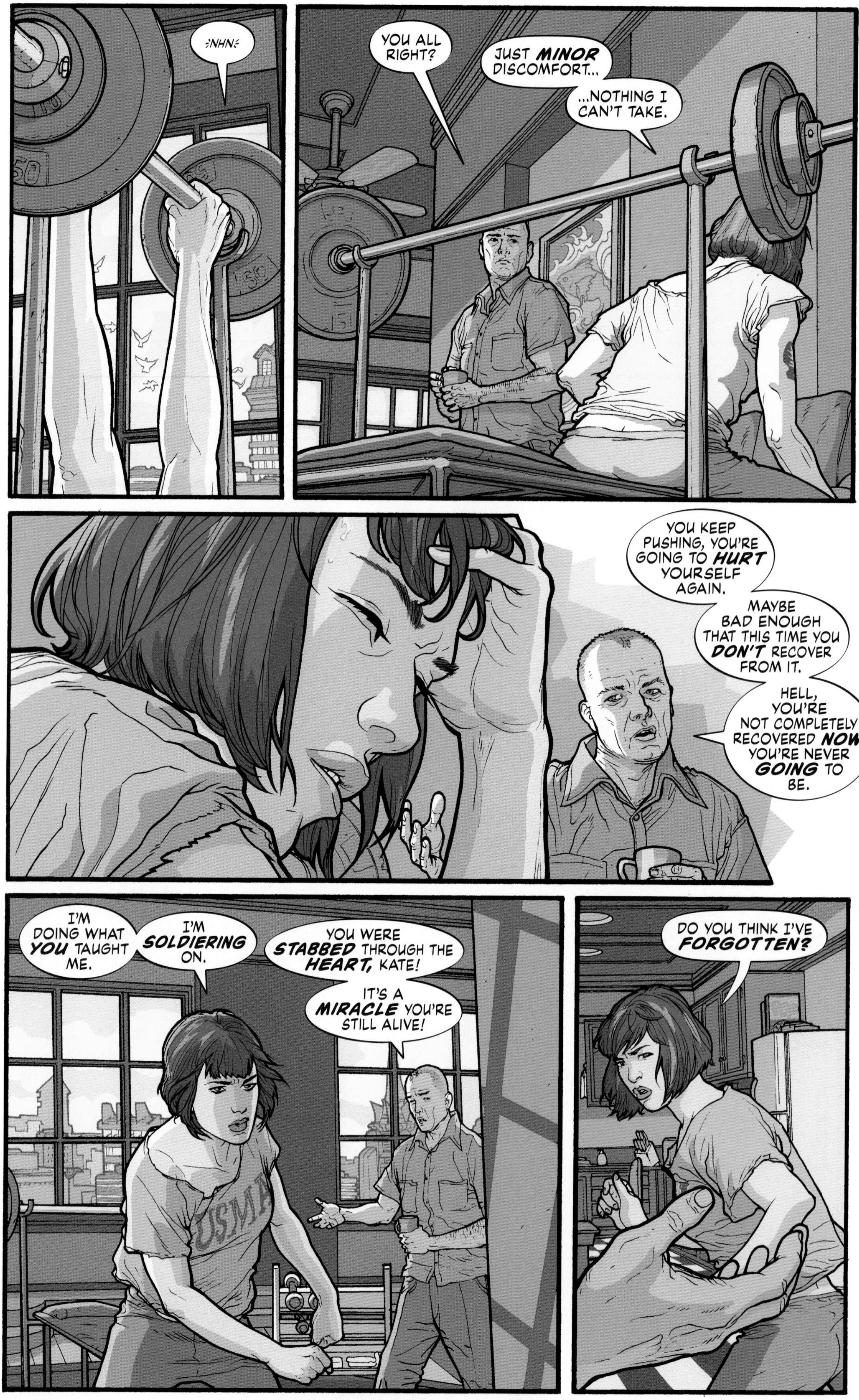
NHN
YOU ALL RIGHT?
JUST MINOR DISCOMFORT...
...NOTHING I CAN'T TAKE.
YOU KEEP PUSHING, YOU'RE GOING TO HURT YOURSELF AGAIN.
MAYBE BAD ENOUGH THAT THIS TIME YOU DON'T RECOVER FROM IT.
HELL, YOU'RE NOT COMPLETELY RECOVERED NOW. YOU'RE NEVER GOING TO BE.
I'M DOING WHAT YOU TAUGHT ME.
I'M SOLDIERING ON.
YOU WERE STABBED THROUGH THE HEART, KATE!
IT'S A MIRACLE YOU'RE STILL ALIVE!
DO YOU THINK I'VE FORGOTTEN?

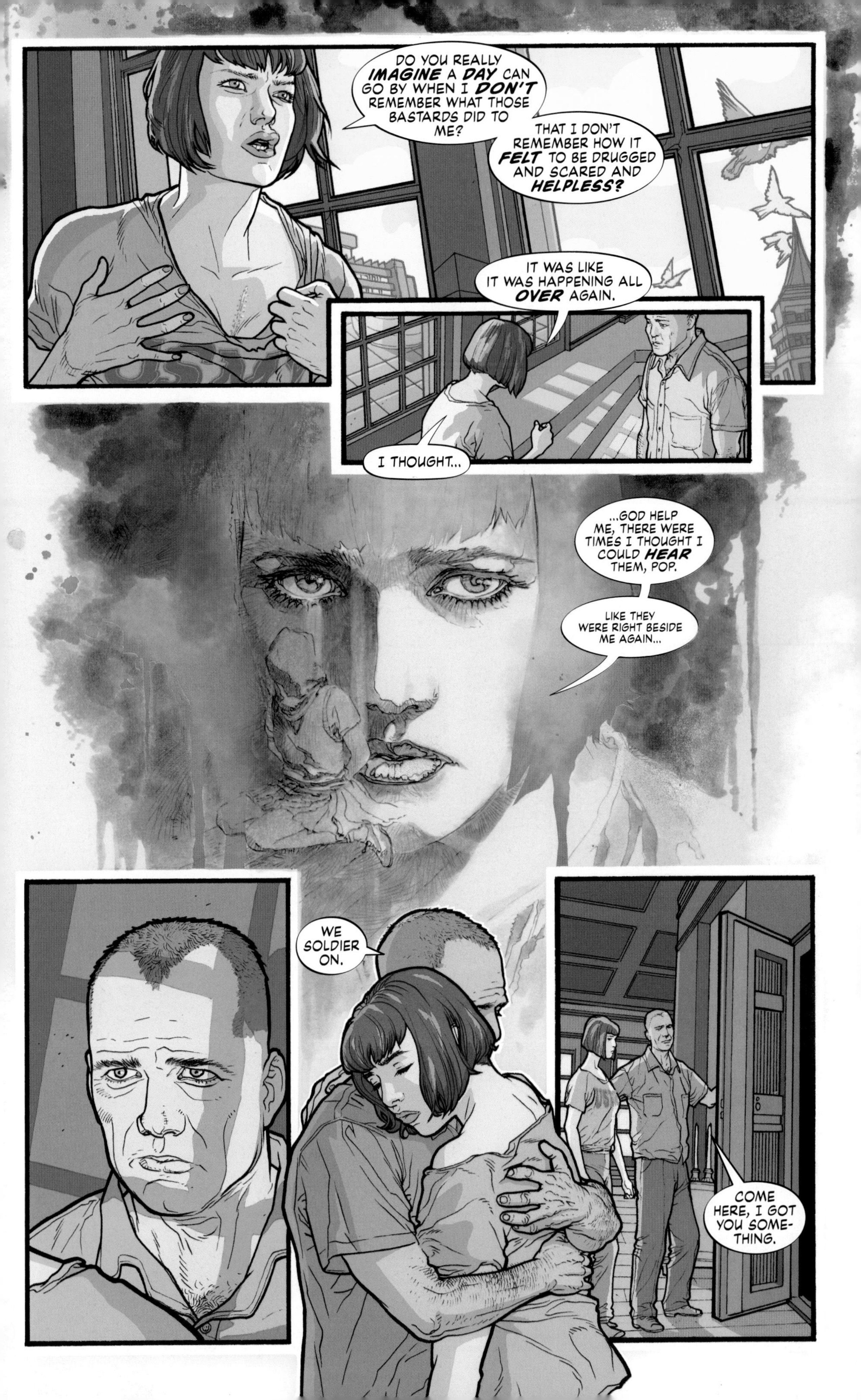
DO YOU REALLY IMAGINE A DAY CAN GO BY WHEN I DON'T REMEMBER WHAT THOSE BASTARDS DID TO ME?
THAT I DON'T REMEMBER HOW IT FELT TO BE DRUGGED AND SCARED AND HELPLESS?
IT WAS LIKE IT WAS HAPPENING ALL OVER AGAIN.
I THOUGHT...
...GOD HELP ME, THERE WERE TIMES I THOUGHT I COULD HEAR THEM, POP.
LIKE THEY WERE RIGHT BESIDE ME AGAIN...
WE SOLDIER ON.
COME HERE, I GOT YOU SOME-THING.

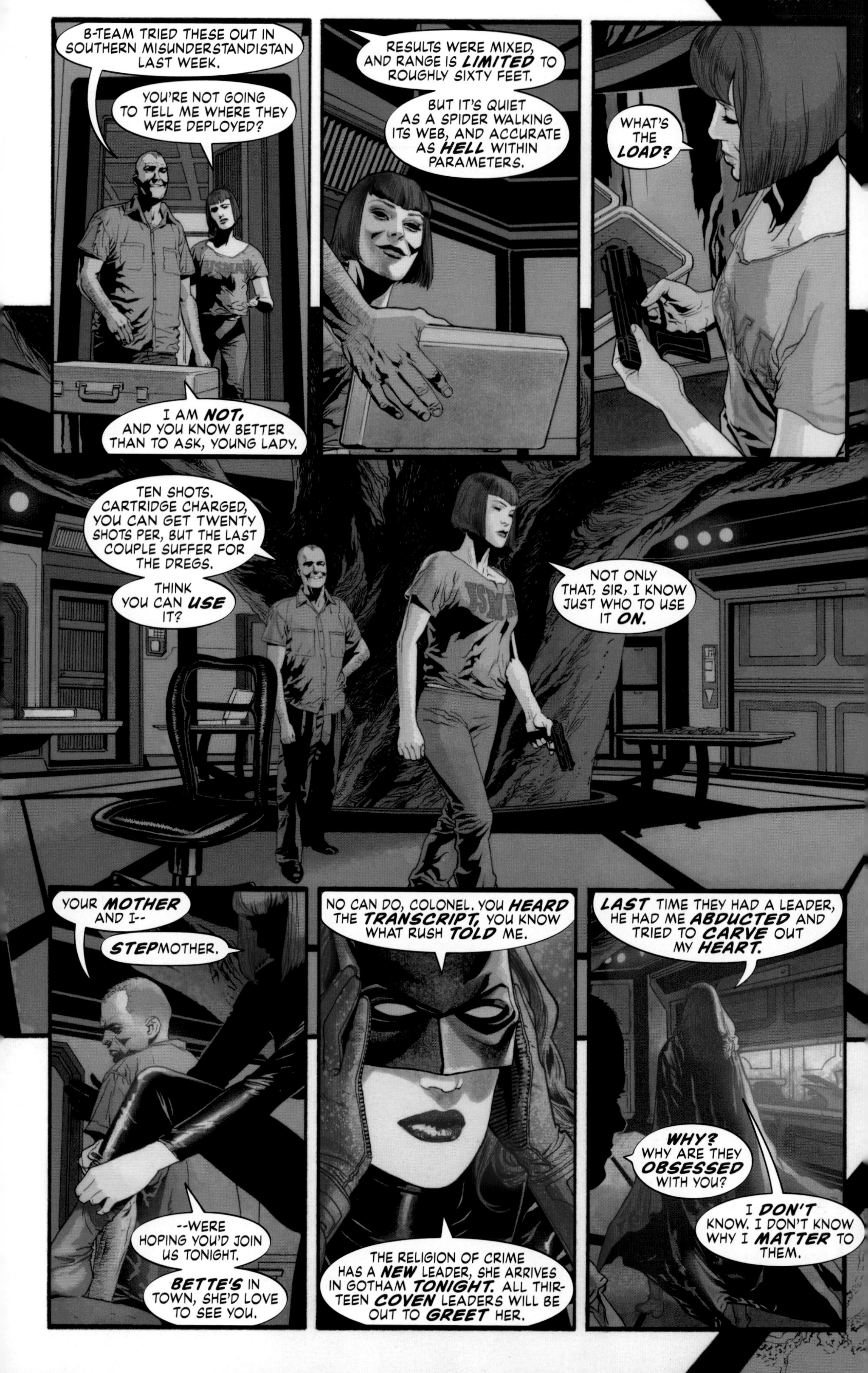
B-TEAM TRIED THESE OUT IN SOUTHERN MISUNDERSTANDISTAN LAST WEEK.
YOU'RE NOT GOING TO TELL ME WHERE THEY WERE DEPLOYED?
I AM NOT, AND YOU KNOW BETTER THAN TO ASK, YOUNG LADY.
RESULTS WERE MIXED, AND RANGE IS LIMITED TO ROUGHLY SIXTY FEET.
BUT IT'S QUIET AS A SPIDER WALKING ITS WEB, AND ACCURATE AS HELL WITHIN PARAMETERS.
WHAT'S THE LOAD?
TEN SHOTS. CARTRIDGE CHARGED, YOU CAN GET TWENTY SHOTS PER, BUT THE LAST COUPLE SUFFER FOR THE DREGS.
THINK YOU CAN USE IT?
NOT ONLY THAT, SIR, I KNOW JUST WHO TO USE IT ON.
YOUR MOTHER AND I--
STEPMOTHER.
--WERE HOPING YOU'D JOIN US TONIGHT.
BETTE'S IN TOWN, SHE'D LOVE TO SEE YOU.
NO CAN DO, COLONEL. YOU HEARD THE TRANSCRIPT, YOU KNOW WHAT RUSH TOLD ME.
THE RELIGION OF CRIME HAS A NEW LEADER, SHE ARRIVES IN GOTHAM TONIGHT. ALL THIRTEEN COVEN LEADERS WILL BE OUT TO GREET HER.
LAST TIME THEY HAD A LEADER, HE HAD ME ABDUCTED AND TRIED TO CARVE OUT MY HEART.
WHY? WHY ARE THEY OBSESSED WITH YOU?
I DON'T KNOW. I DON'T KNOW WHY I MATTER TO THEM.

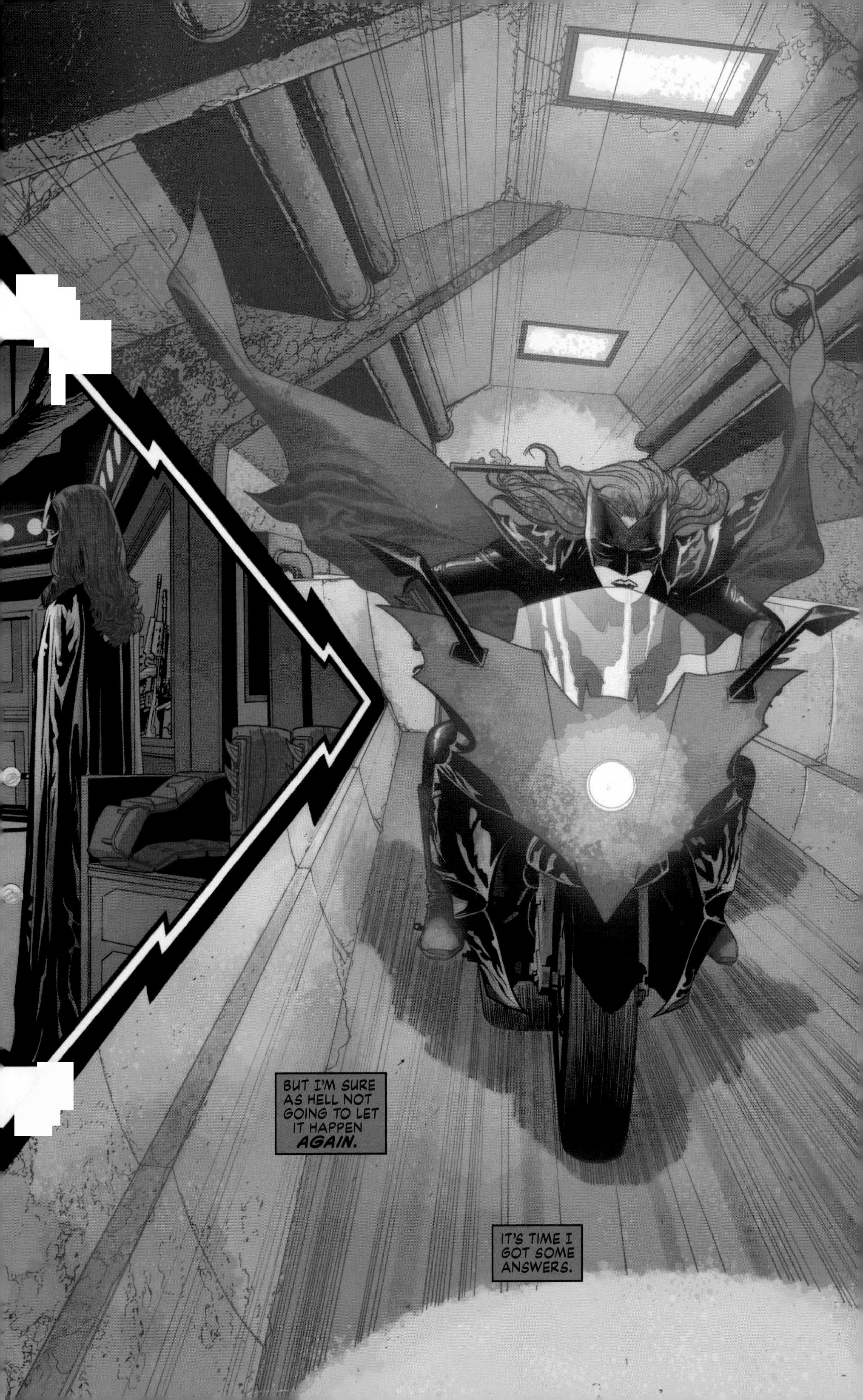
BUT I'M SURE AS HELL NOT GOING TO LET IT HAPPEN *AGAIN.*
IT'S TIME I GOT SOME ANSWERS.

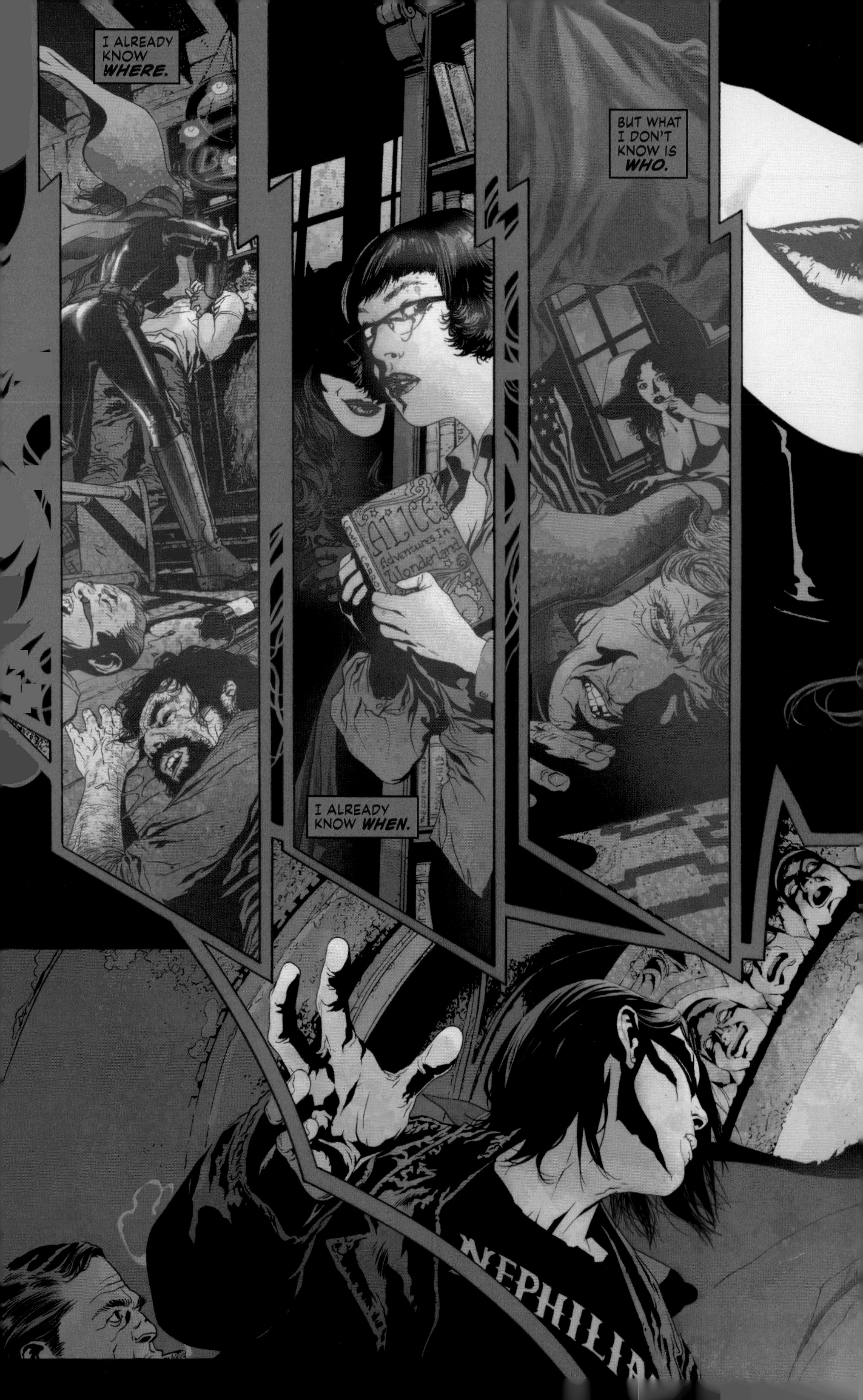
I ALREADY KNOW WHERE.
I ALREADY KNOW WHEN.
BUT WHAT I DON'T KNOW IS WHO.
ALICE'S Adventures In Wonderland
LEWIS CARROLL
NEPHILIM

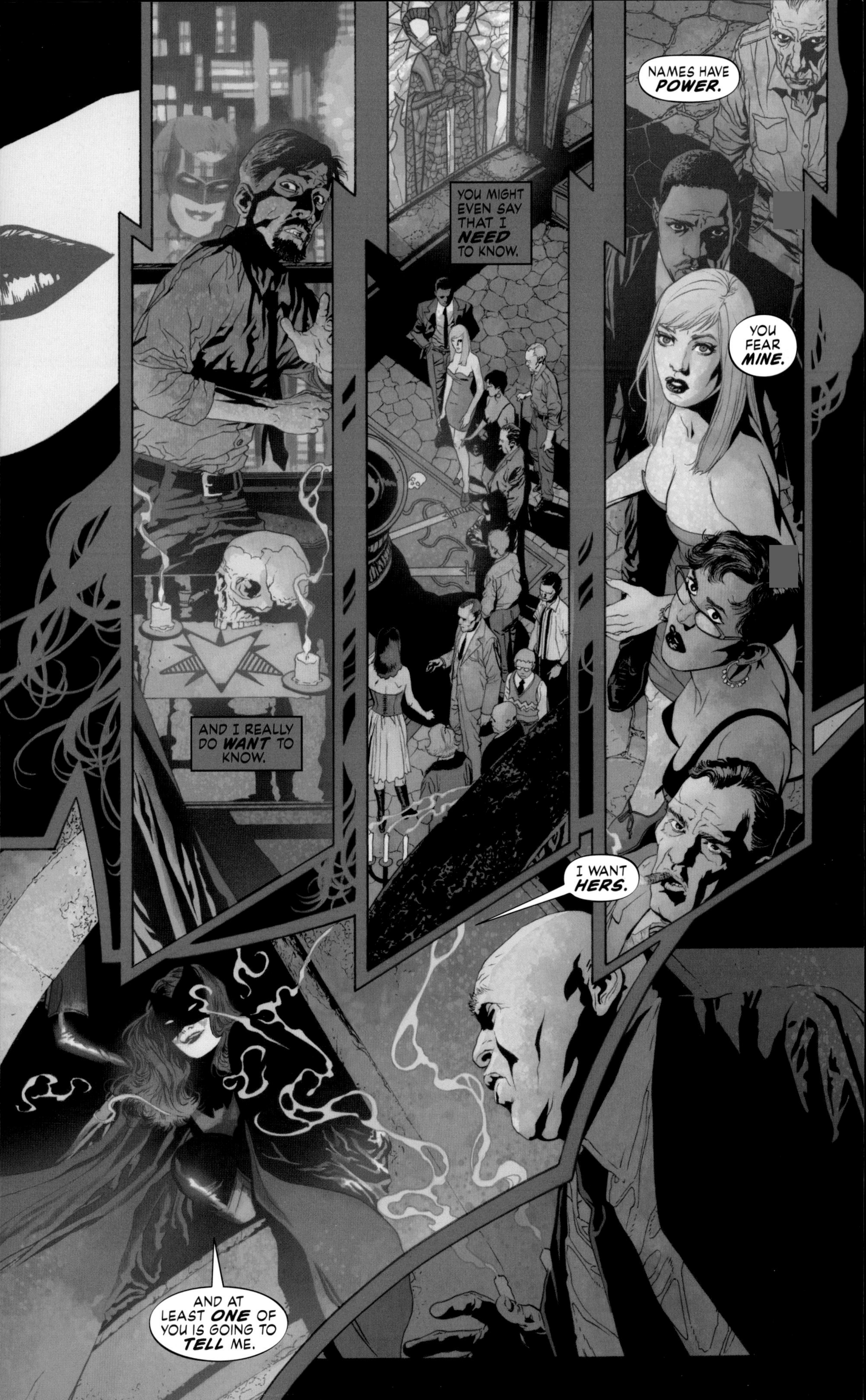
AND I REALLY DO WANT TO KNOW.
YOU MIGHT EVEN SAY THAT I NEED TO KNOW.
NAMES HAVE POWER.
YOU FEAR MINE.
I WANT HERS.
AND AT LEAST ONE OF YOU IS GOING TO TELL ME.

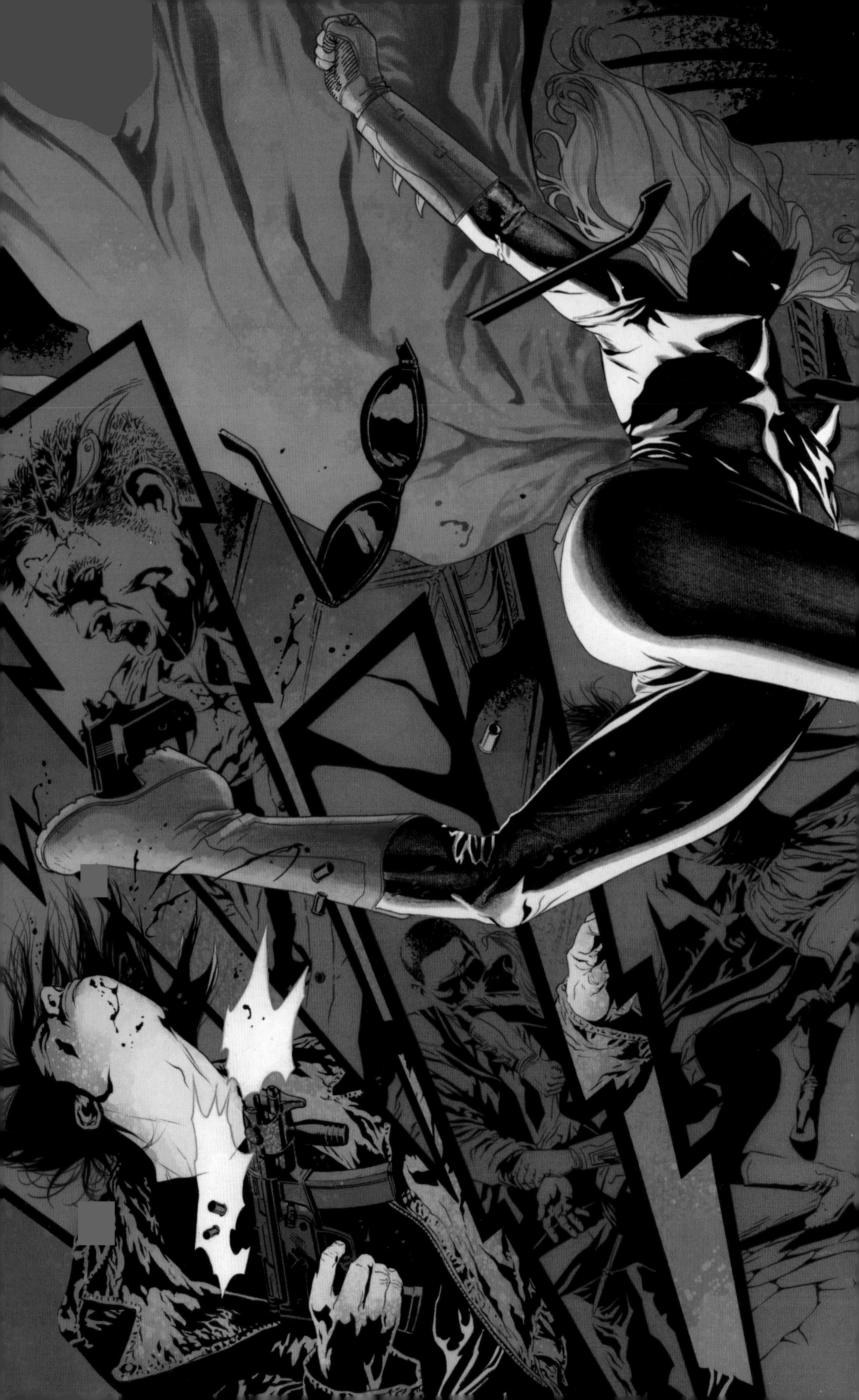

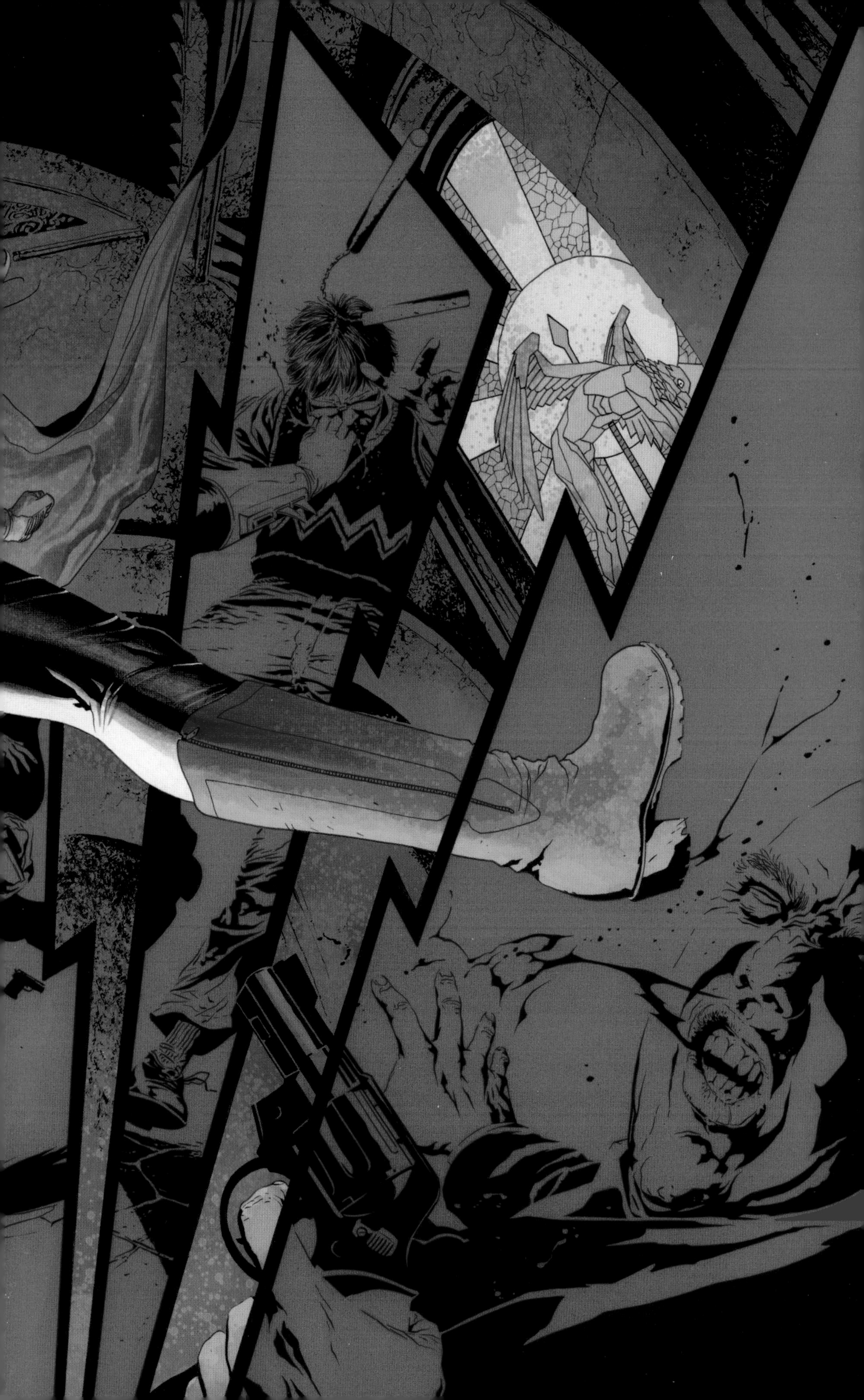

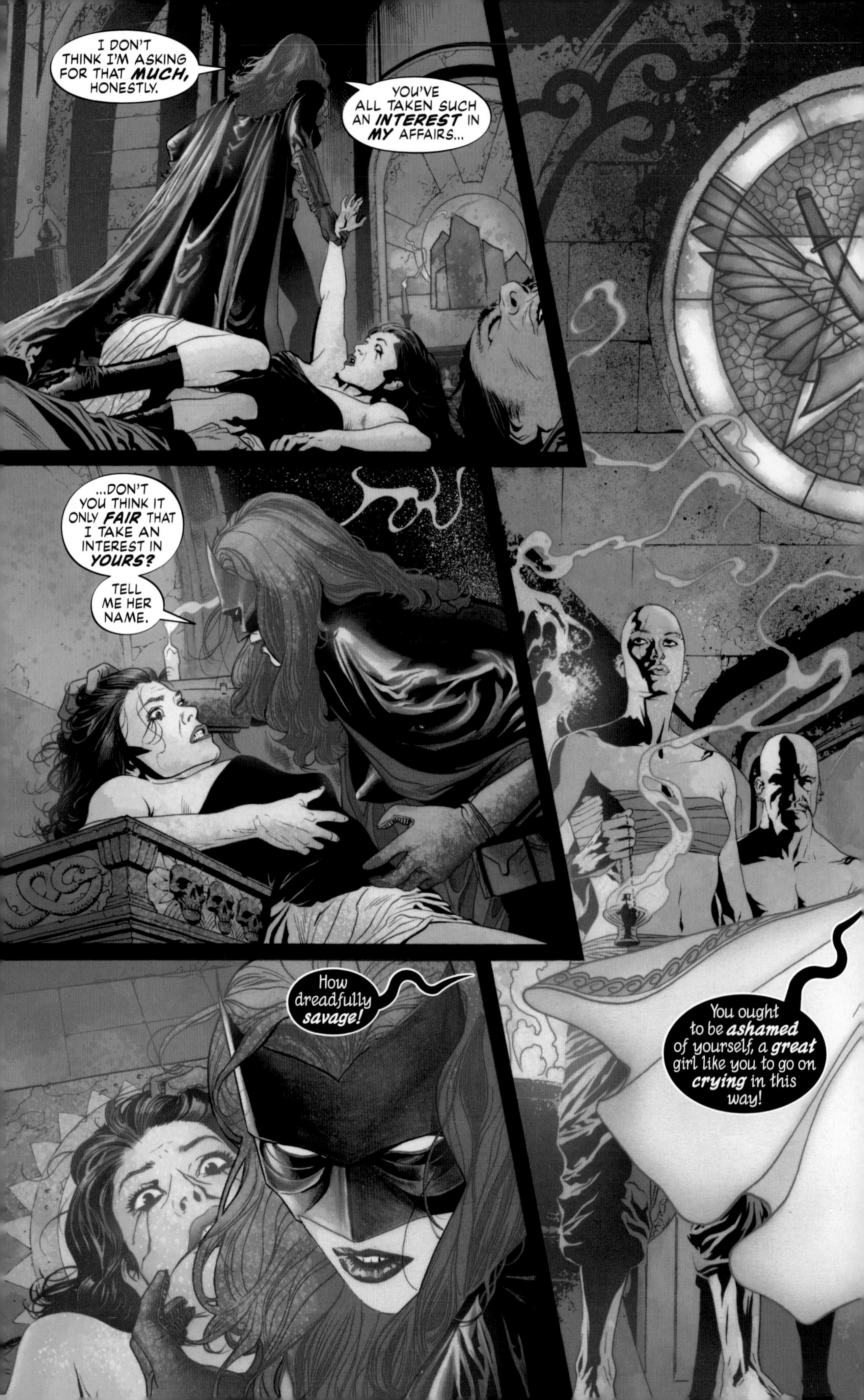

I DON'T THINK I'M ASKING FOR THAT MUCH, HONESTLY.
YOU'VE ALL TAKEN SUCH AN INTEREST IN MY AFFAIRS...
...DON'T YOU THINK IT ONLY FAIR THAT I TAKE AN INTEREST IN YOURS?
TELL ME HER NAME.
How dreadfully savage!
You ought to be ashamed of yourself, a great girl like you to go on crying in this way!

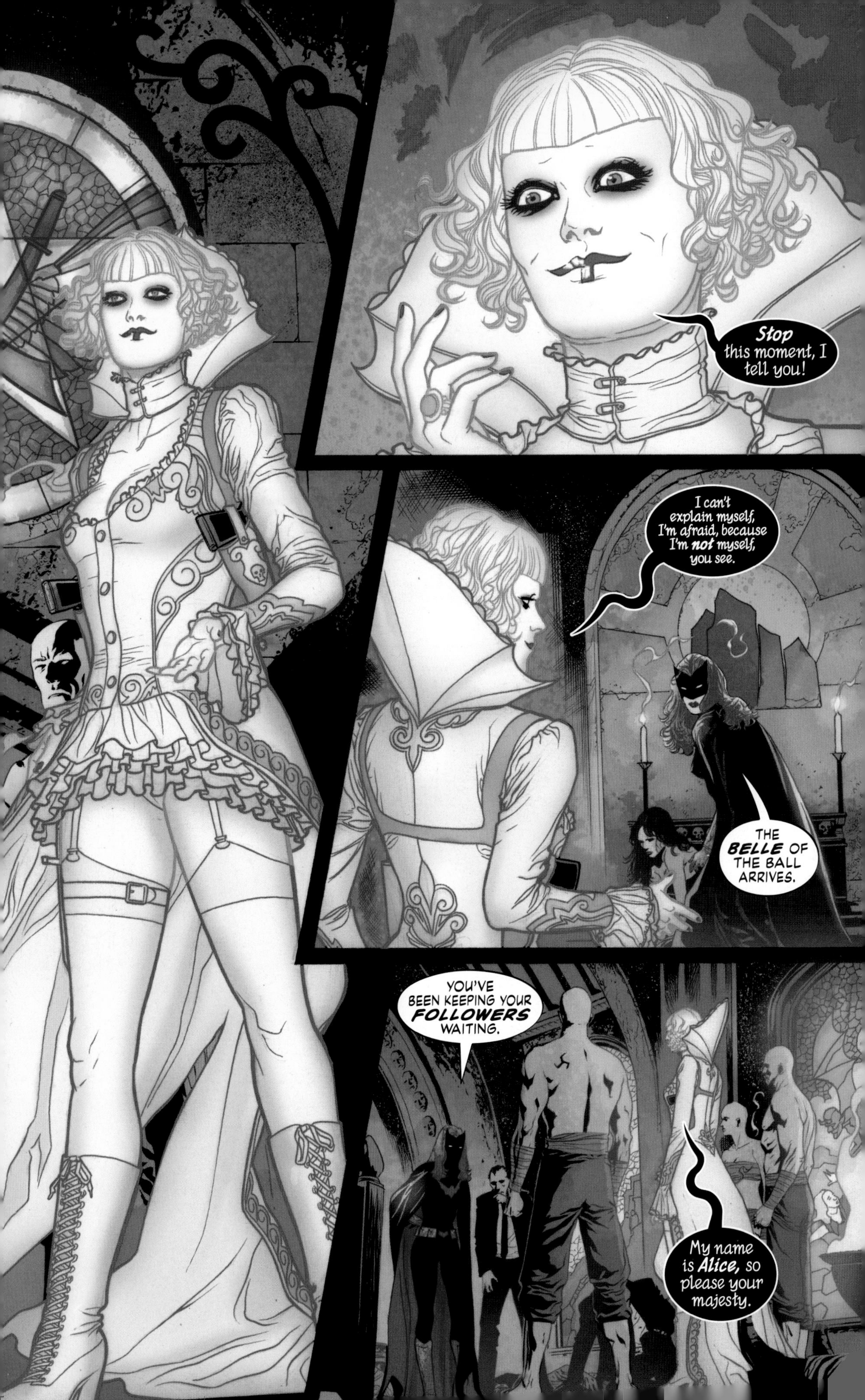
Stop this moment, I tell you!
I can't explain myself, I'm afraid, because I'm not myself, you see.
THE BELLE OF THE BALL ARRIVES.
YOU'VE BEEN KEEPING YOUR FOLLOWERS WAITING.
My name is Alice, so please your majesty.

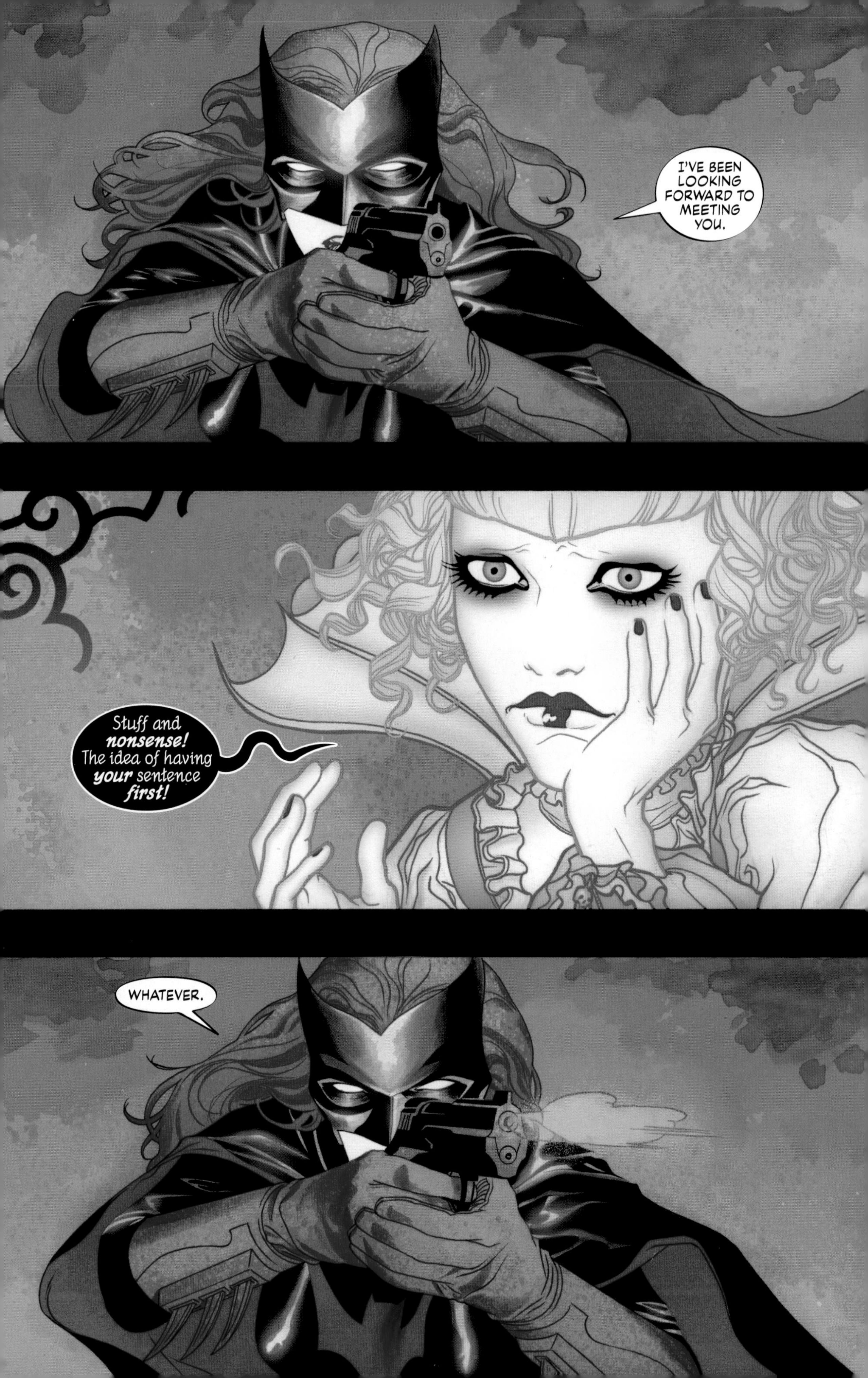
I'VE BEEN LOOKING FORWARD TO MEETING YOU.
Stuff and ***nonsense!*** The idea of having ***your*** sentence ***first!***
WHATEVER.

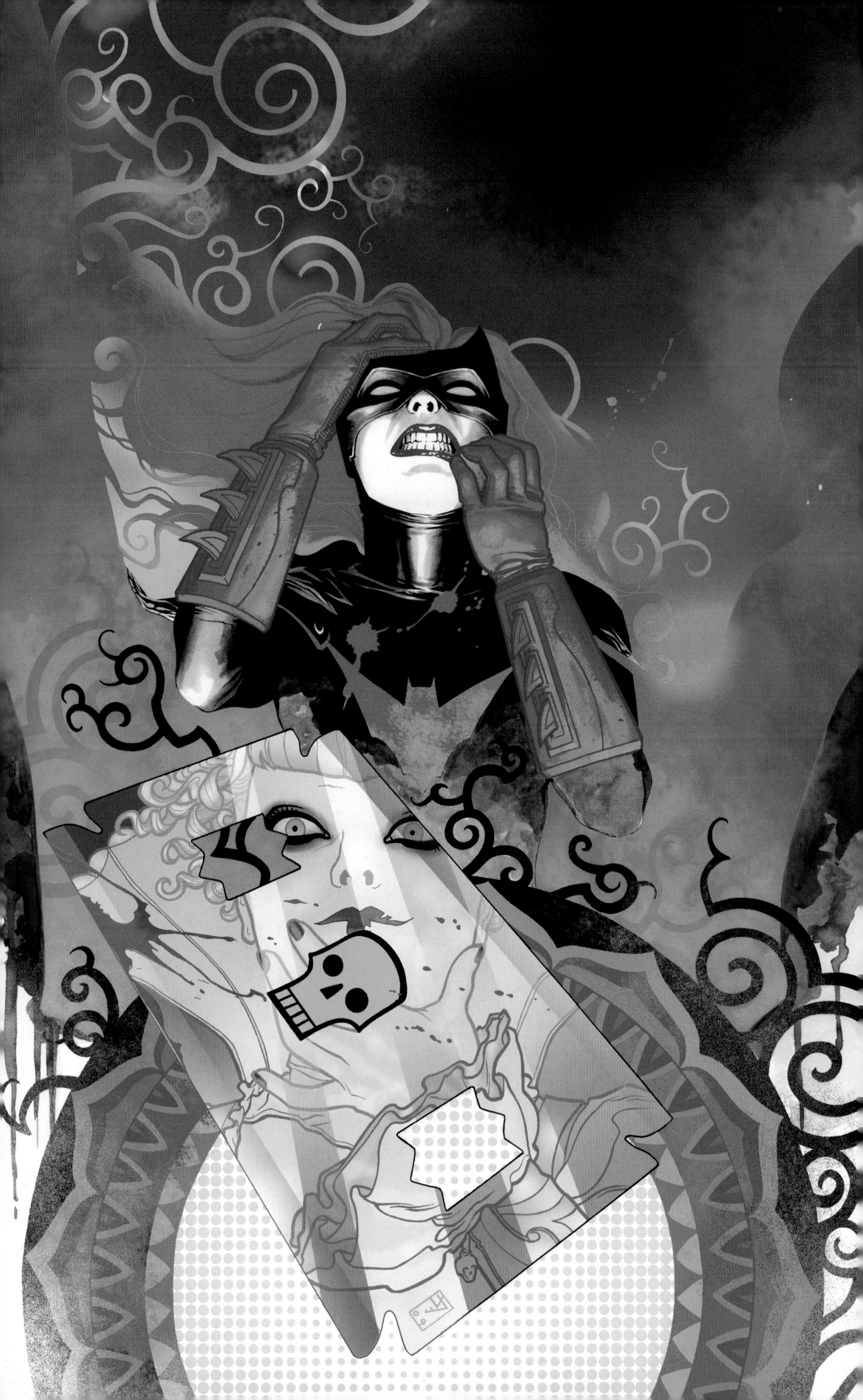

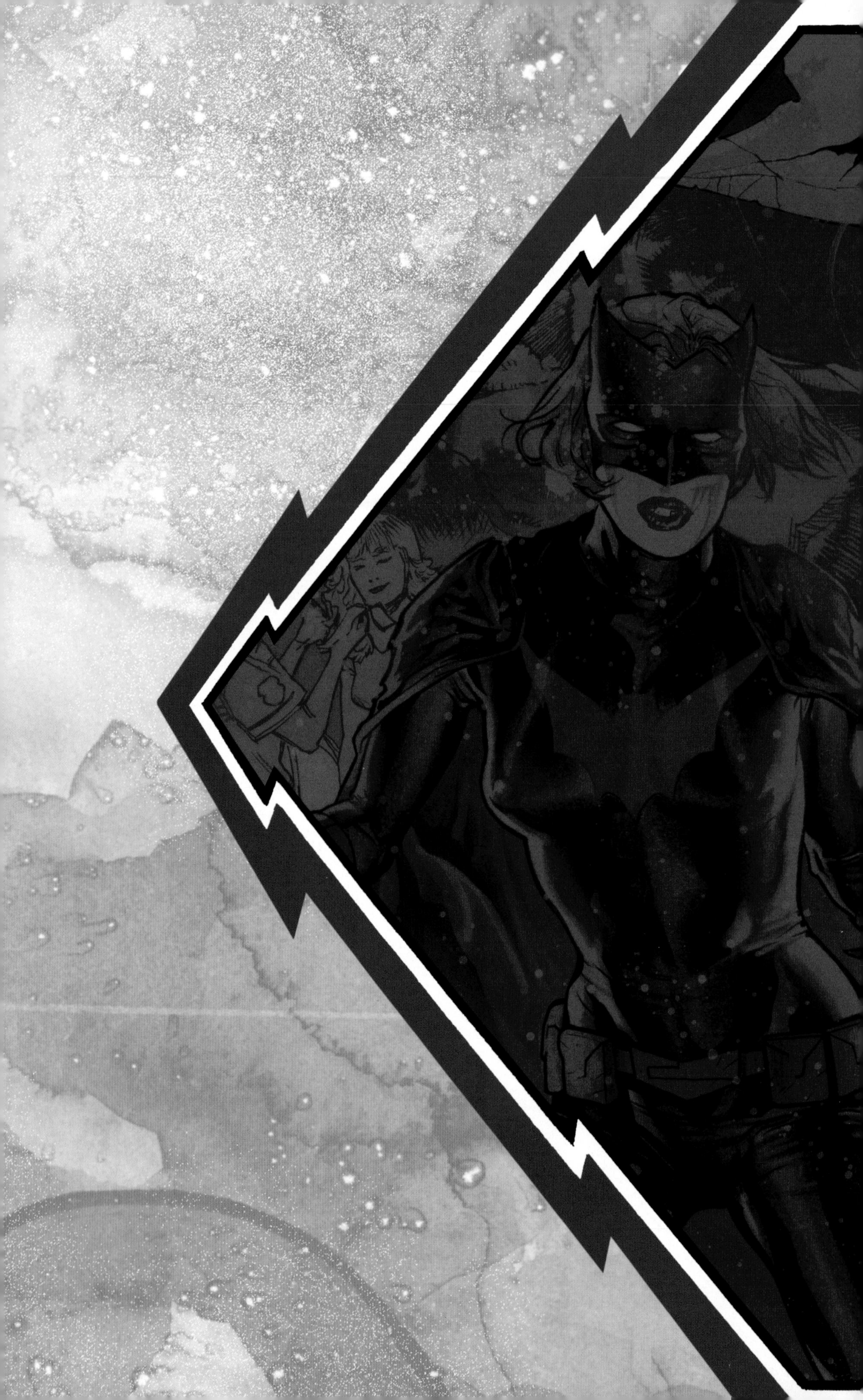

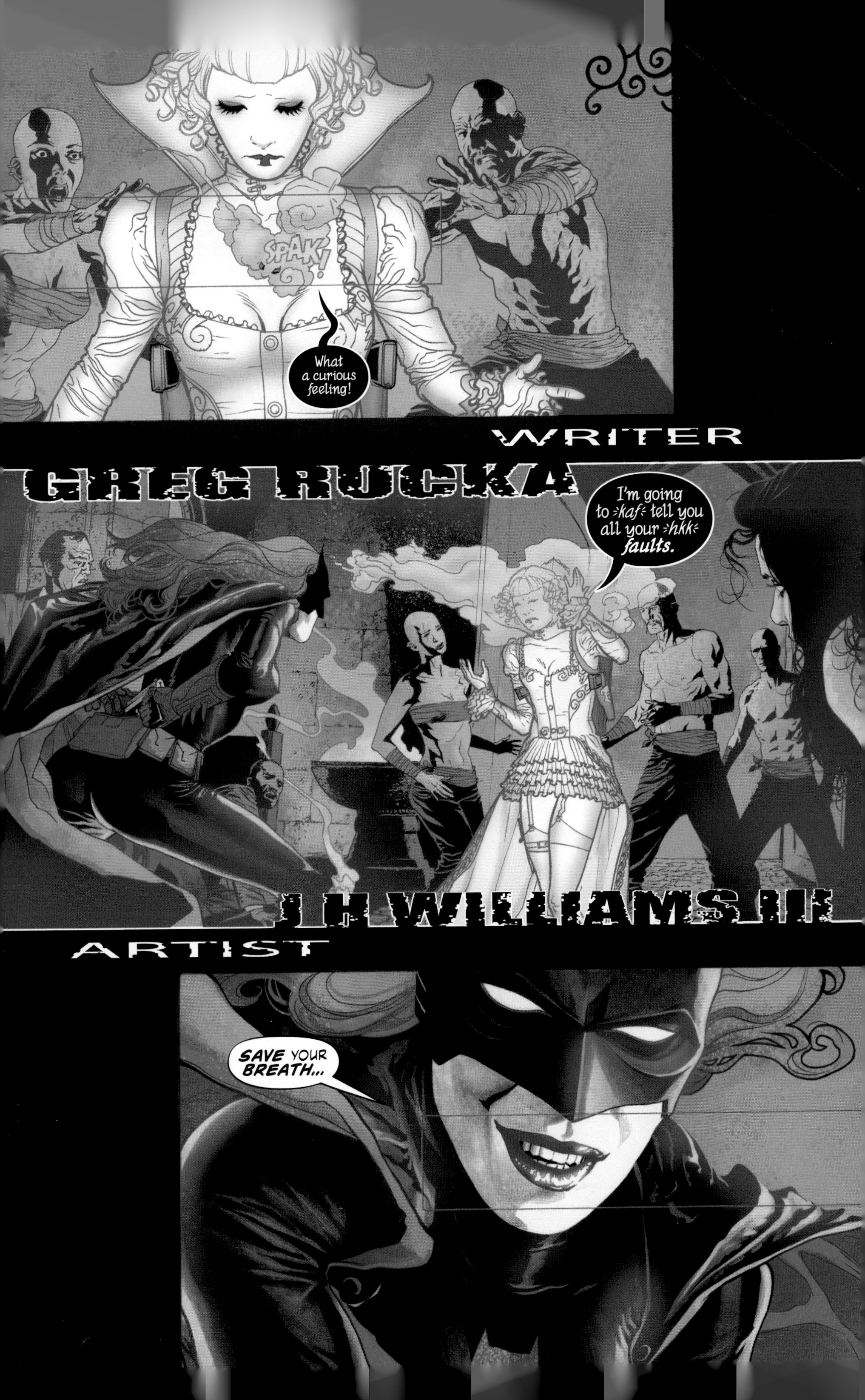
SPAK!
What a curious feeling!
WRITER
GREG RUCKA
I'm going to kaf tell you all your hkk faults.
J H WILLIAMS III
ARTIST
SAVE YOUR BREATH...

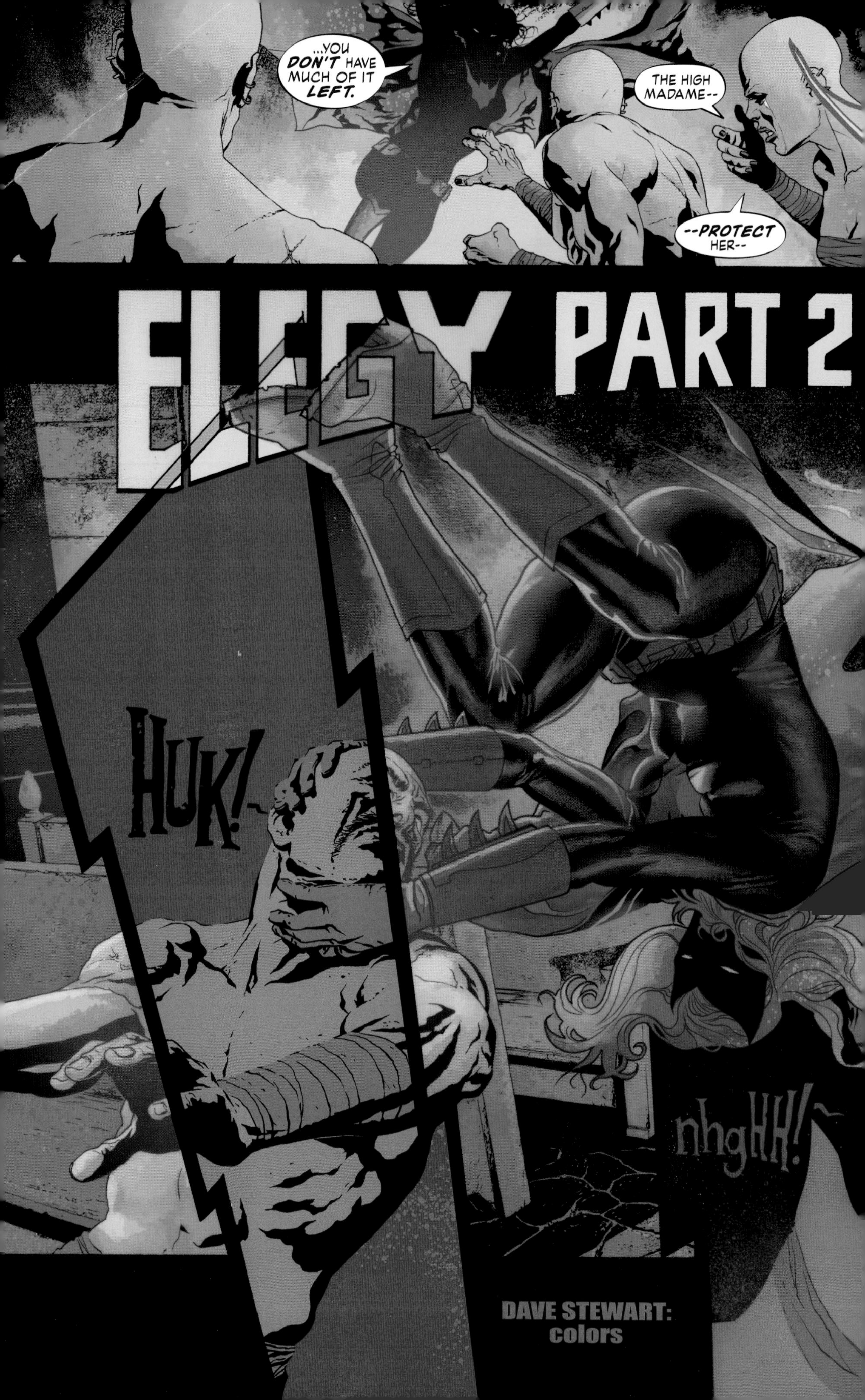
...YOU DON'T HAVE MUCH OF IT LEFT.
THE HIGH MADAME--
--PROTECT HER--
ELEGY PART 2
HUK!
nhgHH!
DAVE STEWART: colors

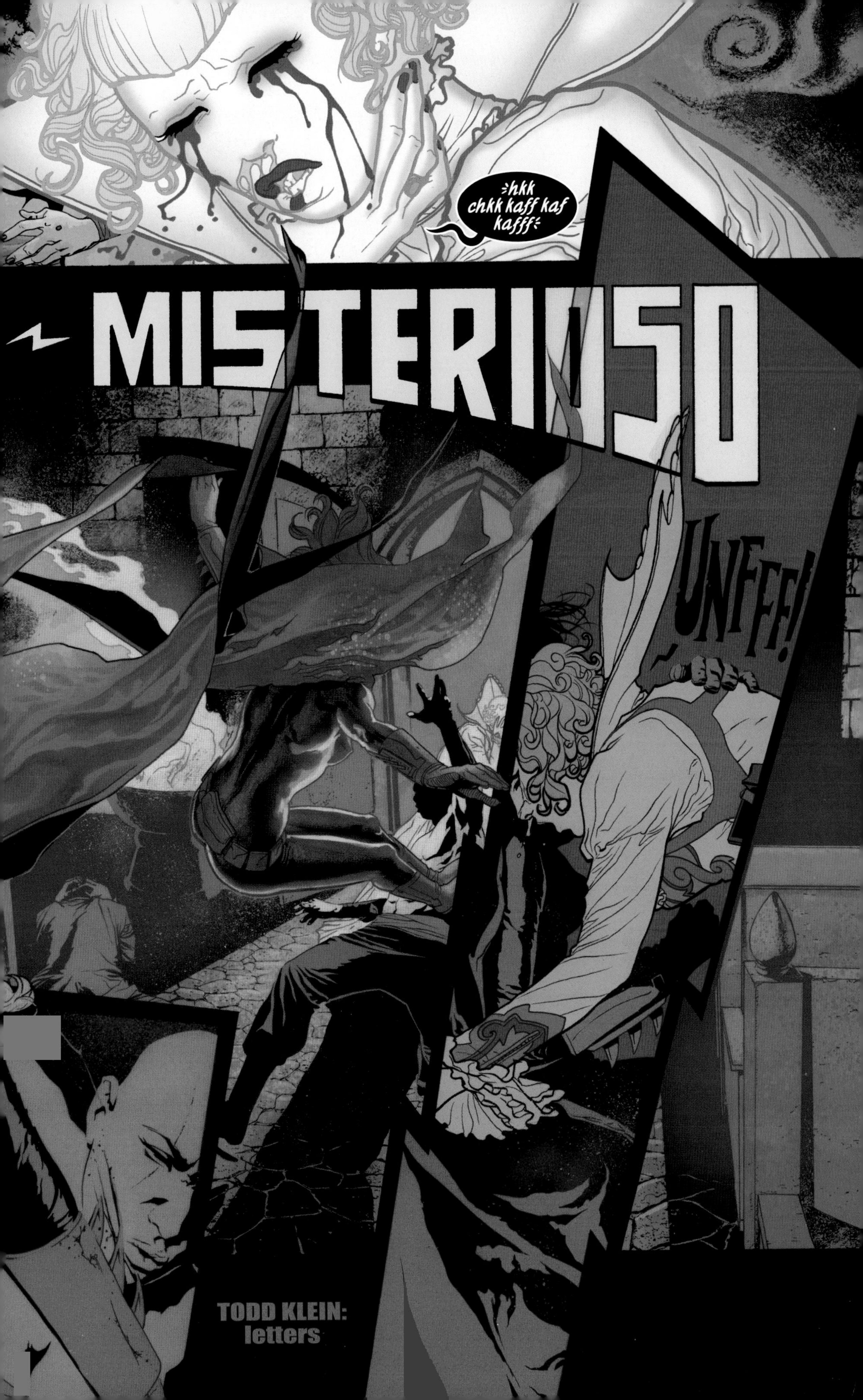
hkk chkk kaff kaf kafff
MISTERIOSO
UNFFF!
TODD KLEIN: letters

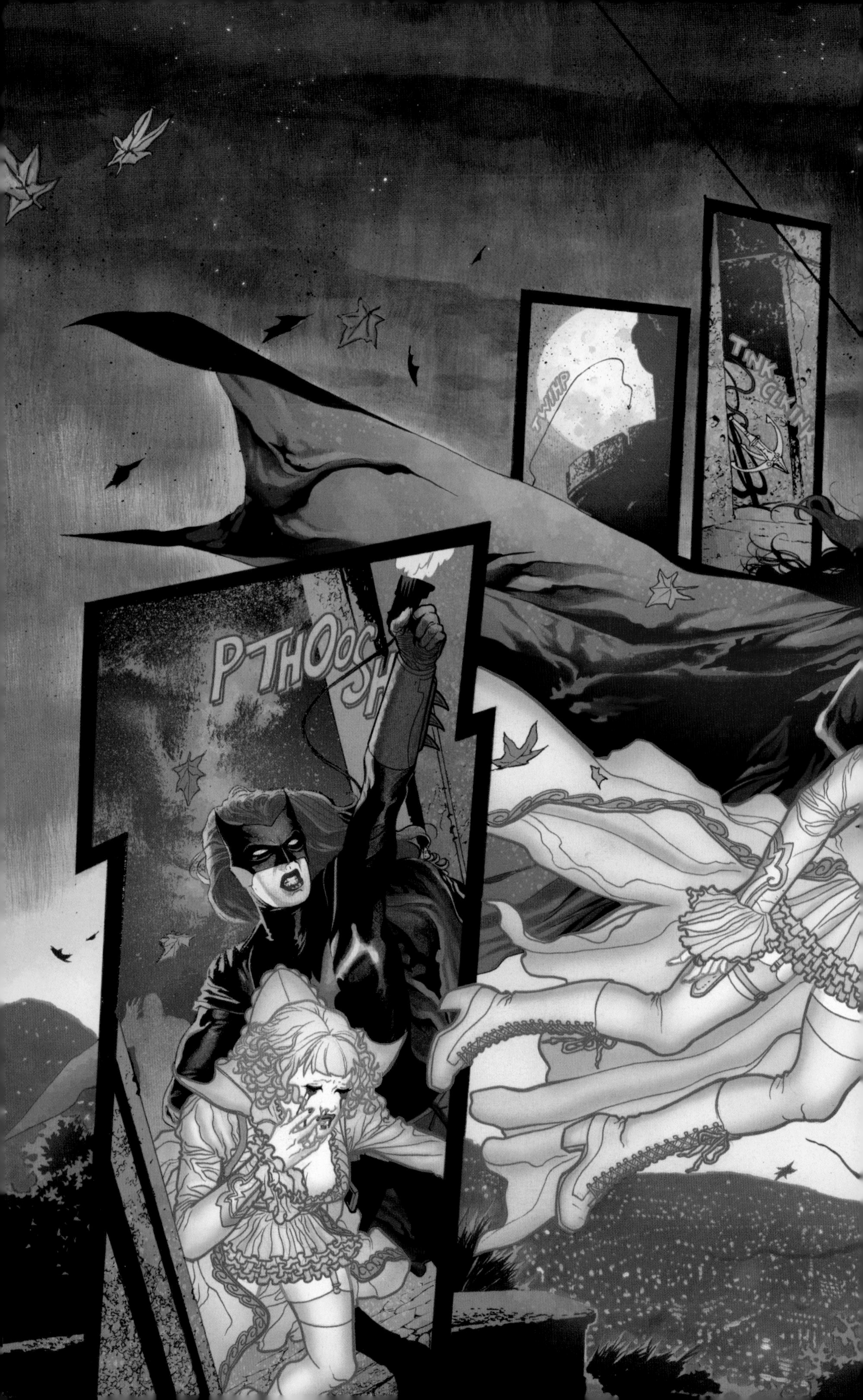
TWIIIP
TINK CLKINK
PTHOOSH

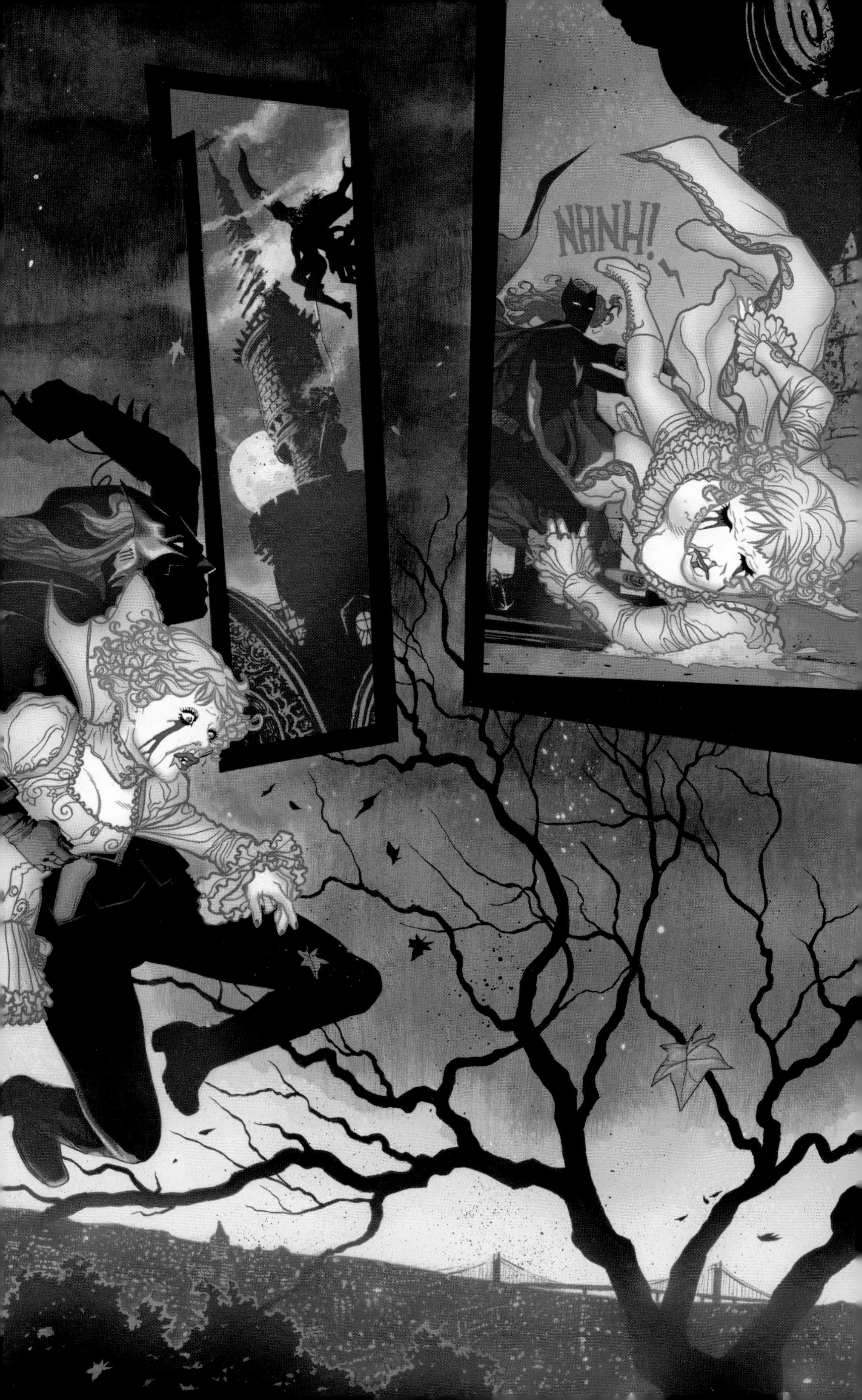
NHNH!

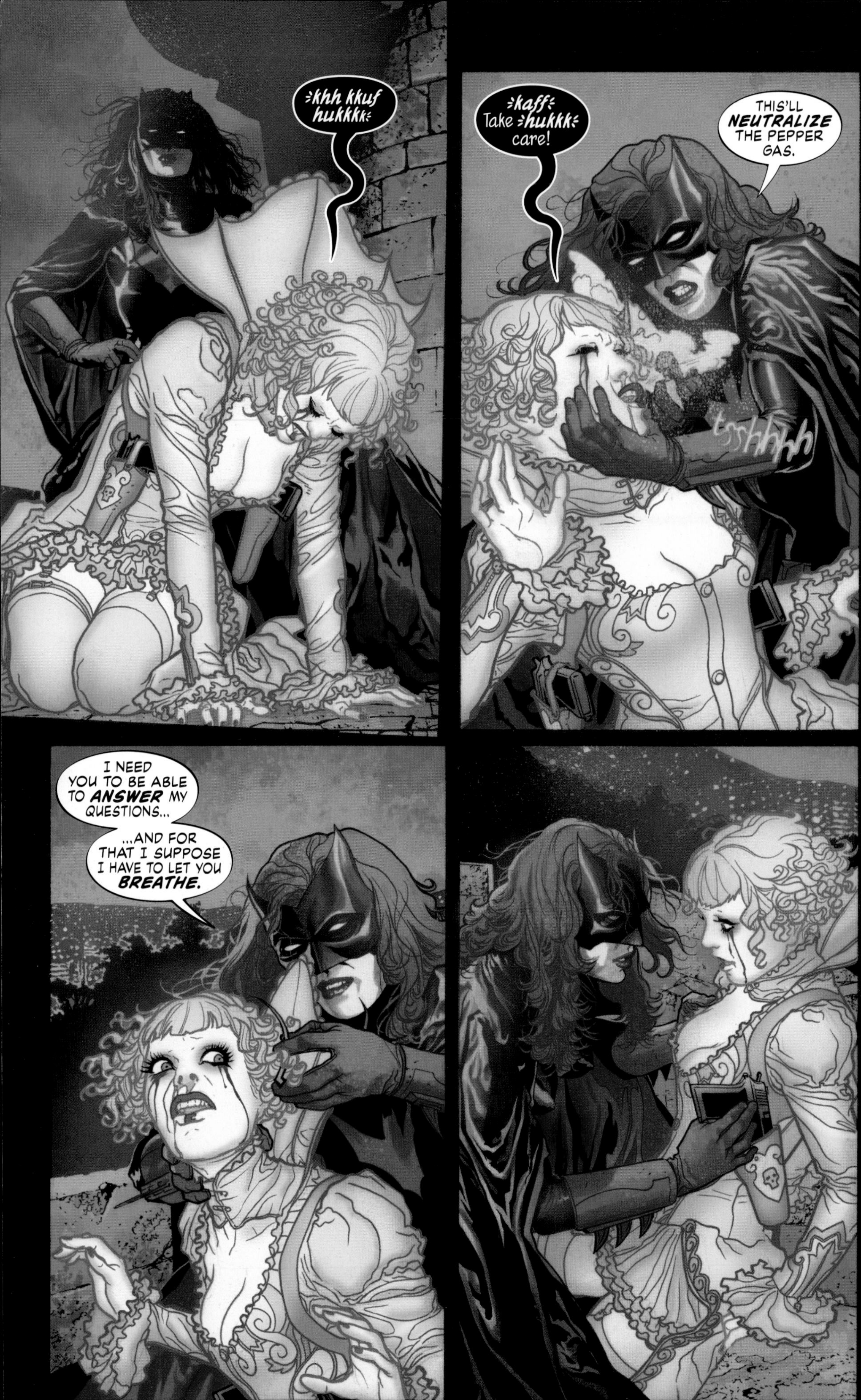
khh kkuf hukkkk
kaff Take *hukkk* care!
THIS'LL **NEUTRALIZE** THE PEPPER GAS.
tsshhhh
I NEED YOU TO BE ABLE TO **ANSWER** MY QUESTIONS...
...AND FOR THAT I SUPPOSE I HAVE TO LET YOU **BREATHE.**

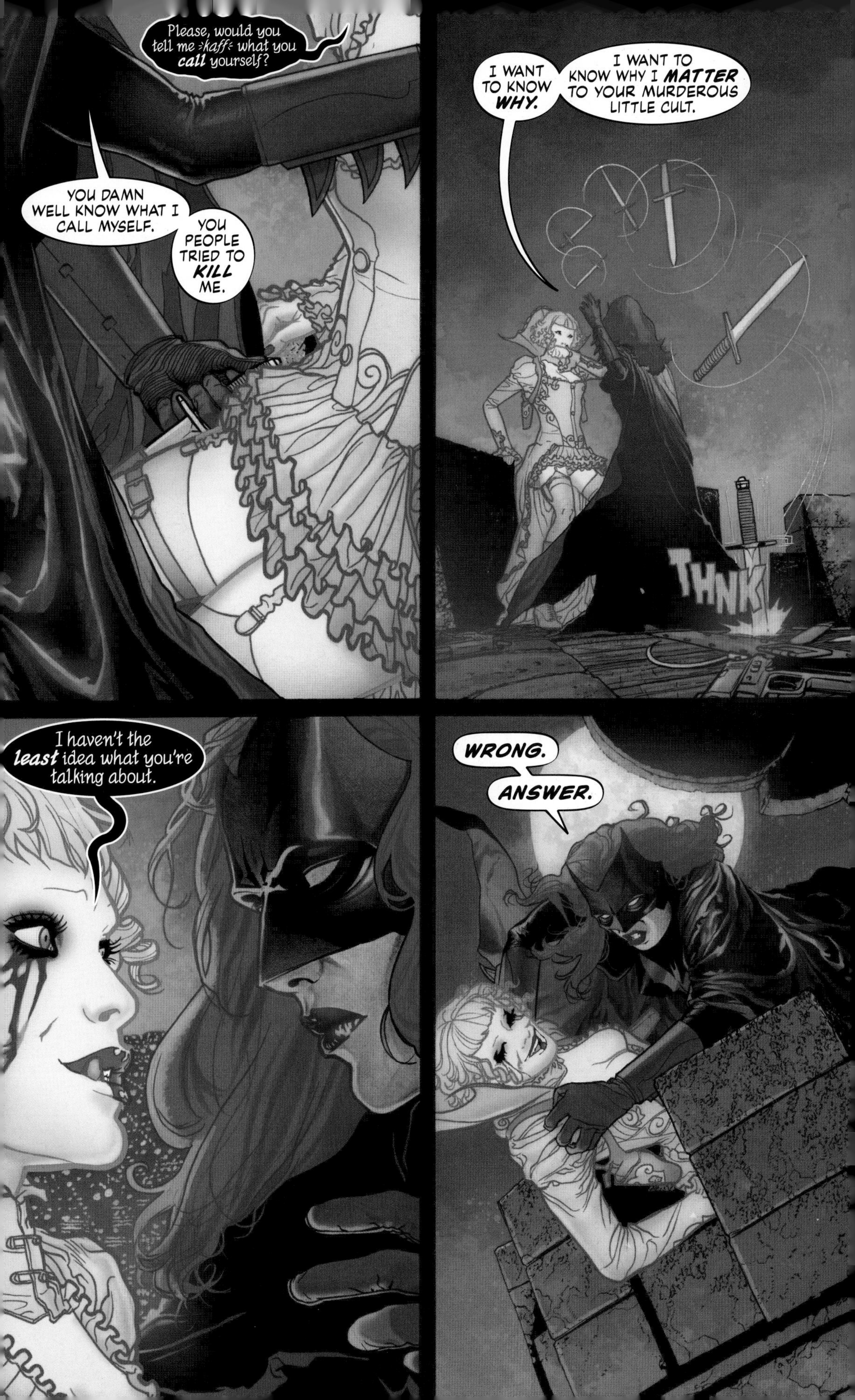
Please, would you tell me =kaff= what you call yourself?
YOU DAMN WELL KNOW WHAT I CALL MYSELF.
YOU PEOPLE TRIED TO KILL ME.
I WANT TO KNOW WHY.
I WANT TO KNOW WHY I MATTER TO YOUR MURDEROUS LITTLE CULT.
THNK
I haven't the least idea what you're talking about.
WRONG.
ANSWER.

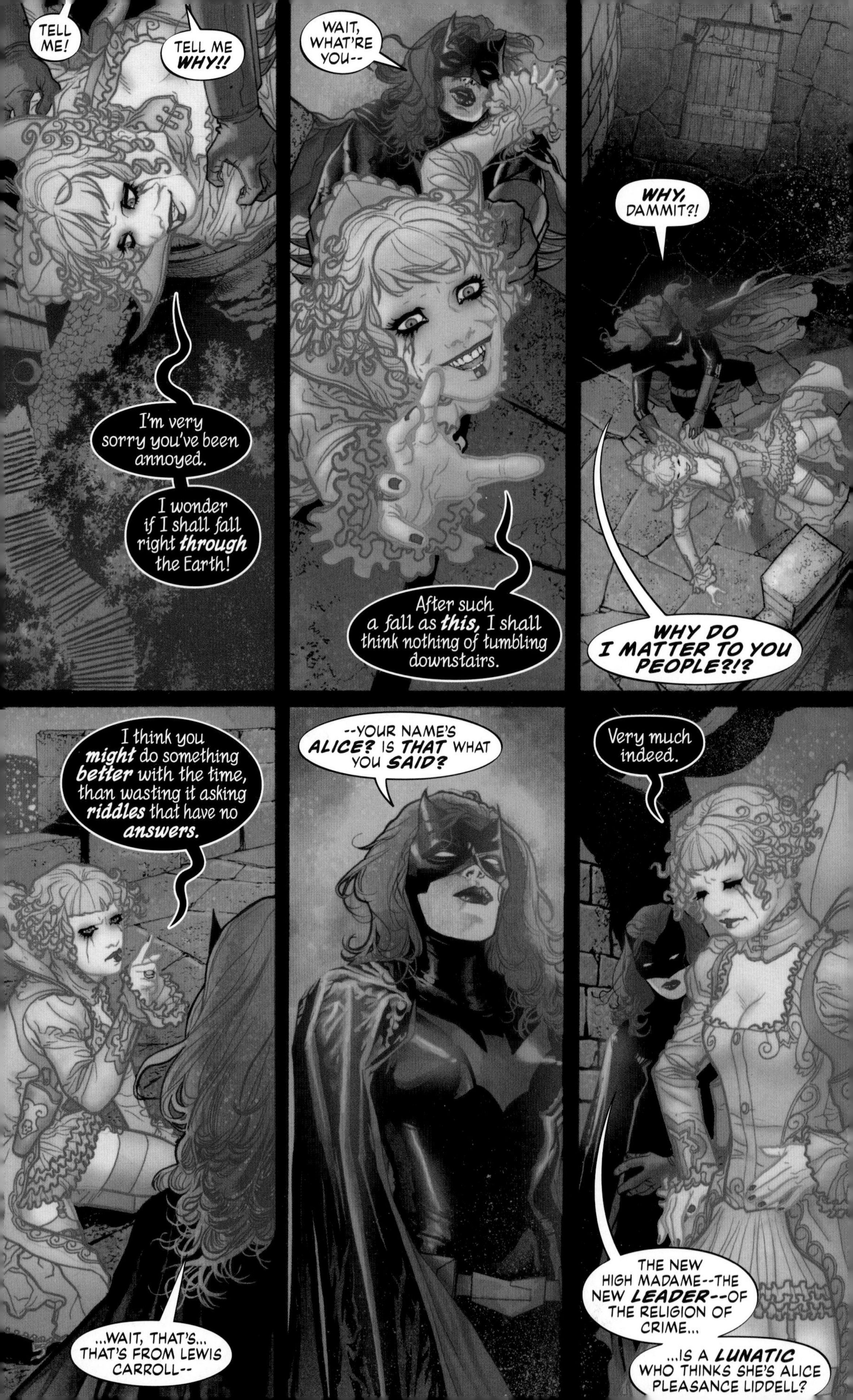
TELL ME!
TELL ME WHY!!
I'm very sorry you've been annoyed.
I wonder if I shall fall right through the Earth!
WAIT, WHAT'RE YOU--
After such a fall as this, I shall think nothing of tumbling downstairs.
WHY, DAMMIT?!
WHY DO I MATTER TO YOU PEOPLE?!?
I think you might do something better with the time, than wasting it asking riddles that have no answers.
...WAIT, THAT'S... THAT'S FROM LEWIS CARROLL--
--YOUR NAME'S ALICE? IS THAT WHAT YOU SAID?
Very much indeed.
THE NEW HIGH MADAME--THE NEW LEADER--OF THE RELIGION OF CRIME...
...IS A LUNATIC WHO THINKS SHE'S ALICE PLEASANCE LIDDELL?

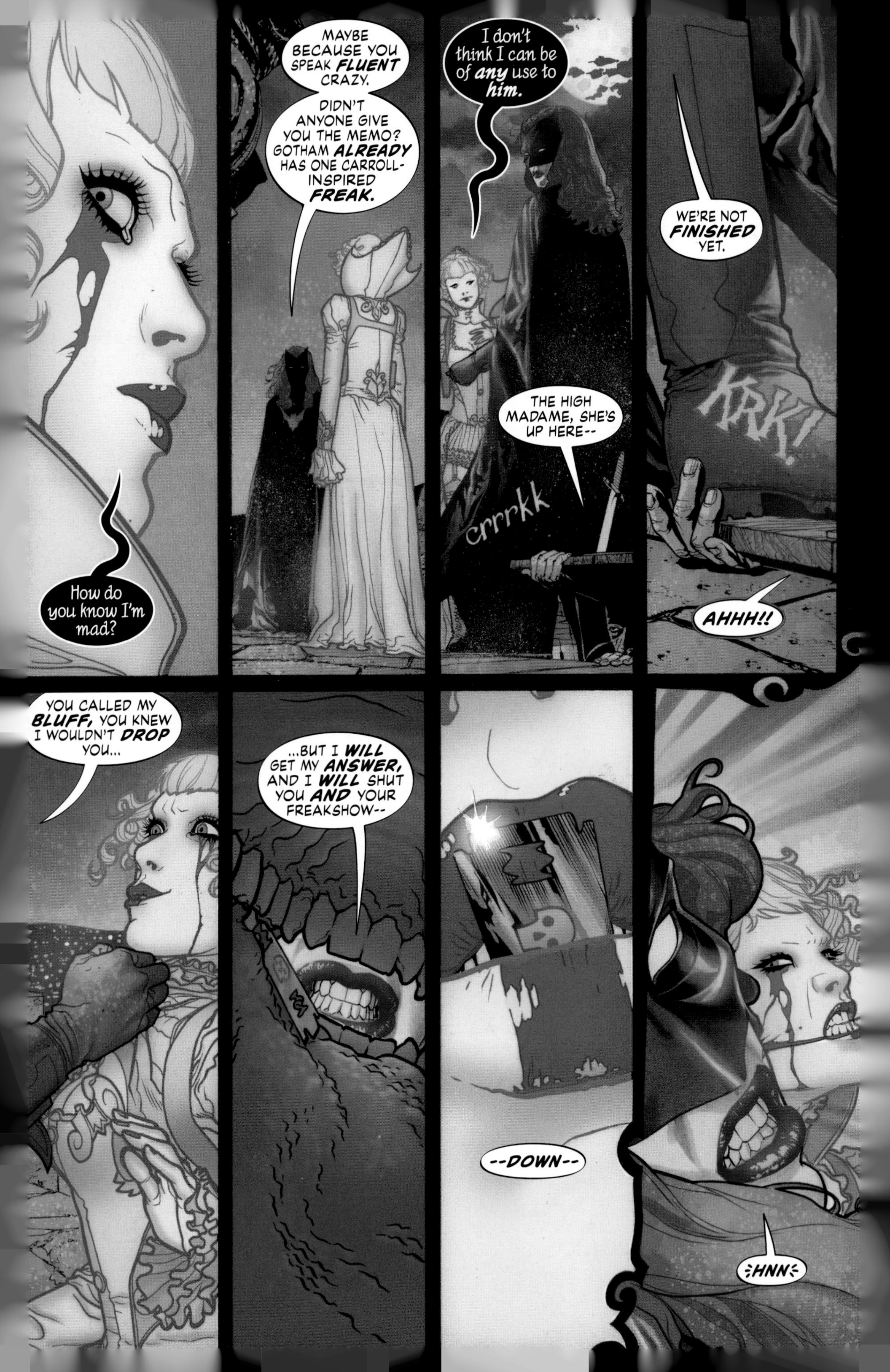
How do you know I'm mad?
MAYBE BECAUSE YOU SPEAK FLUENT CRAZY.
DIDN'T ANYONE GIVE YOU THE MEMO? GOTHAM ALREADY HAS ONE CARROLL-INSPIRED FREAK.
I don't think I can be of any use to him.
THE HIGH MADAME, SHE'S UP HERE--
crrrkk
WE'RE NOT FINISHED YET.
KRK!
AHHH!!
YOU CALLED MY BLUFF, YOU KNEW I WOULDN'T DROP YOU...
...BUT I WILL GET MY ANSWER, AND I WILL SHUT YOU AND YOUR FREAKSHOW--
--DOWN--
HNN

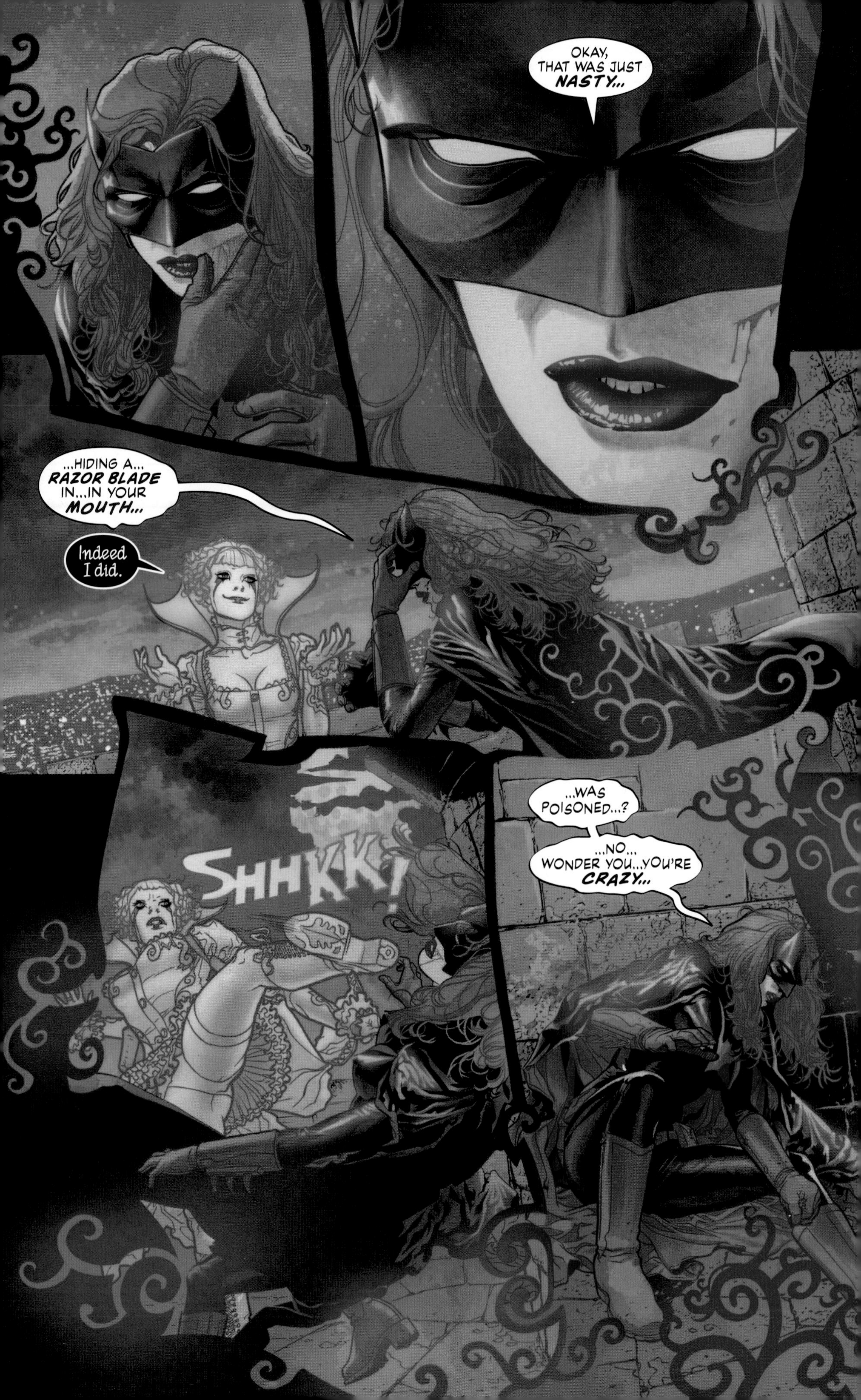
OKAY, THAT WAS JUST NASTY...
...HIDING A... RAZOR BLADE IN...IN YOUR MOUTH...
Indeed I did.
SHHKK!
...WAS POISONED...?
...NO... WONDER YOU...YOU'RE CRAZY...

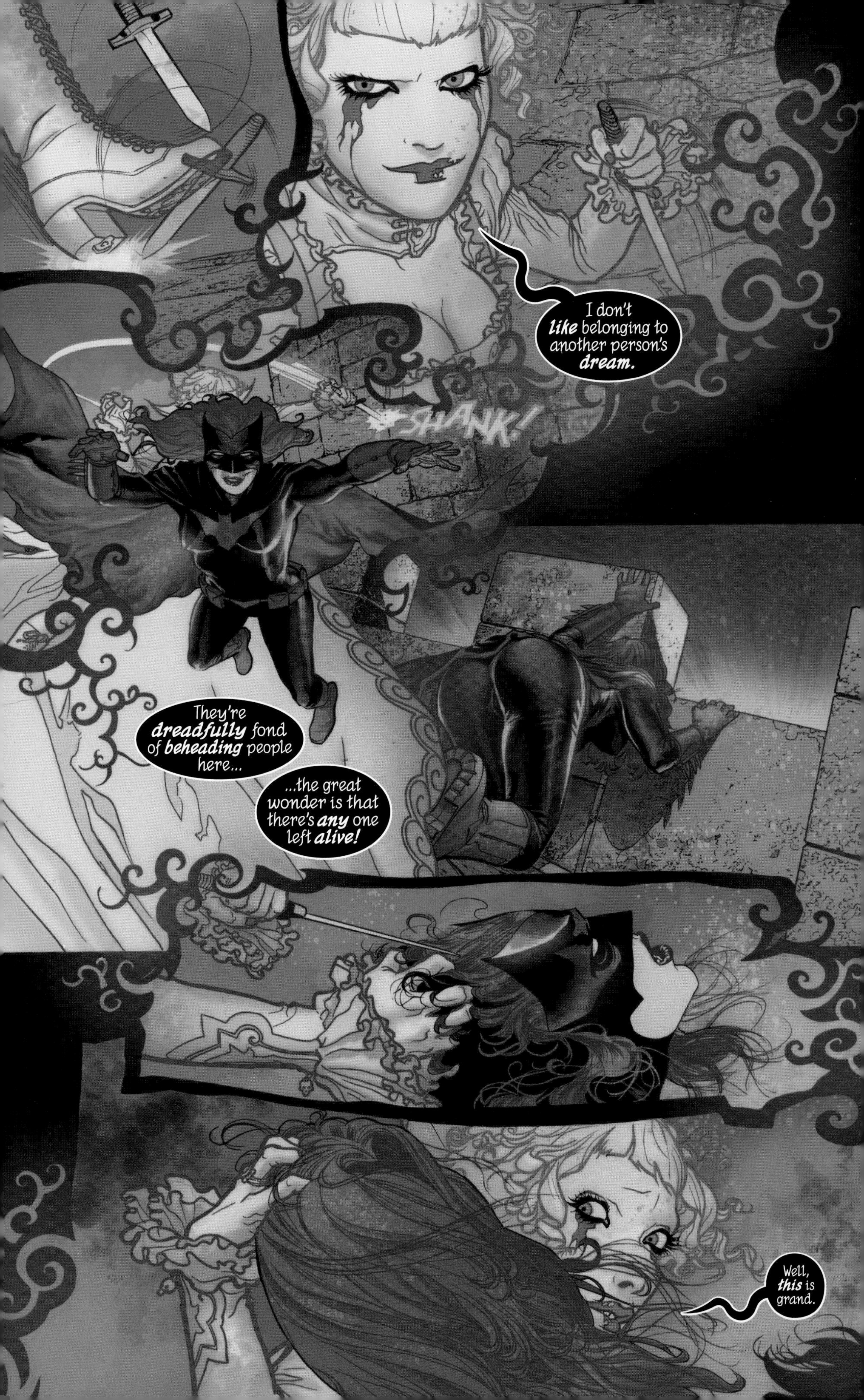
I don't like belonging to another person's dream.
SHANK!
They're dreadfully fond of beheading people here...
...the great wonder is that there's any one left alive!
Well, this is grand.

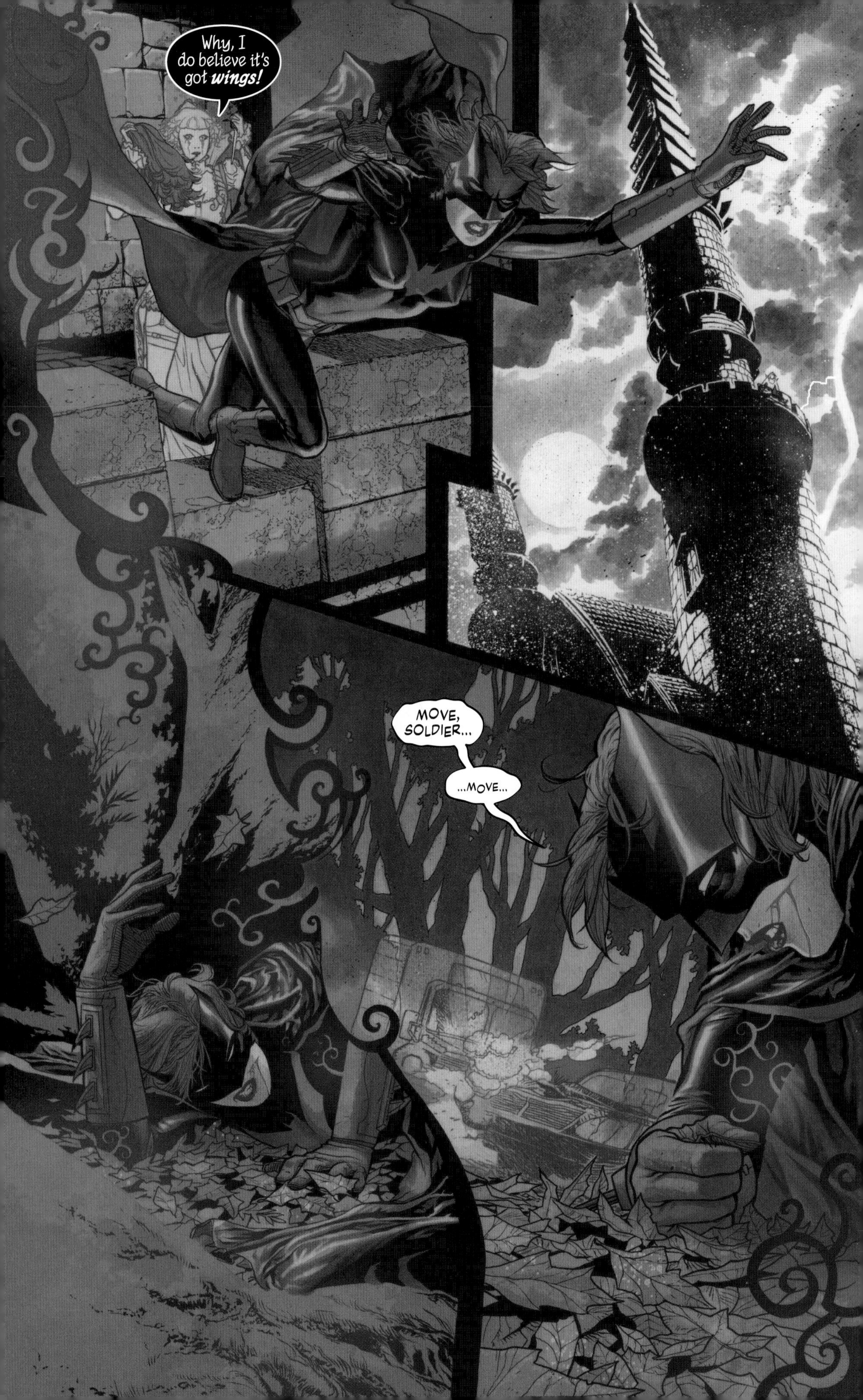
Why, I do believe it's got ***wings!***
MOVE, SOLDIER...
...MOVE...

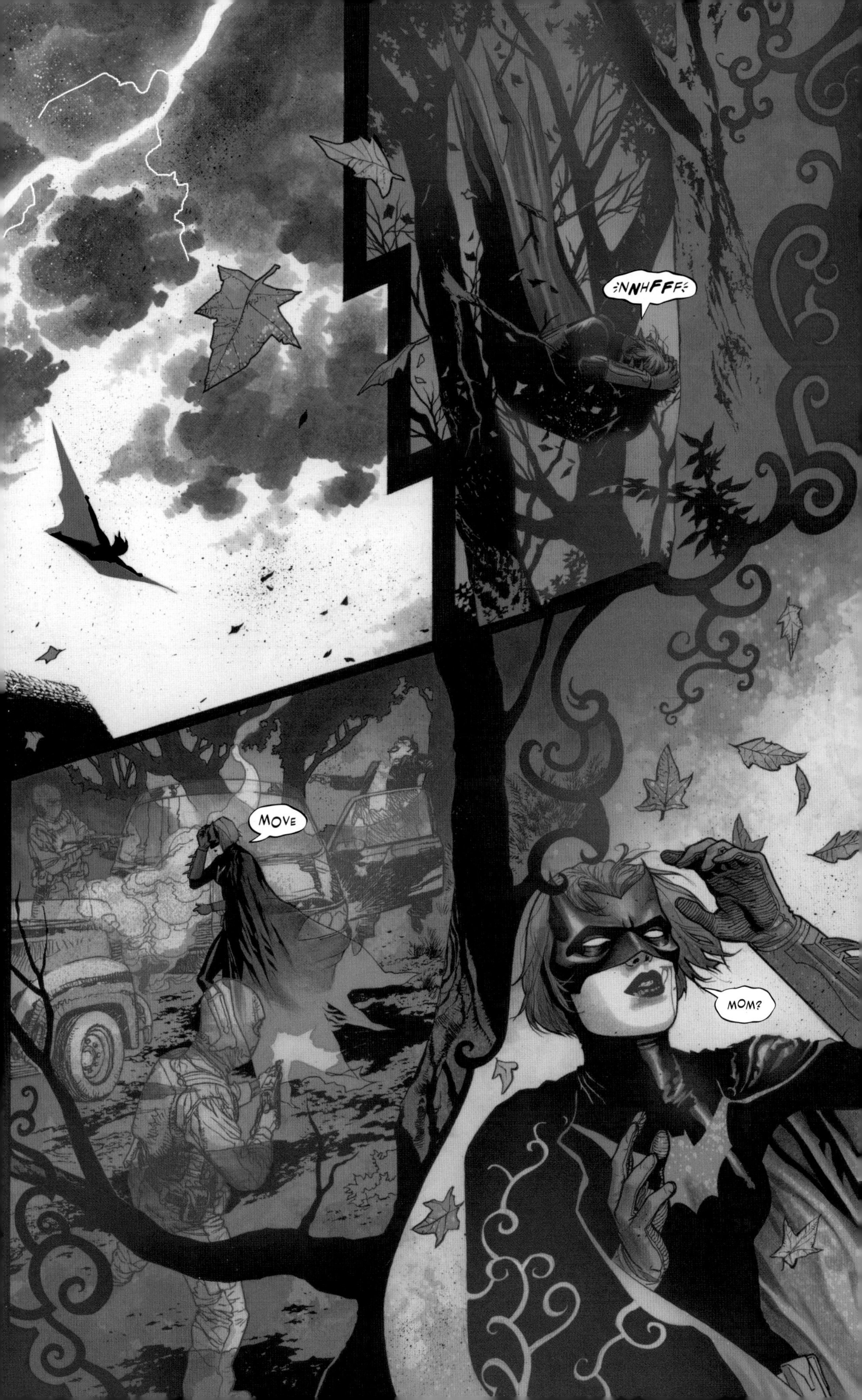
NNHFFF
MOVE
MOM?

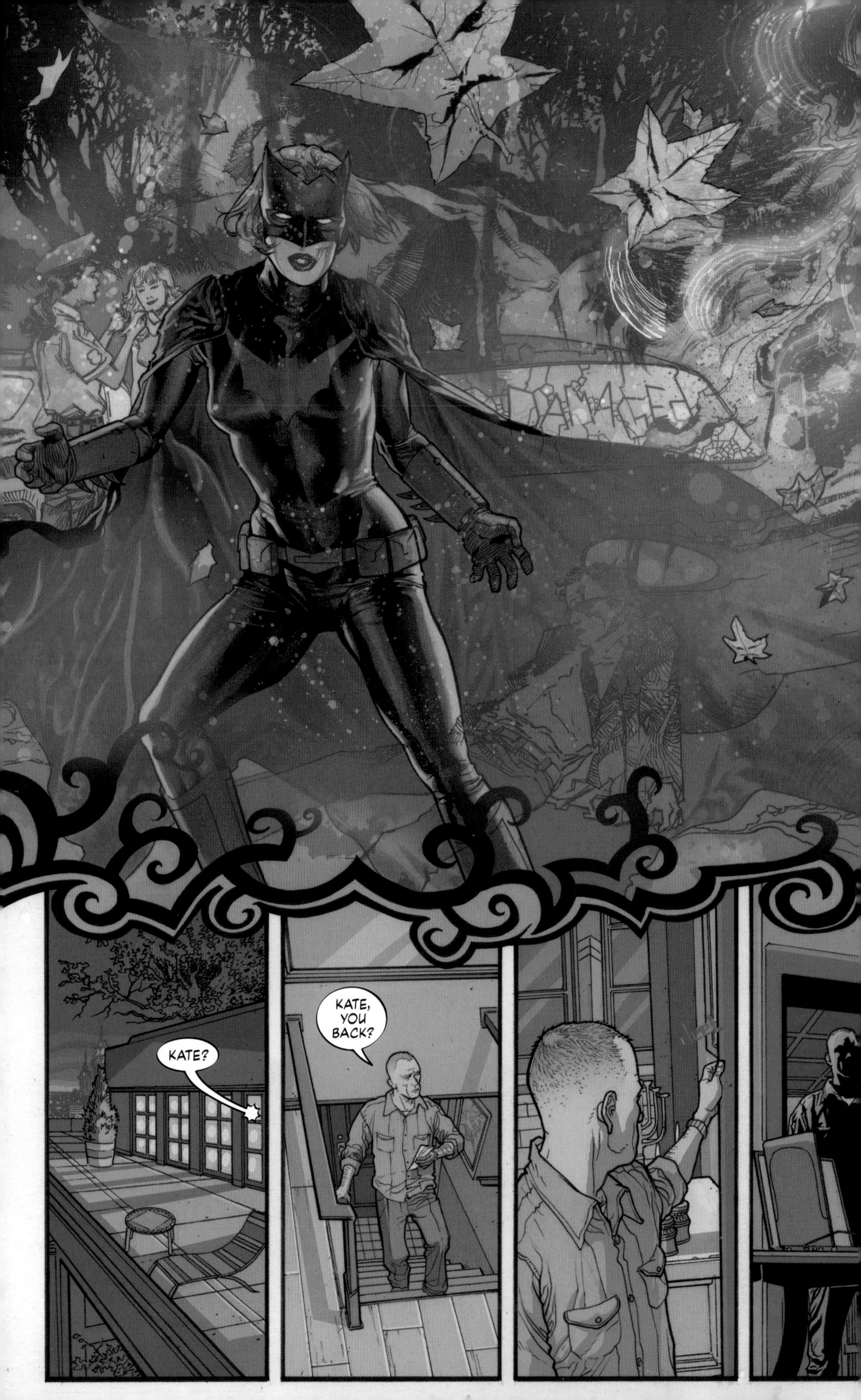
DAMAGED
KATE?
KATE, YOU BACK?

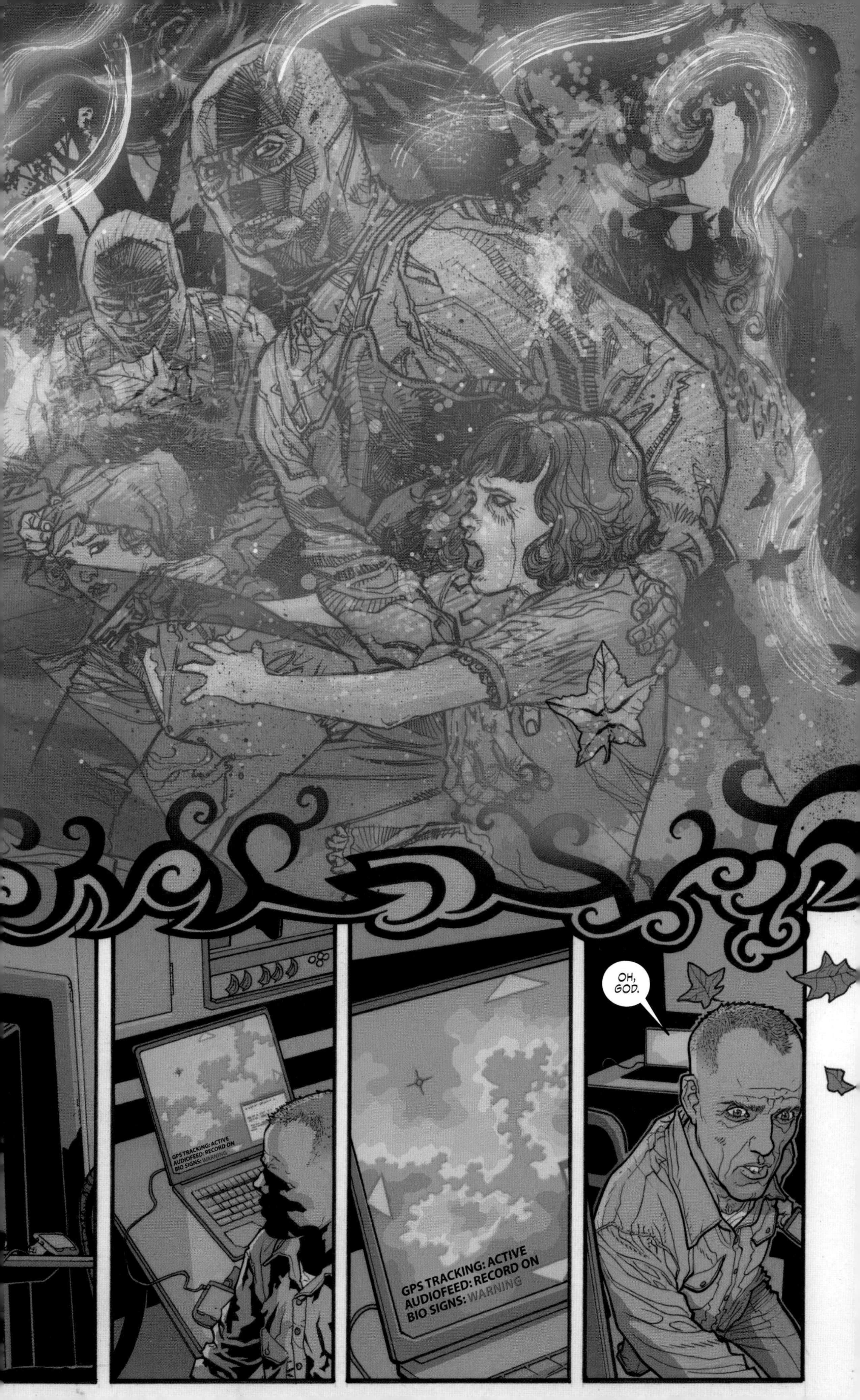
GPS TRACKING: ACTIVE
AUDIOFEED: RECORD ON
BIO SIGNS: WARNING
GPS TRACKING: ACTIVE
AUDIOFEED: RECORD ON
BIO SIGNS: WARNING
OH, GOD.

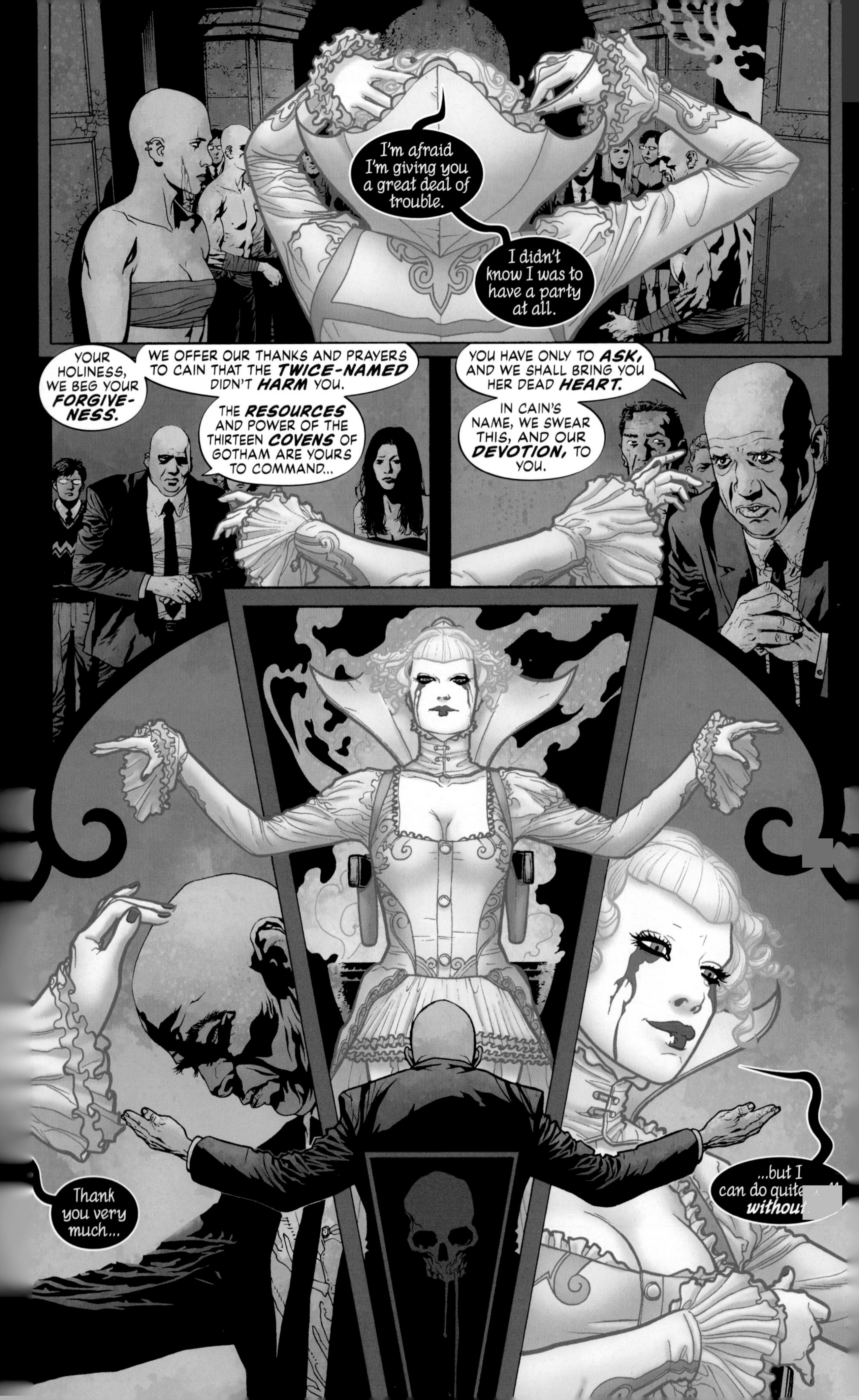
I'm afraid I'm giving you a great deal of trouble.
I didn't know I was to have a party at all.
YOUR HOLINESS, WE BEG YOUR **FORGIVE-NESS.**
WE OFFER OUR THANKS AND PRAYERS TO CAIN THAT THE **TWICE-NAMED** DIDN'T **HARM** YOU.
THE **RESOURCES** AND POWER OF THE THIRTEEN **COVENS** OF GOTHAM ARE YOURS TO COMMAND...
YOU HAVE ONLY TO **ASK,** AND WE SHALL BRING YOU HER DEAD **HEART.**
IN CAIN'S NAME, WE SWEAR THIS, AND OUR **DEVOTION,** TO YOU.
Thank you very much...
...but I can do quite
without

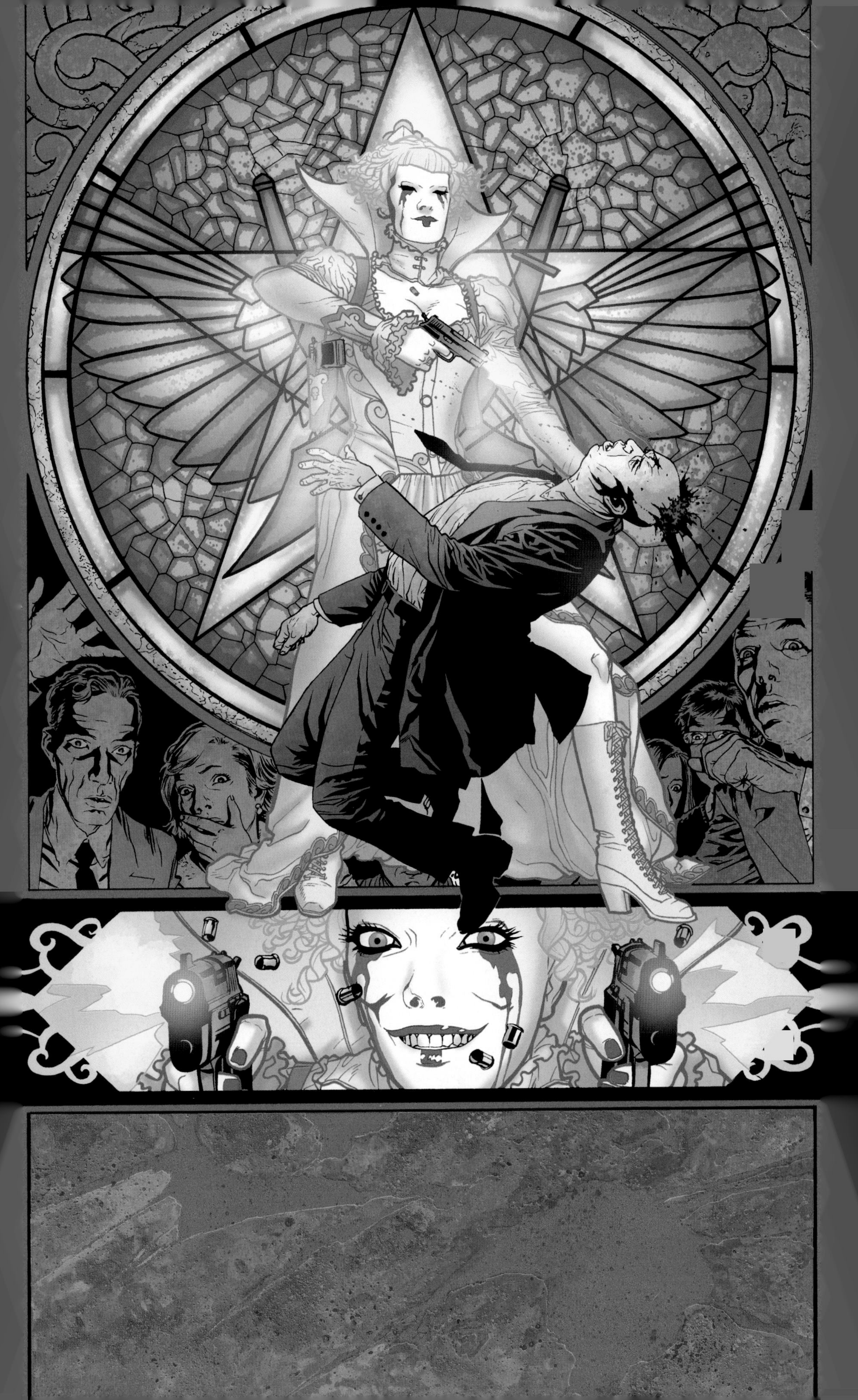

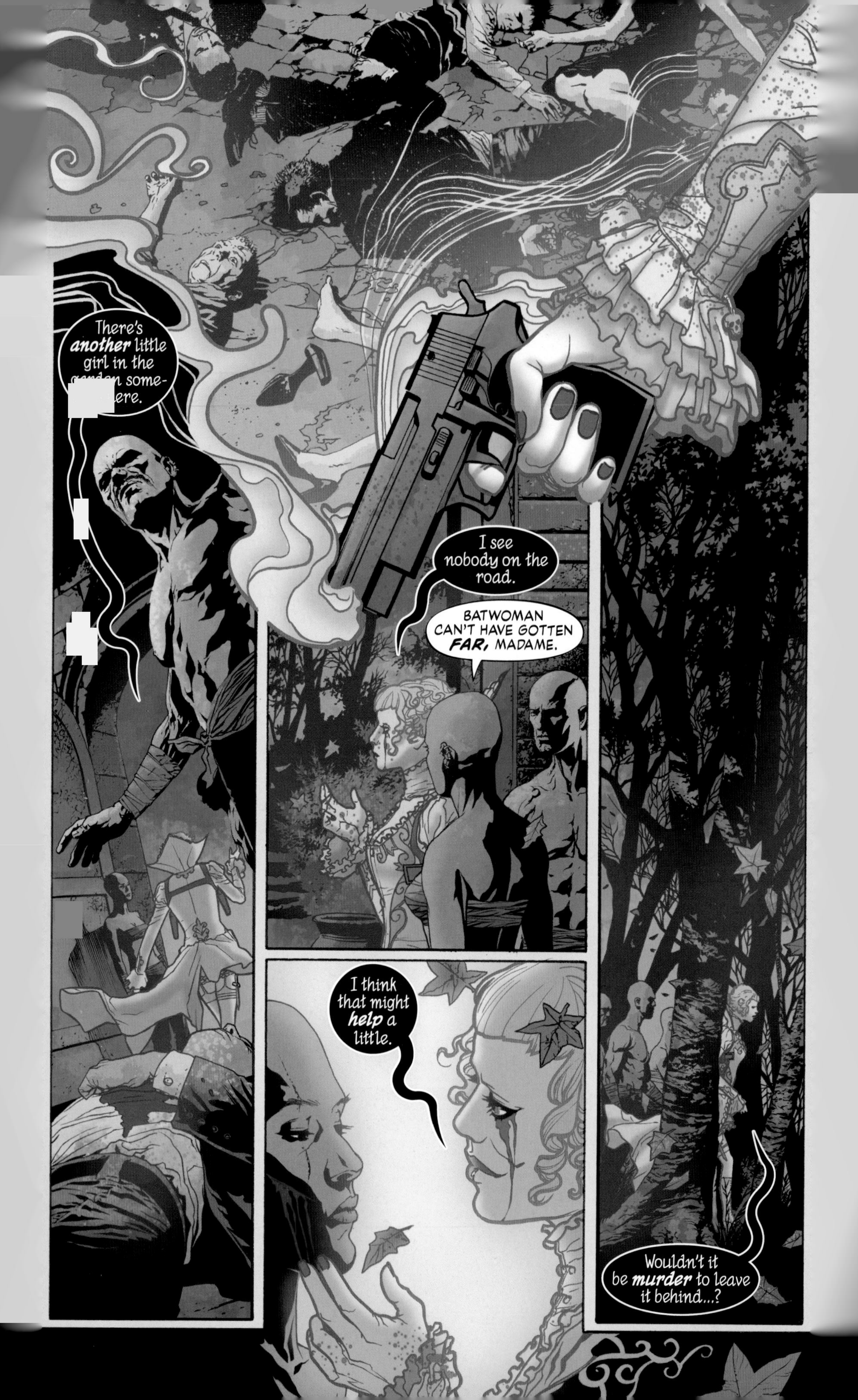
There's **another** little girl in the garden some- …ere.
I see nobody on the road.
BATWOMAN CAN'T HAVE GOTTEN **FAR,** MADAME.
I think that might **help** a little.
Wouldn't it be **murder** to leave it behind...?

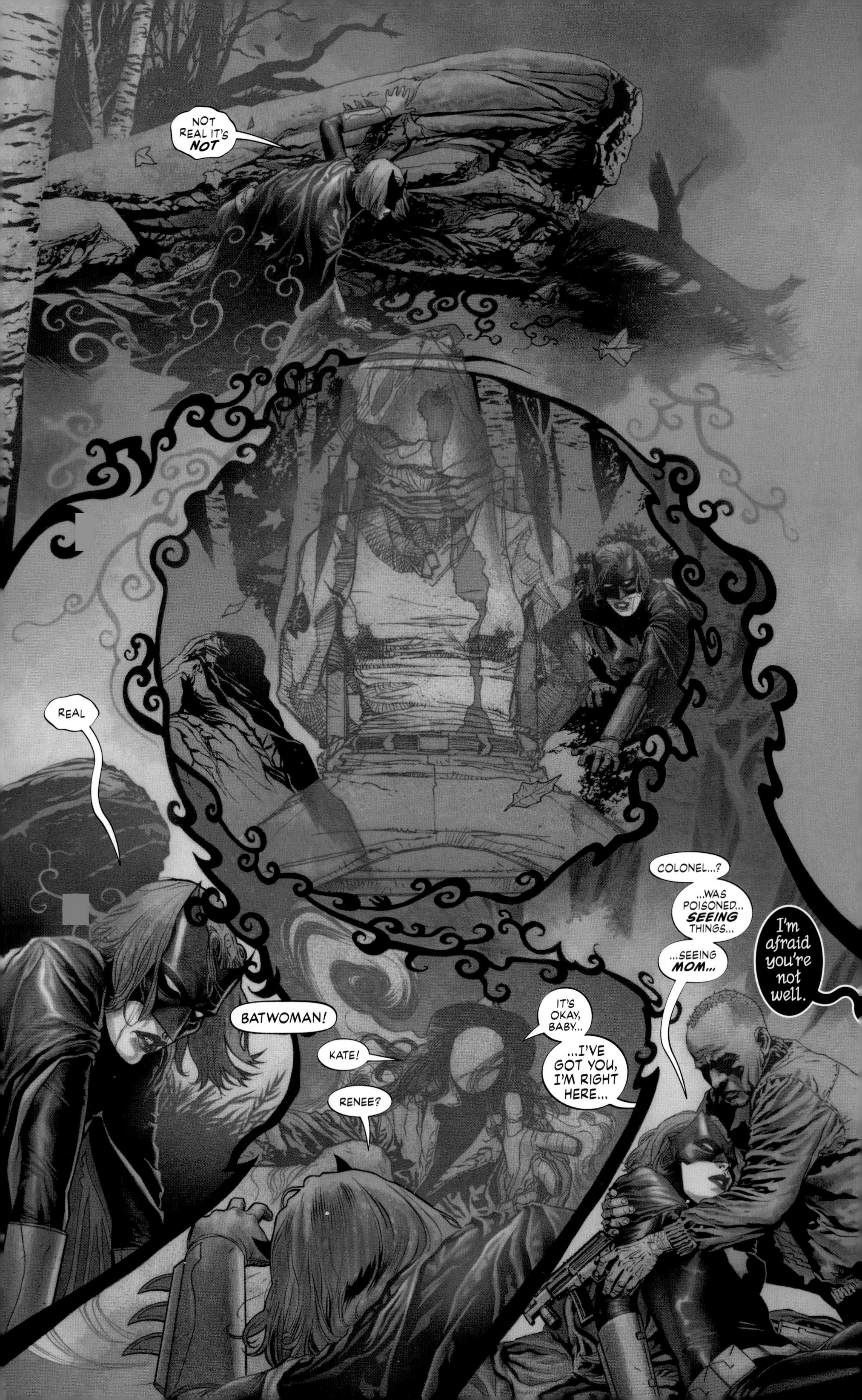
NOT REAL IT'S **NOT**
REAL
BATWOMAN!
KATE!
RENEE?
IT'S OKAY, BABY...
...I'VE GOT YOU, I'M RIGHT HERE...
COLONEL...?
...WAS POISONED... **SEEING** THINGS...
...SEEING **MOM**...
I'm afraid you're not well.

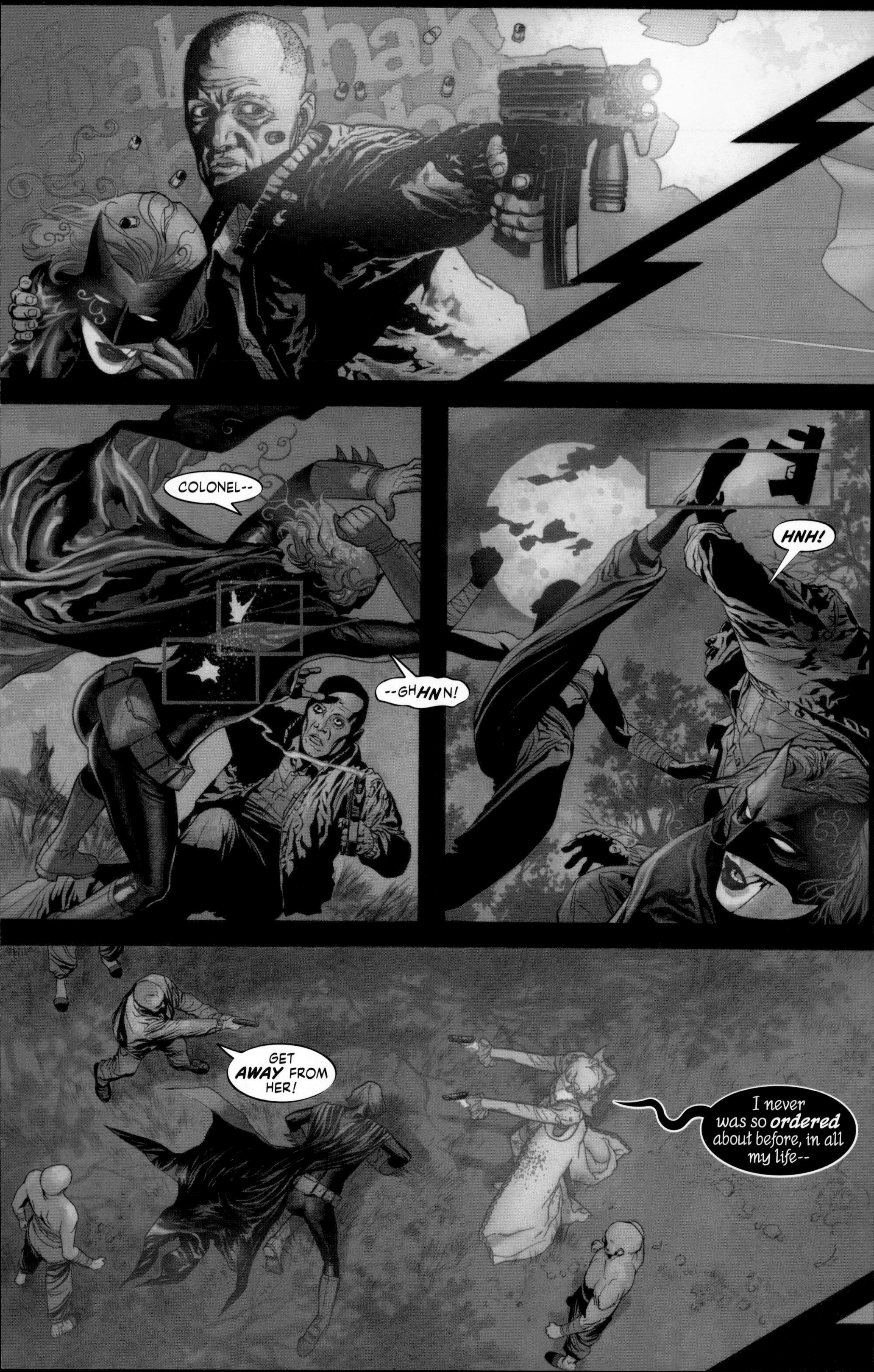
COLONEL--
--GHHNN!
HNH!
GET AWAY FROM HER!
I never was so ordered about before, in all my life--

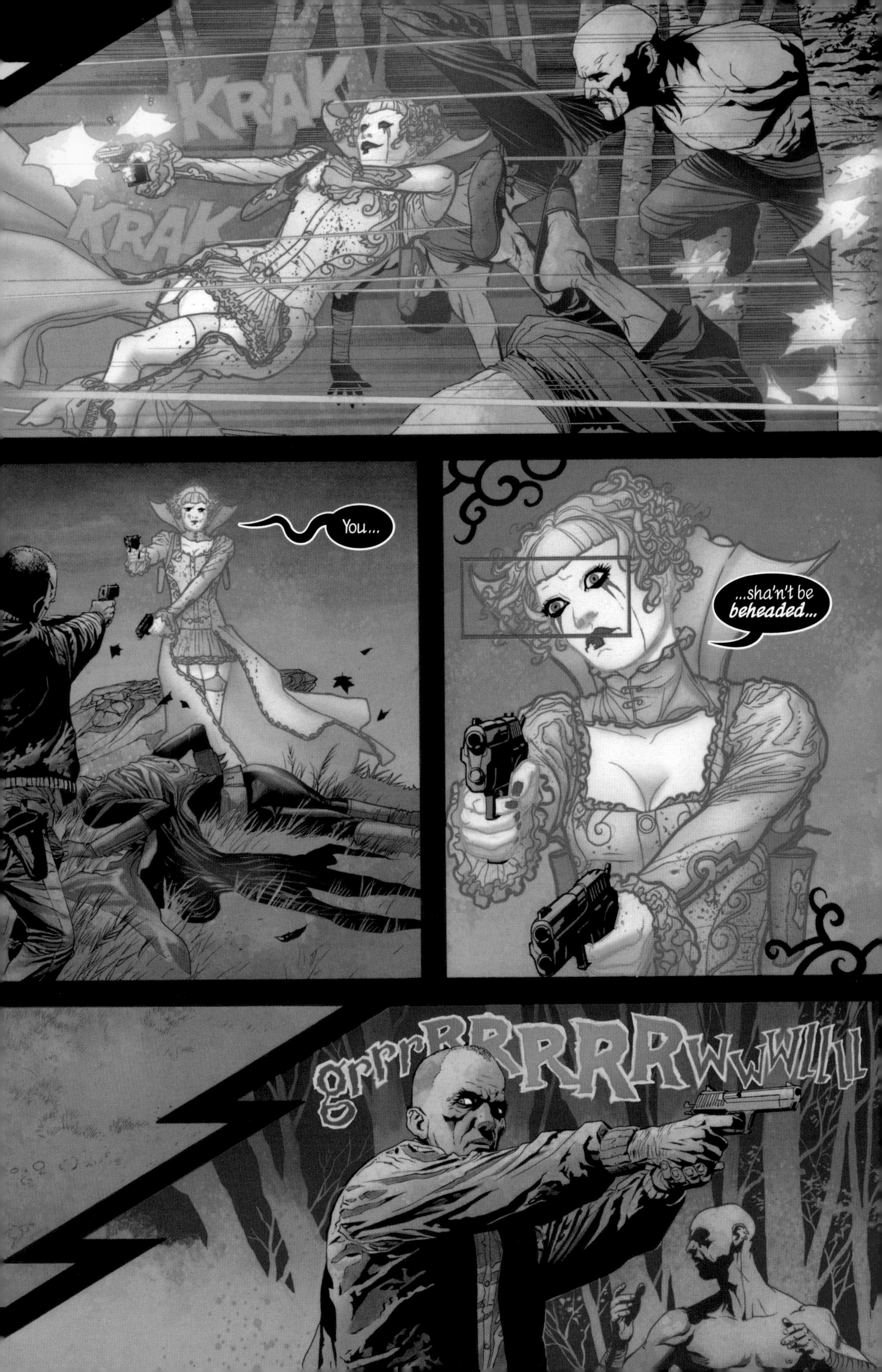
KRAK
KRAK
You...
...sha'n't be *beheaded*...
grrrRRRRRwwWlll

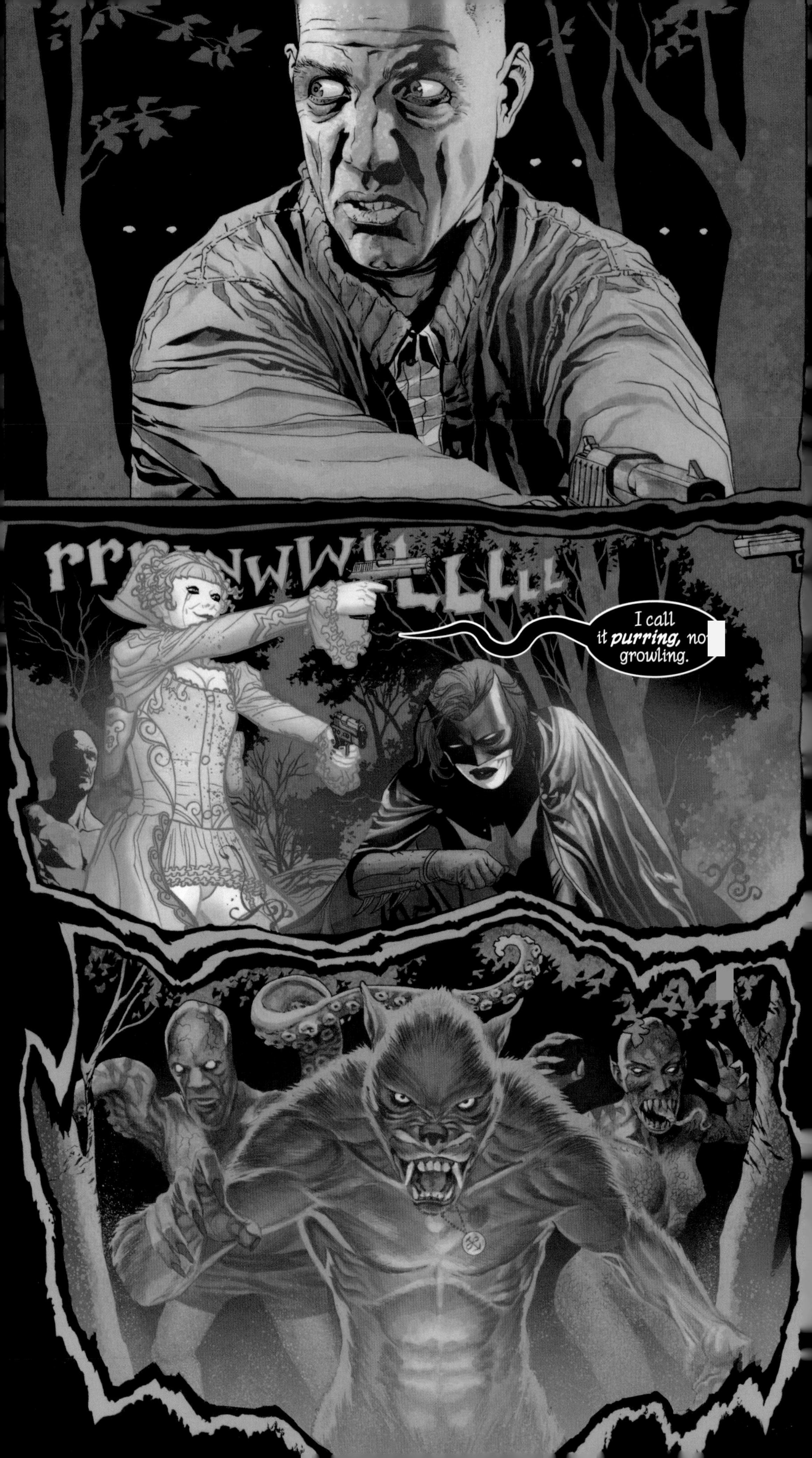
I call it *purring,* no growling.

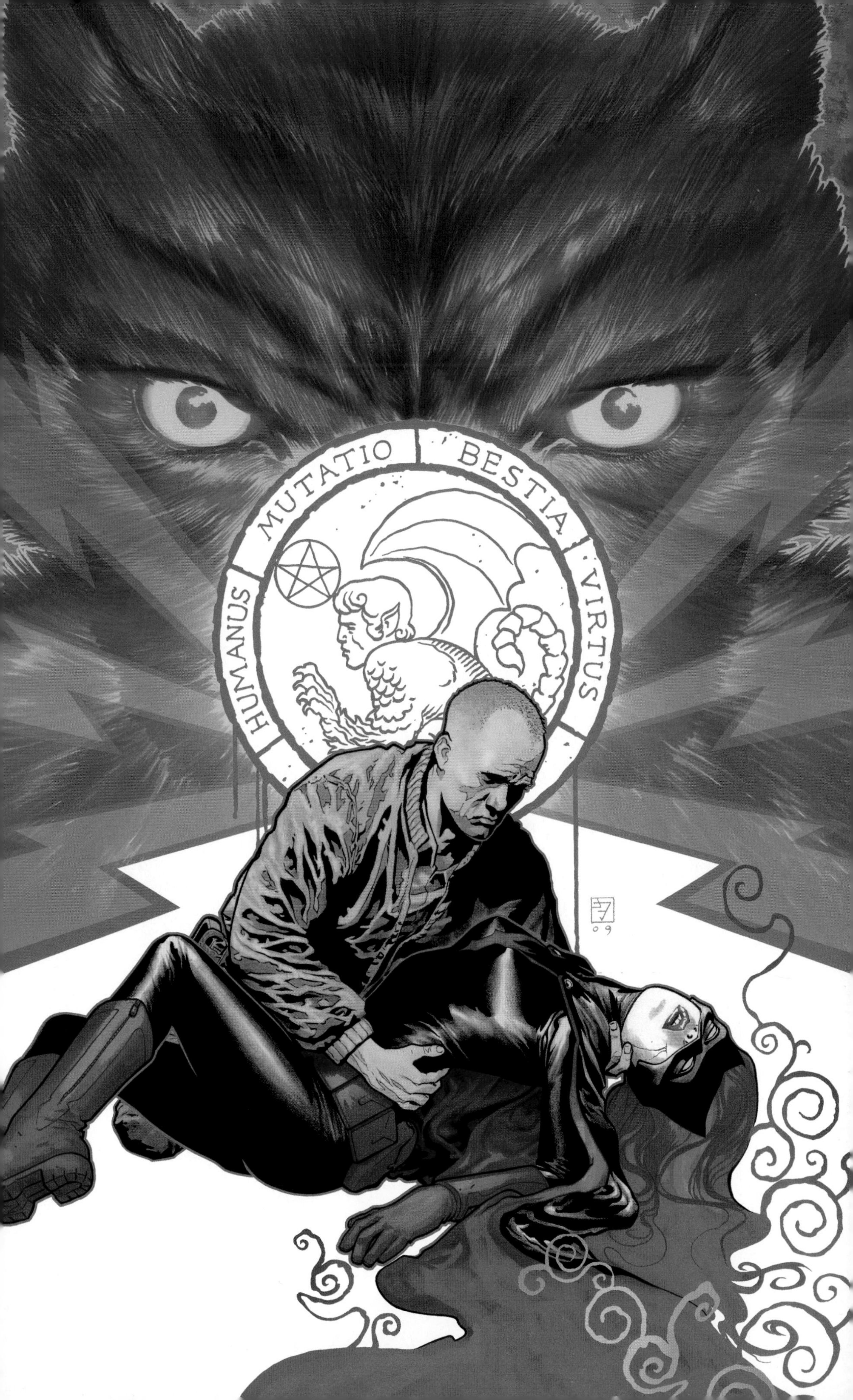

HUMANUS
MUTATIO
BESTIA
VIRTUS

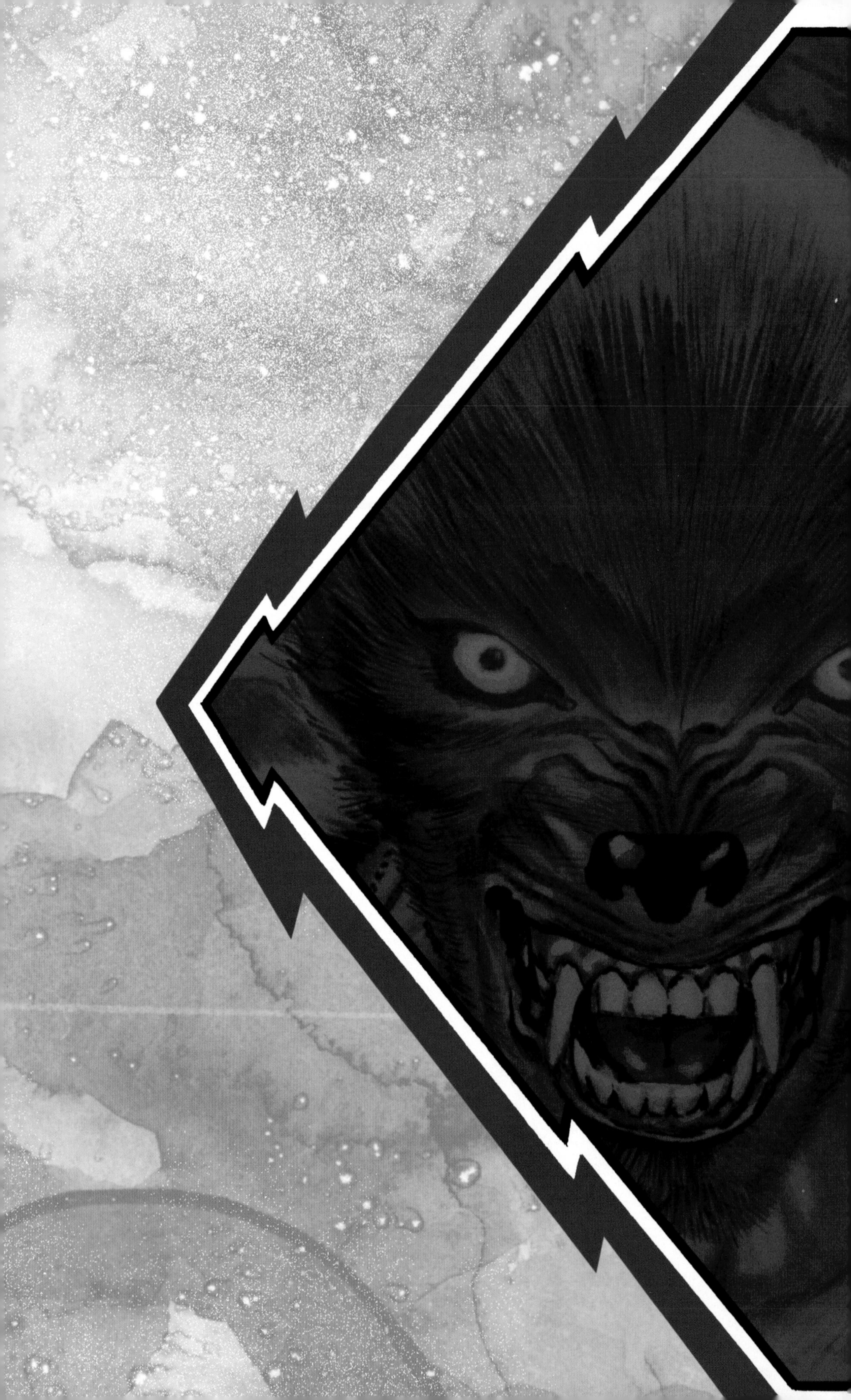

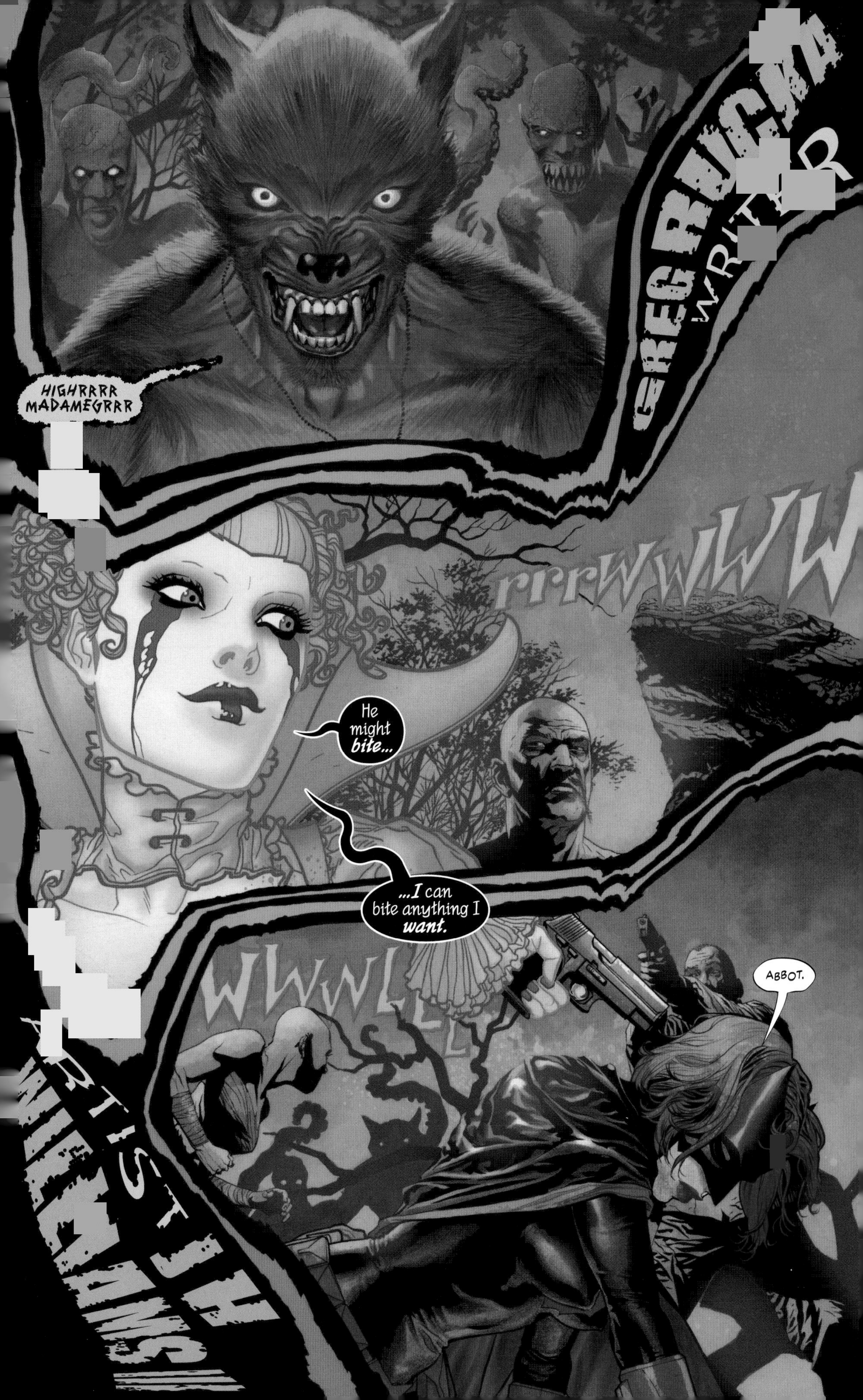
HIGHRRRR MADAMEGRRR
rrrWWWWW
He might *bite*...
...I can bite anything I *want.*
WWWLLL
ABBOT.
ARTIST

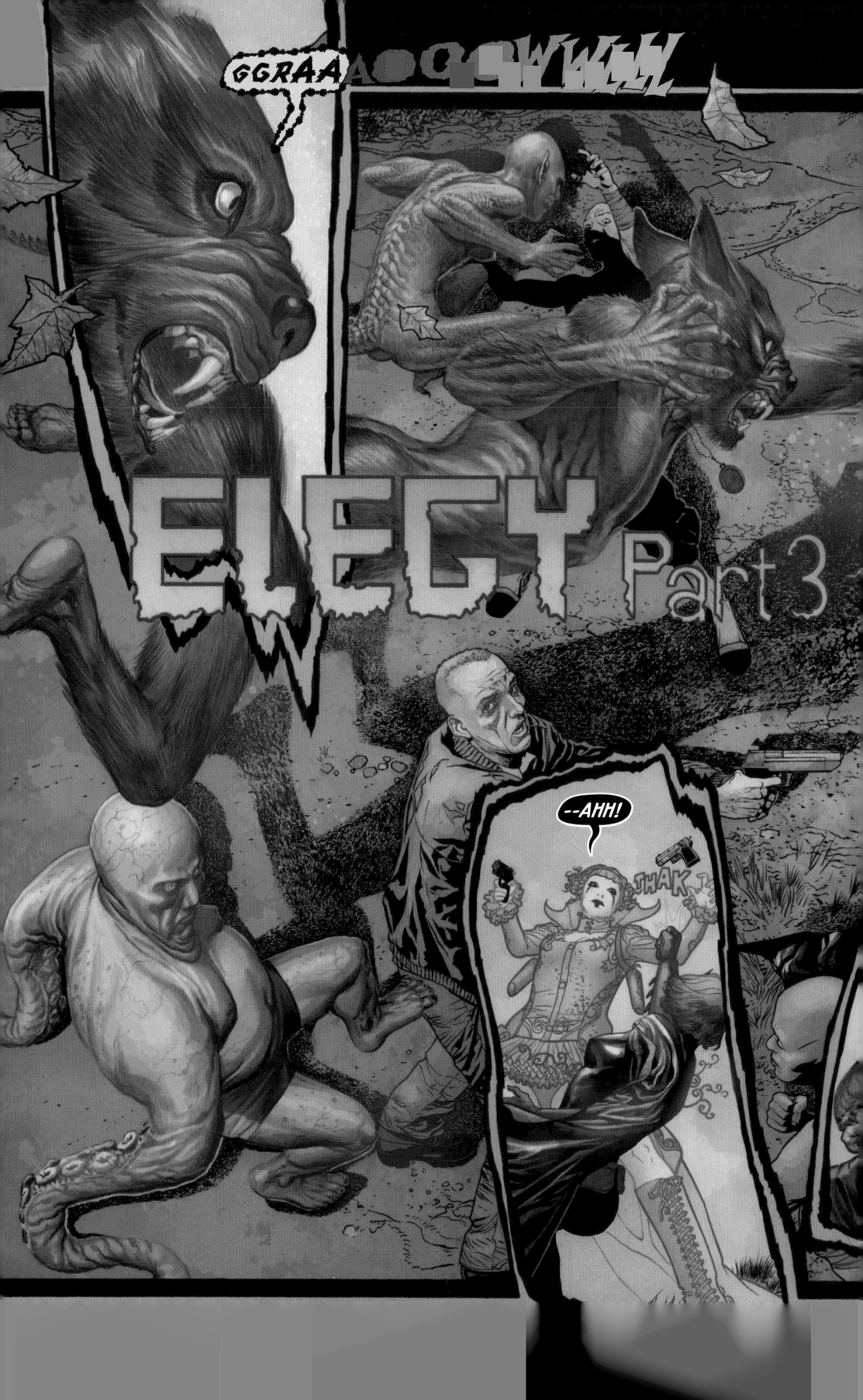
GGRAA
ELEGY Part 3
--AHH!
THAK

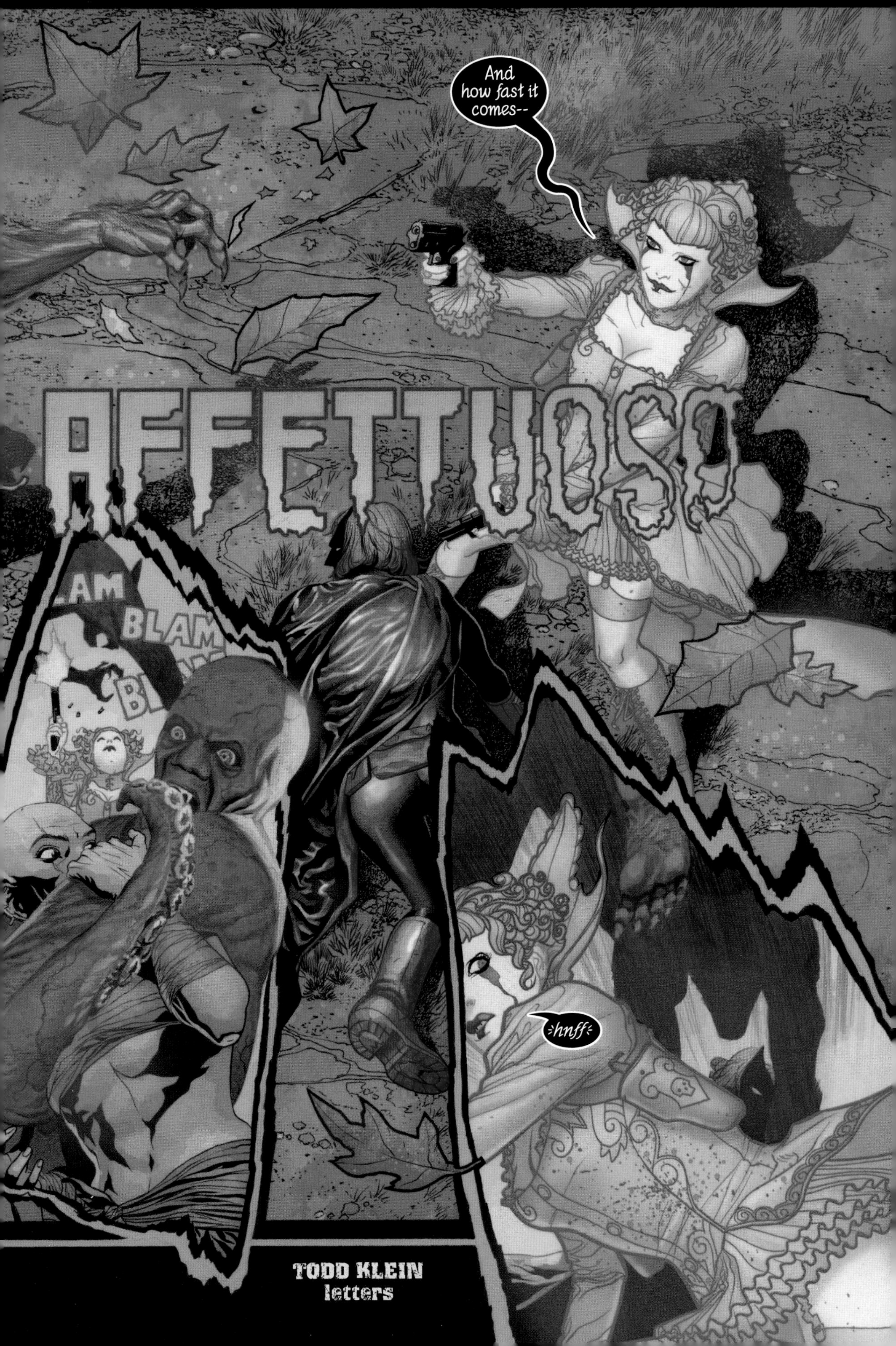
And how fast it comes--
AFFETTUOSO
BLAM
BLAM
hnff
TODD KLEIN
letters

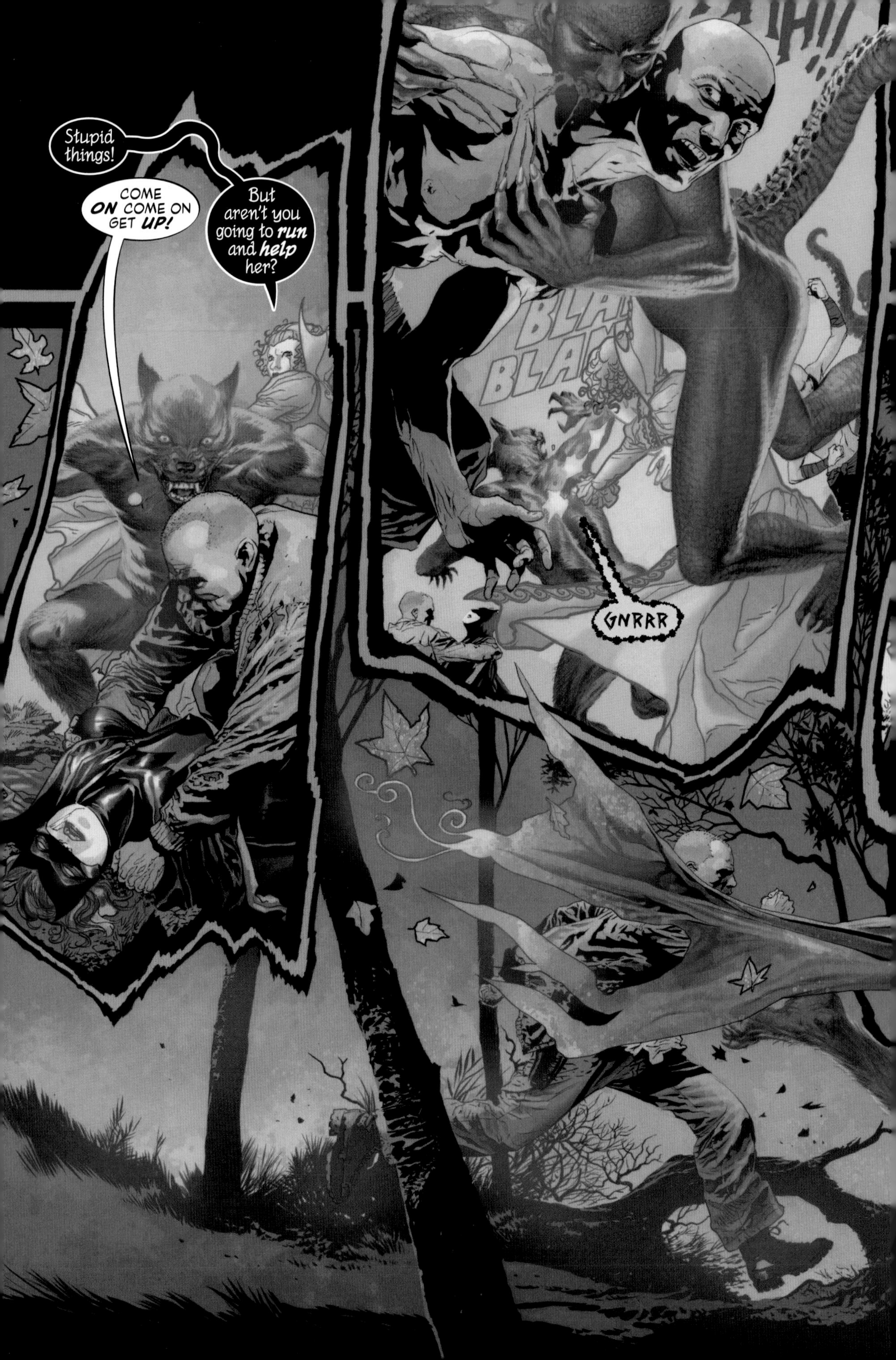

Stupid things!
COME ON COME ON GET UP!
But aren't you going to run and help her?
BLA! BLA!
GNRRR

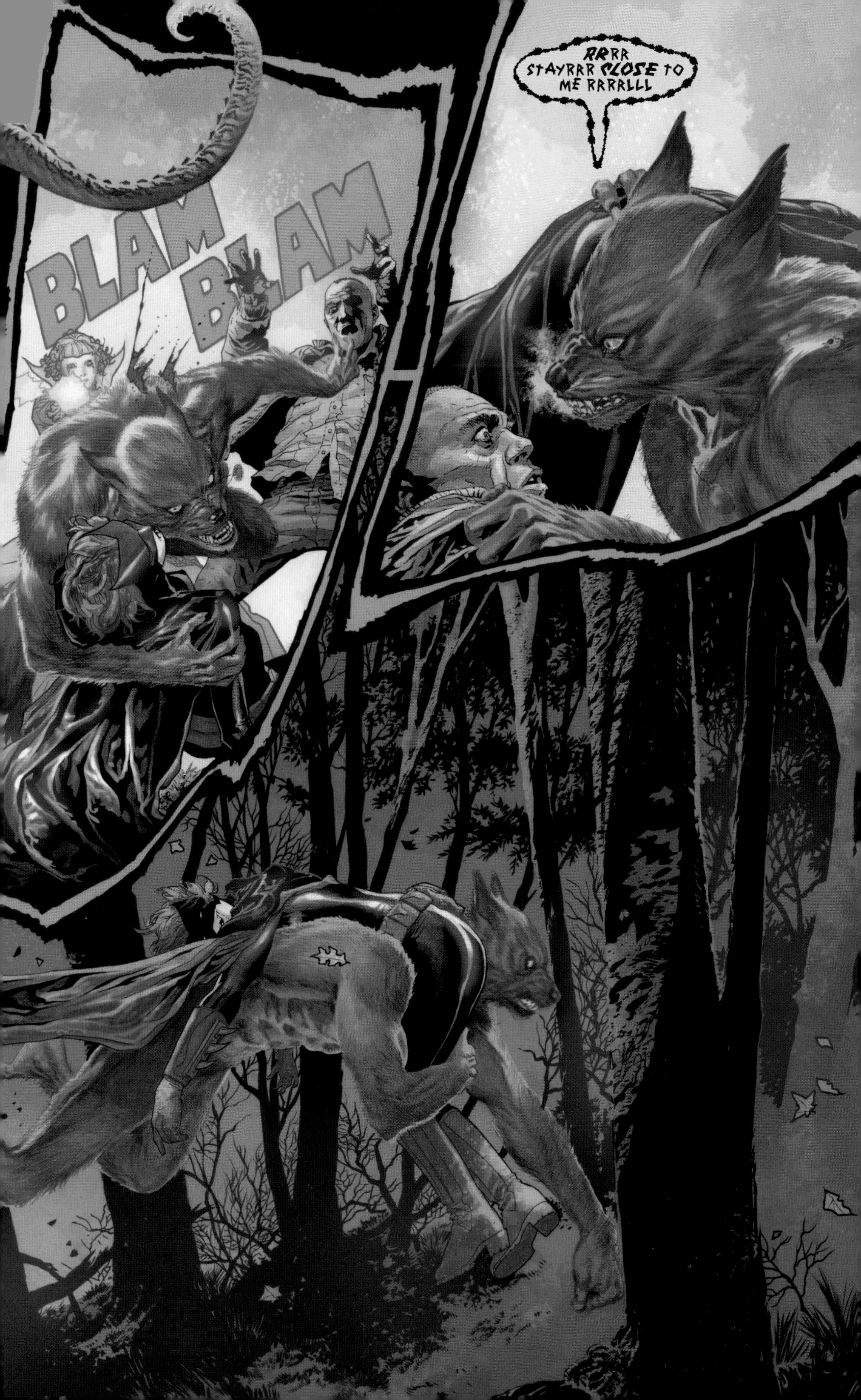
BLAM
BLAM
RRRR STAYRRR CLOSE TO ME RRRRLLL

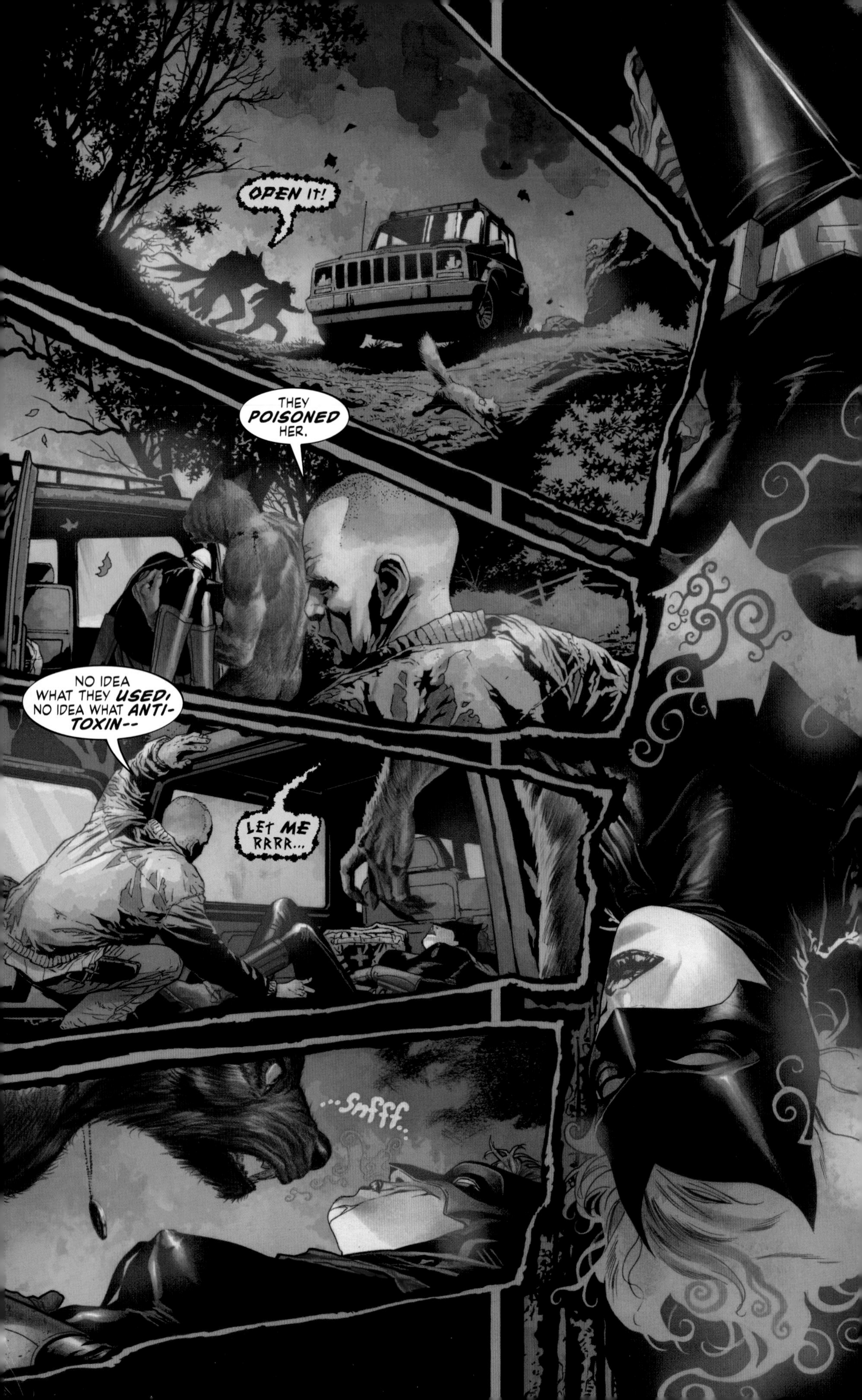
OPEN IT!
THEY POISONED HER.
NO IDEA WHAT THEY USED, NO IDEA WHAT ANTI-TOXIN--
LET ME RRRR...
...Snfff...

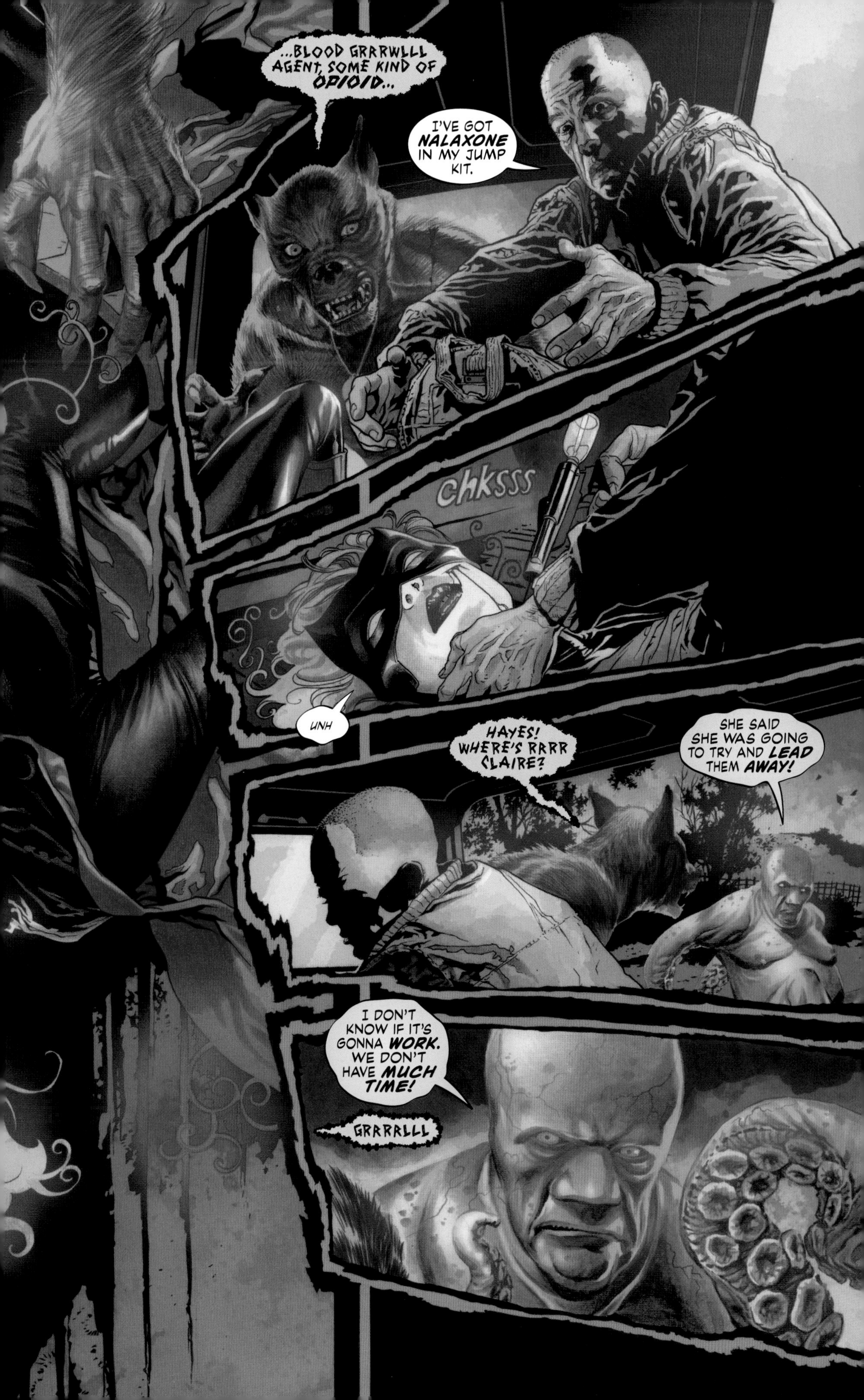
...BLOOD GRRRWLLL AGENT, SOME KIND OF OPIOID...
I'VE GOT NALAXONE IN MY JUMP KIT.
chksss
UNH
HAYES! WHERE'S RRRR CLAIRE?
SHE SAID SHE WAS GOING TO TRY AND LEAD THEM AWAY!
I DON'T KNOW IF IT'S GONNA WORK. WE DON'T HAVE MUCH TIME!
GRRRRLLL

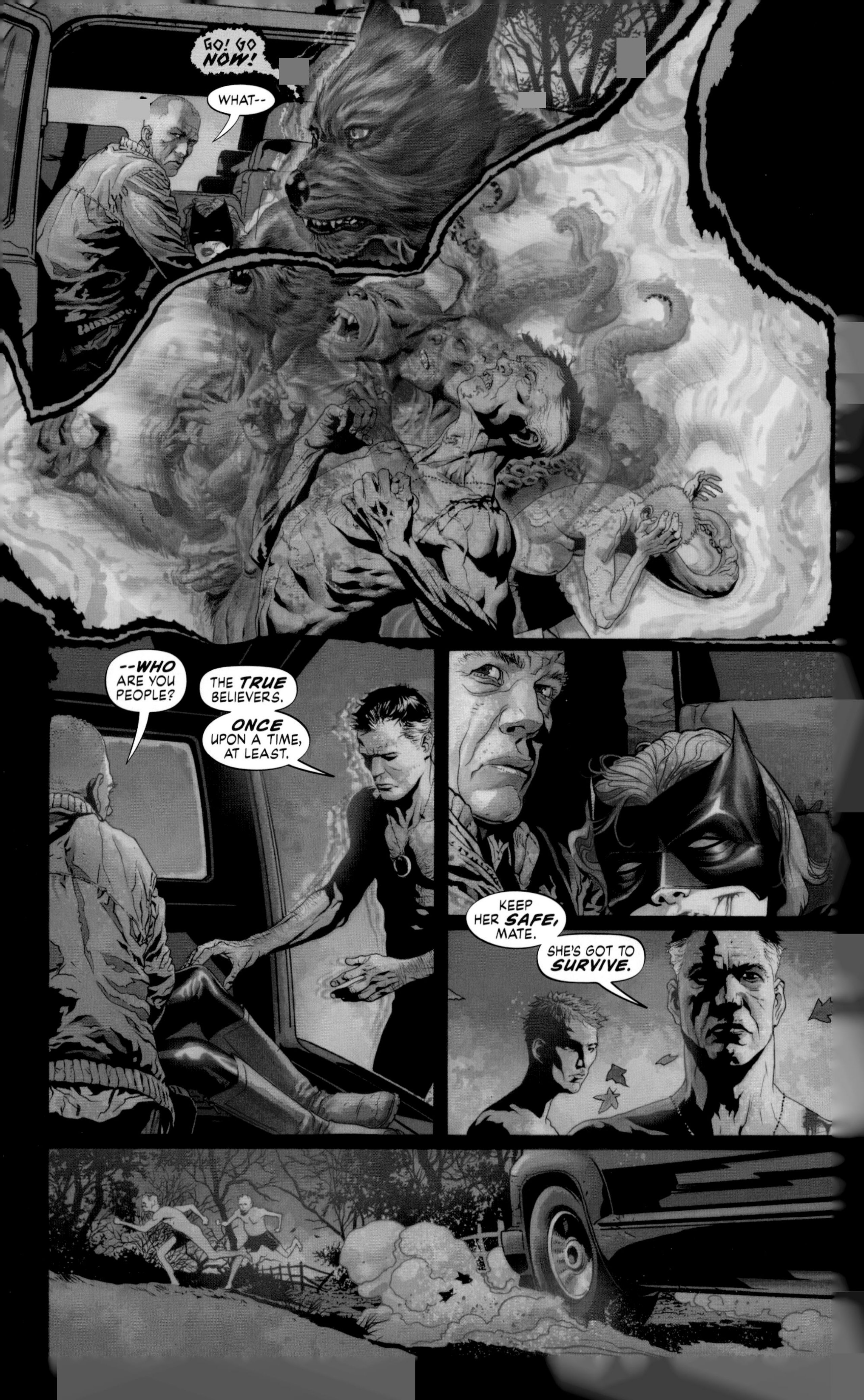
GO! GO NOW!
WHAT--
--WHO ARE YOU PEOPLE?
THE TRUE BELIEVERS.
ONCE UPON A TIME, AT LEAST.
KEEP HER SAFE, MATE.
SHE'S GOT TO SURVIVE.

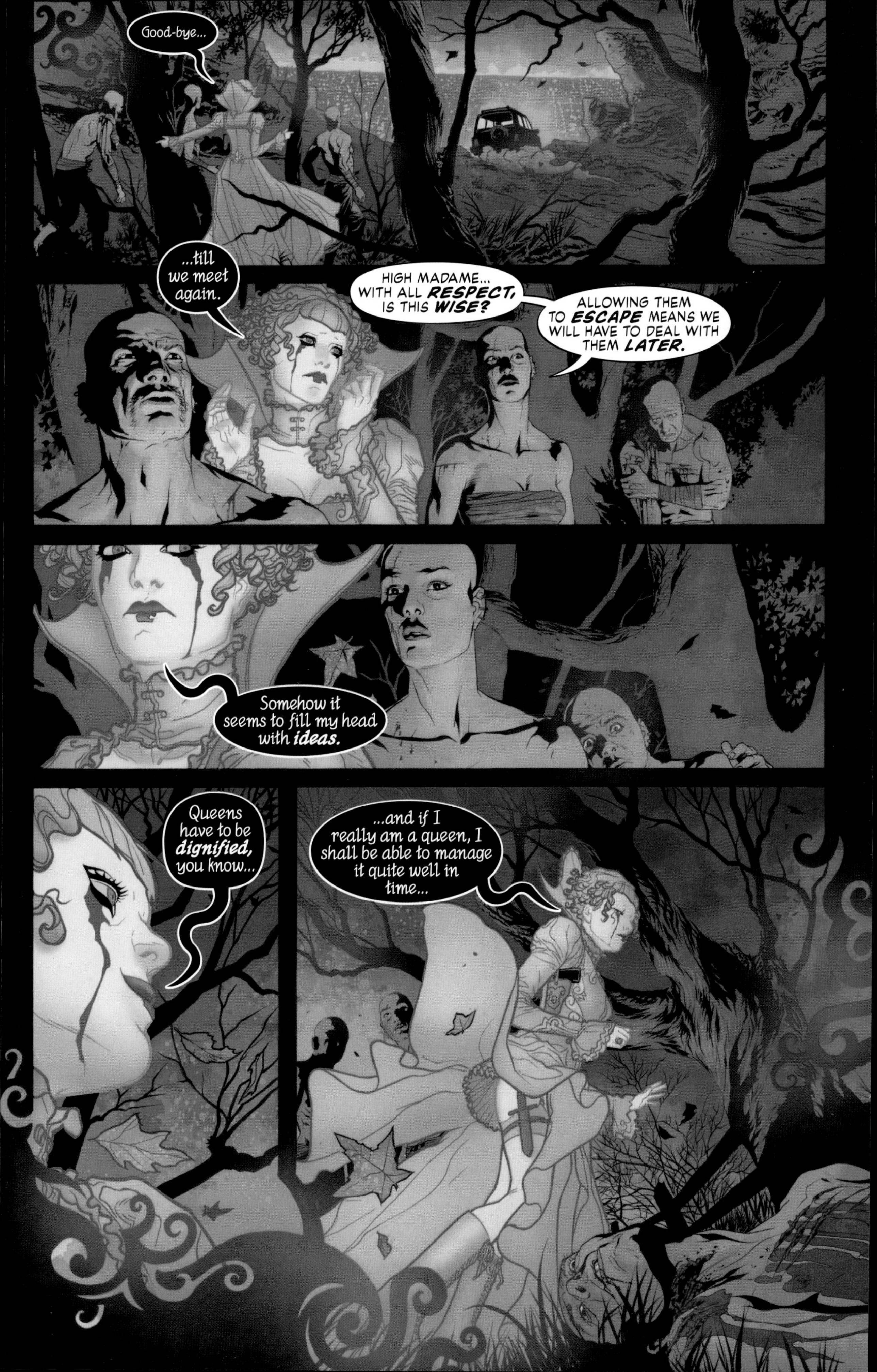
Good-bye...
...till we meet again.
HIGH MADAME... WITH ALL RESPECT, IS THIS WISE?
ALLOWING THEM TO ESCAPE MEANS WE WILL HAVE TO DEAL WITH THEM LATER.
Somehow it seems to fill my head with ideas.
Queens have to be dignified, you know...
...and if I really am a queen, I shall be able to manage it quite well in time...

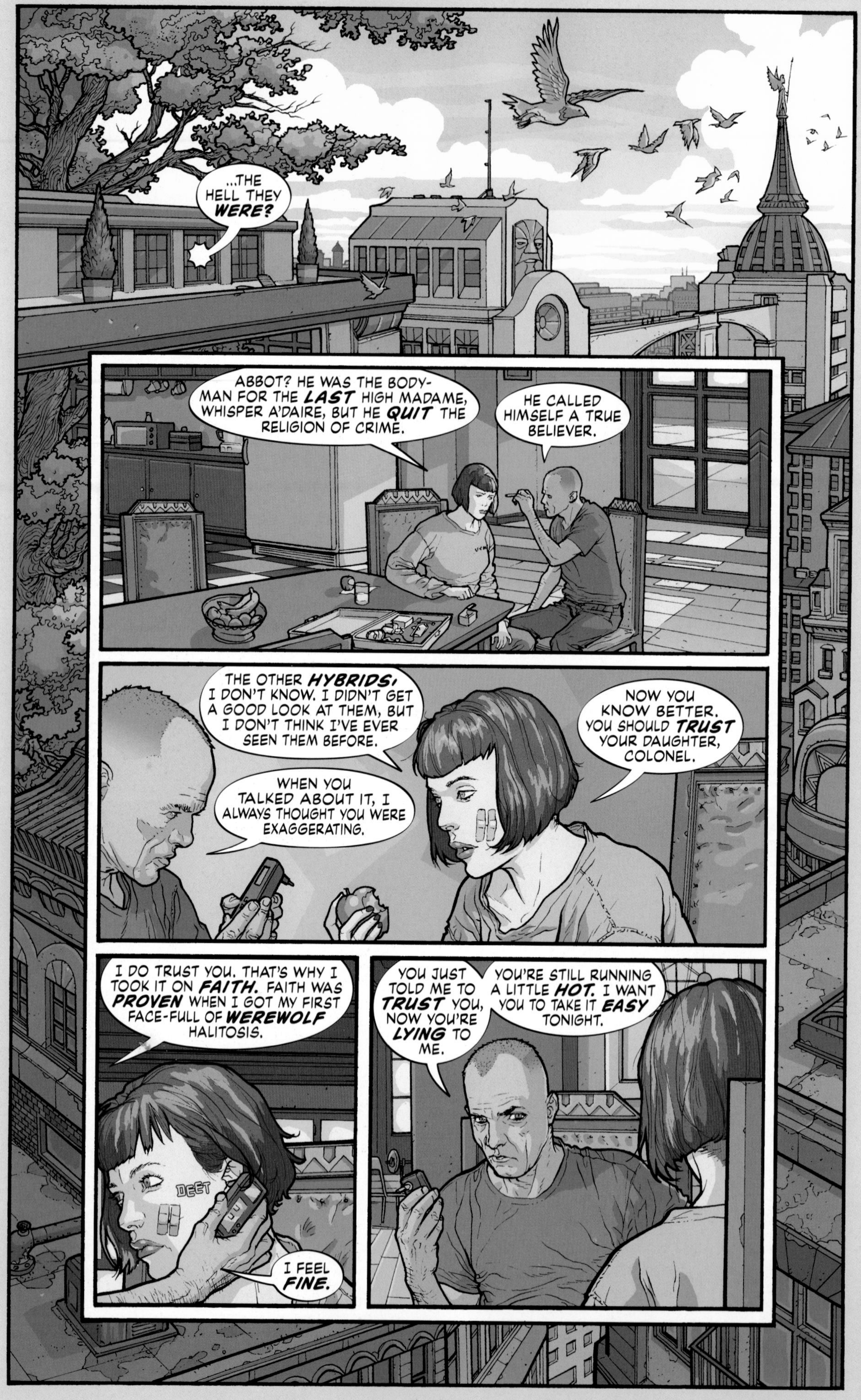
...THE HELL THEY WERE?
ABBOT? HE WAS THE BODY-MAN FOR THE LAST HIGH MADAME, WHISPER A'DAIRE, BUT HE QUIT THE RELIGION OF CRIME.
HE CALLED HIMSELF A TRUE BELIEVER.
THE OTHER HYBRIDS, I DON'T KNOW. I DIDN'T GET A GOOD LOOK AT THEM, BUT I DON'T THINK I'VE EVER SEEN THEM BEFORE.
WHEN YOU TALKED ABOUT IT, I ALWAYS THOUGHT YOU WERE EXAGGERATING.
NOW YOU KNOW BETTER. YOU SHOULD TRUST YOUR DAUGHTER, COLONEL.
I DO TRUST YOU. THAT'S WHY I TOOK IT ON FAITH. FAITH WAS PROVEN WHEN I GOT MY FIRST FACE-FULL OF WEREWOLF HALITOSIS.
DEET
I FEEL FINE.
YOU'RE STILL RUNNING A LITTLE HOT. I WANT YOU TO TAKE IT EASY TONIGHT.
YOU JUST TOLD ME TO TRUST YOU, NOW YOU'RE LYING TO ME.

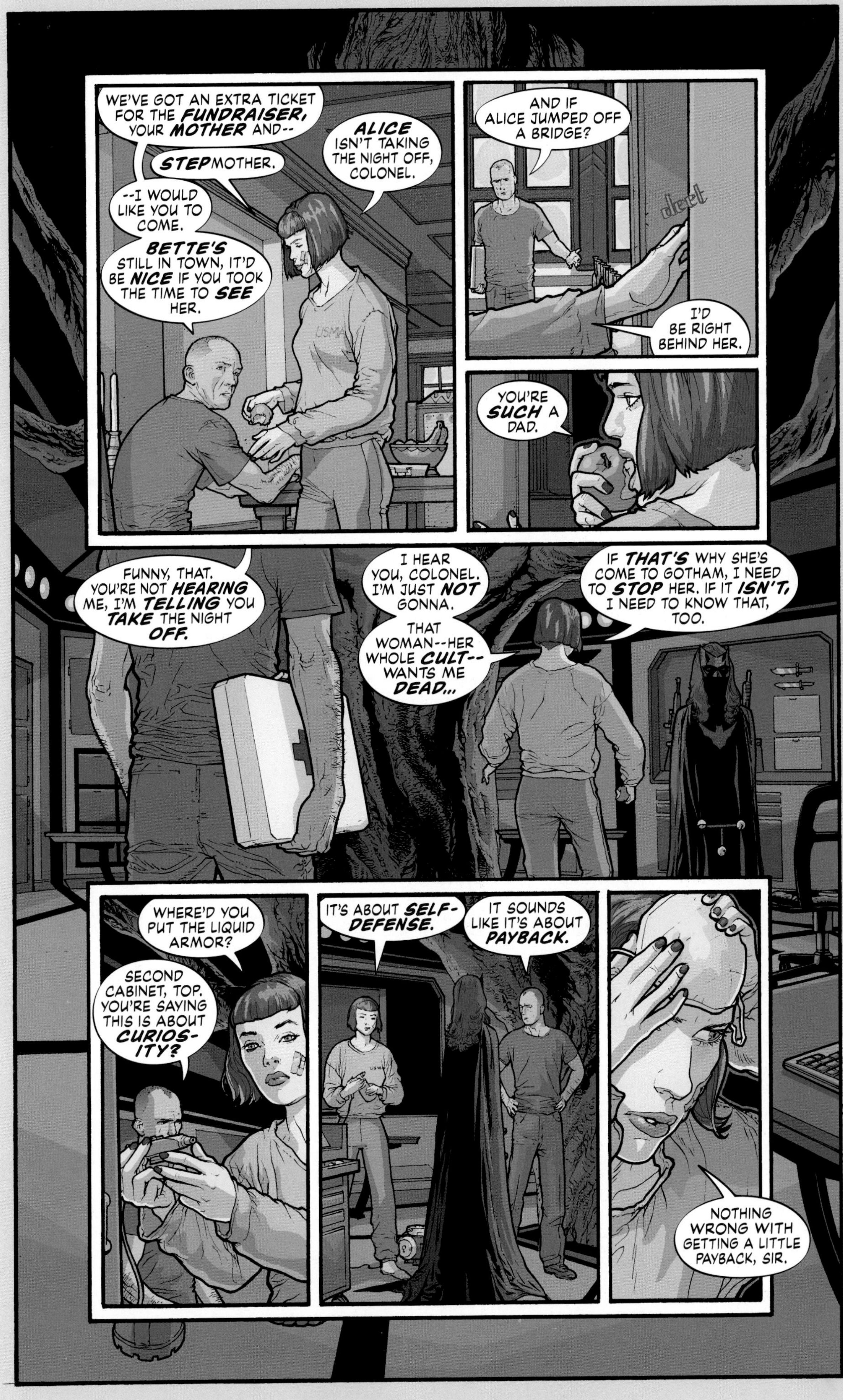
WE'VE GOT AN EXTRA TICKET FOR THE FUNDRAISER, YOUR MOTHER AND--
STEPMOTHER.
--I WOULD LIKE YOU TO COME.
BETTE'S STILL IN TOWN, IT'D BE NICE IF YOU TOOK THE TIME TO SEE HER.
ALICE ISN'T TAKING THE NIGHT OFF, COLONEL.
AND IF ALICE JUMPED OFF A BRIDGE?
I'D BE RIGHT BEHIND HER.
YOU'RE SUCH A DAD.
FUNNY, THAT. YOU'RE NOT HEARING ME, I'M TELLING YOU TAKE THE NIGHT OFF.
I HEAR YOU, COLONEL. I'M JUST NOT GONNA.
THAT WOMAN--HER WHOLE CULT--WANTS ME DEAD...
IF THAT'S WHY SHE'S COME TO GOTHAM, I NEED TO STOP HER. IF IT ISN'T, I NEED TO KNOW THAT, TOO.
WHERE'D YOU PUT THE LIQUID ARMOR?
SECOND CABINET, TOP. YOU'RE SAYING THIS IS ABOUT CURIOSITY?
IT'S ABOUT SELF-DEFENSE.
IT SOUNDS LIKE IT'S ABOUT PAYBACK.
NOTHING WRONG WITH GETTING A LITTLE PAYBACK, SIR.

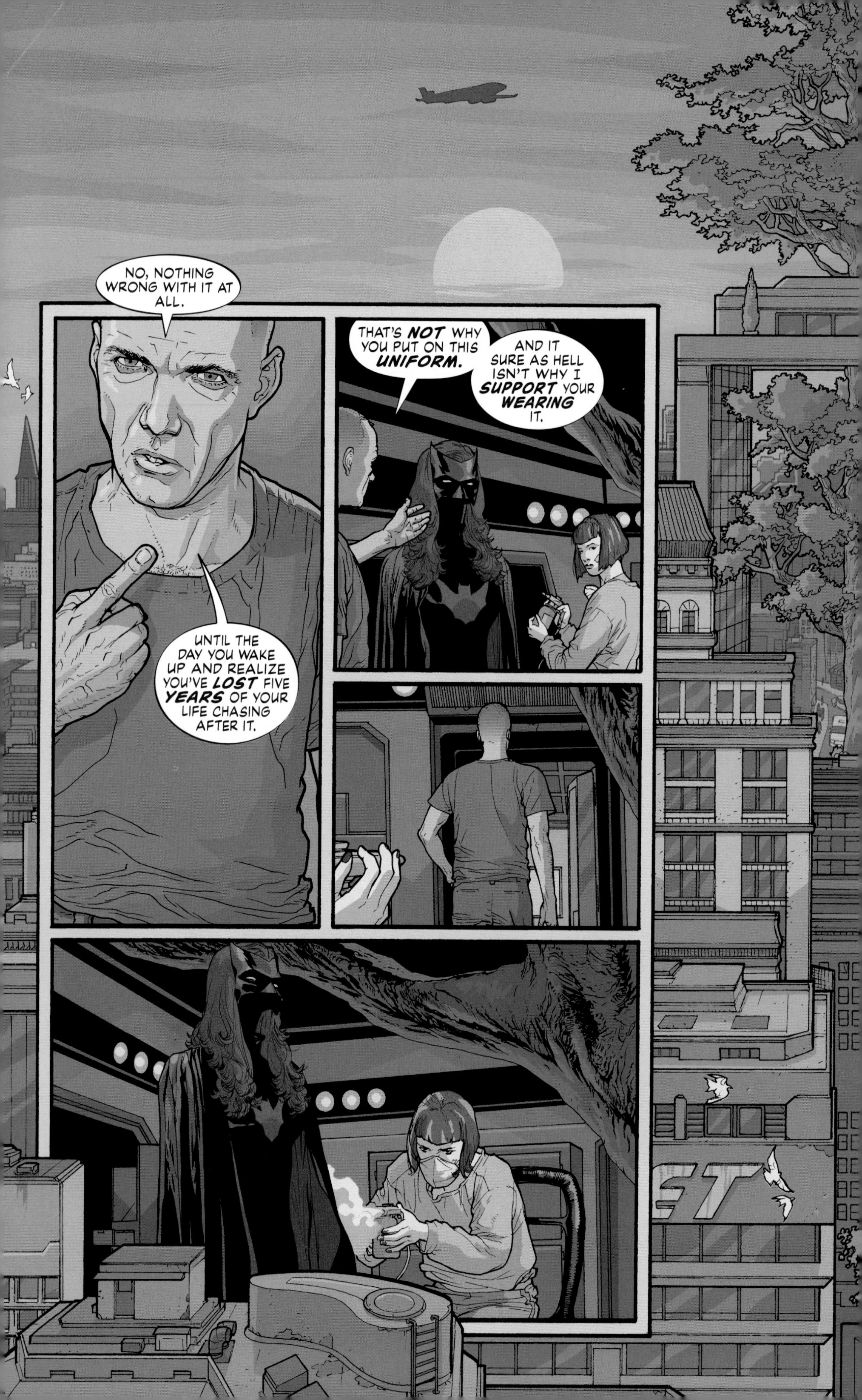
NO, NOTHING WRONG WITH IT AT ALL.
UNTIL THE DAY YOU WAKE UP AND REALIZE YOU'VE LOST FIVE YEARS OF YOUR LIFE CHASING AFTER IT.
THAT'S NOT WHY YOU PUT ON THIS UNIFORM.
AND IT SURE AS HELL ISN'T WHY I SUPPORT YOUR WEARING IT.

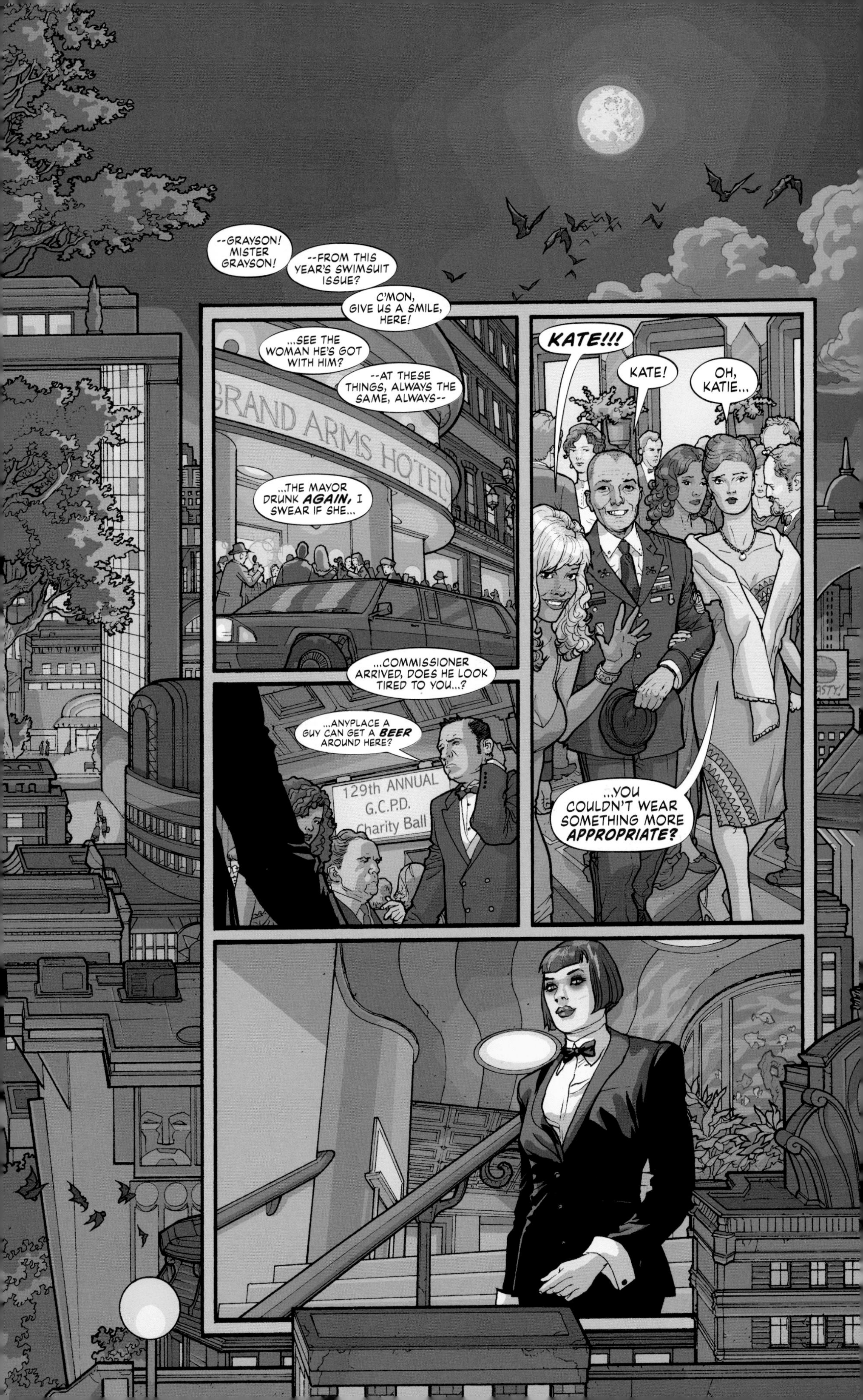
--GRAYSON! MISTER GRAYSON!
--FROM THIS YEAR'S SWIMSUIT ISSUE?
C'MON, GIVE US A SMILE, HERE!
...SEE THE WOMAN HE'S GOT WITH HIM?
--AT THESE THINGS, ALWAYS THE SAME, ALWAYS--
GRAND ARMS HOTEL
...THE MAYOR DRUNK AGAIN, I SWEAR IF SHE...
KATE!!!
KATE!
OH, KATIE...
...COMMISSIONER ARRIVED, DOES HE LOOK TIRED TO YOU...?
...ANYPLACE A GUY CAN GET A BEER AROUND HERE?
129th ANNUAL G.C.P.D. Charity Ball
...YOU COULDN'T WEAR SOMETHING MORE APPROPRIATE?

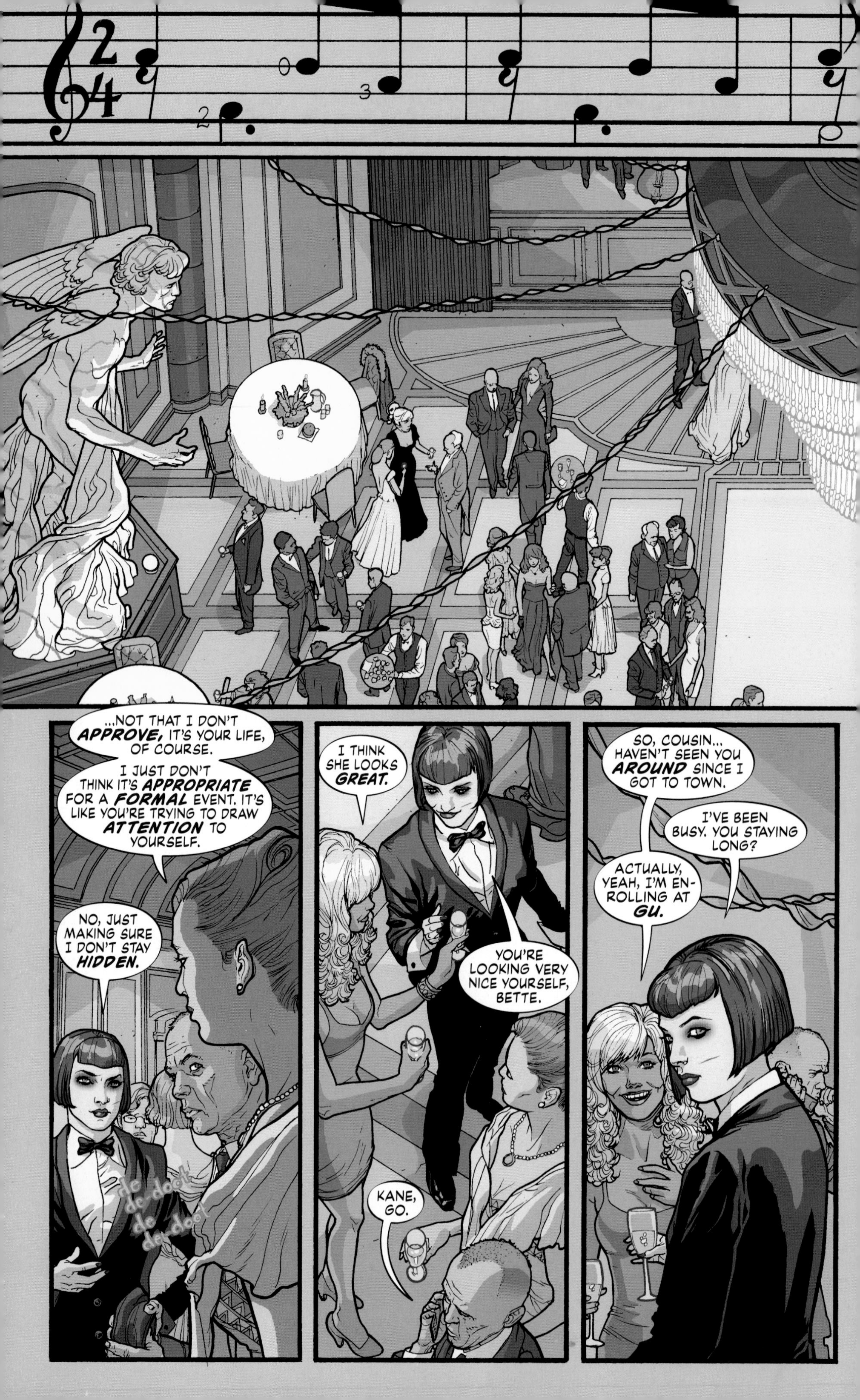
...NOT THAT I DON'T APPROVE, IT'S YOUR LIFE, OF COURSE.
I JUST DON'T THINK IT'S APPROPRIATE FOR A FORMAL EVENT. IT'S LIKE YOU'RE TRYING TO DRAW ATTENTION TO YOURSELF.
NO, JUST MAKING SURE I DON'T STAY HIDDEN.
de de-doot de de-doot
I THINK SHE LOOKS GREAT.
YOU'RE LOOKING VERY NICE YOURSELF, BETTE.
KANE, GO.
SO, COUSIN... HAVEN'T SEEN YOU AROUND SINCE I GOT TO TOWN.
I'VE BEEN BUSY. YOU STAYING LONG?
ACTUALLY, YEAH, I'M EN-ROLLING AT GU.

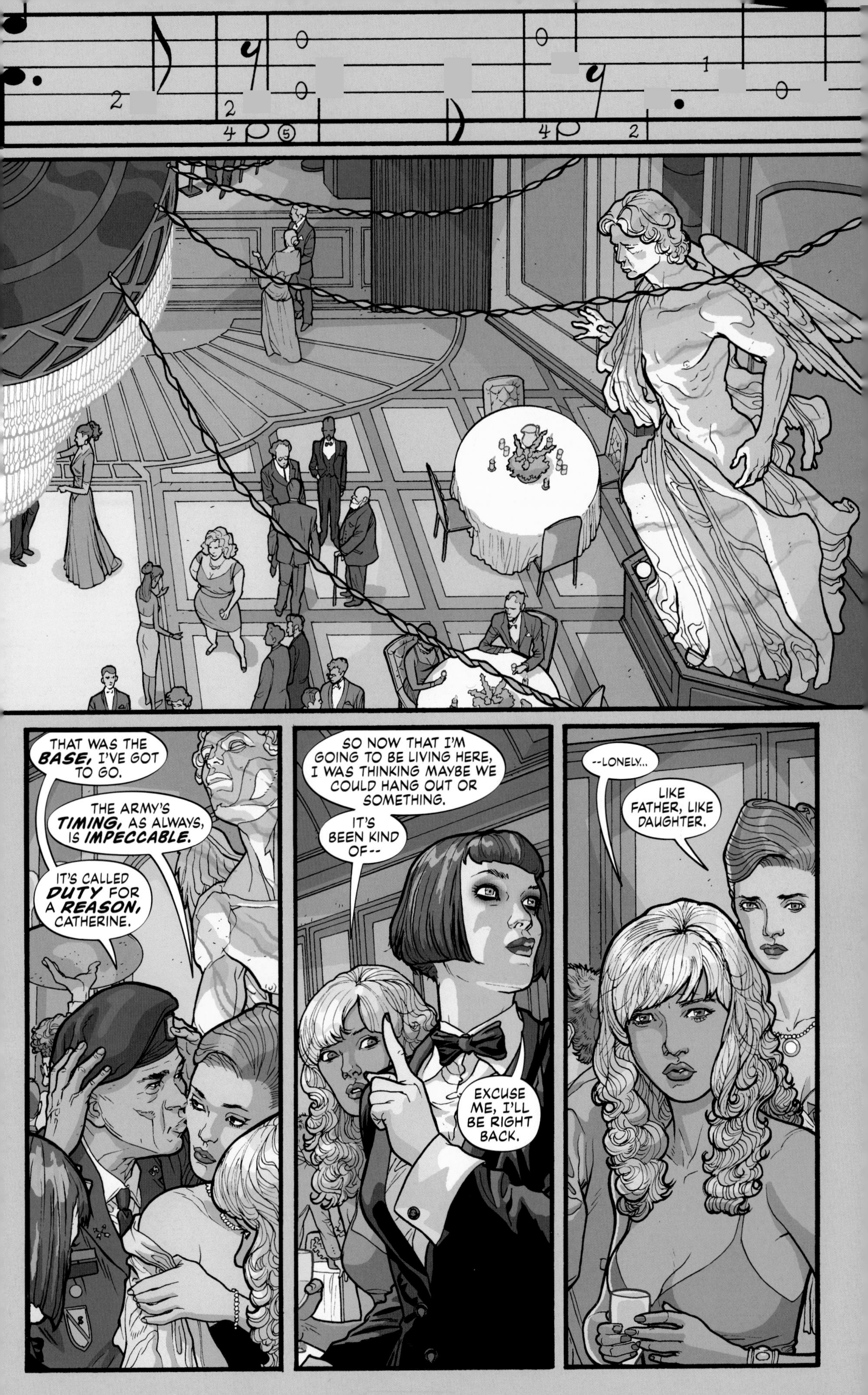
THAT WAS THE BASE, I'VE GOT TO GO.
THE ARMY'S TIMING, AS ALWAYS, IS IMPECCABLE.
IT'S CALLED DUTY FOR A REASON, CATHERINE.
SO NOW THAT I'M GOING TO BE LIVING HERE, I WAS THINKING MAYBE WE COULD HANG OUT OR SOMETHING.
IT'S BEEN KIND OF--
EXCUSE ME, I'LL BE RIGHT BACK.
--LONELY...
LIKE FATHER, LIKE DAUGHTER.

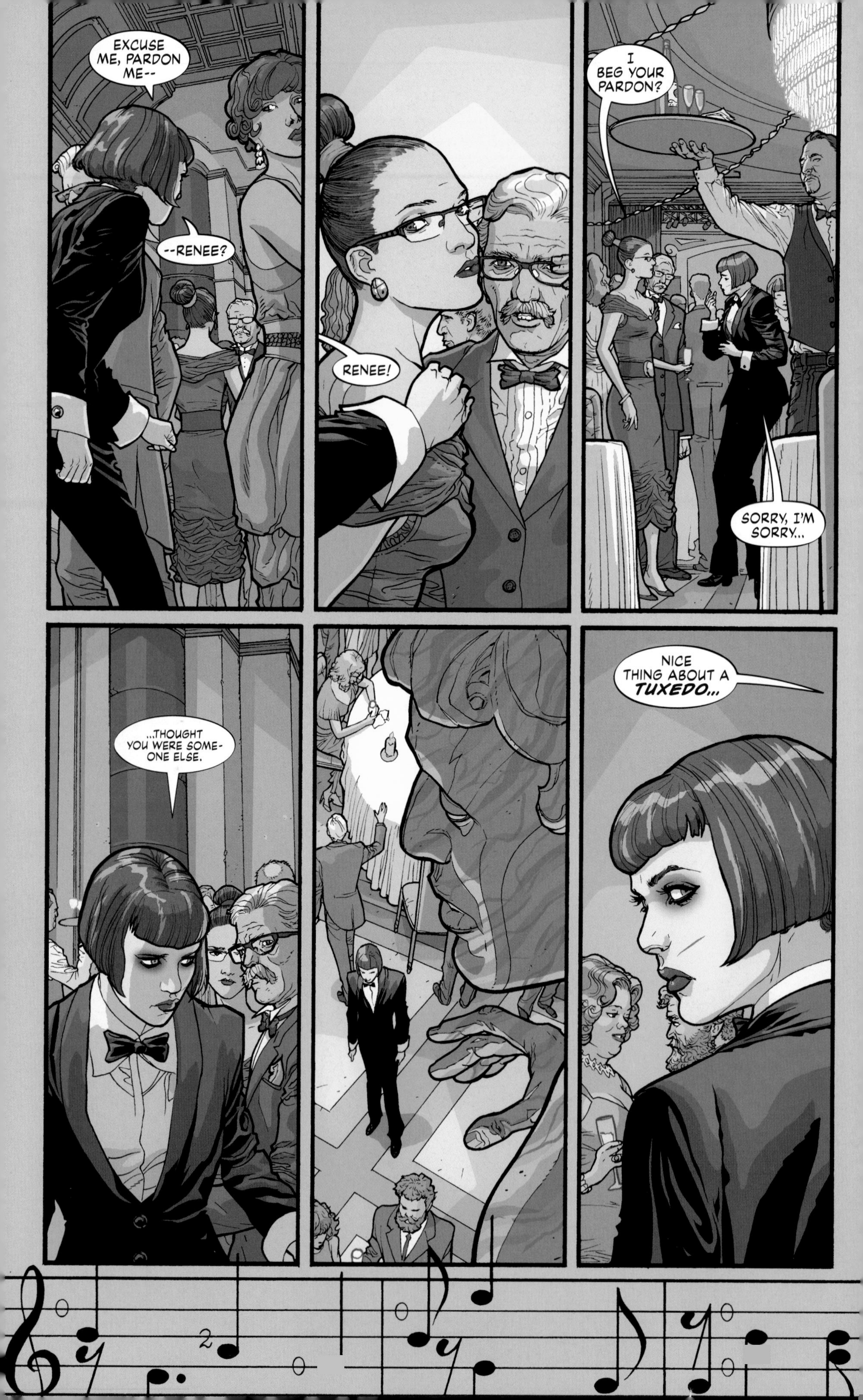
EXCUSE ME, PARDON ME--
--RENEE?
RENEE!
I BEG YOUR PARDON?
SORRY, I'M SORRY...
...THOUGHT YOU WERE SOME-ONE ELSE.
NICE THING ABOUT A *TUXEDO...*

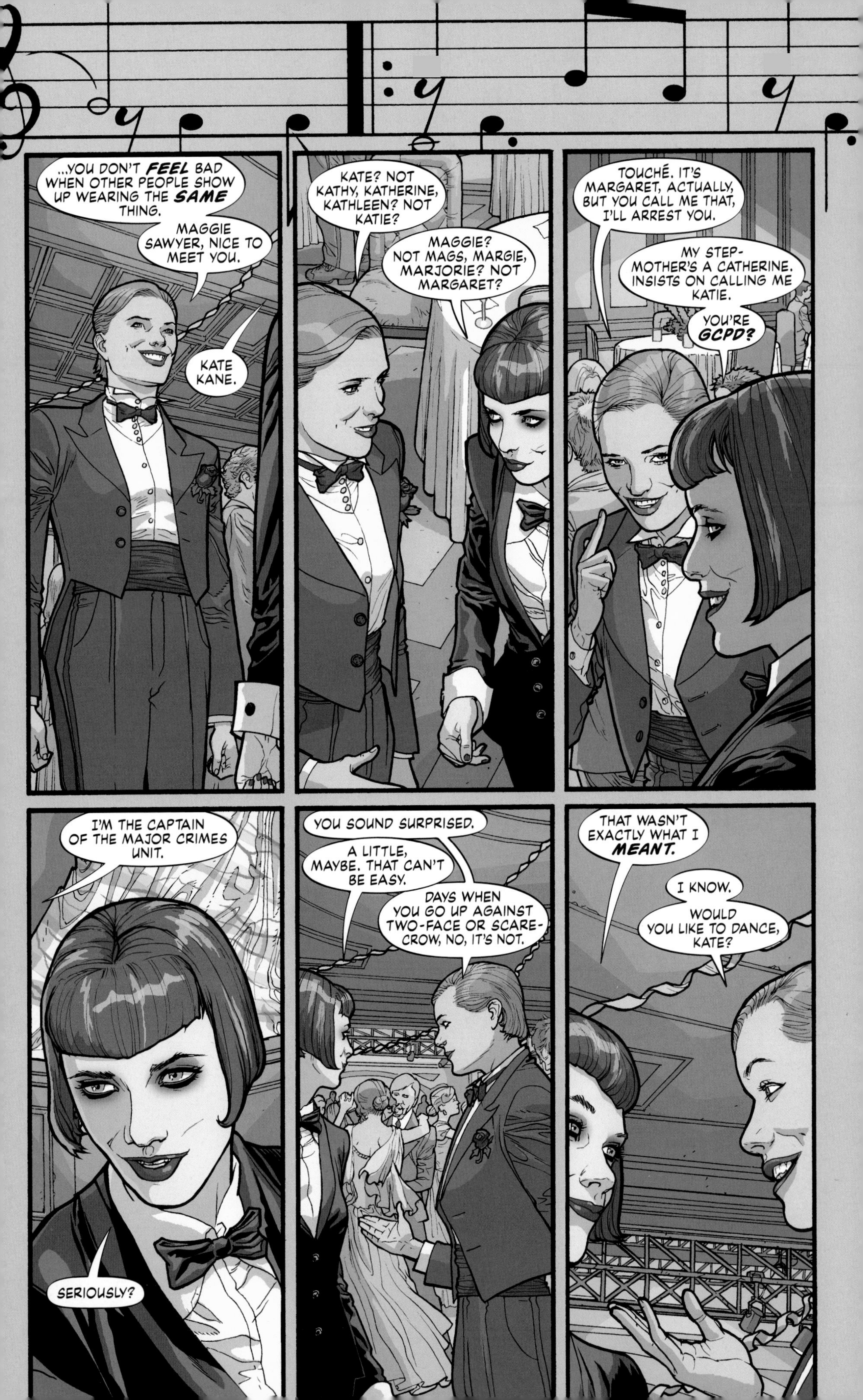
...YOU DON'T FEEL BAD WHEN OTHER PEOPLE SHOW UP WEARING THE SAME THING.
MAGGIE SAWYER, NICE TO MEET YOU.
KATE KANE.
KATE? NOT KATHY, KATHERINE, KATHLEEN? NOT KATIE?
MAGGIE? NOT MAGS, MARGIE, MARJORIE? NOT MARGARET?
TOUCHÉ. IT'S MARGARET, ACTUALLY, BUT YOU CALL ME THAT, I'LL ARREST YOU.
MY STEP-MOTHER'S A CATHERINE. INSISTS ON CALLING ME KATIE.
YOU'RE GCPD?
I'M THE CAPTAIN OF THE MAJOR CRIMES UNIT.
SERIOUSLY?
YOU SOUND SURPRISED.
A LITTLE, MAYBE. THAT CAN'T BE EASY.
DAYS WHEN YOU GO UP AGAINST TWO-FACE OR SCARE-CROW, NO, IT'S NOT.
THAT WASN'T EXACTLY WHAT I MEANT.
I KNOW.
WOULD YOU LIKE TO DANCE, KATE?

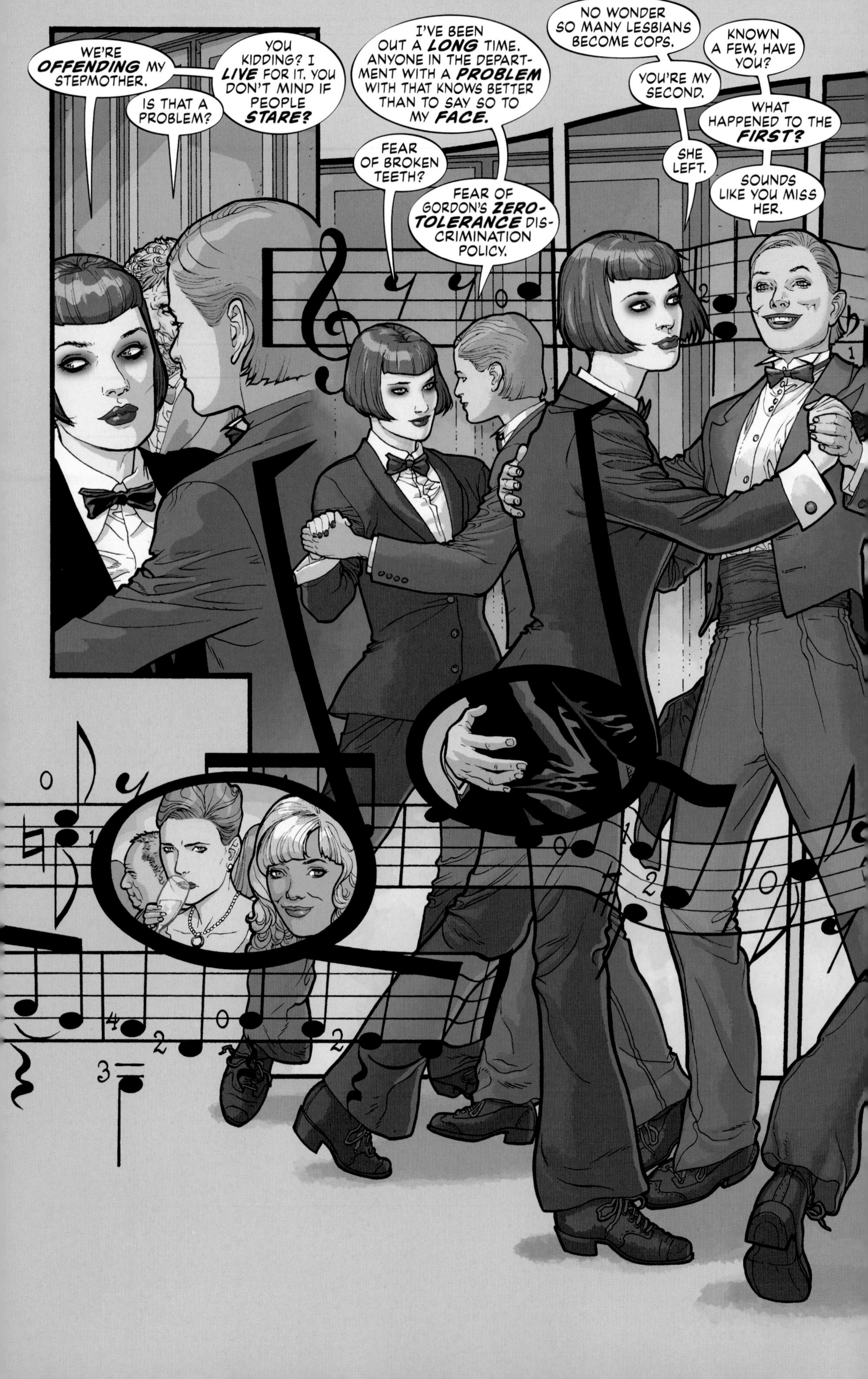

WE'RE **OFFENDING** MY STEPMOTHER.
IS THAT A PROBLEM?
YOU KIDDING? I **LIVE** FOR IT. YOU DON'T MIND IF PEOPLE **STARE?**
I'VE BEEN OUT A **LONG** TIME. ANYONE IN THE DEPART-MENT WITH A **PROBLEM** WITH THAT KNOWS BETTER THAN TO SAY SO TO MY **FACE.**
FEAR OF BROKEN TEETH?
FEAR OF GORDON'S **ZERO-TOLERANCE** DIS-CRIMINATION POLICY.
NO WONDER SO MANY LESBIANS BECOME COPS.
KNOWN A FEW, HAVE YOU?
YOU'RE MY SECOND.
WHAT HAPPENED TO THE **FIRST?**
SHE LEFT.
SOUNDS LIKE YOU MISS HER.

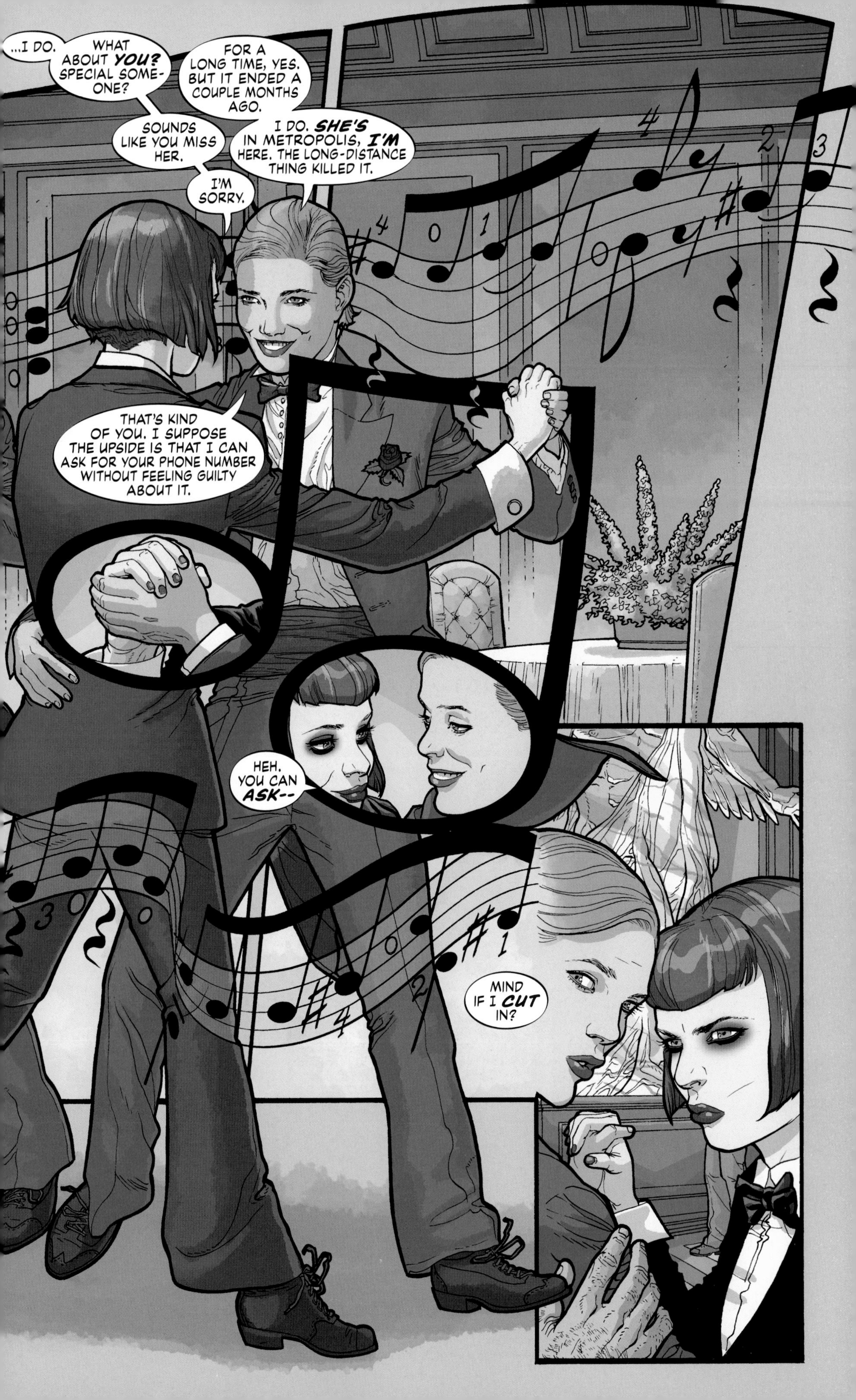
...I DO.
WHAT ABOUT **YOU?** SPECIAL SOME-ONE?
FOR A LONG TIME, YES. BUT IT ENDED A COUPLE MONTHS AGO.
SOUNDS LIKE YOU MISS HER.
I DO. **SHE'S** IN METROPOLIS, **I'M** HERE. THE LONG-DISTANCE THING KILLED IT.
I'M SORRY.
THAT'S KIND OF YOU. I SUPPOSE THE UPSIDE IS THAT I CAN ASK FOR YOUR PHONE NUMBER WITHOUT FEELING GUILTY ABOUT IT.
HEH. YOU CAN **ASK--**
MIND IF I **CUT** IN?

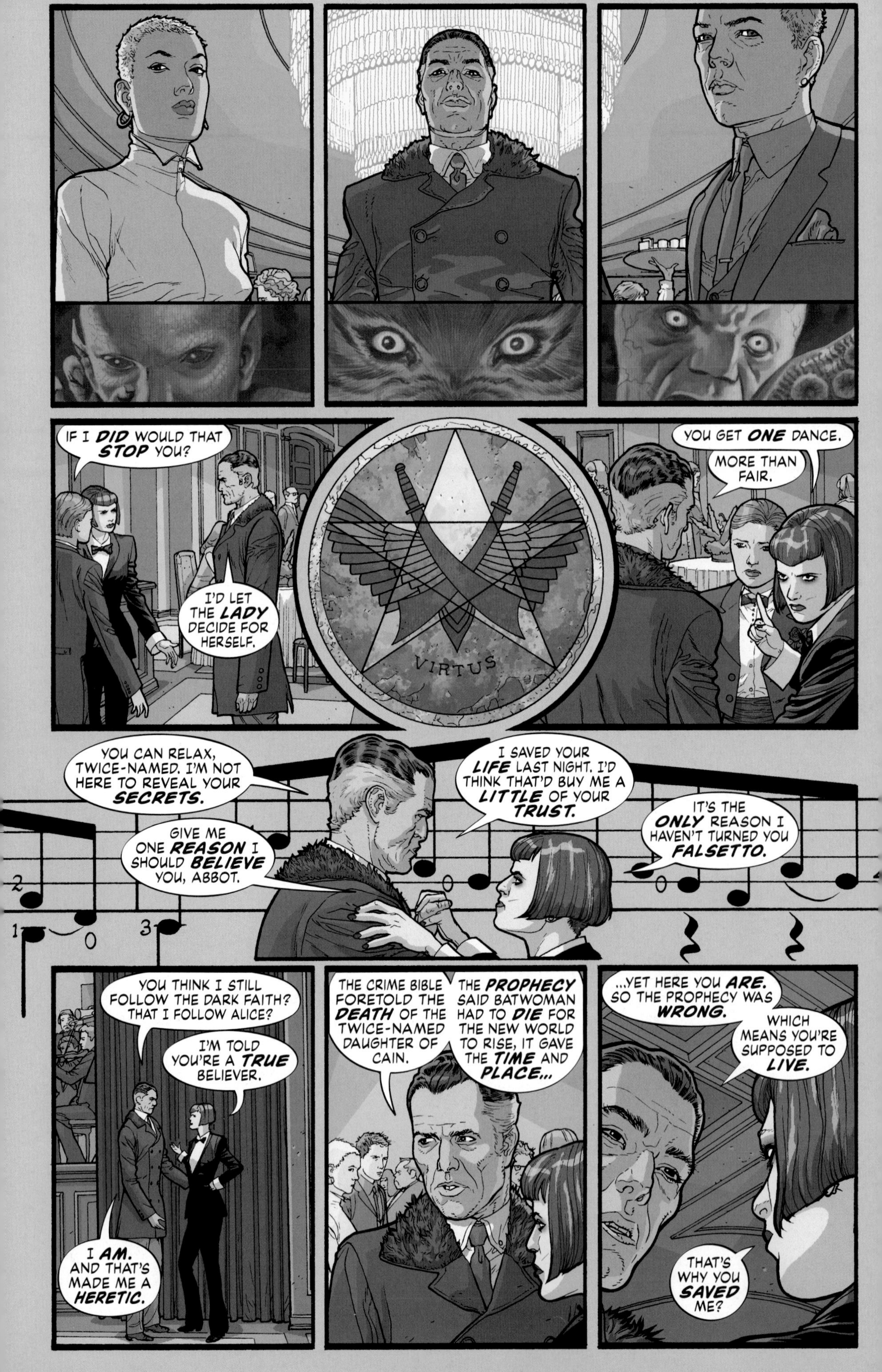

IF I DID WOULD THAT STOP YOU?
I'D LET THE LADY DECIDE FOR HERSELF.
VIRTUS
YOU GET ONE DANCE.
MORE THAN FAIR.
YOU CAN RELAX, TWICE-NAMED. I'M NOT HERE TO REVEAL YOUR SECRETS.
GIVE ME ONE REASON I SHOULD BELIEVE YOU, ABBOT.
I SAVED YOUR LIFE LAST NIGHT. I'D THINK THAT'D BUY ME A LITTLE OF YOUR TRUST.
IT'S THE ONLY REASON I HAVEN'T TURNED YOU FALSETTO.
YOU THINK I STILL FOLLOW THE DARK FAITH? THAT I FOLLOW ALICE?
I'M TOLD YOU'RE A TRUE BELIEVER.
I AM. AND THAT'S MADE ME A HERETIC.
THE CRIME BIBLE FORETOLD THE DEATH OF THE TWICE-NAMED DAUGHTER OF CAIN.
THE PROPHECY SAID BATWOMAN HAD TO DIE FOR THE NEW WORLD TO RISE, IT GAVE THE TIME AND PLACE...
...YET HERE YOU ARE. SO THE PROPHECY WAS WRONG.
WHICH MEANS YOU'RE SUPPOSED TO LIVE.
THAT'S WHY YOU SAVED ME?

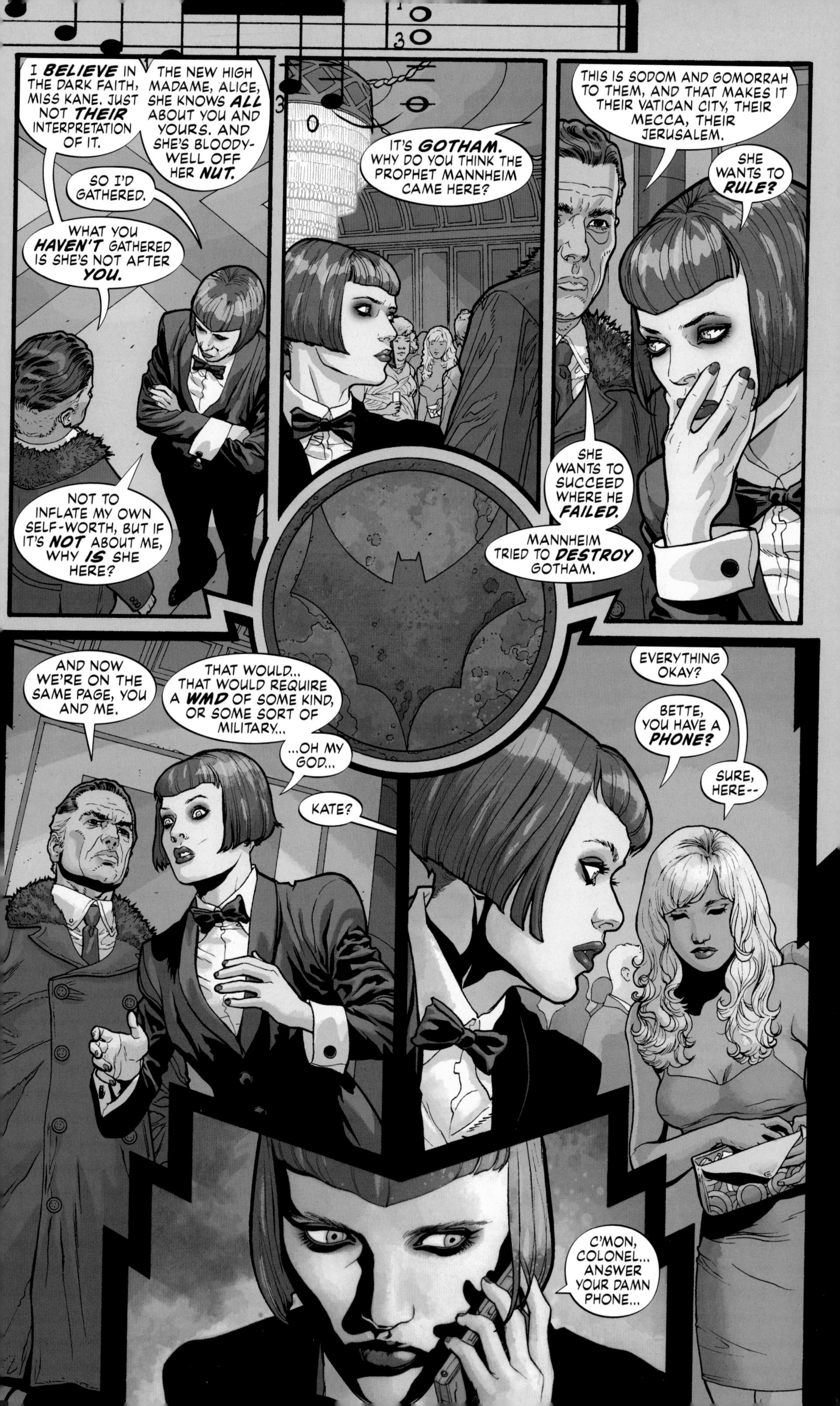

I BELIEVE IN THE DARK FAITH, MISS KANE. JUST NOT THEIR INTERPRETATION OF IT.
THE NEW HIGH MADAME, ALICE, SHE KNOWS ALL ABOUT YOU AND YOURS. AND SHE'S BLOODY-WELL OFF HER NUT.
SO I'D GATHERED.
WHAT YOU HAVEN'T GATHERED IS SHE'S NOT AFTER YOU.
NOT TO INFLATE MY OWN SELF-WORTH, BUT IF IT'S NOT ABOUT ME, WHY IS SHE HERE?
IT'S GOTHAM. WHY DO YOU THINK THE PROPHET MANNHEIM CAME HERE?
THIS IS SODOM AND GOMORRAH TO THEM, AND THAT MAKES IT THEIR VATICAN CITY, THEIR MECCA, THEIR JERUSALEM.
SHE WANTS TO RULE?
SHE WANTS TO SUCCEED WHERE HE FAILED.
MANNHEIM TRIED TO DESTROY GOTHAM.
AND NOW WE'RE ON THE SAME PAGE, YOU AND ME.
THAT WOULD... THAT WOULD REQUIRE A WMD OF SOME KIND, OR SOME SORT OF MILITARY...
...OH MY GOD...
KATE?
EVERYTHING OKAY?
BETTE, YOU HAVE A PHONE?
SURE, HERE--
C'MON, COLONEL... ANSWER YOUR DAMN PHONE...

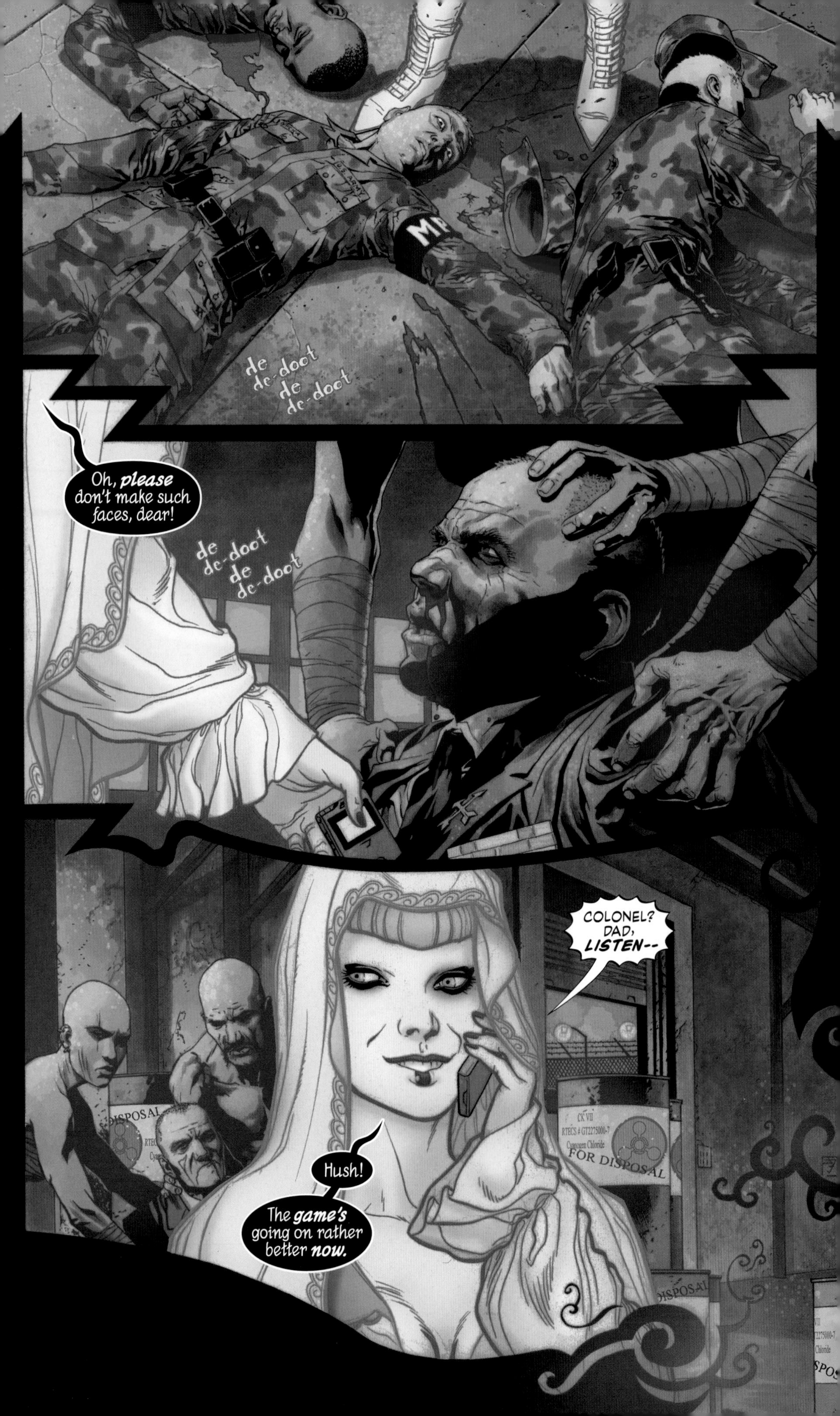
de-doot
de-doot
de
de-doot
Oh, please don't make such faces, dear!
de-doot
de-doot
de
de-doot
COLONEL? DAD, LISTEN--
Hush!
The game's going on rather better now.
DISPOSAL
CK VII
RTECS # GT2275000-7
Cyanogen Chloride
FOR DISPOSAL

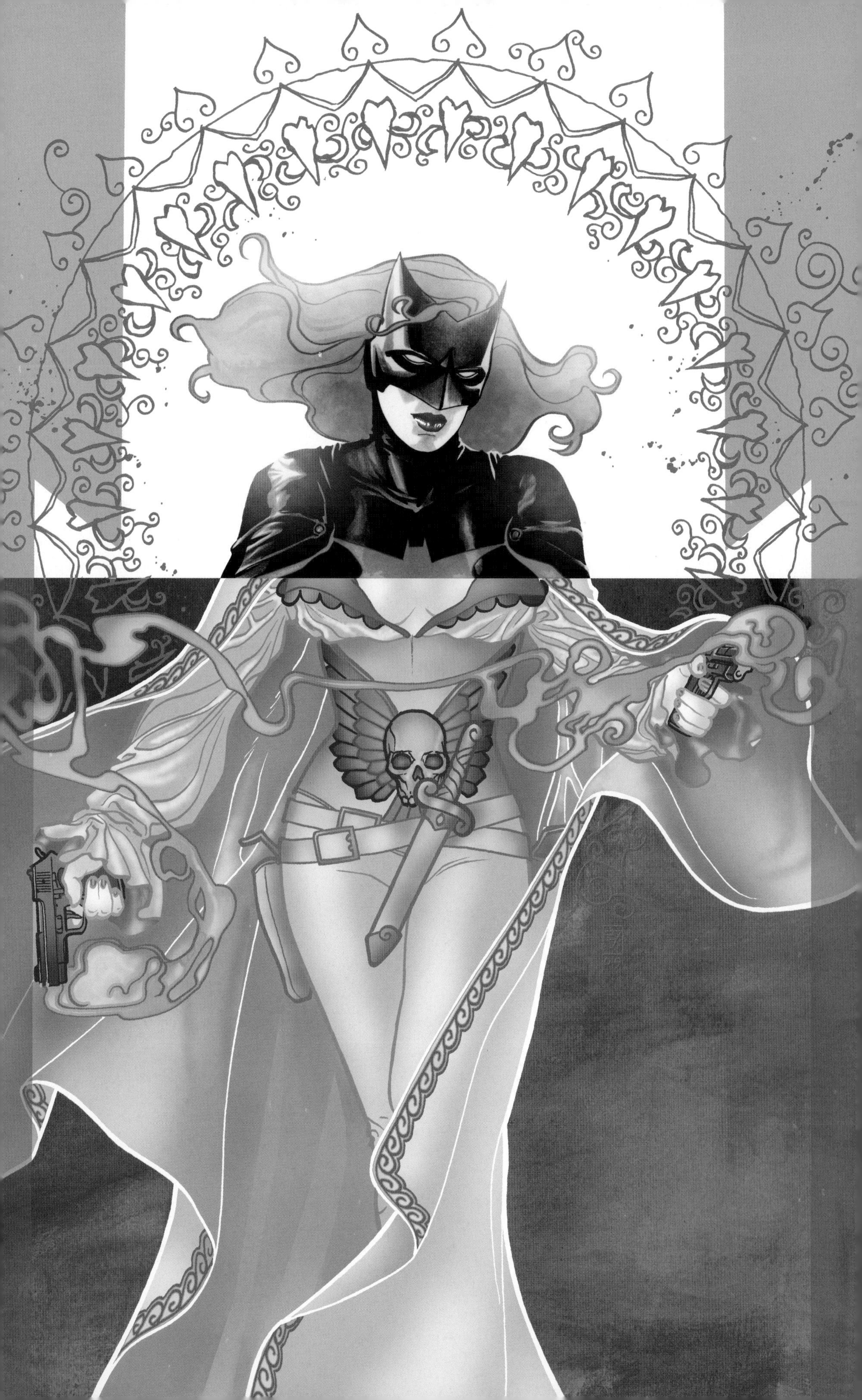

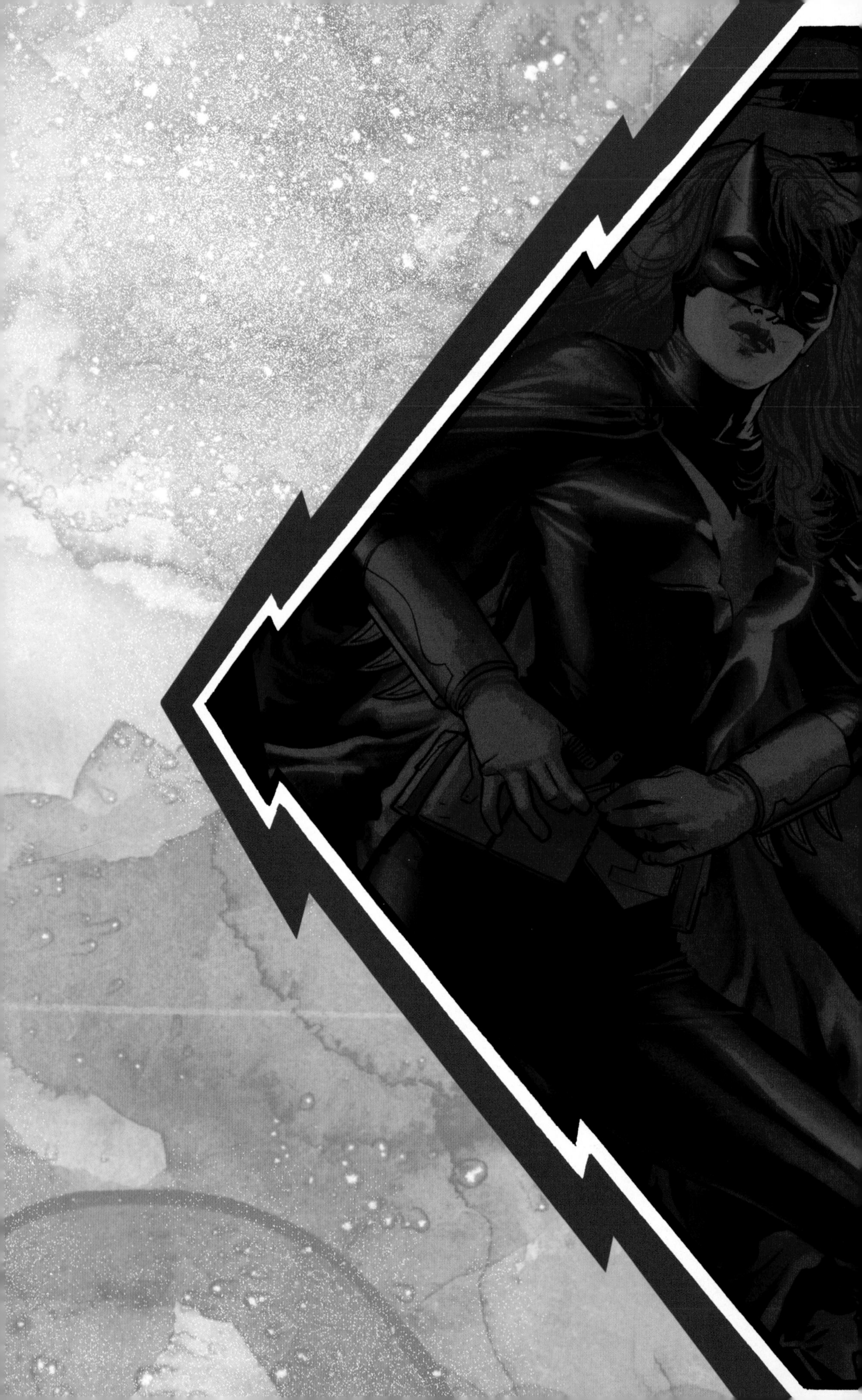

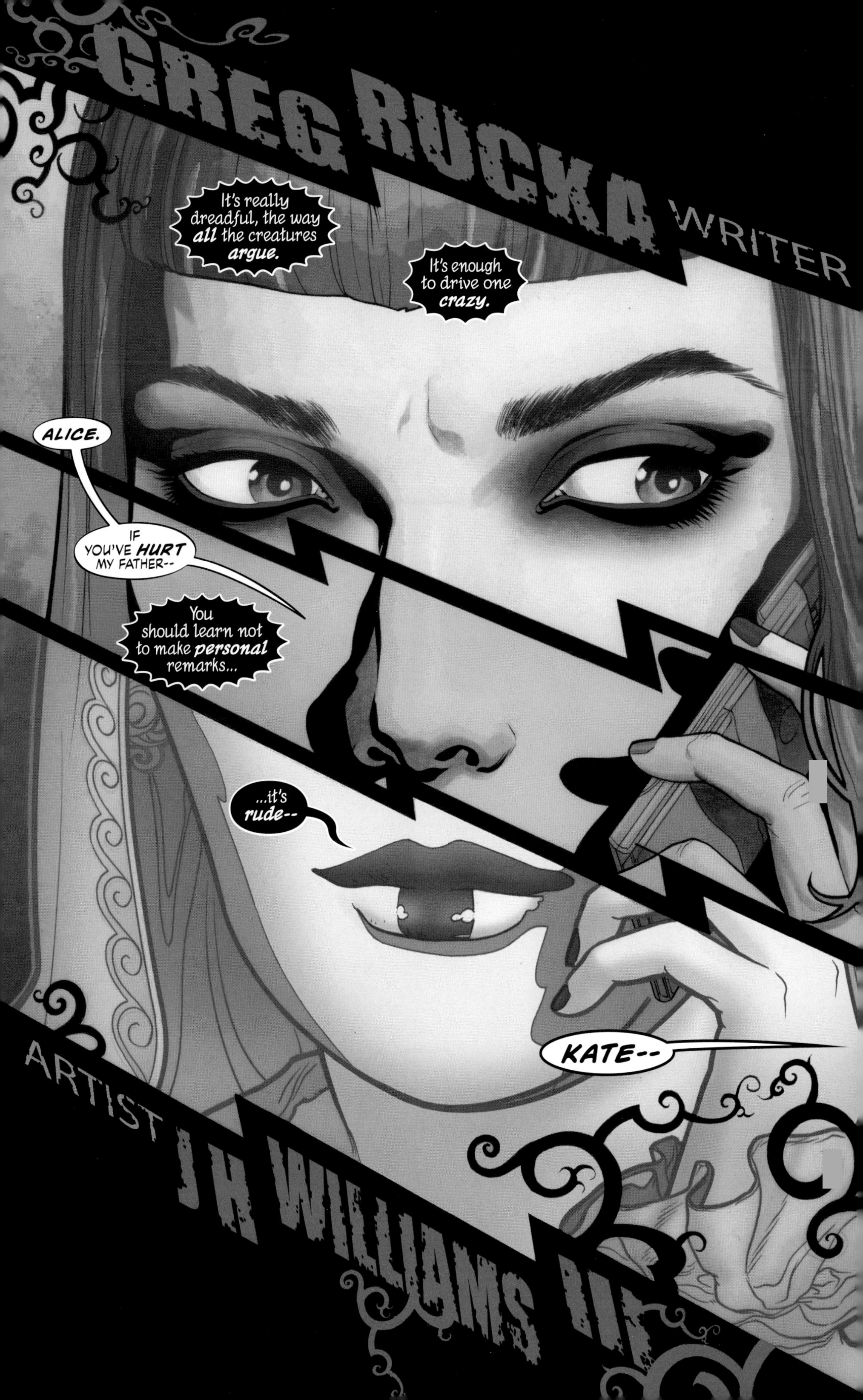
GREG RUCKA WRITER
It's really dreadful, the way all the creatures argue.
It's enough to drive one crazy.
ALICE.
IF YOU'VE HURT MY FATHER--
You should learn not to make personal remarks...
...it's rude--
KATE--
ARTIST J H WILLIAMS III

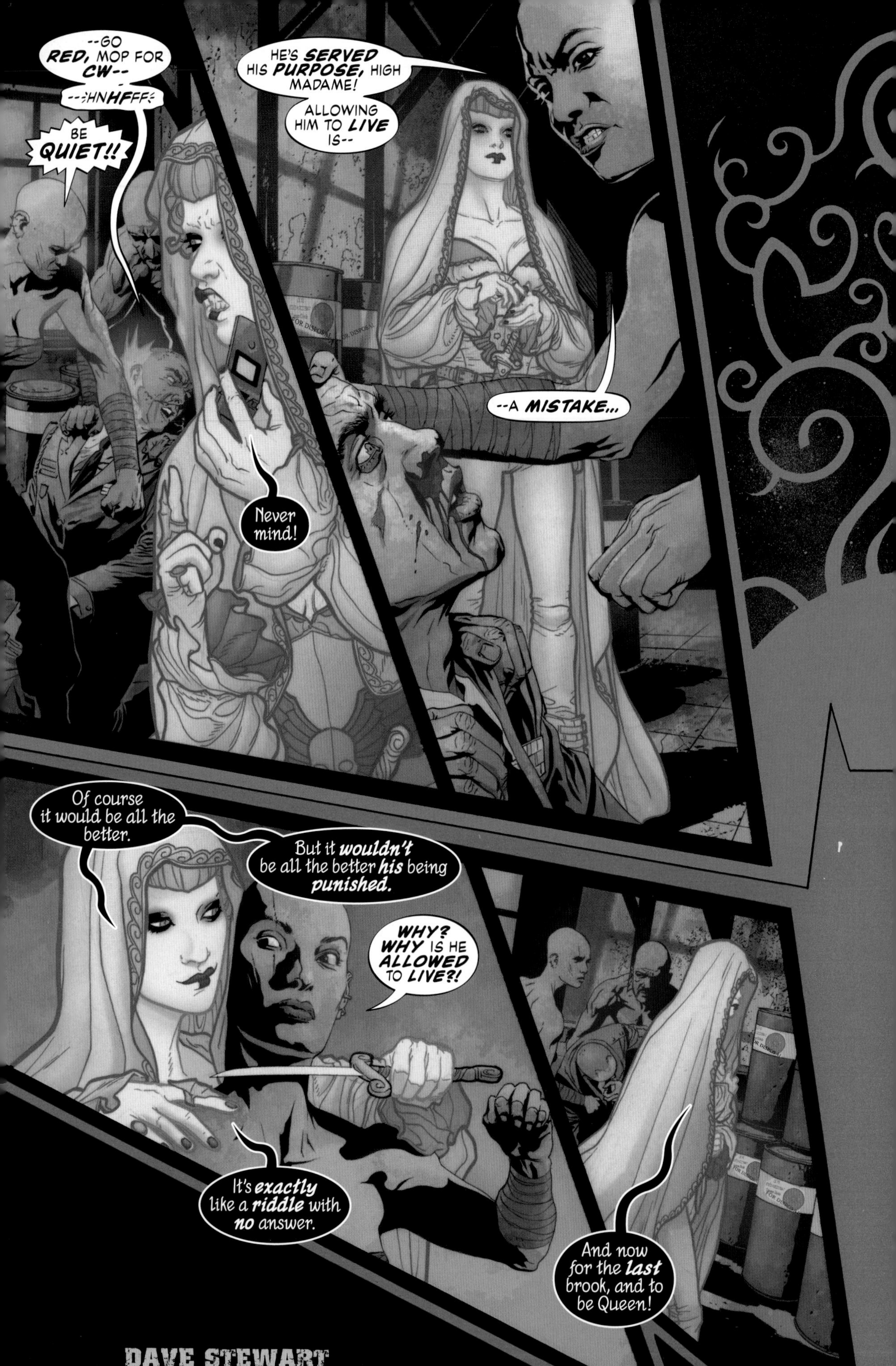

--GO RED, MOP FOR CW--
--HNHFFF--
BE QUIET!!
HE'S SERVED HIS PURPOSE, HIGH MADAME!
ALLOWING HIM TO LIVE IS--
--A MISTAKE...
Never mind!
Of course it would be all the better.
But it wouldn't be all the better his being punished.
WHY? WHY IS HE ALLOWED TO LIVE?!
It's exactly like a riddle with no answer.
And now for the last brook, and to be Queen!

DAVE STEWART
colors

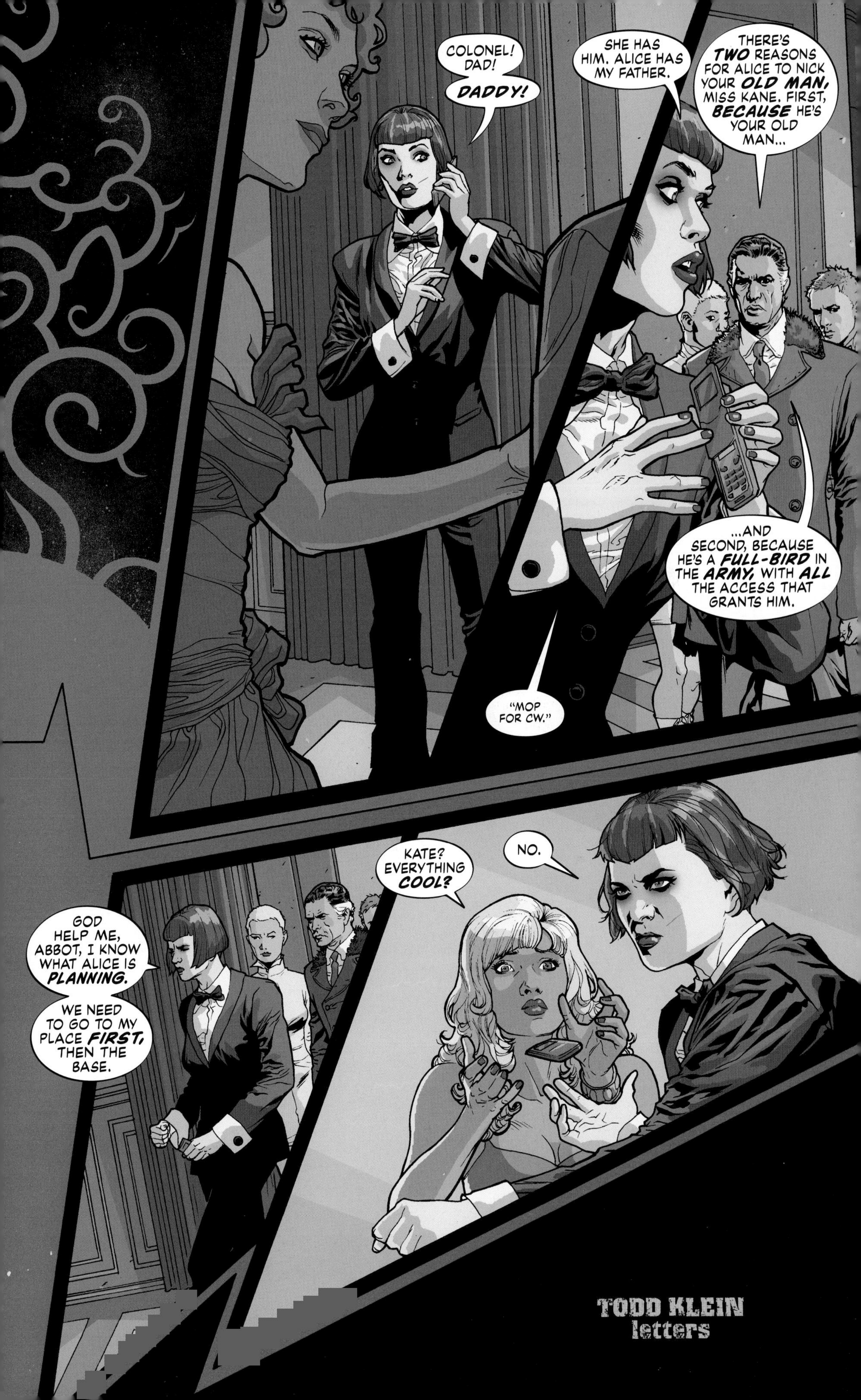
COLONEL! DAD! DADDY!
SHE HAS HIM. ALICE HAS MY FATHER.
THERE'S TWO REASONS FOR ALICE TO NICK YOUR OLD MAN, MISS KANE. FIRST, BECAUSE HE'S YOUR OLD MAN...
...AND SECOND, BECAUSE HE'S A FULL-BIRD IN THE ARMY, WITH ALL THE ACCESS THAT GRANTS HIM.
"MOP FOR CW."
GOD HELP ME, ABBOT, I KNOW WHAT ALICE IS PLANNING.
WE NEED TO GO TO MY PLACE FIRST, THEN THE BASE.
KATE? EVERYTHING COOL?
NO.
TODD KLEIN
letters

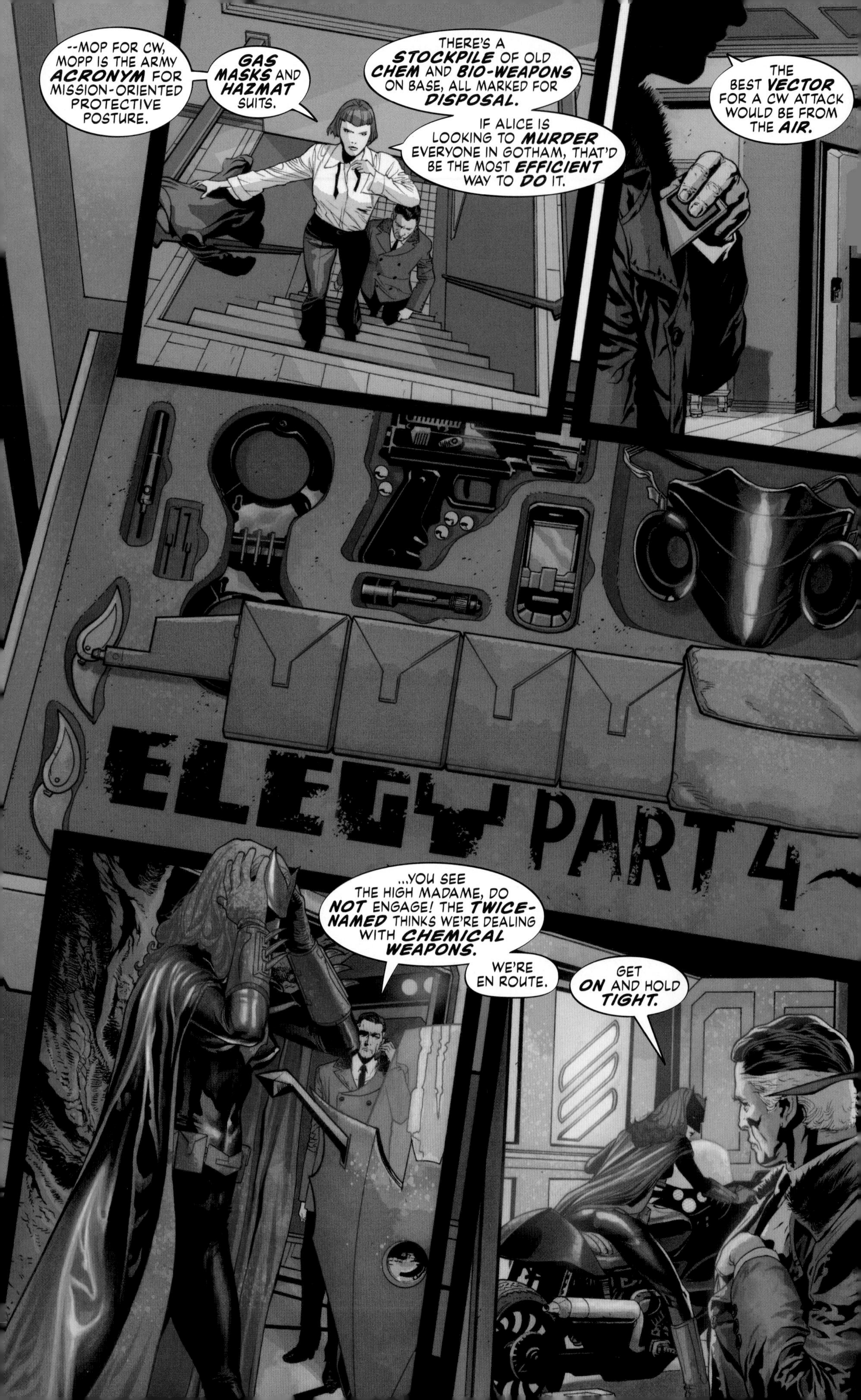
--MOP FOR CW, MOPP IS THE ARMY ACRONYM FOR MISSION-ORIENTED PROTECTIVE POSTURE.
GAS MASKS AND HAZMAT SUITS.
THERE'S A STOCKPILE OF OLD CHEM AND BIO-WEAPONS ON BASE, ALL MARKED FOR DISPOSAL.
IF ALICE IS LOOKING TO MURDER EVERYONE IN GOTHAM, THAT'D BE THE MOST EFFICIENT WAY TO DO IT.
THE BEST VECTOR FOR A CW ATTACK WOULD BE FROM THE AIR.
ELEGY PART 4
...YOU SEE THE HIGH MADAME, DO NOT ENGAGE! THE TWICE-NAMED THINKS WE'RE DEALING WITH CHEMICAL WEAPONS.
WE'RE EN ROUTE.
GET ON AND HOLD TIGHT.

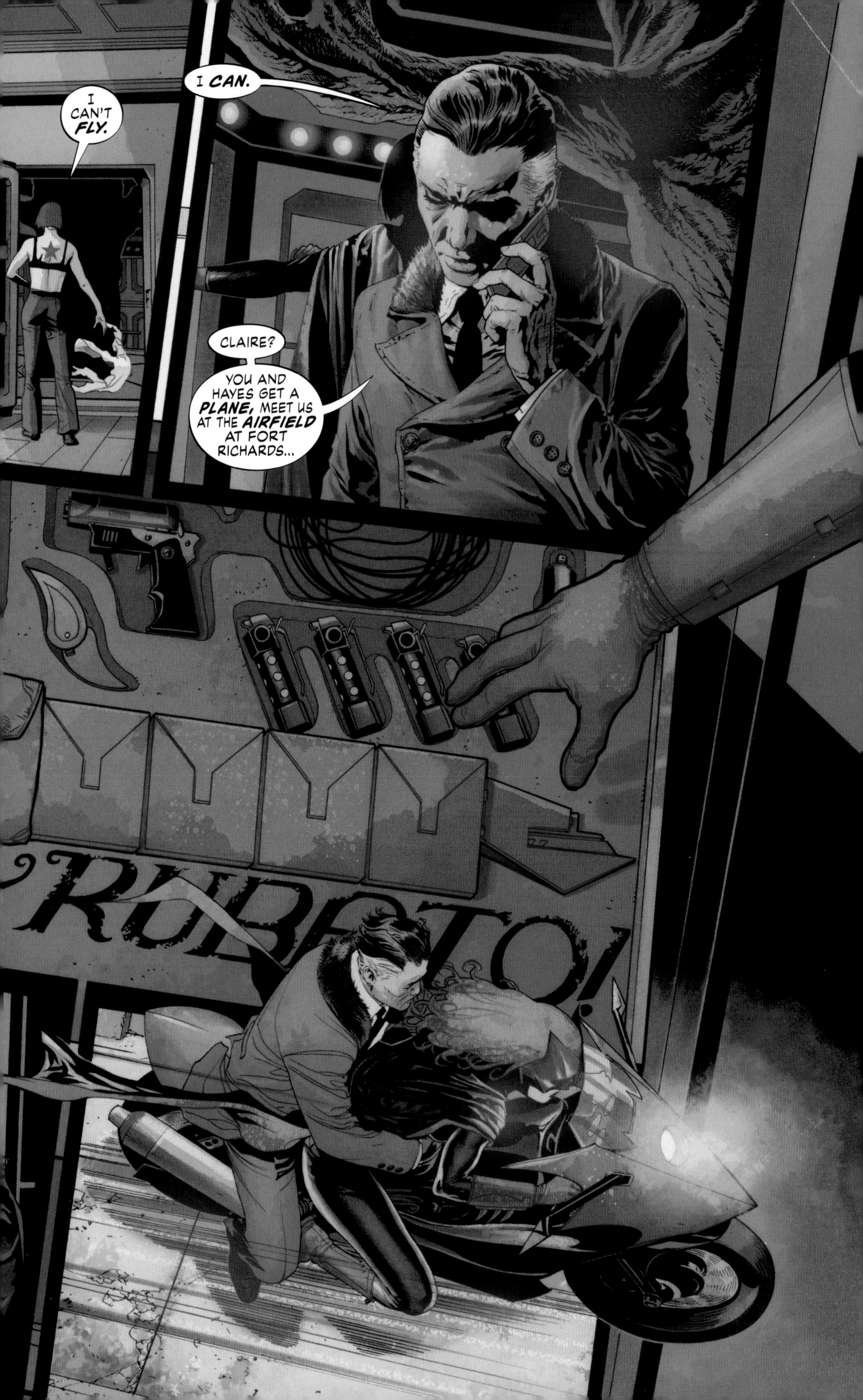
I CAN'T FLY.
I CAN.
CLAIRE?
YOU AND HAYES GET A PLANE, MEET US AT THE AIRFIELD AT FORT RICHARDS...

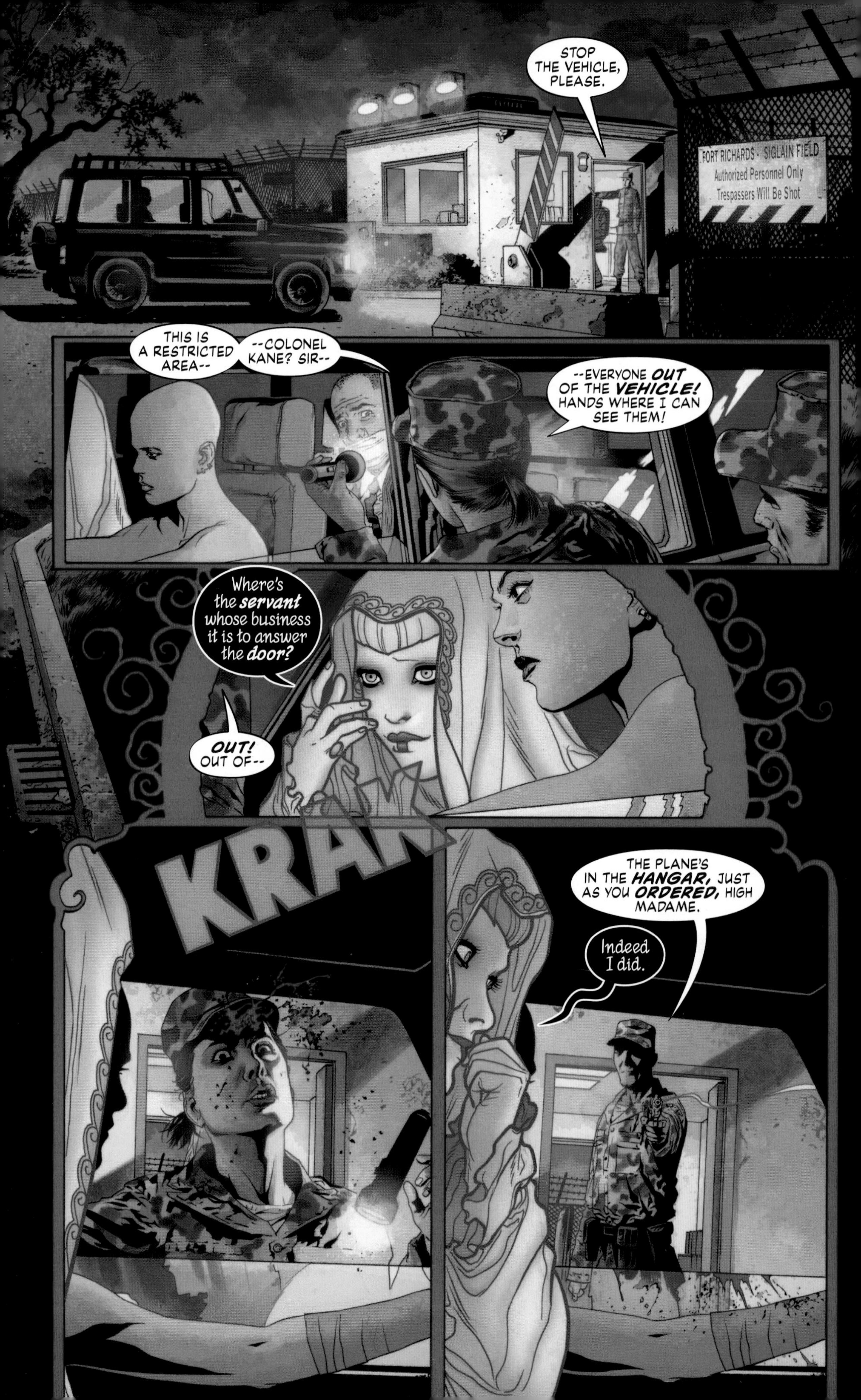
STOP THE VEHICLE, PLEASE.
FORT RICHARDS · SIGLAIN FIELD
Authorized Personnel Only
Trespassers Will Be Shot
THIS IS A RESTRICTED AREA--
--COLONEL KANE? SIR--
--EVERYONE OUT OF THE VEHICLE! HANDS WHERE I CAN SEE THEM!
Where's the servant whose business it is to answer the door?
OUT! OUT OF--
KRAK
THE PLANE'S IN THE HANGAR, JUST AS YOU ORDERED, HIGH MADAME.
Indeed I did.

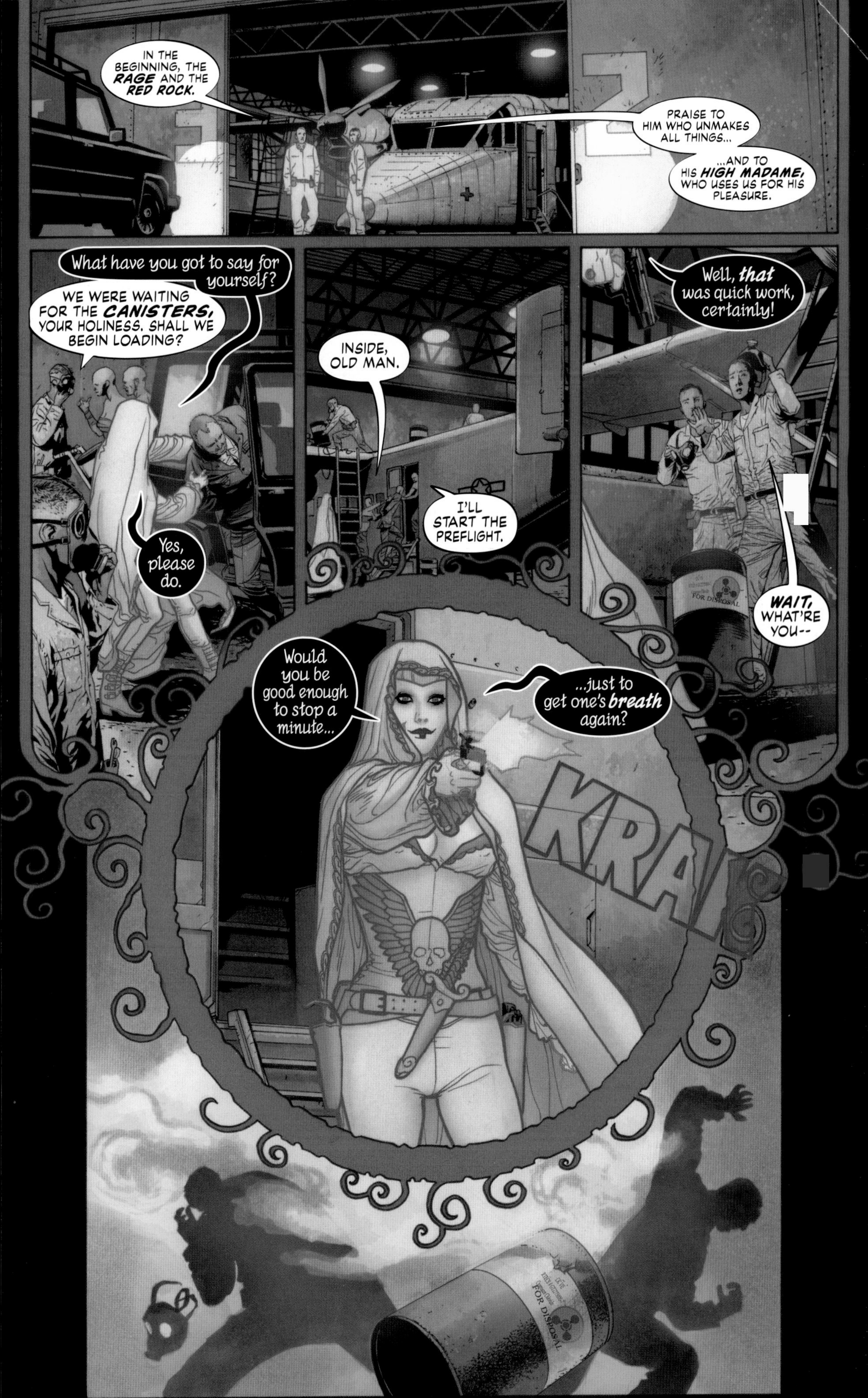
IN THE BEGINNING, THE RAGE AND THE RED ROCK.
PRAISE TO HIM WHO UNMAKES ALL THINGS...
...AND TO HIS HIGH MADAME, WHO USES US FOR HIS PLEASURE.
What have you got to say for yourself?
WE WERE WAITING FOR THE CANISTERS, YOUR HOLINESS. SHALL WE BEGIN LOADING?
Yes, please do.
INSIDE, OLD MAN.
I'LL START THE PREFLIGHT.
Well, that was quick work, certainly!
WAIT, WHAT'RE YOU--
FOR DISPOSAL
Would you be good enough to stop a minute...
...just to get one's breath again?
KRA
FOR DISPOSAL

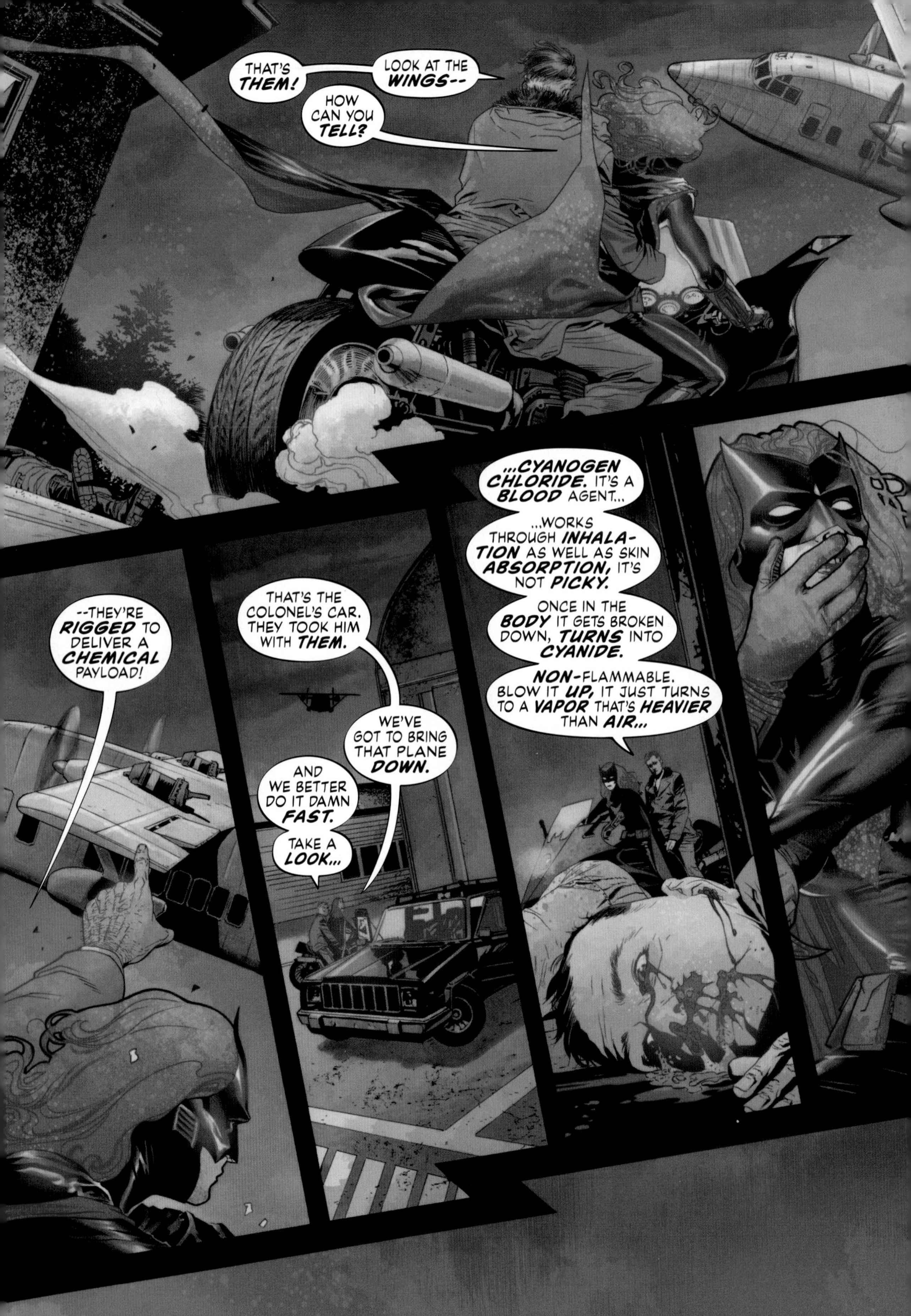
THAT'S THEM!
LOOK AT THE WINGS--
HOW CAN YOU TELL?
--THEY'RE RIGGED TO DELIVER A CHEMICAL PAYLOAD!
THAT'S THE COLONEL'S CAR. THEY TOOK HIM WITH THEM.
WE'VE GOT TO BRING THAT PLANE DOWN.
AND WE BETTER DO IT DAMN FAST.
TAKE A LOOK...
...CYANOGEN CHLORIDE. IT'S A BLOOD AGENT...
...WORKS THROUGH INHALATION AS WELL AS SKIN ABSORPTION, IT'S NOT PICKY.
ONCE IN THE BODY IT GETS BROKEN DOWN, TURNS INTO CYANIDE.
NON-FLAMMABLE. BLOW IT UP, IT JUST TURNS TO A VAPOR THAT'S HEAVIER THAN AIR...

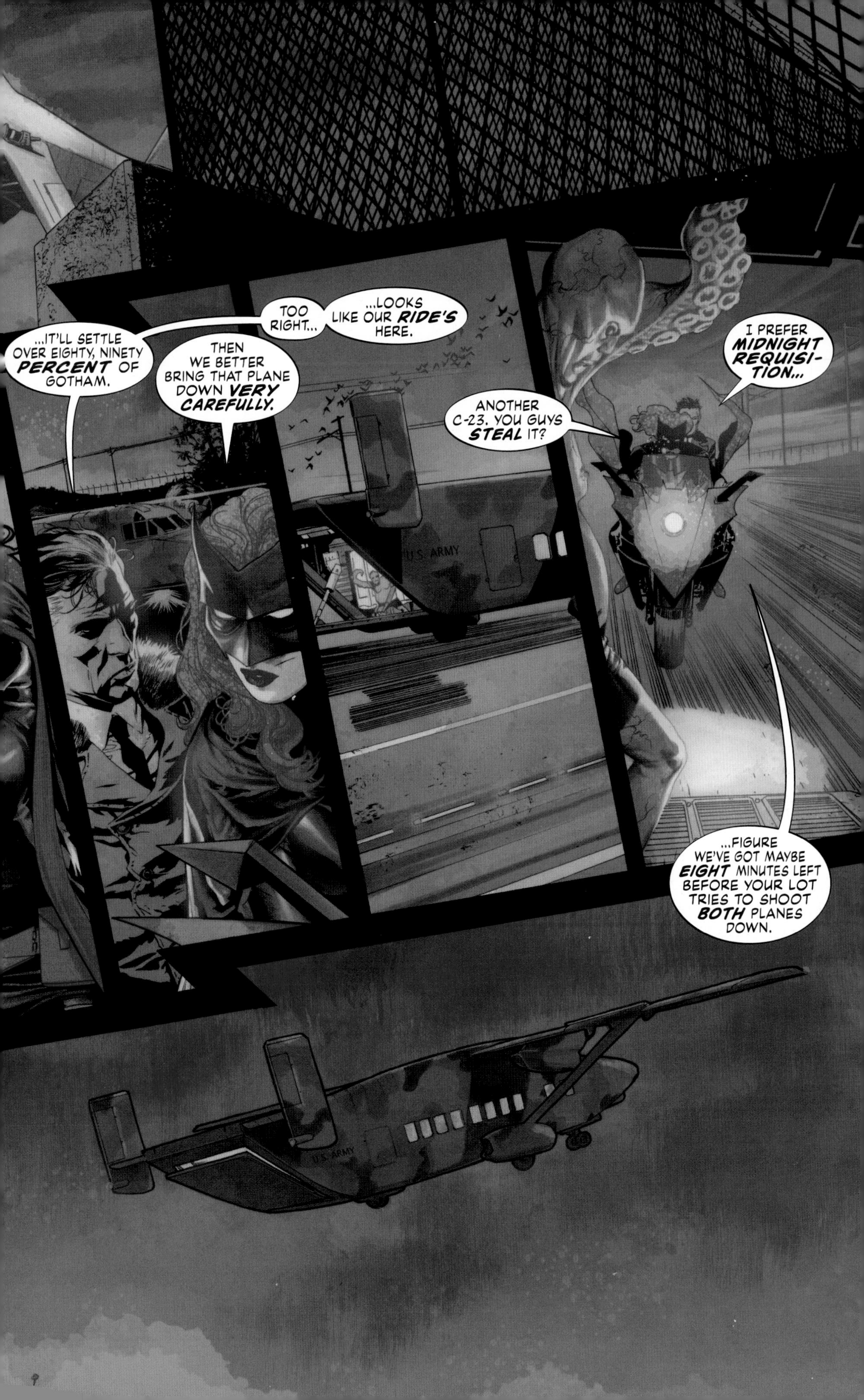
...IT'LL SETTLE OVER EIGHTY, NINETY PERCENT OF GOTHAM.
THEN WE BETTER BRING THAT PLANE DOWN VERY CAREFULLY.
TOO RIGHT...
...LOOKS LIKE OUR RIDE'S HERE.
U.S. ARMY
ANOTHER C-23. YOU GUYS STEAL IT?
I PREFER MIDNIGHT REQUISITION...
...FIGURE WE'VE GOT MAYBE EIGHT MINUTES LEFT BEFORE YOUR LOT TRIES TO SHOOT BOTH PLANES DOWN.

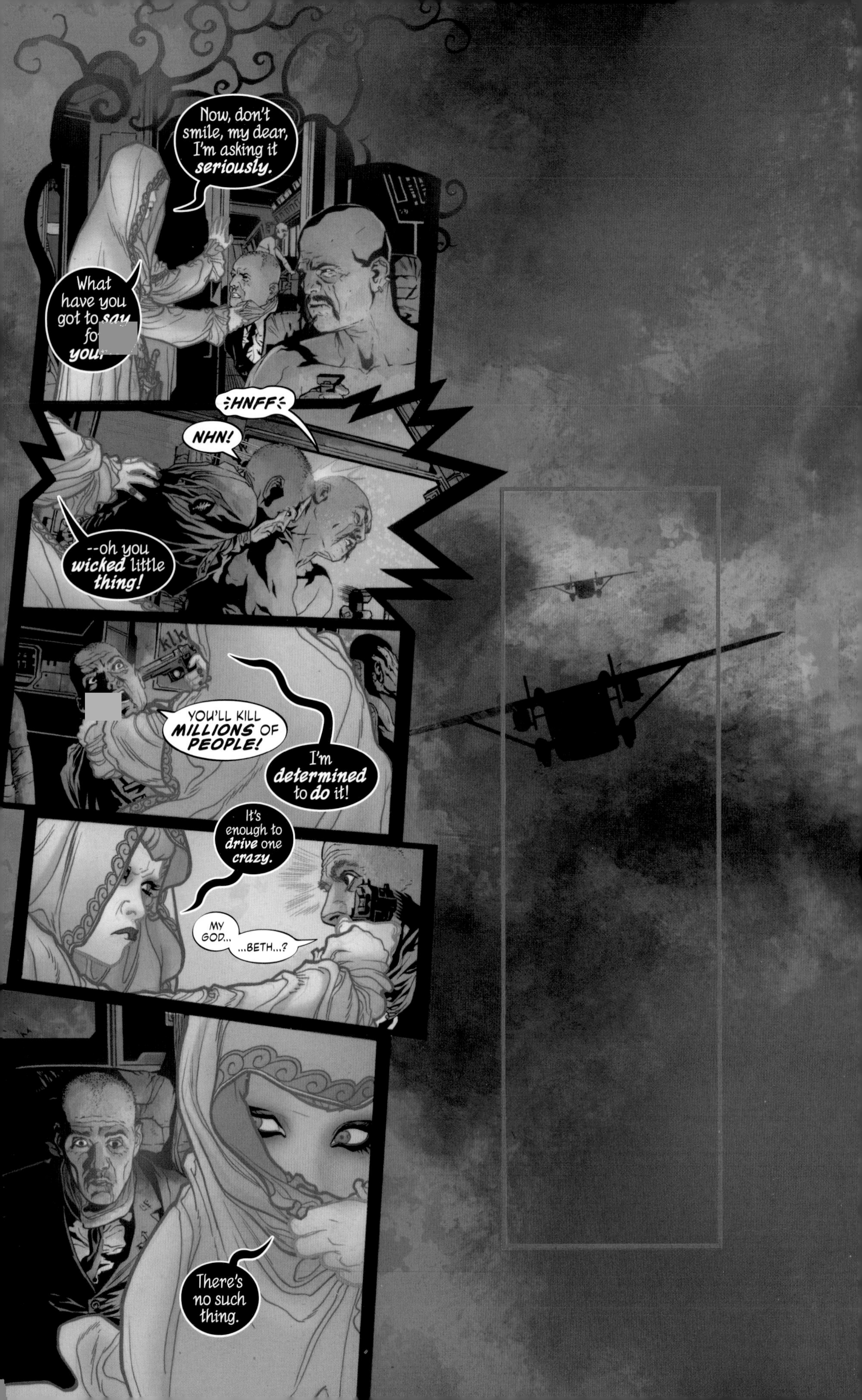

Now, don't smile, my dear, I'm asking it seriously.
What have you got to say fo you?
HNFF
NHN!
--oh you wicked little thing!
klk
YOU'LL KILL MILLIONS OF PEOPLE!
I'm determined to do it!
It's enough to drive one crazy.
MY GOD...
...BETH...?
There's no such thing.

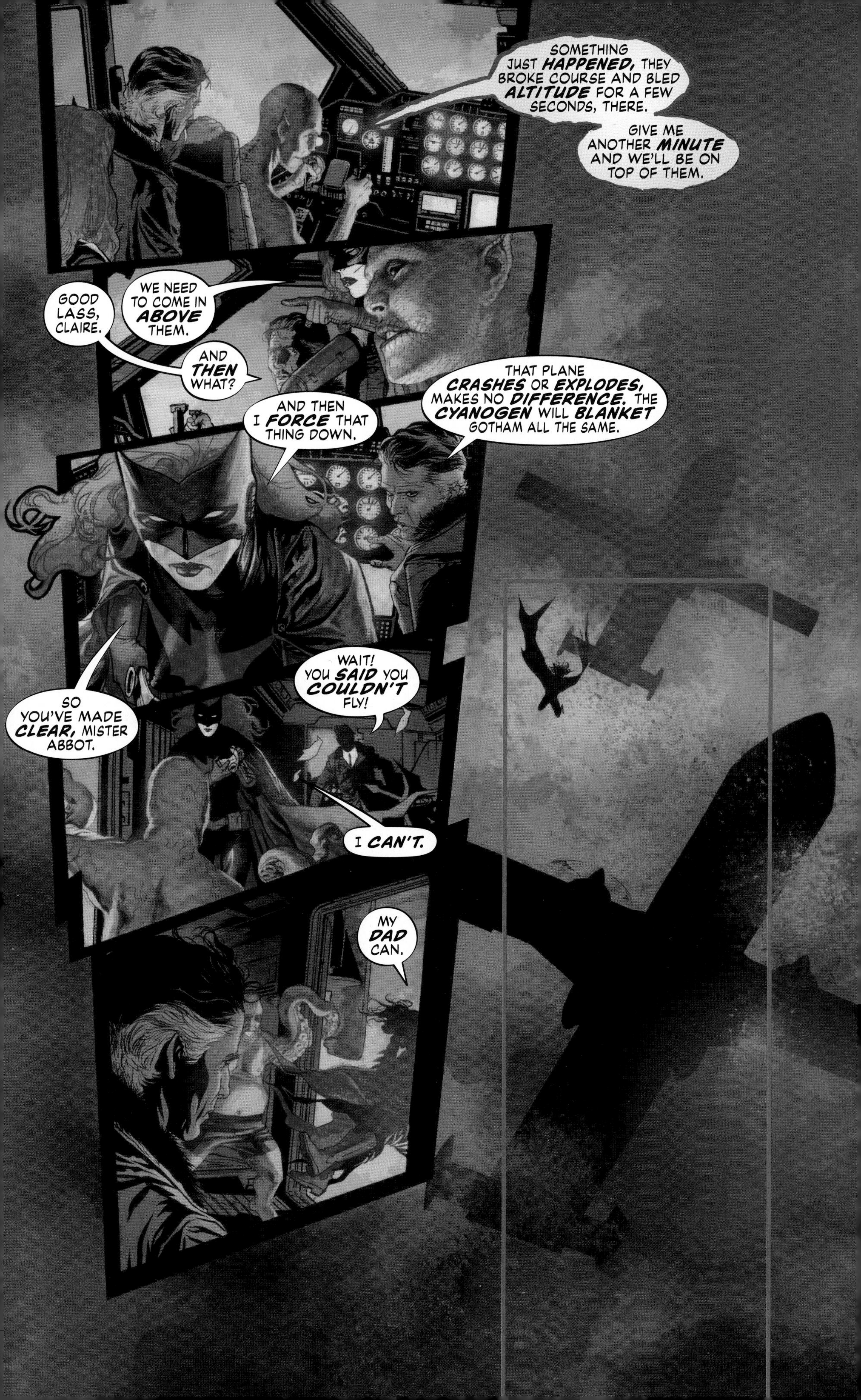
SOMETHING JUST HAPPENED, THEY BROKE COURSE AND BLED ALTITUDE FOR A FEW SECONDS, THERE.
GIVE ME ANOTHER MINUTE AND WE'LL BE ON TOP OF THEM.
WE NEED TO COME IN ABOVE THEM.
GOOD LASS, CLAIRE.
AND THEN WHAT?
AND THEN I FORCE THAT THING DOWN.
THAT PLANE CRASHES OR EXPLODES, MAKES NO DIFFERENCE. THE CYANOGEN WILL BLANKET GOTHAM ALL THE SAME.
SO YOU'VE MADE CLEAR, MISTER ABBOT.
WAIT! YOU SAID YOU COULDN'T FLY!
I CAN'T.
MY DAD CAN.

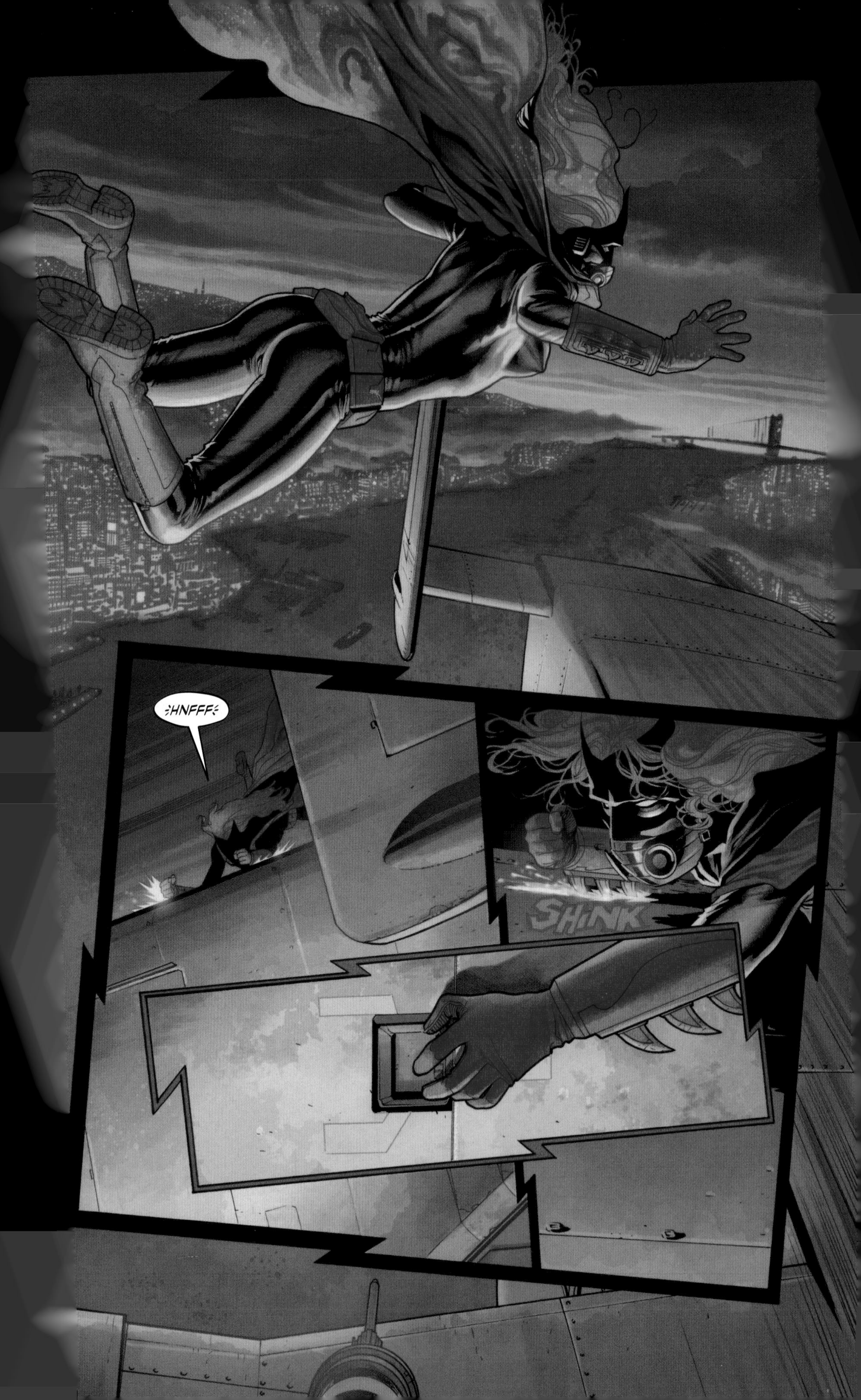
HNFFF
SHINK

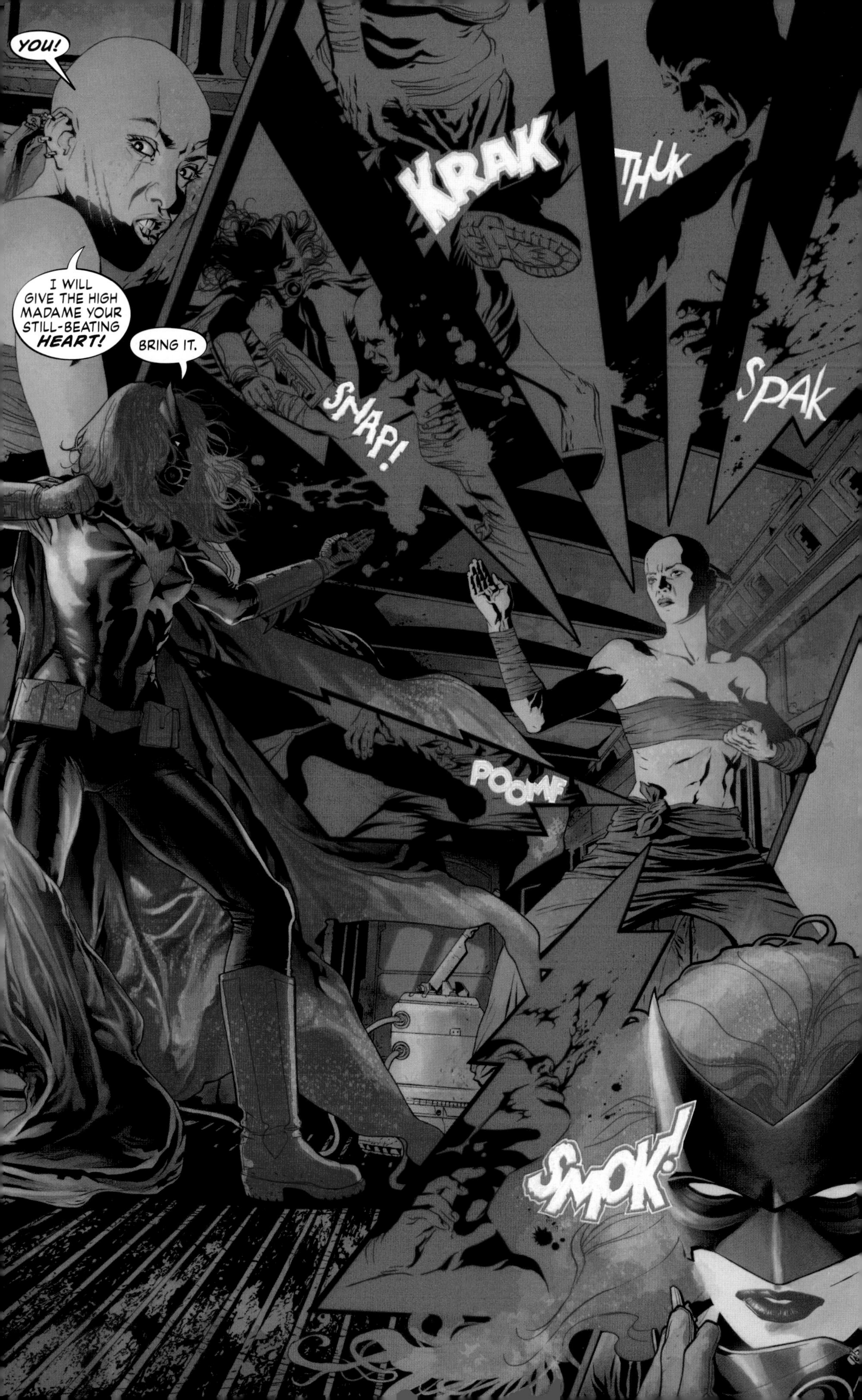
YOU!
I WILL GIVE THE HIGH MADAME YOUR STILL-BEATING HEART!
BRING IT.
KRAK
THUK
SNAP!
SPAK
POOMF
SMOK!

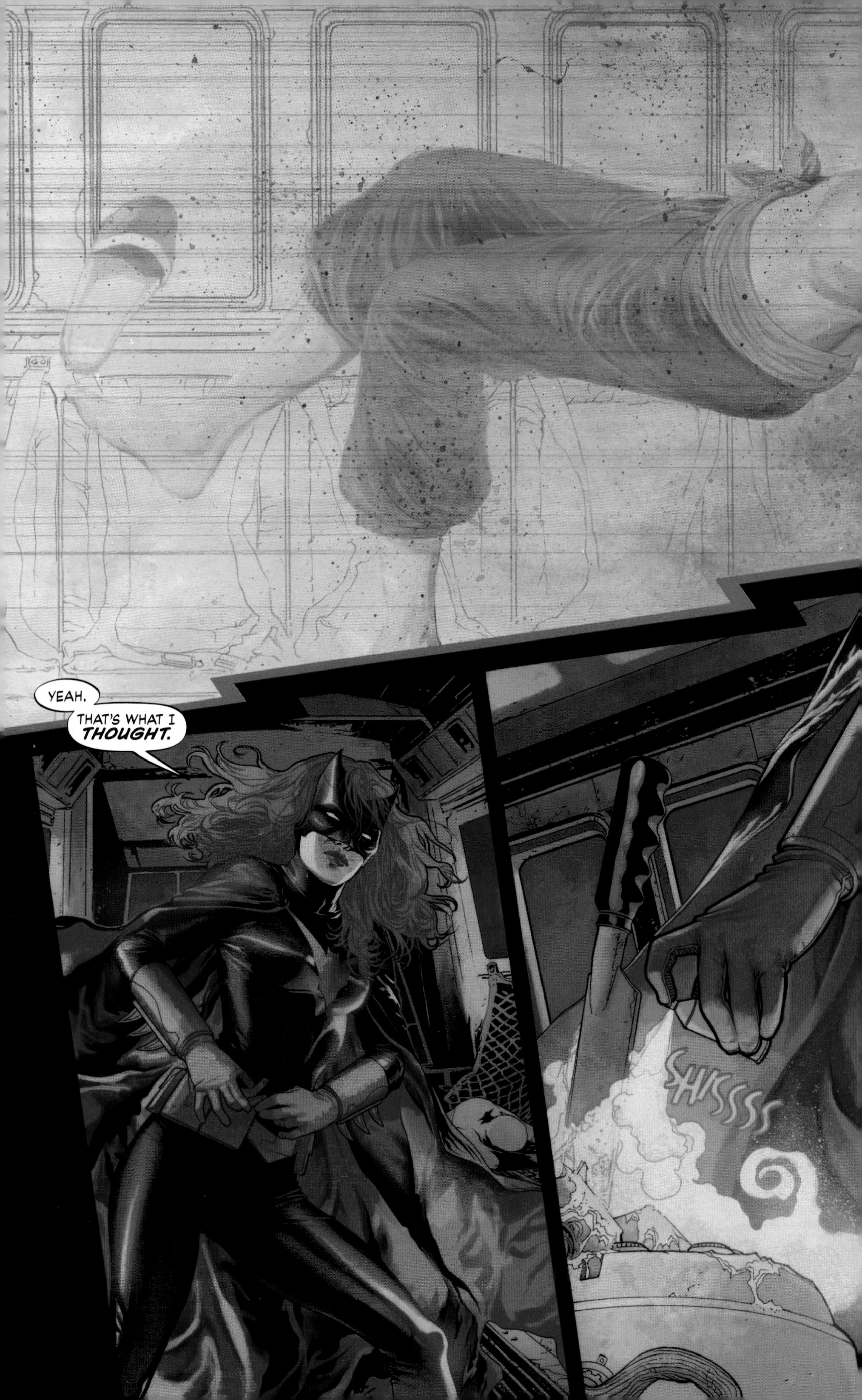
YEAH.
THAT'S WHAT I THOUGHT.
SHISSSS

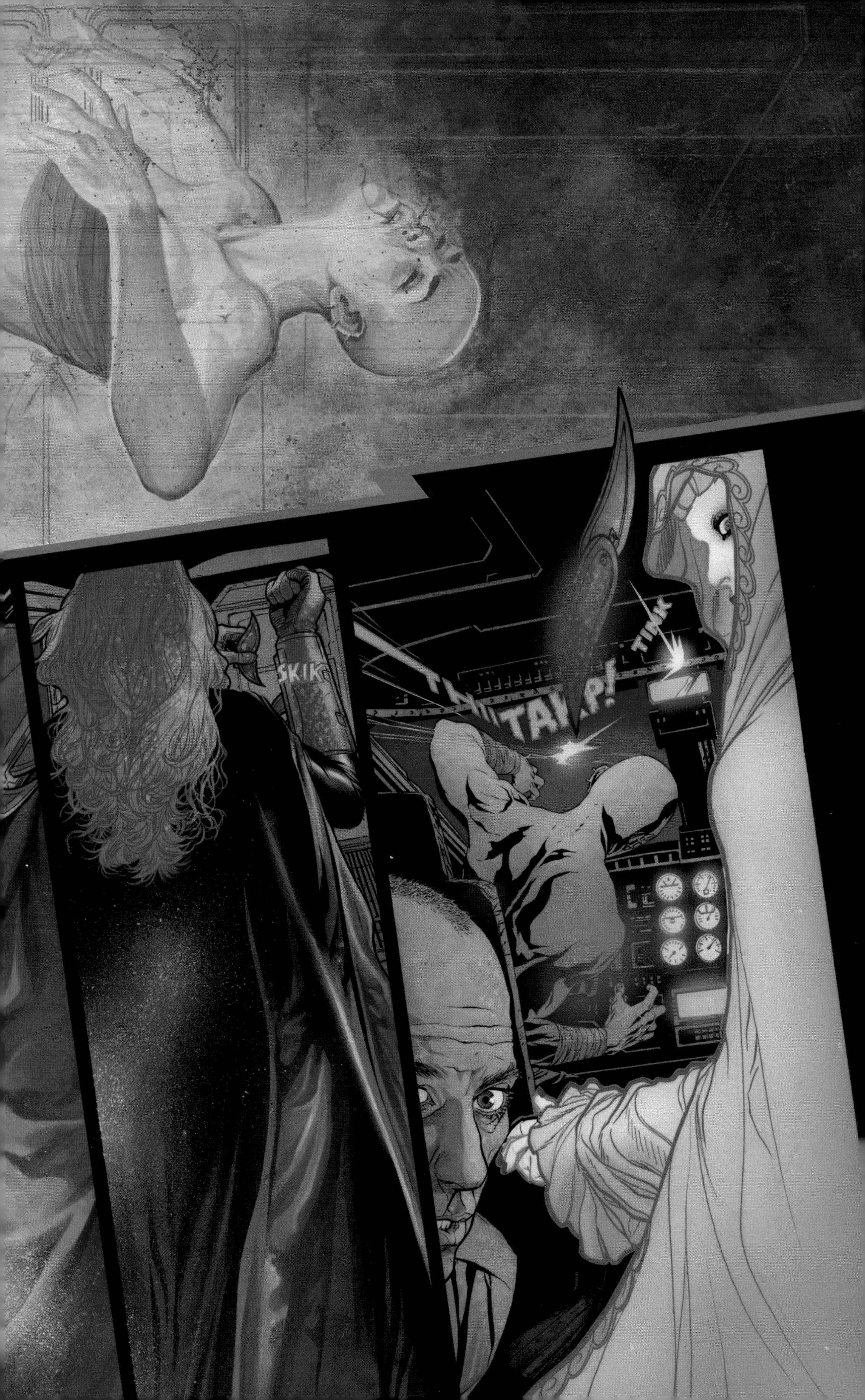
SKIK
TINK

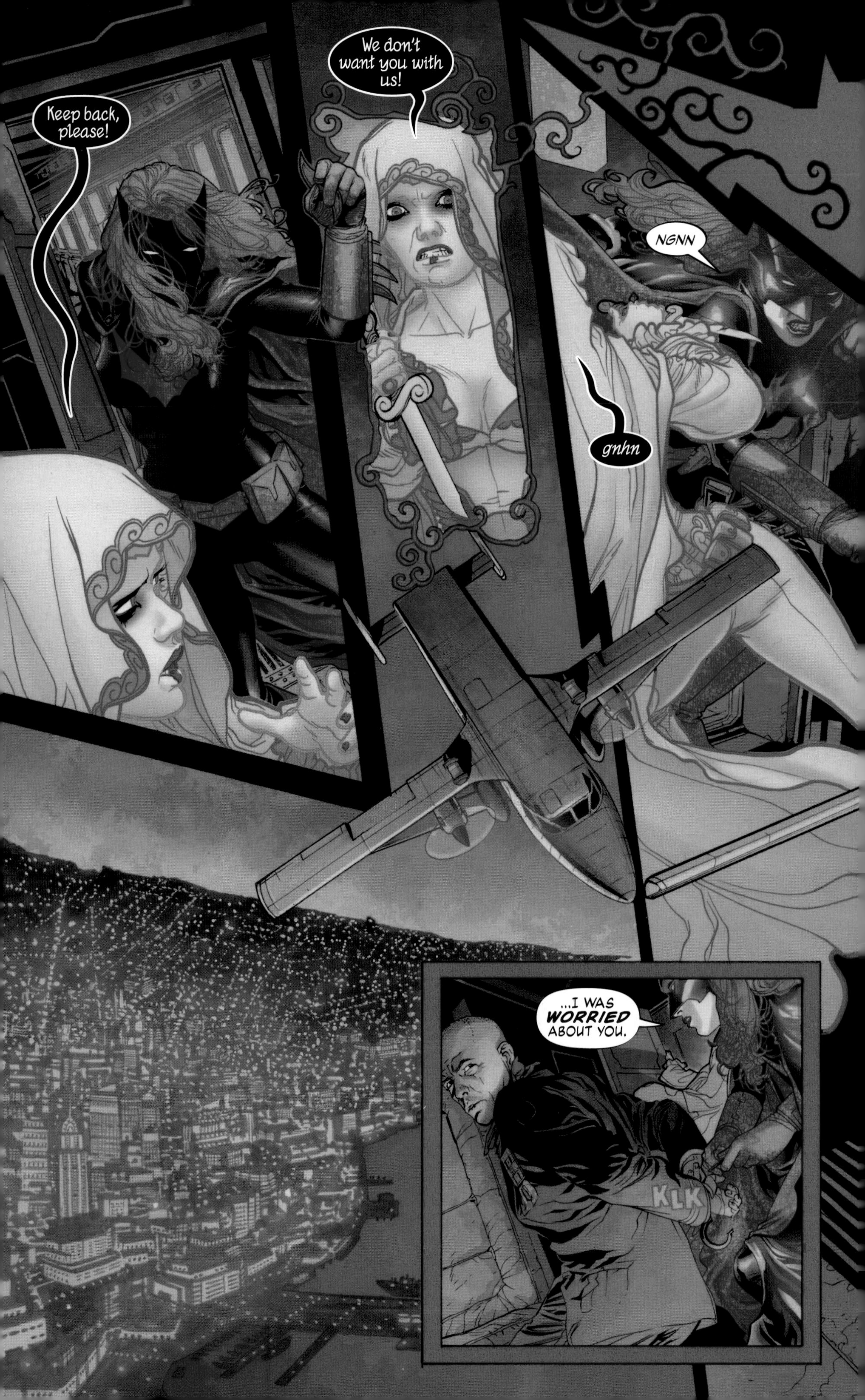

Keep back, please!
We don't want you with us!
NGNN
gnhn
...I WAS WORRIED ABOUT YOU.
KLK

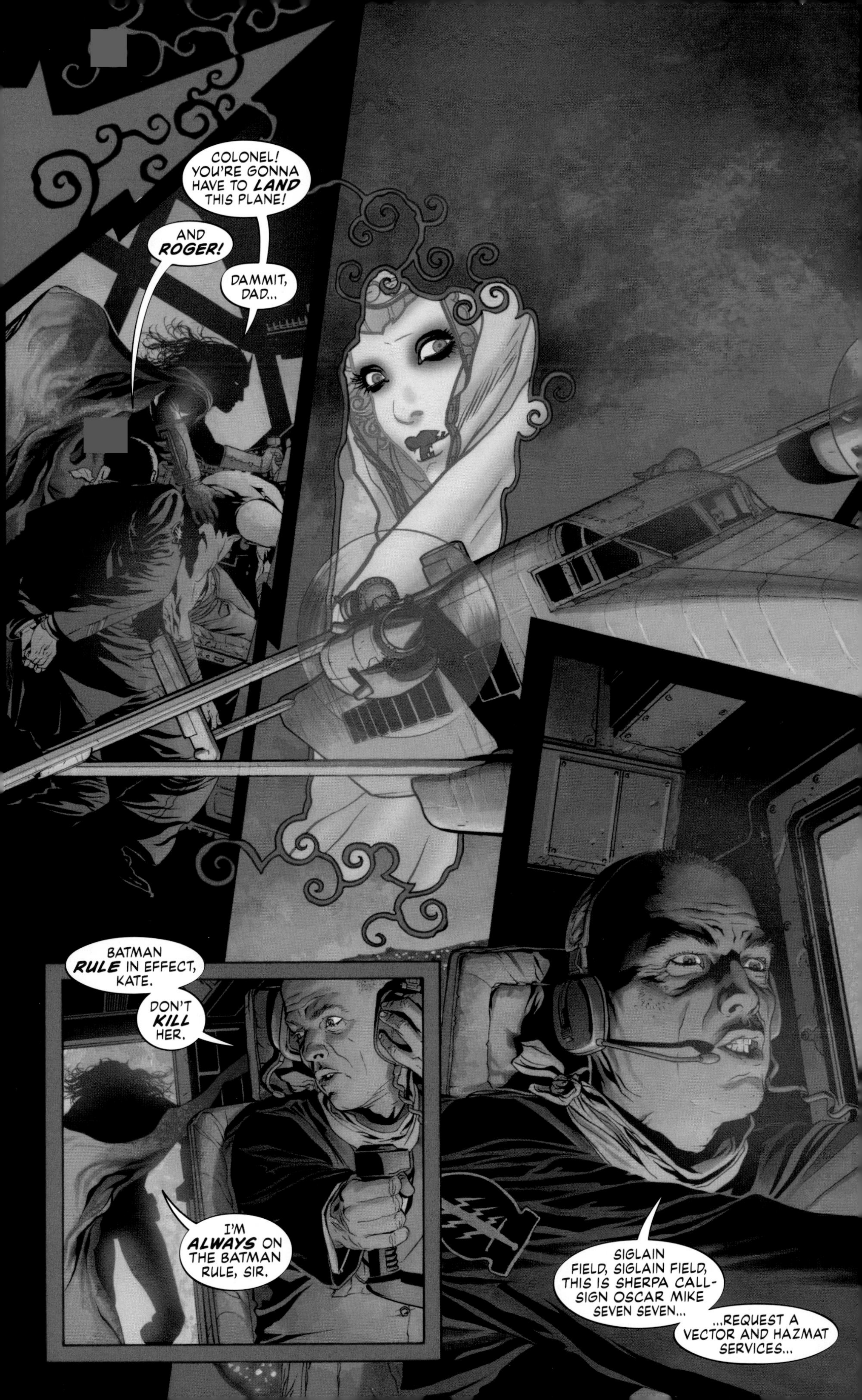
COLONEL! YOU'RE GONNA HAVE TO LAND THIS PLANE!
AND ROGER!
DAMMIT, DAD...
BATMAN RULE IN EFFECT, KATE.
DON'T KILL HER.
I'M ALWAYS ON THE BATMAN RULE, SIR.
SIGLAIN FIELD, SIGLAIN FIELD, THIS IS SHERPA CALL-SIGN OSCAR MIKE SEVEN SEVEN...
...REQUEST A VECTOR AND HAZMAT SERVICES...

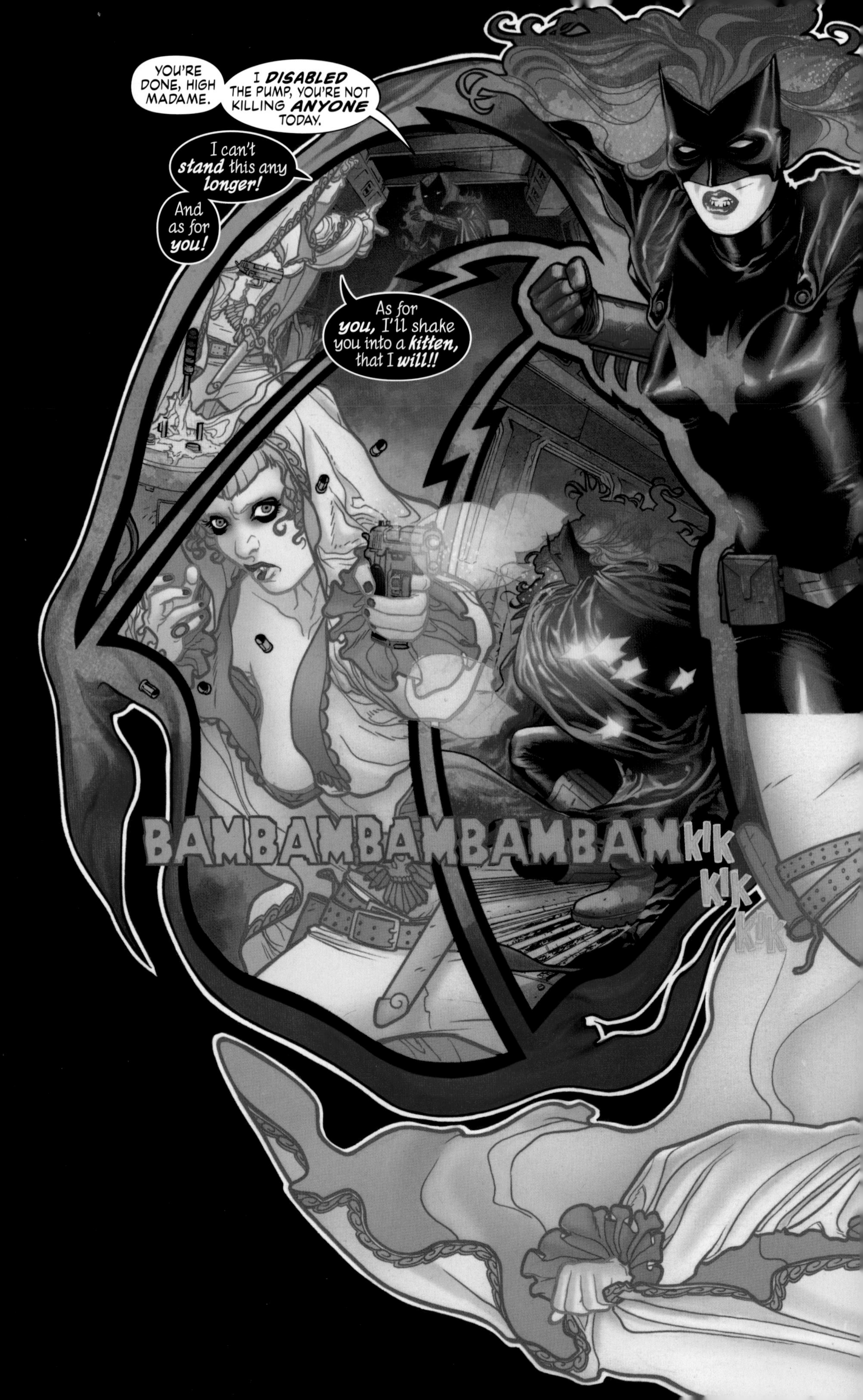
YOU'RE DONE, HIGH MADAME.
I DISABLED THE PUMP, YOU'RE NOT KILLING ANYONE TODAY.
I can't stand this any longer!
And as for you!
As for you, I'll shake you into a kitten, that I will!!
BAMBAMBAMBAMBAMBAM
KIK KIK KIK

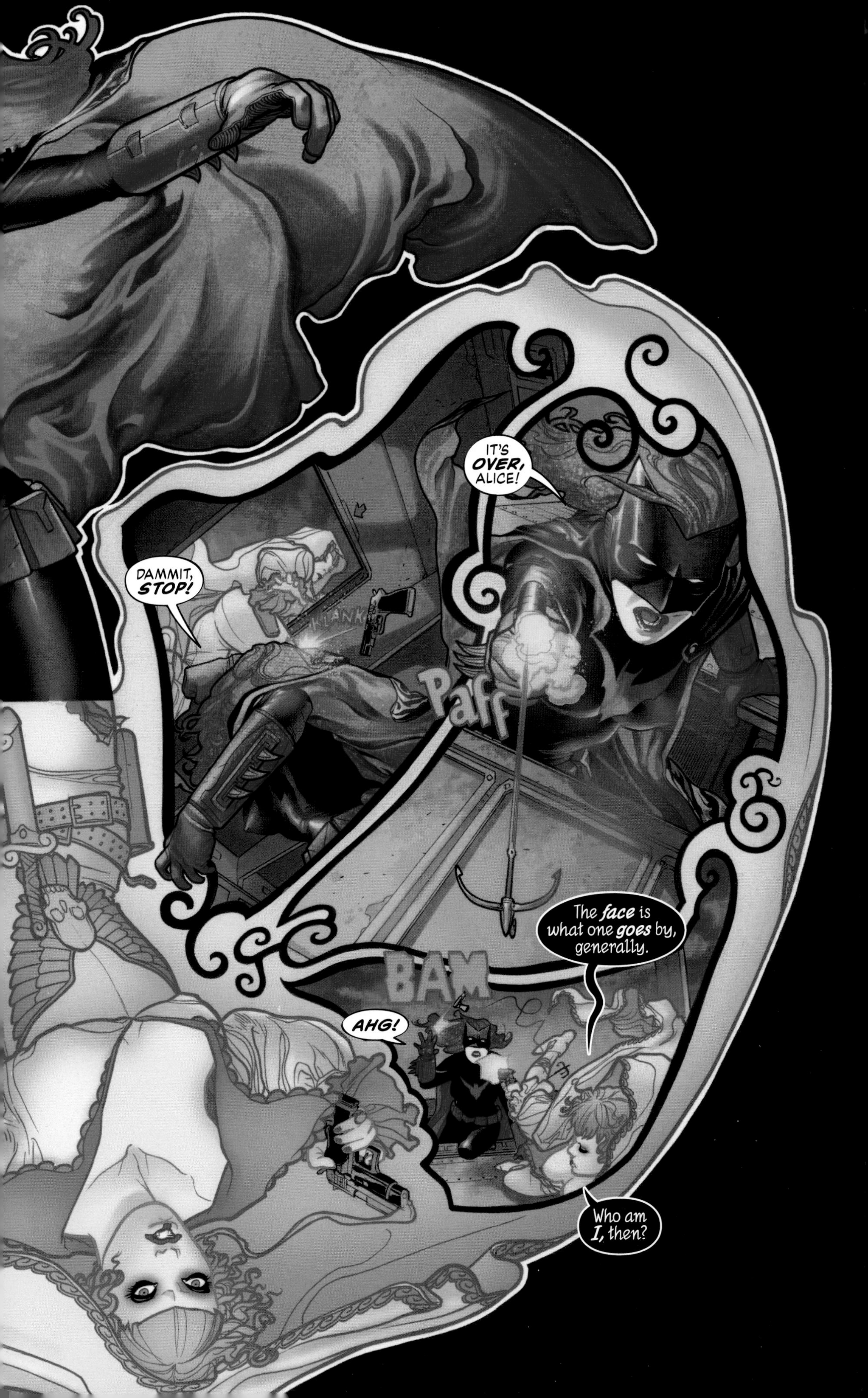
IT'S OVER, ALICE!
DAMMIT, STOP!
KLANK
Paff
The face is what one goes by, generally.
BAM
AHG!
Who am I, then?

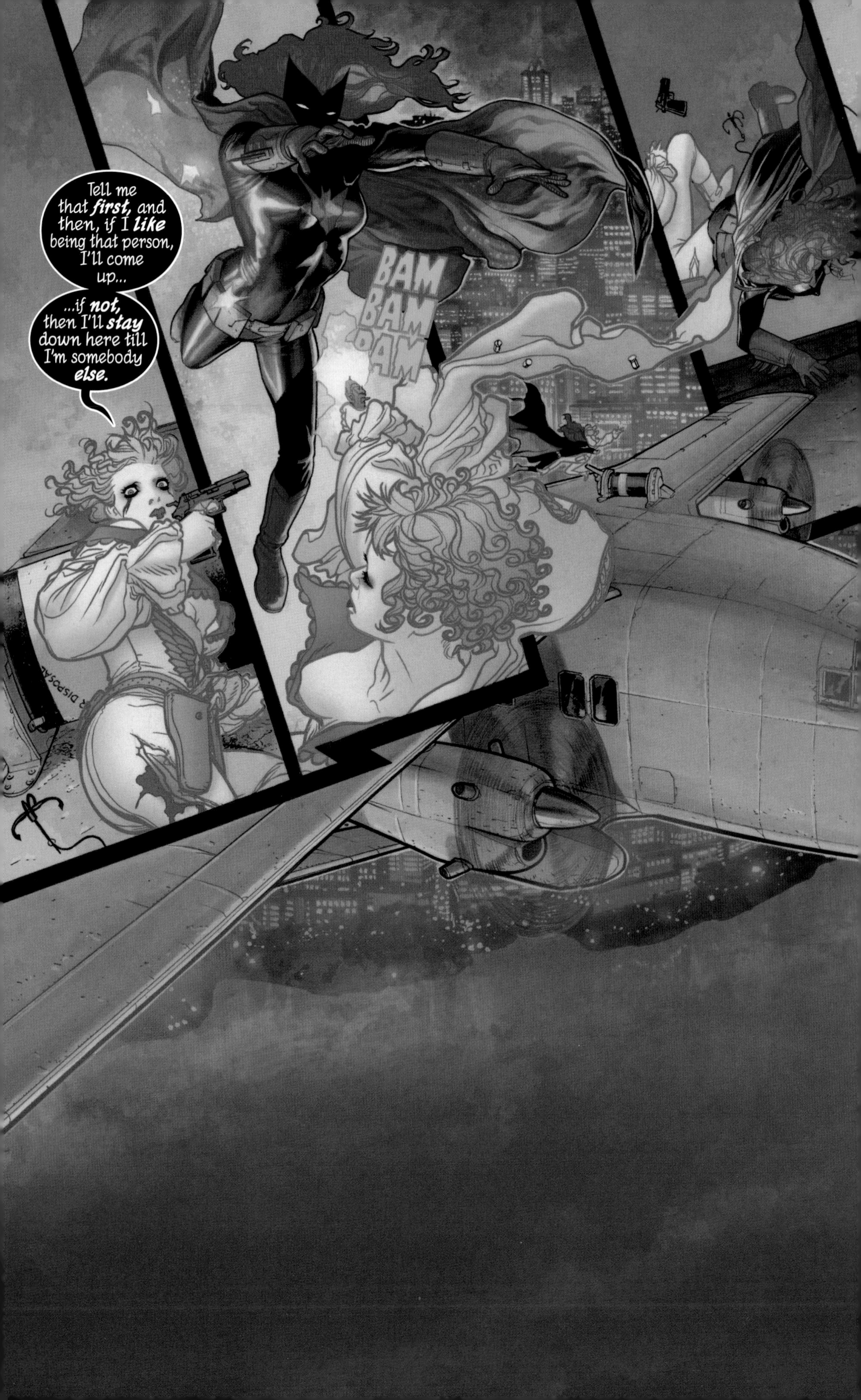
Tell me that first, and then, if I like being that person, I'll come up...
...if not, then I'll stay down here till I'm somebody else.
BAM
BAM

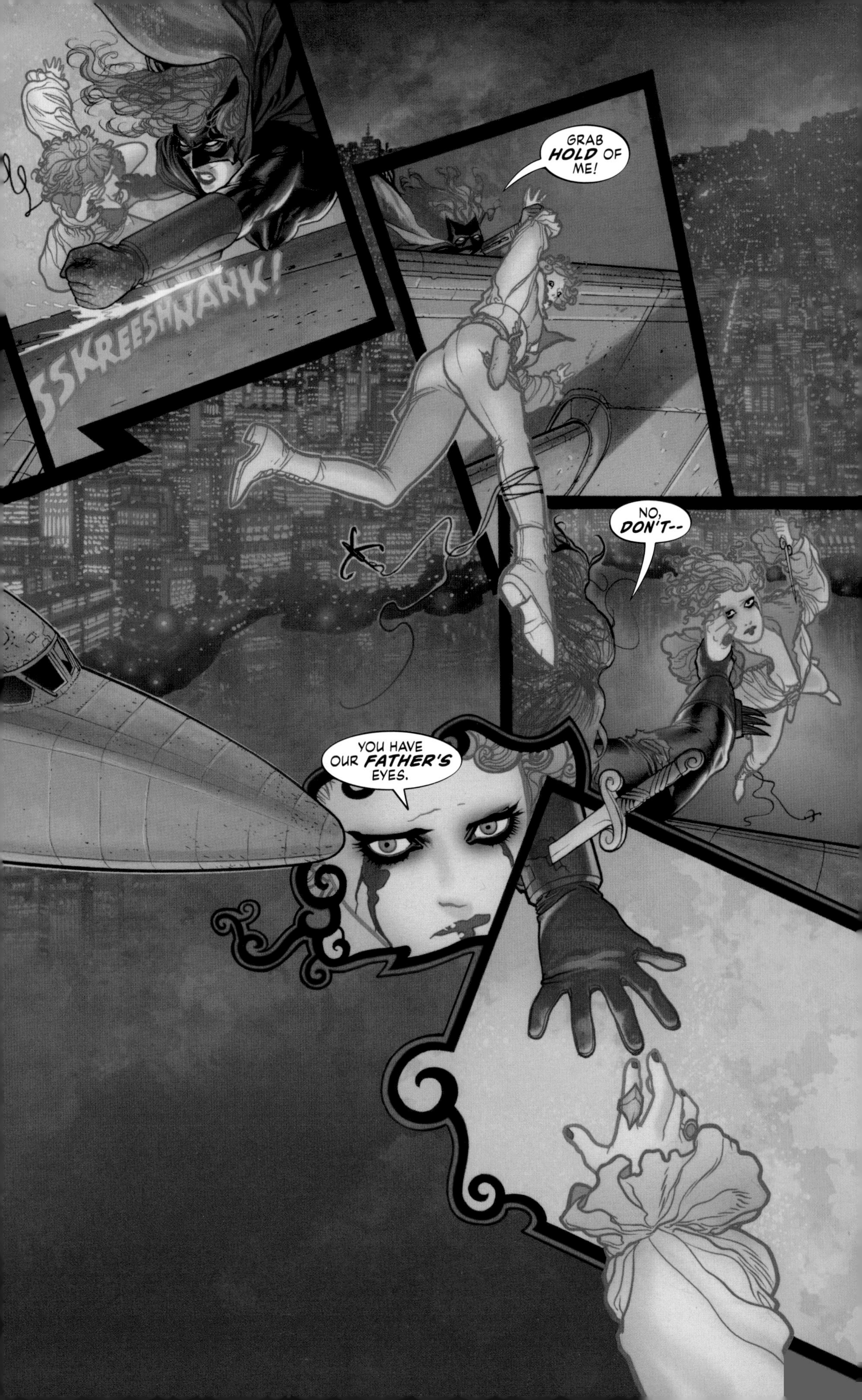
SSKREESHNANK!
GRAB HOLD OF ME!
NO, DON'T--
YOU HAVE OUR FATHER'S EYES.

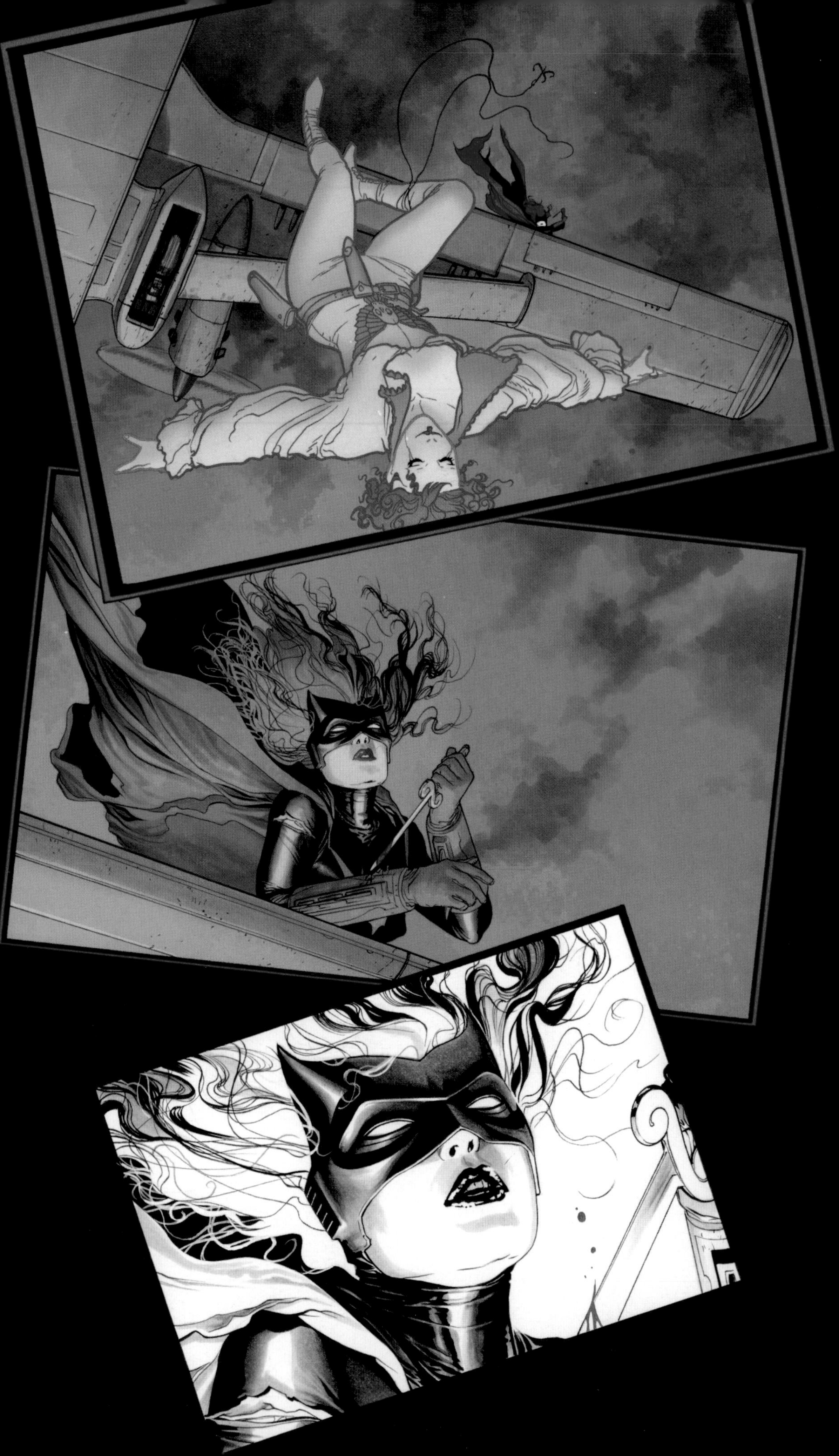

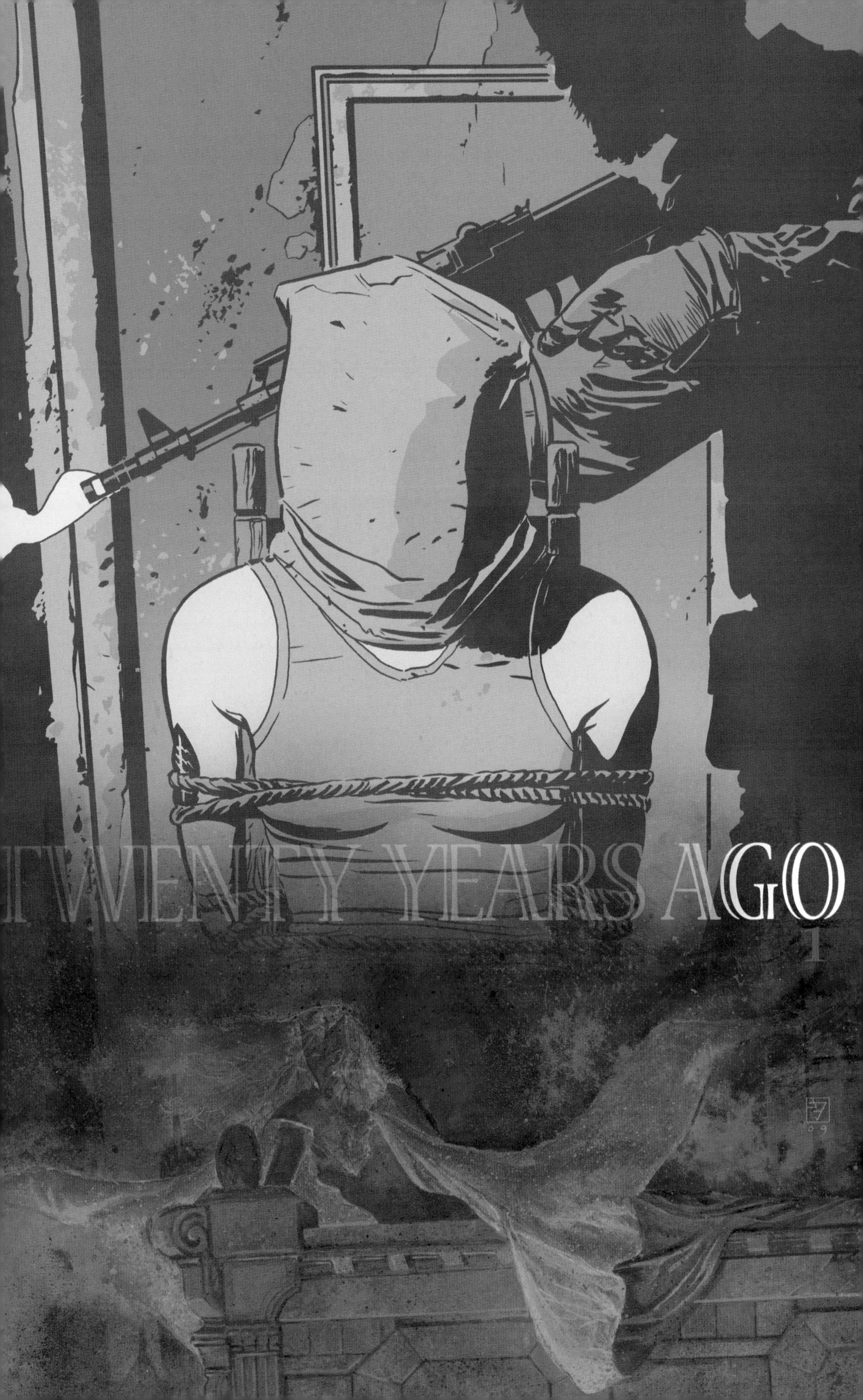
TWENTY YEARS AGO
1

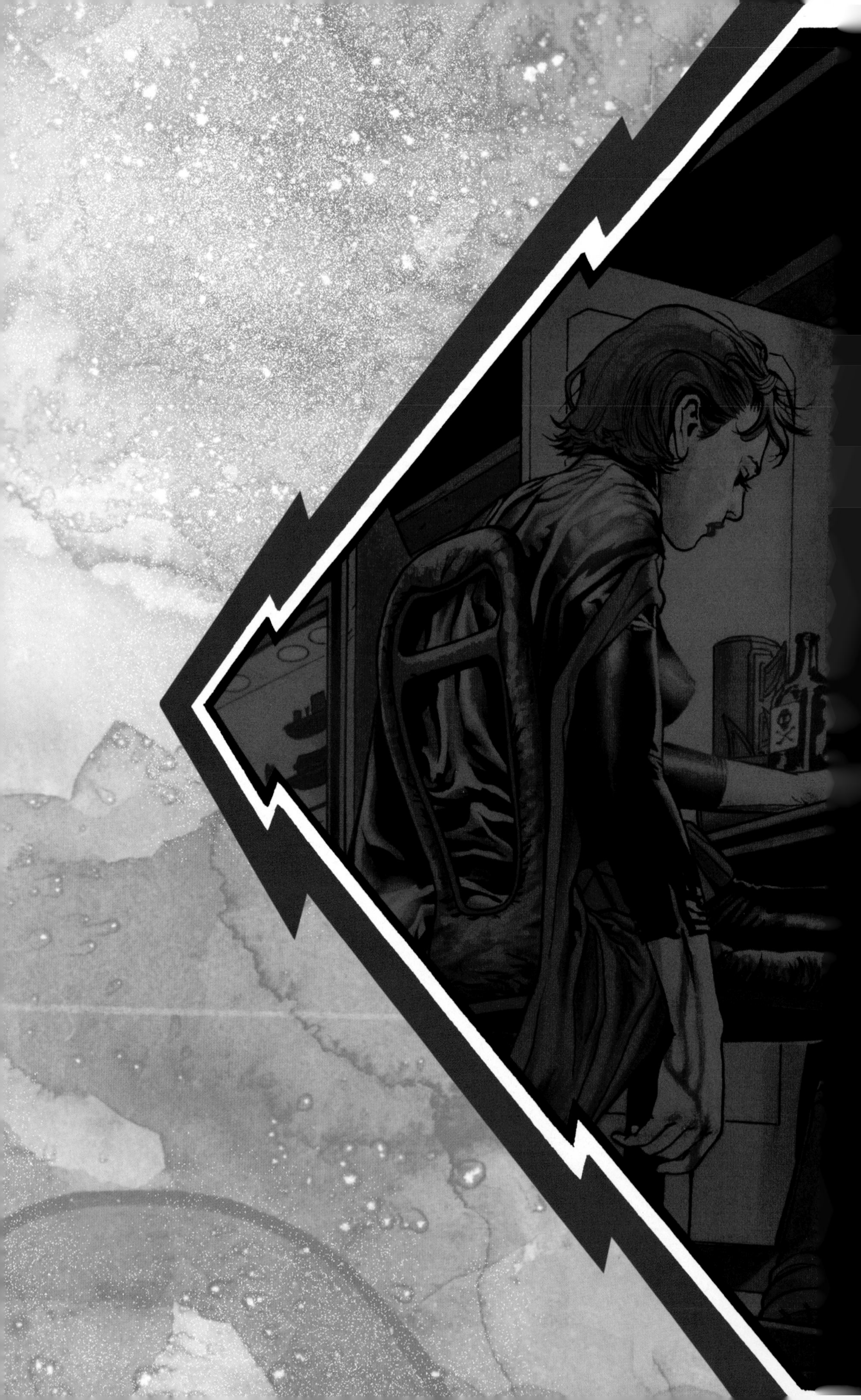

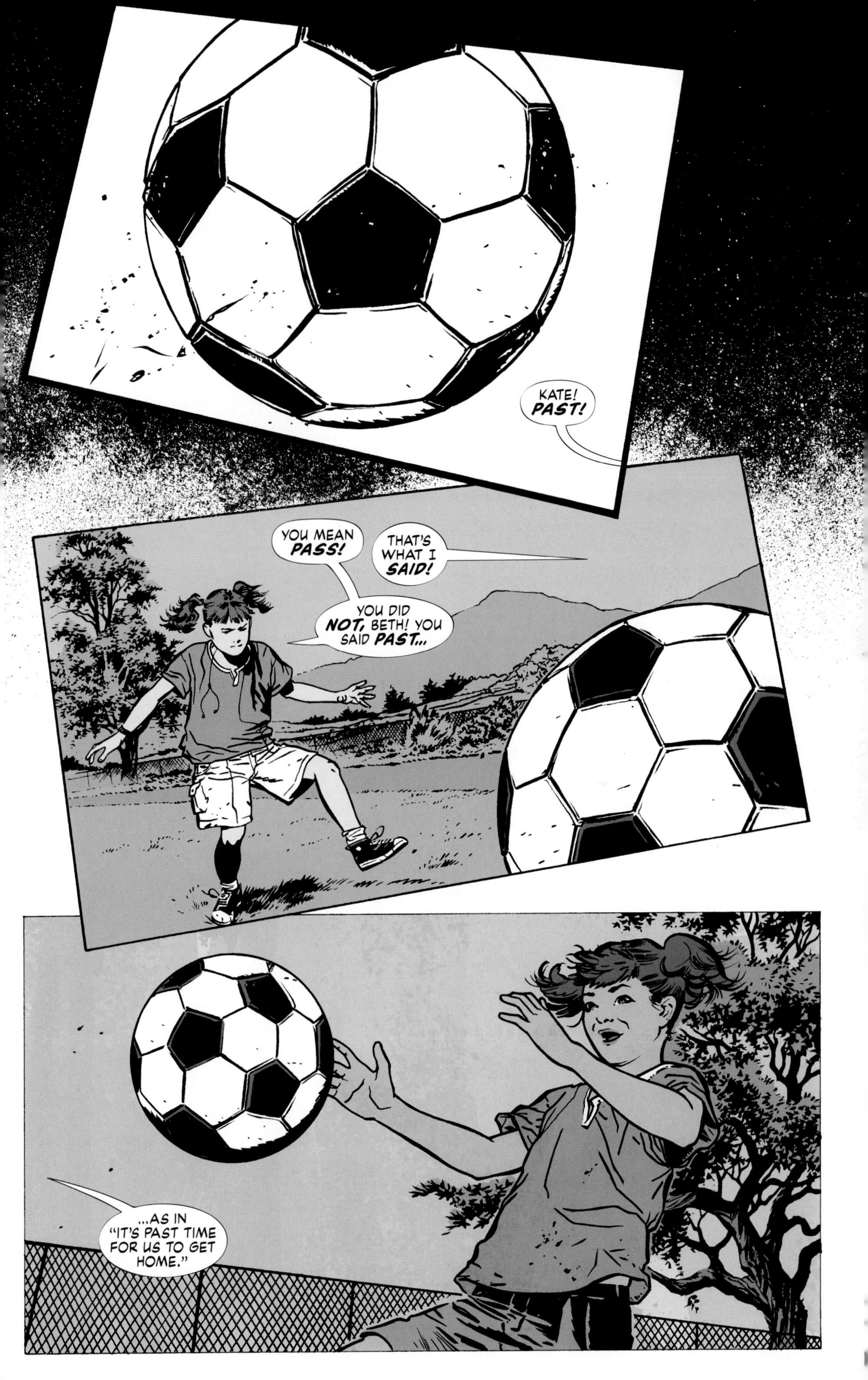
KATE! PAST!
YOU MEAN PASS!
THAT'S WHAT I SAID!
YOU DID NOT, BETH! YOU SAID PAST...
...AS IN "IT'S PAST TIME FOR US TO GET HOME."

GREG RUCKA
WRITER

DAVE STEWART
COLORS

J.H. WILLIAMS III
ARTIST

TODD KLEIN
LETTERS

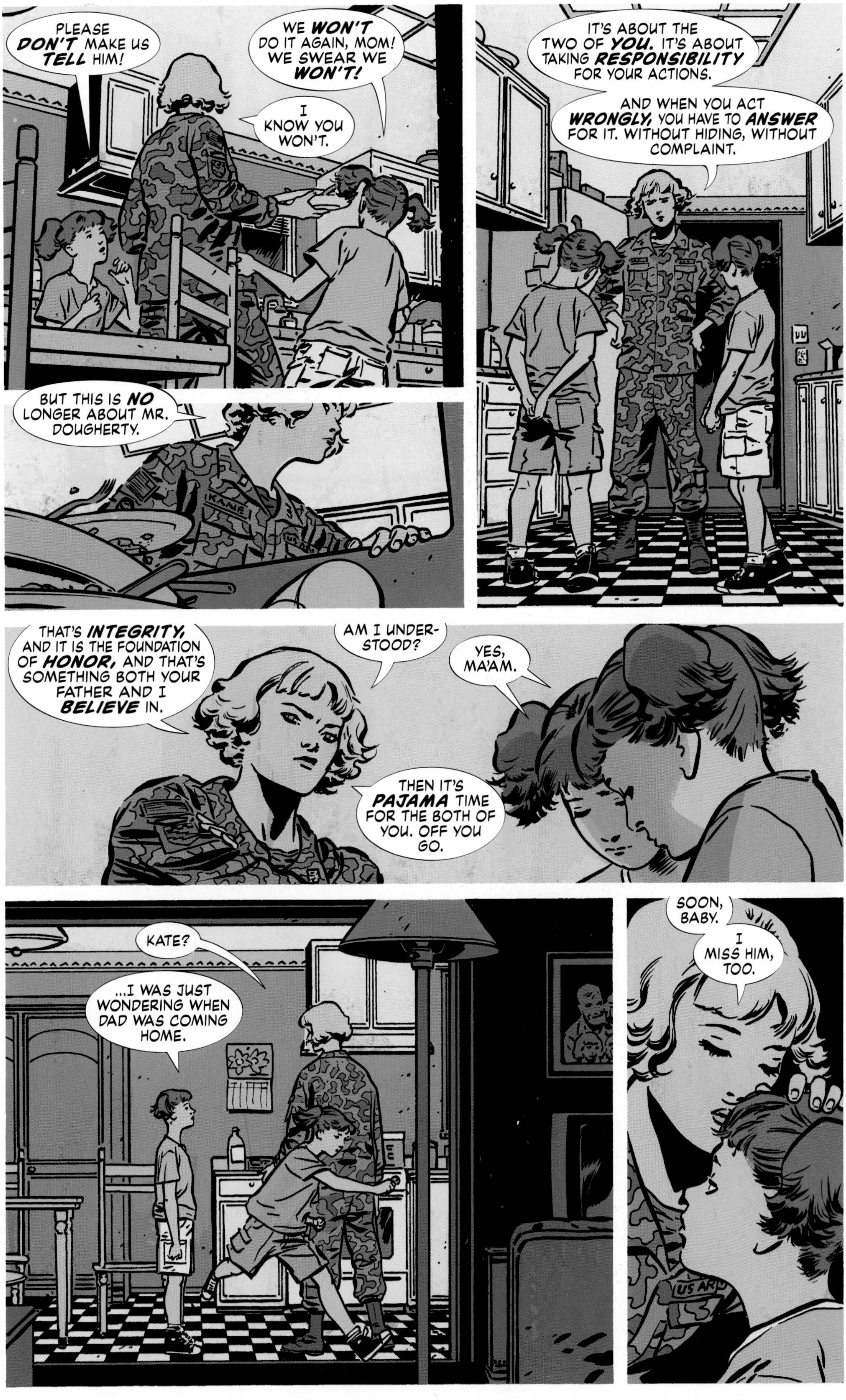
PLEASE DON'T MAKE US TELL HIM!
WE WON'T DO IT AGAIN, MOM! WE SWEAR WE WON'T!
I KNOW YOU WON'T.
BUT THIS IS NO LONGER ABOUT MR. DOUGHERTY.
IT'S ABOUT THE TWO OF YOU. IT'S ABOUT TAKING RESPONSIBILITY FOR YOUR ACTIONS.
AND WHEN YOU ACT WRONGLY, YOU HAVE TO ANSWER FOR IT. WITHOUT HIDING, WITHOUT COMPLAINT.
KANE
THAT'S INTEGRITY, AND IT IS THE FOUNDATION OF HONOR, AND THAT'S SOMETHING BOTH YOUR FATHER AND I BELIEVE IN.
AM I UNDER-STOOD?
YES, MA'AM.
THEN IT'S PAJAMA TIME FOR THE BOTH OF YOU. OFF YOU GO.
KATE?
...I WAS JUST WONDERING WHEN DAD WAS COMING HOME.
SOON, BABY.
I MISS HIM, TOO.

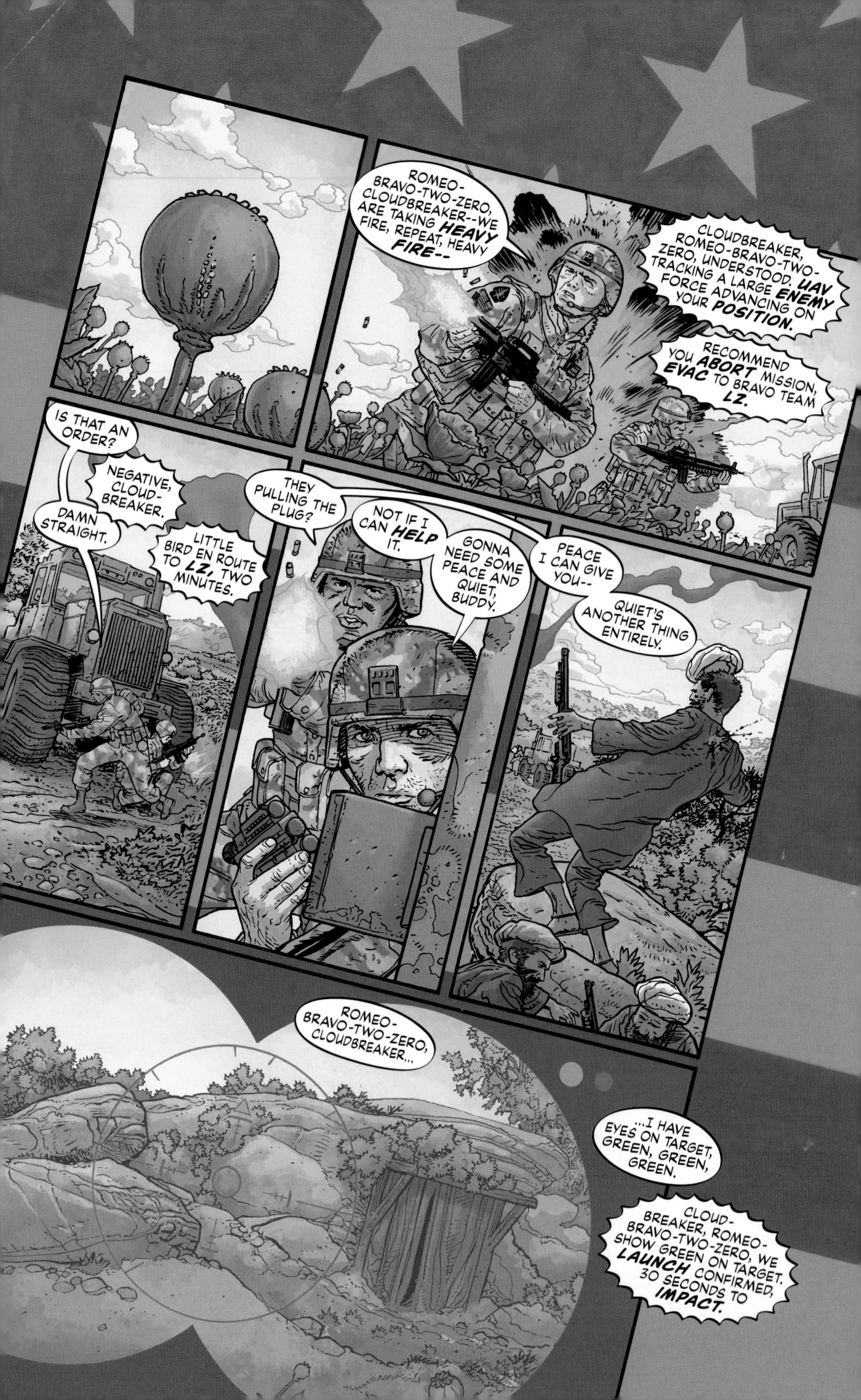
ROMEO-BRAVO-TWO-ZERO, CLOUDBREAKER--WE ARE TAKING HEAVY FIRE, REPEAT, HEAVY FIRE--
CLOUDBREAKER, ROMEO-BRAVO-TWO-ZERO, UNDERSTOOD. UAV TRACKING A LARGE ENEMY FORCE ADVANCING ON YOUR POSITION.
RECOMMEND YOU ABORT MISSION, EVAC TO BRAVO TEAM LZ.
IS THAT AN ORDER?
NEGATIVE, CLOUDBREAKER.
DAMN STRAIGHT.
LITTLE BIRD EN ROUTE TO LZ, TWO MINUTES.
THEY PULLING THE PLUG?
NOT IF I CAN HELP IT.
GONNA NEED SOME PEACE AND QUIET, BUDDY.
PEACE I CAN GIVE YOU--
QUIET'S ANOTHER THING ENTIRELY.
ROMEO-BRAVO-TWO-ZERO, CLOUDBREAKER...
...I HAVE EYES ON TARGET. GREEN, GREEN, GREEN.
CLOUDBREAKER, ROMEO-BRAVO-TWO-ZERO, WE SHOW GREEN ON TARGET. LAUNCH CONFIRMED, 30 SECONDS TO IMPACT.

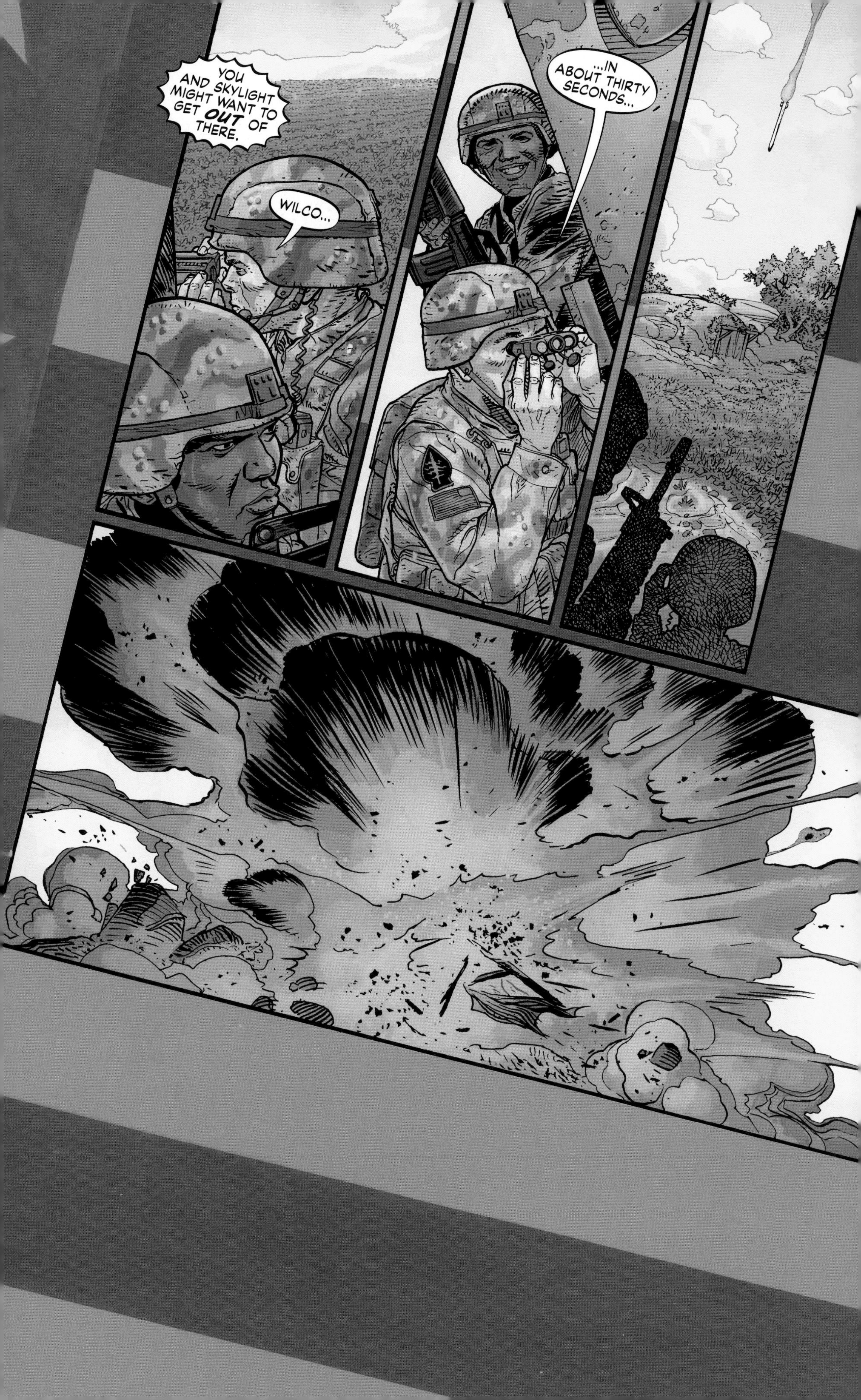
YOU AND SKYLIGHT MIGHT WANT TO GET OUT OF THERE.
WILCO...
...IN ABOUT THIRTY SECONDS...

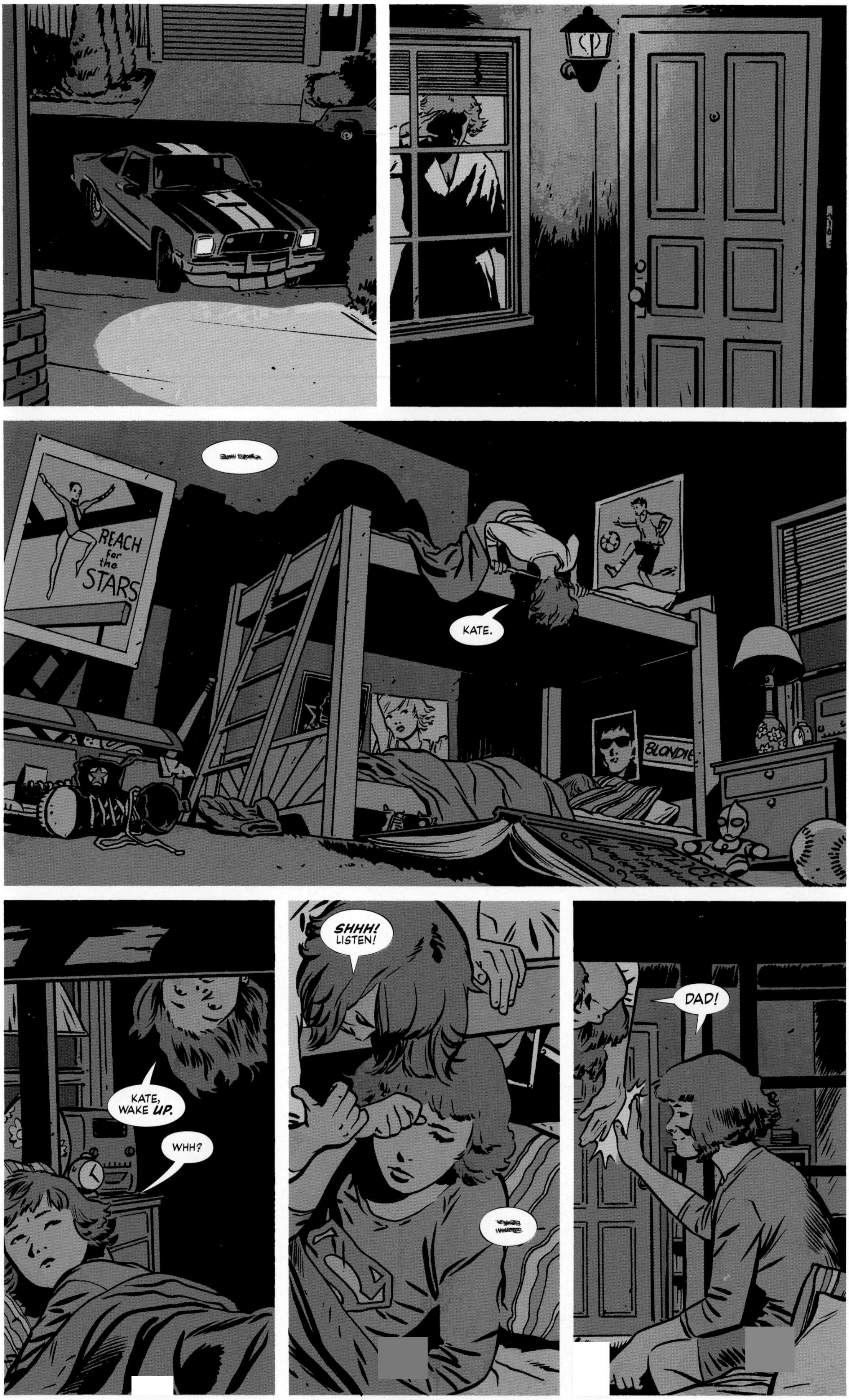
REACH for the STARS
KATE.
BLONDIE
KATE, WAKE UP.
WHH?
SHHH! LISTEN!
DAD!

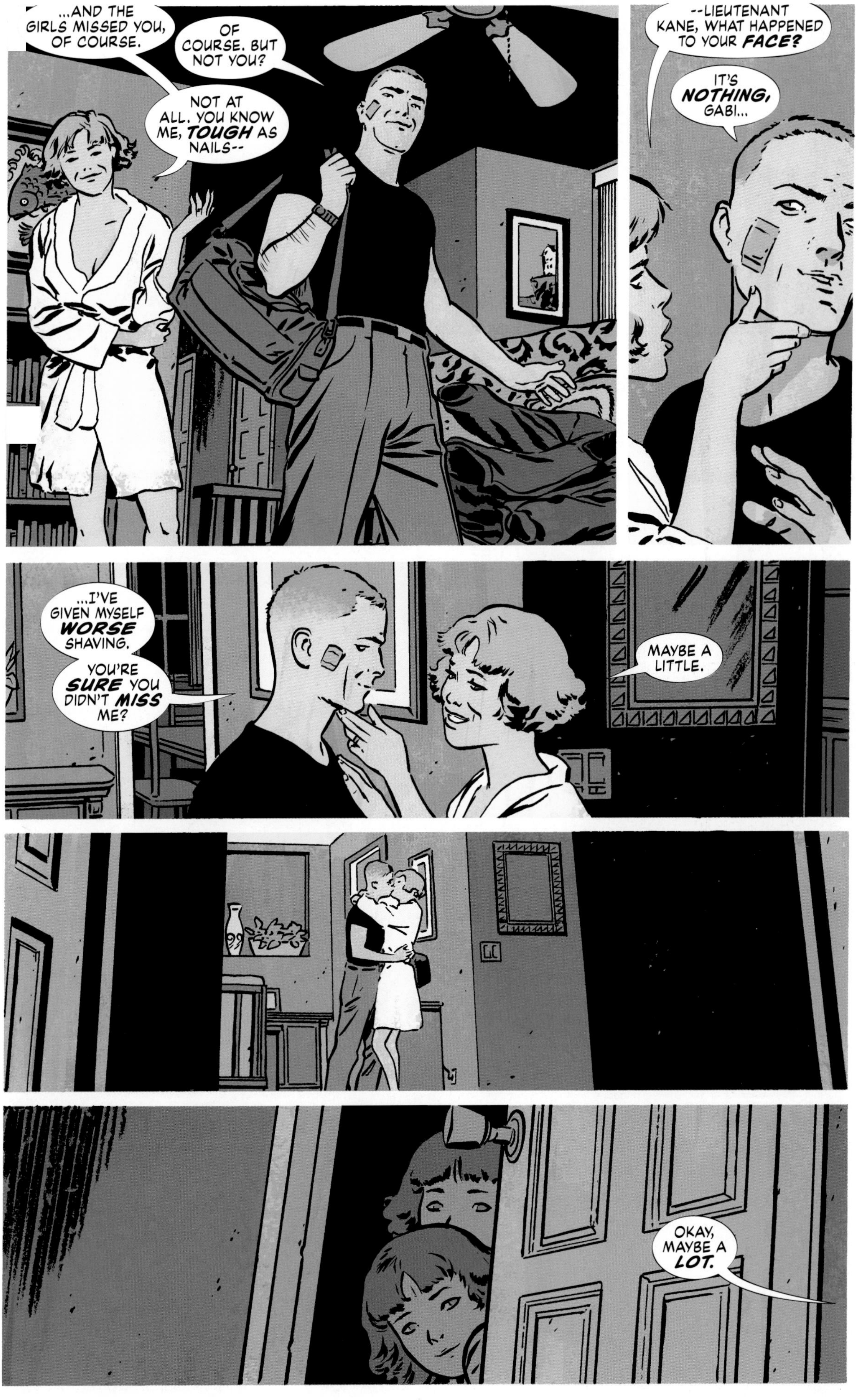
...AND THE GIRLS MISSED YOU, OF COURSE.
OF COURSE. BUT NOT YOU?
NOT AT ALL. YOU KNOW ME, TOUGH AS NAILS--
--LIEUTENANT KANE, WHAT HAPPENED TO YOUR FACE?
IT'S NOTHING, GABI...
...I'VE GIVEN MYSELF WORSE SHAVING.
YOU'RE SURE YOU DIDN'T MISS ME?
MAYBE A LITTLE.
OKAY, MAYBE A LOT.

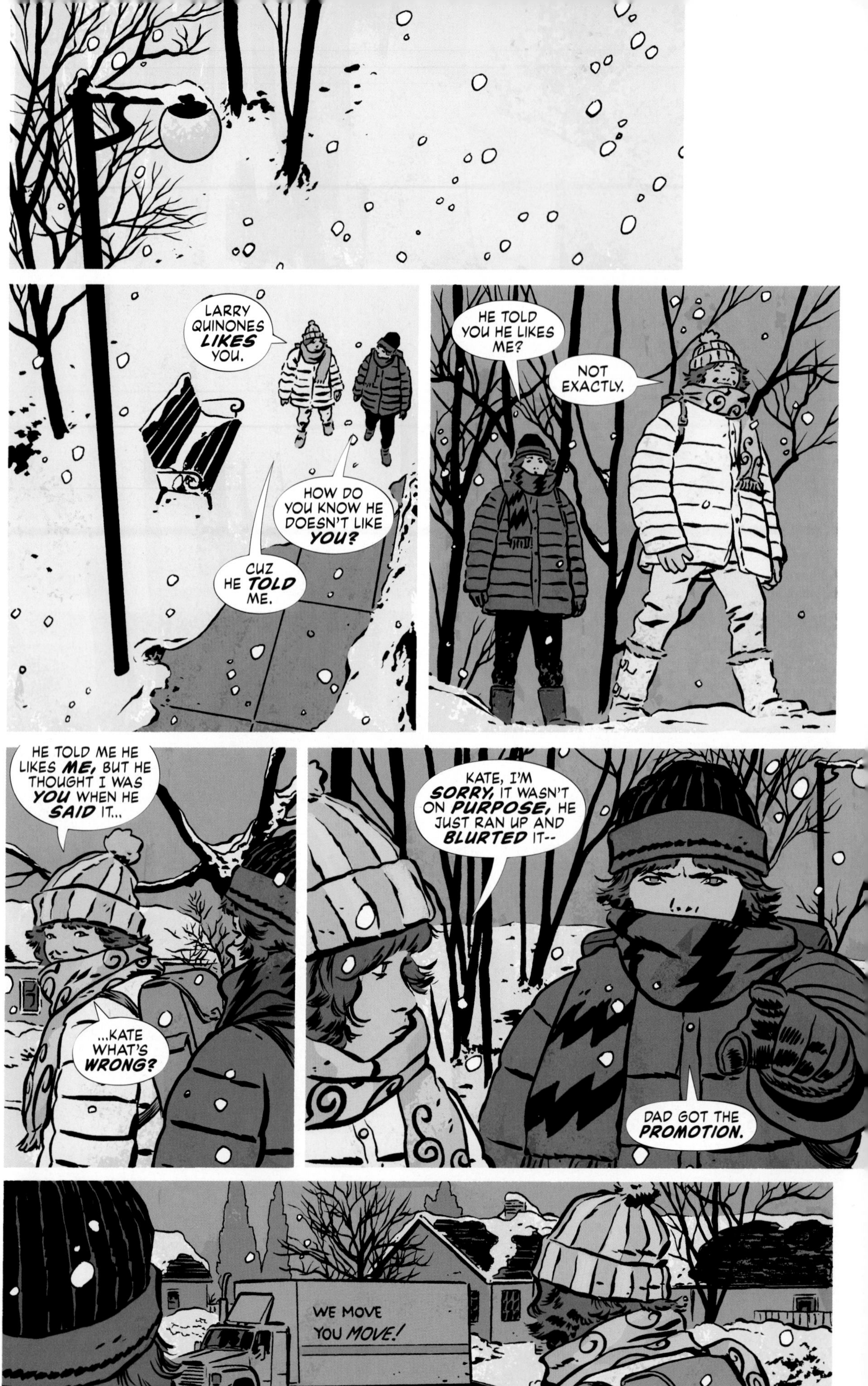
LARRY QUINONES *LIKES* YOU.
HOW DO YOU KNOW HE DOESN'T LIKE *YOU?*
CUZ HE *TOLD* ME.
HE TOLD YOU HE LIKES ME?
NOT EXACTLY.
HE TOLD ME HE LIKES *ME,* BUT HE THOUGHT I WAS *YOU* WHEN HE *SAID* IT...
...KATE WHAT'S *WRONG?*
KATE, I'M *SORRY,* IT WASN'T ON *PURPOSE,* HE JUST RAN UP AND *BLURTED* IT--
DAD GOT THE *PROMOTION.*
WE MOVE YOU *MOVE!*

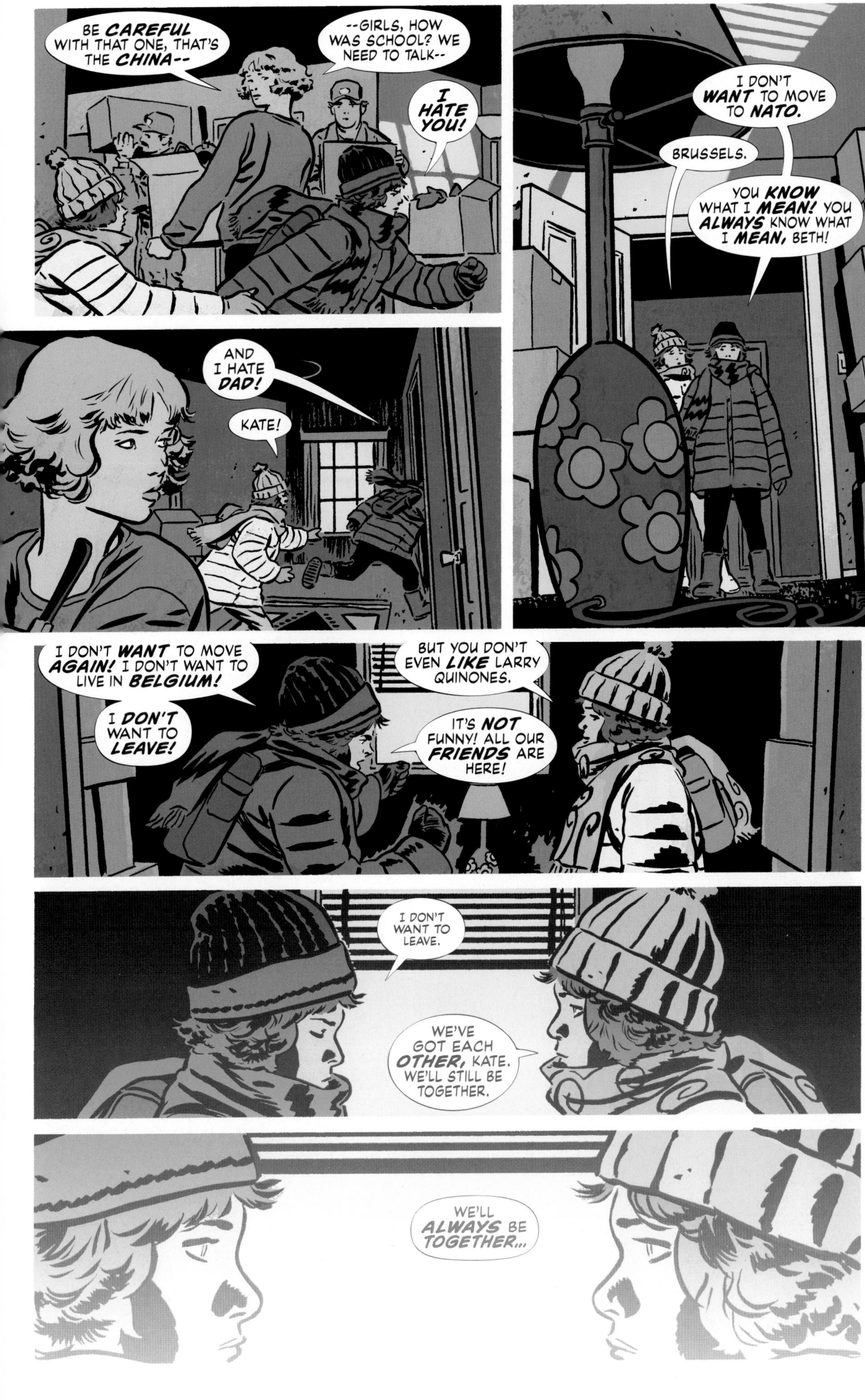

BE CAREFUL WITH THAT ONE, THAT'S THE CHINA--
--GIRLS, HOW WAS SCHOOL? WE NEED TO TALK--
I HATE YOU!
AND I HATE DAD!
KATE!
I DON'T WANT TO MOVE TO NATO.
BRUSSELS.
YOU KNOW WHAT I MEAN! YOU ALWAYS KNOW WHAT I MEAN, BETH!
I DON'T WANT TO MOVE AGAIN! I DON'T WANT TO LIVE IN BELGIUM!
I DON'T WANT TO LEAVE!
BUT YOU DON'T EVEN LIKE LARRY QUINONES.
IT'S NOT FUNNY! ALL OUR FRIENDS ARE HERE!
I DON'T WANT TO LEAVE.
WE'VE GOT EACH OTHER, KATE. WE'LL STILL BE TOGETHER.
WE'LL ALWAYS BE TOGETHER...

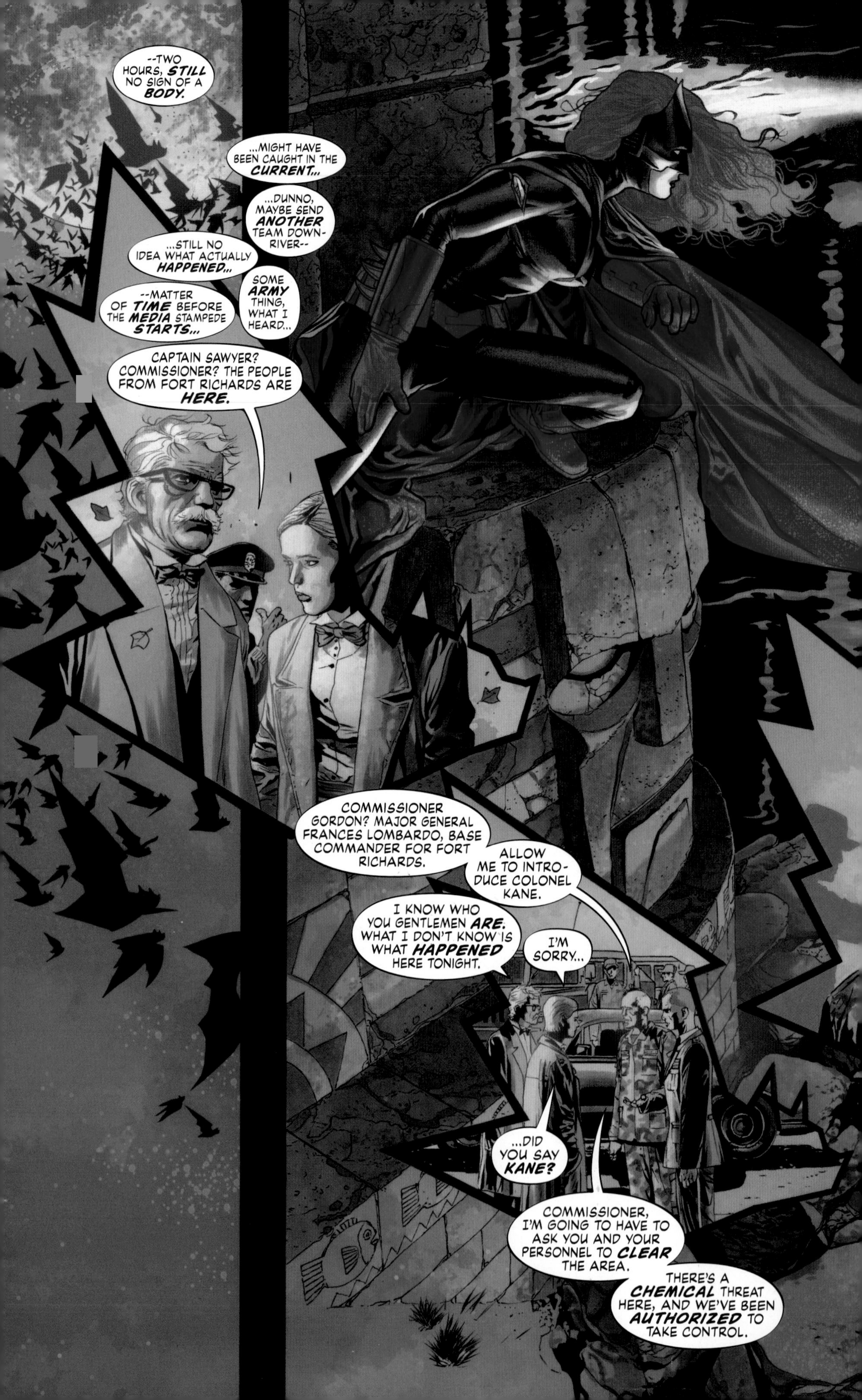

--TWO HOURS, STILL NO SIGN OF A BODY.
...MIGHT HAVE BEEN CAUGHT IN THE CURRENT...
...DUNNO, MAYBE SEND ANOTHER TEAM DOWN-RIVER--
...STILL NO IDEA WHAT ACTUALLY HAPPENED...
SOME ARMY THING, WHAT I HEARD...
--MATTER OF TIME BEFORE THE MEDIA STAMPEDE STARTS...
CAPTAIN SAWYER? COMMISSIONER? THE PEOPLE FROM FORT RICHARDS ARE HERE.
COMMISSIONER GORDON? MAJOR GENERAL FRANCES LOMBARDO, BASE COMMANDER FOR FORT RICHARDS.
ALLOW ME TO INTRO-DUCE COLONEL KANE.
I KNOW WHO YOU GENTLEMEN ARE. WHAT I DON'T KNOW IS WHAT HAPPENED HERE TONIGHT.
I'M SORRY...
...DID YOU SAY KANE?
COMMISSIONER, I'M GOING TO HAVE TO ASK YOU AND YOUR PERSONNEL TO CLEAR THE AREA.
THERE'S A CHEMICAL THREAT HERE, AND WE'VE BEEN AUTHORIZED TO TAKE CONTROL.

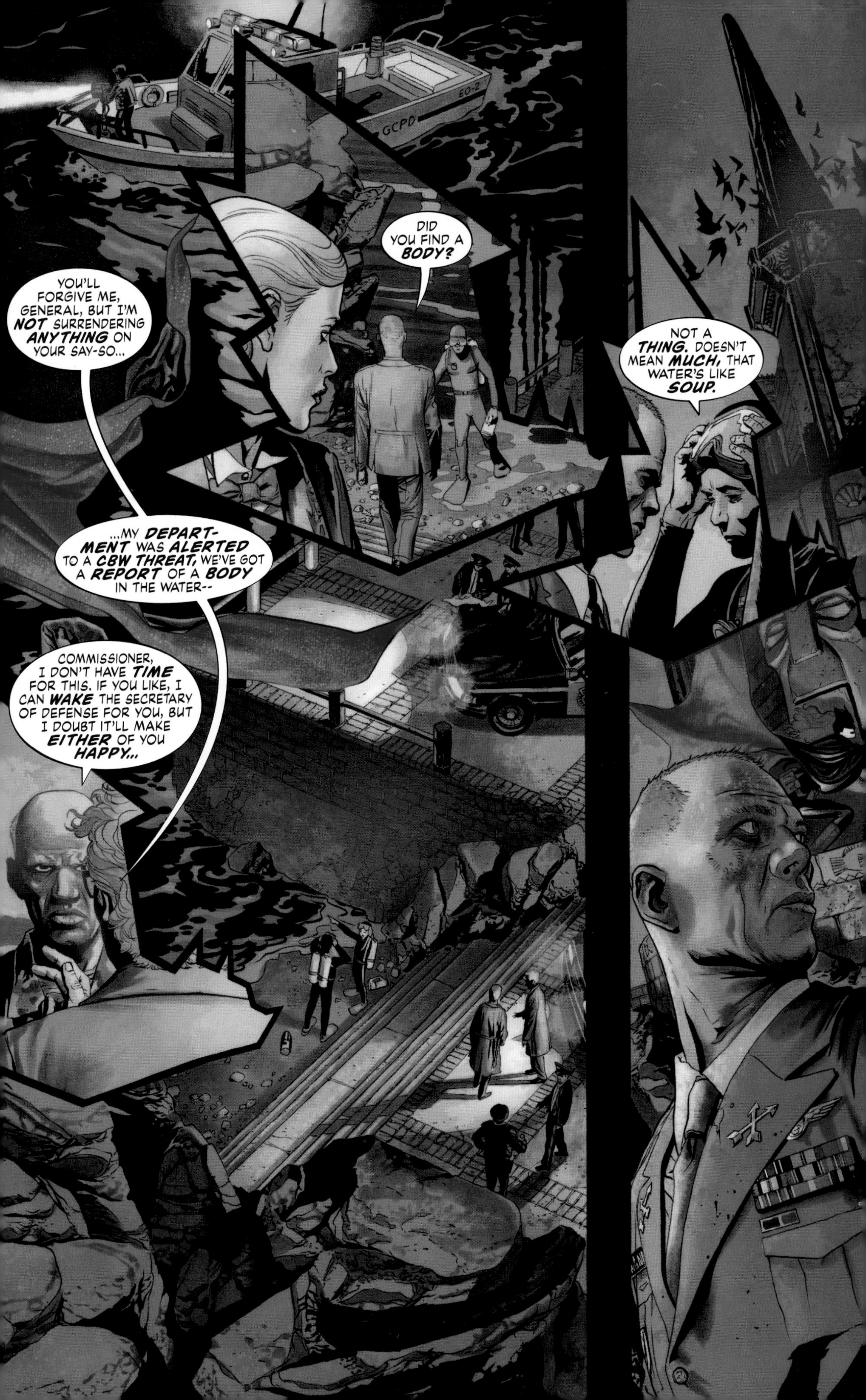
DID YOU FIND A BODY?
YOU'LL FORGIVE ME, GENERAL, BUT I'M NOT SURRENDERING ANYTHING ON YOUR SAY-SO...
NOT A THING. DOESN'T MEAN MUCH, THAT WATER'S LIKE SOUP.
...MY DEPARTMENT WAS ALERTED TO A CBW THREAT, WE'VE GOT A REPORT OF A BODY IN THE WATER--
COMMISSIONER, I DON'T HAVE TIME FOR THIS. IF YOU LIKE, I CAN WAKE THE SECRETARY OF DEFENSE FOR YOU, BUT I DOUBT IT'LL MAKE EITHER OF YOU HAPPY...

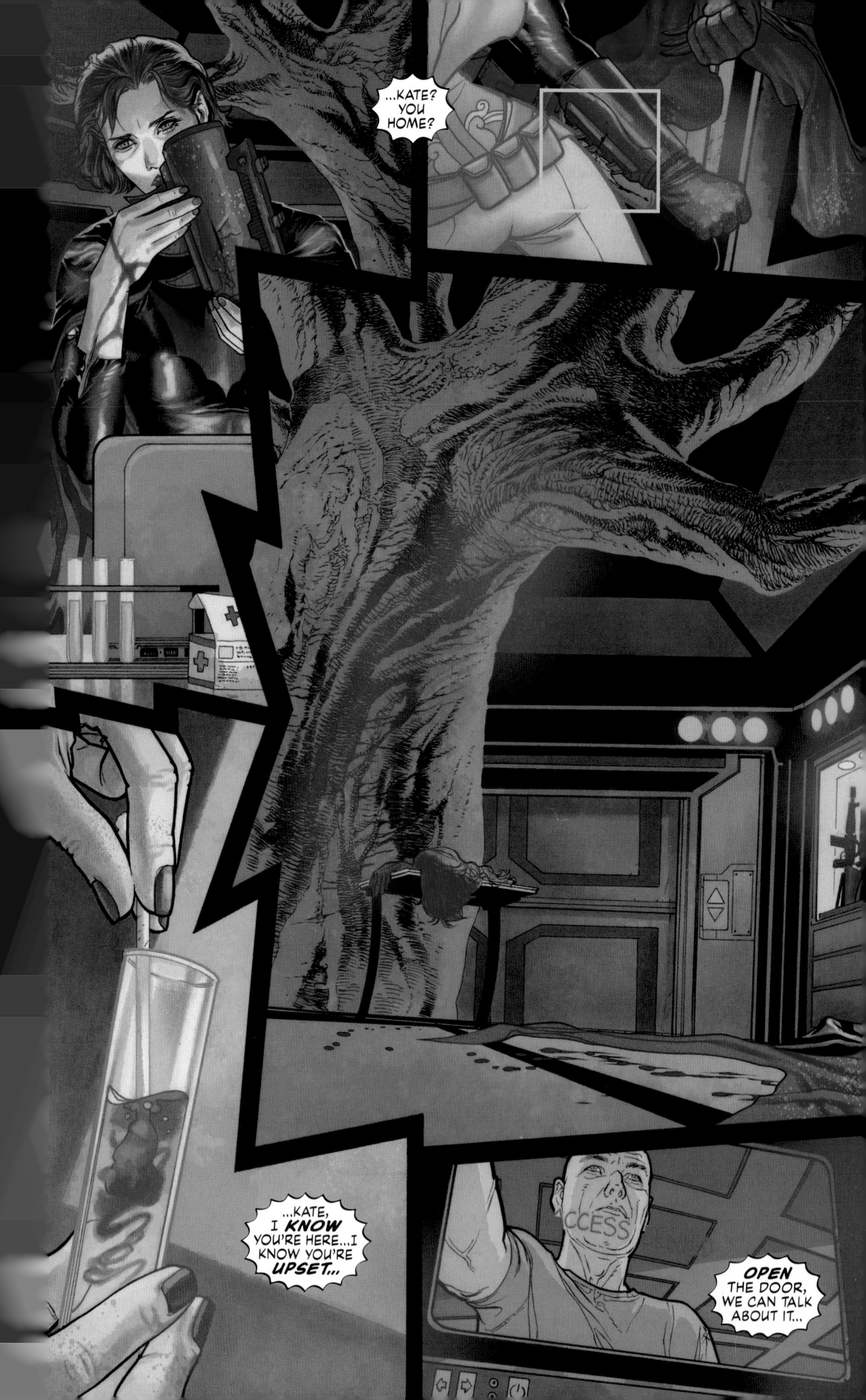
...KATE? YOU HOME?
...KATE, I **KNOW** YOU'RE HERE...I KNOW YOU'RE **UPSET...**
CCESS
OPEN THE DOOR, WE CAN TALK ABOUT IT...

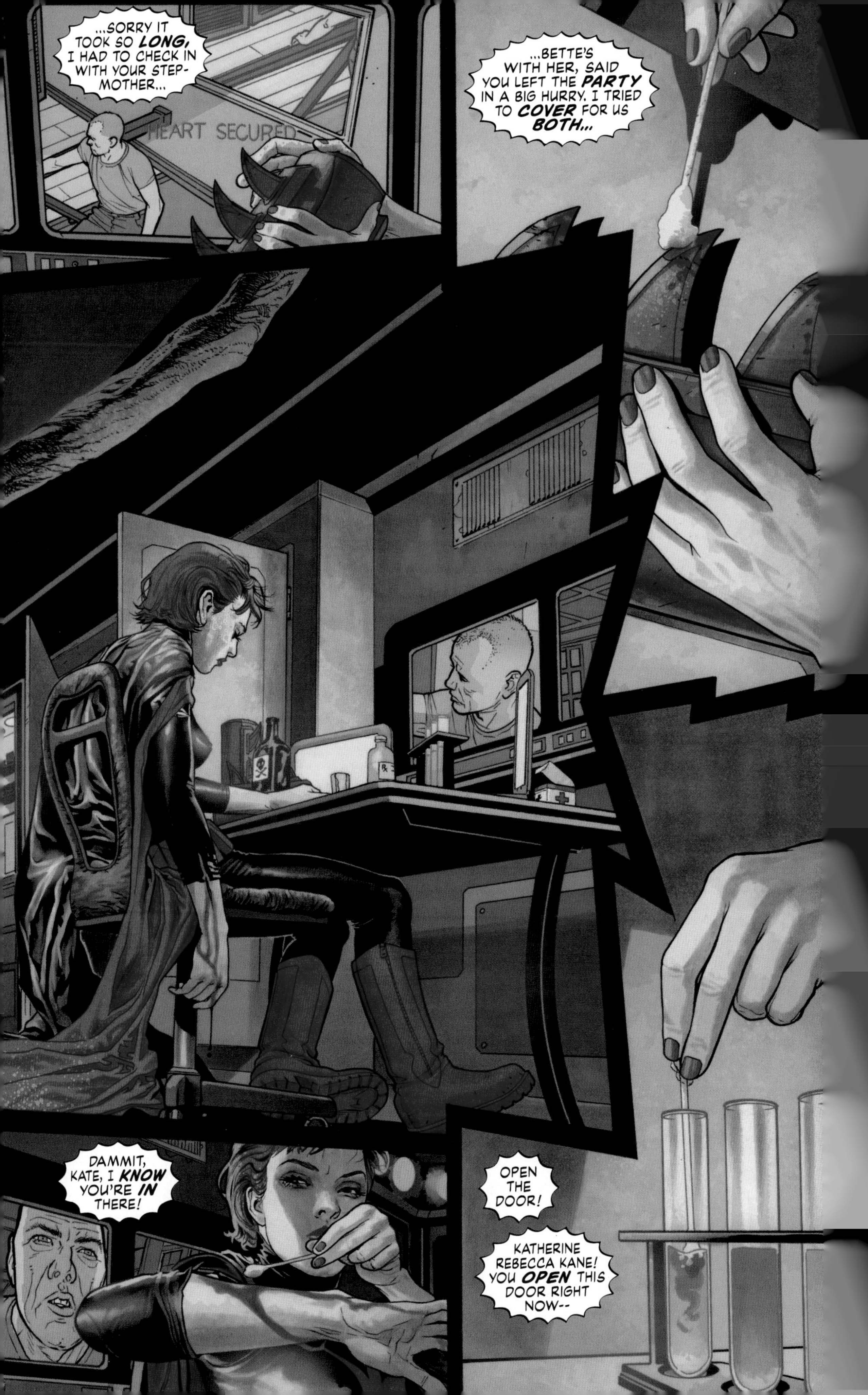
...SORRY IT TOOK SO LONG, I HAD TO CHECK IN WITH YOUR STEP-MOTHER...
HEART SECURED
...BETTE'S WITH HER, SAID YOU LEFT THE PARTY IN A BIG HURRY. I TRIED TO COVER FOR US BOTH...
DAMMIT, KATE, I KNOW YOU'RE IN THERE!
OPEN THE DOOR!
KATHERINE REBECCA KANE! YOU OPEN THIS DOOR RIGHT NOW--

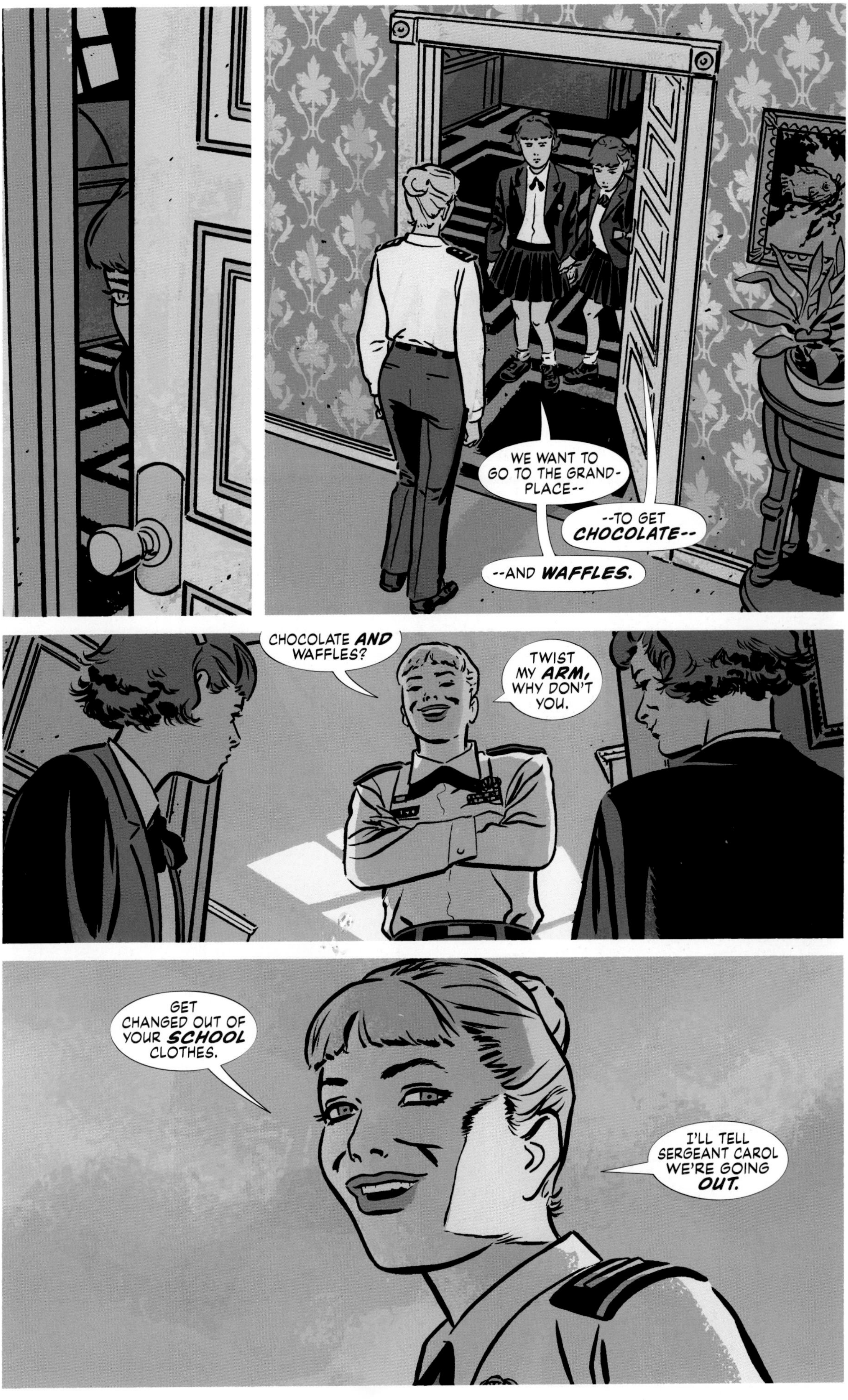
WE WANT TO GO TO THE GRAND-PLACE--
--TO GET CHOCOLATE--
--AND WAFFLES.
CHOCOLATE AND WAFFLES?
TWIST MY ARM, WHY DON'T YOU.
GET CHANGED OUT OF YOUR SCHOOL CLOTHES.
I'LL TELL SERGEANT CAROL WE'RE GOING OUT.

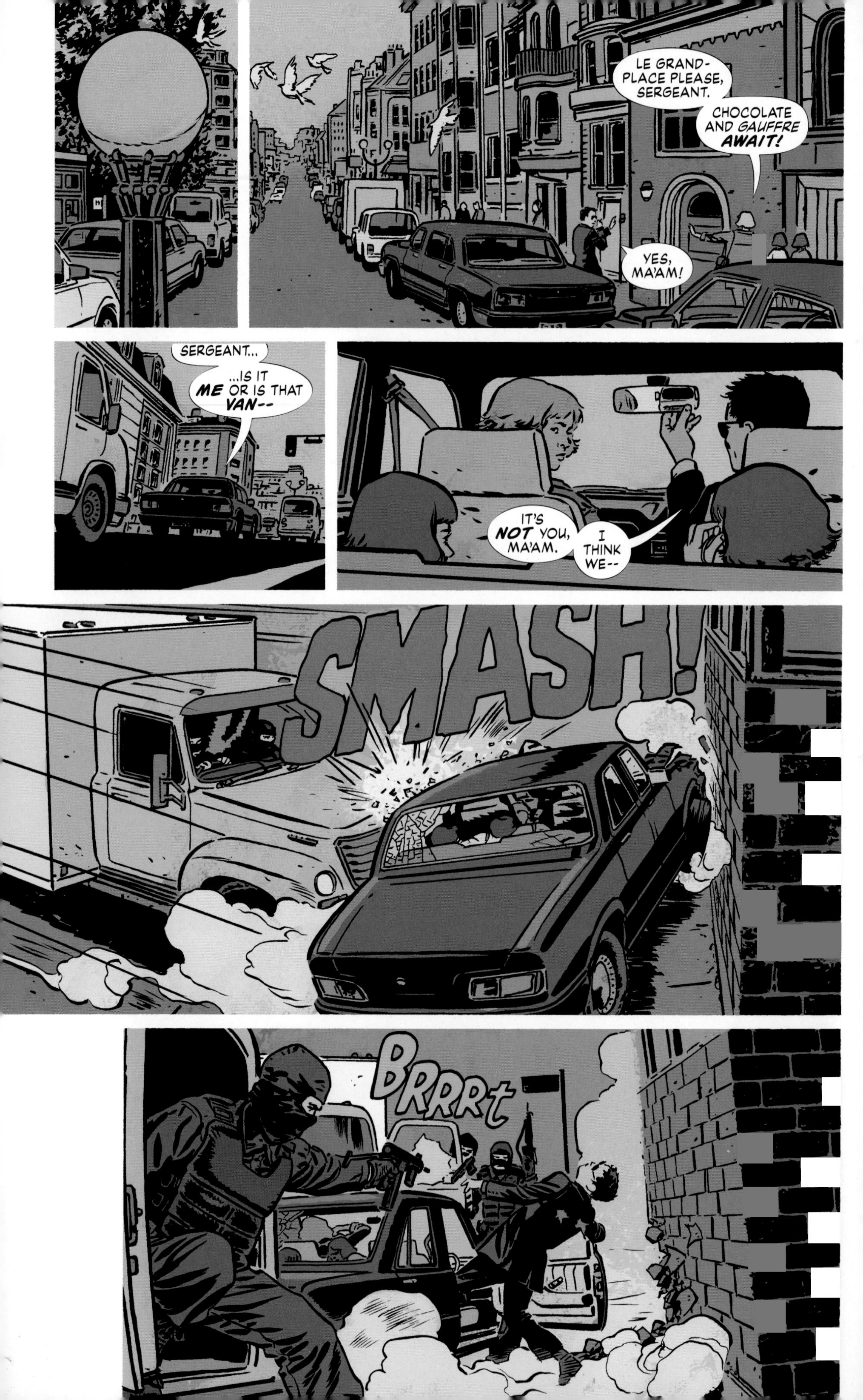
LE GRAND-PLACE PLEASE, SERGEANT.
CHOCOLATE AND GAUFFRE AWAIT!
YES, MA'AM!
SERGEANT...
...IS IT ME OR IS THAT VAN--
IT'S NOT YOU, MA'AM.
I THINK WE--
SMASH!
BRRRt

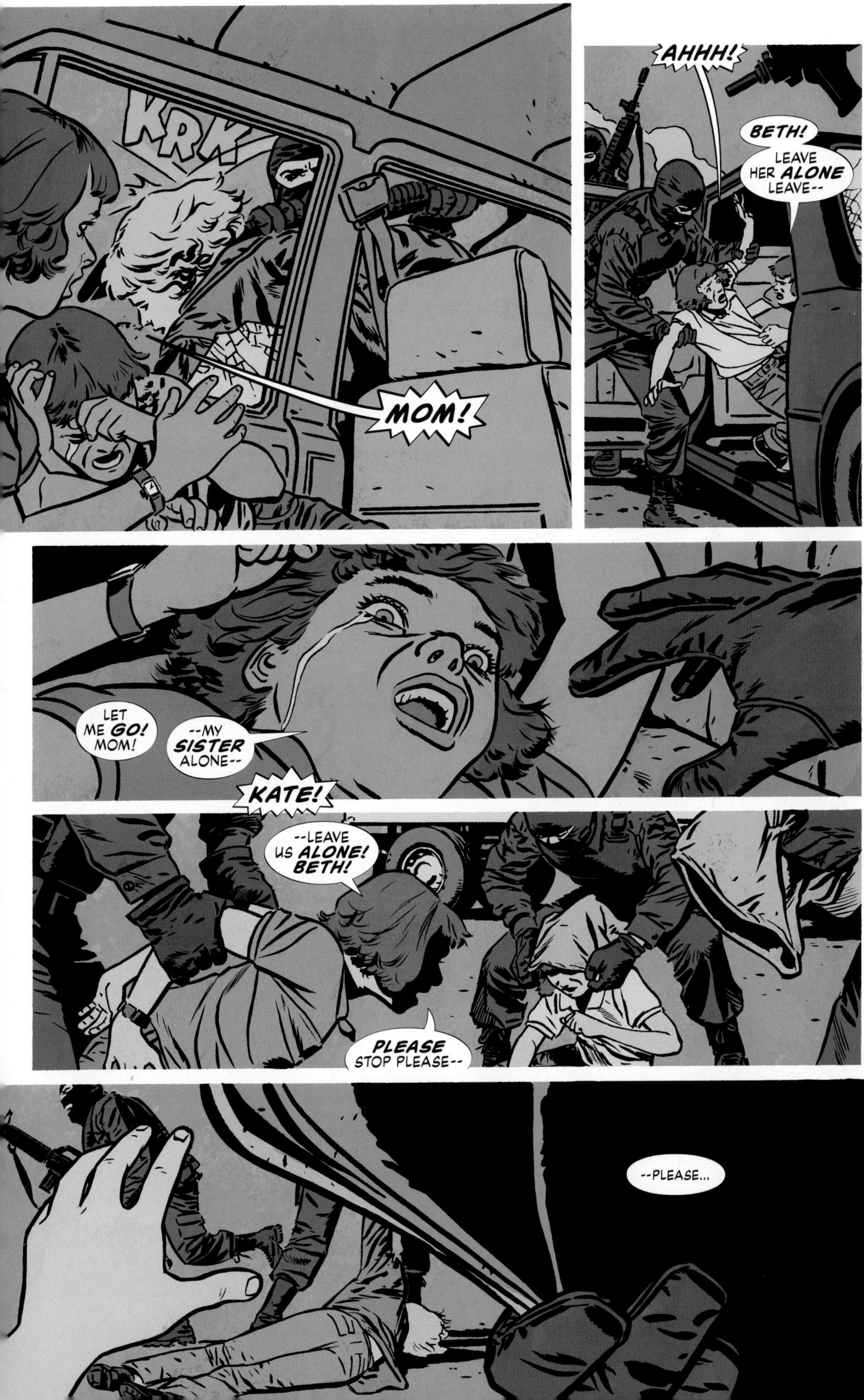
KRK
MOM!
AHHH!
BETH!
LEAVE HER ALONE LEAVE--
LET ME GO! MOM!
--MY SISTER ALONE--
KATE!
--LEAVE US ALONE! BETH!
PLEASE STOP PLEASE--
--PLEASE...

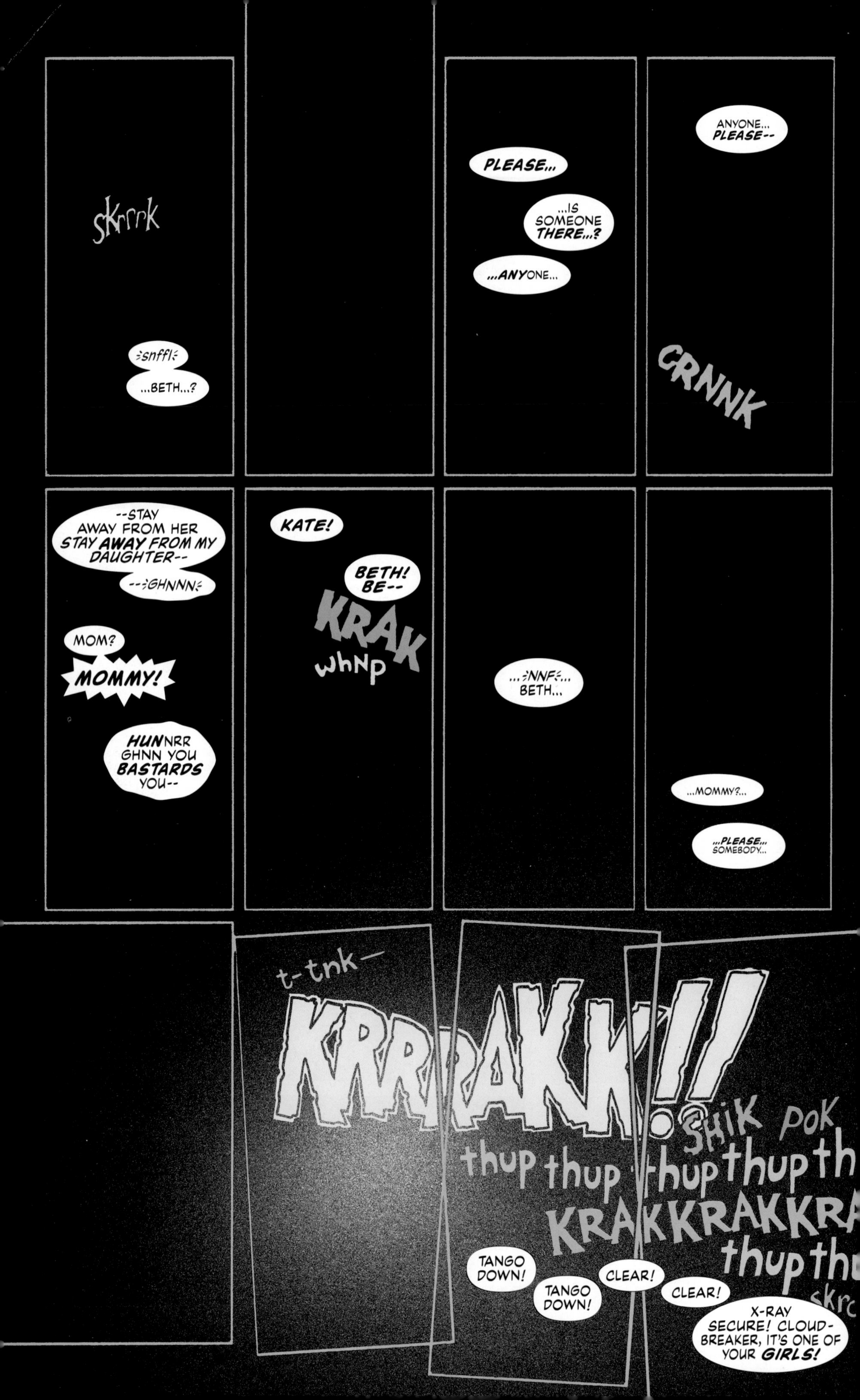

sKrrrk
snffl
...BETH...?
PLEASE...
...IS SOMEONE THERE...?
...ANYONE...
ANYONE... PLEASE--
CRNNK
--STAY AWAY FROM HER STAY AWAY FROM MY DAUGHTER--
--GHNNN
MOM?
MOMMY!
HUNNRR GHNN YOU BASTARDS YOU--
KATE!
BETH! BE--
KRAK
whNp
...NNF... BETH...
...MOMMY?...
...PLEASE... SOMEBODY...
t-tnk—
KRRRAKK!!
SHIK POK
thup thup thup thup th
KRAKKRAKKRA
thup th
TANGO DOWN!
TANGO DOWN!
CLEAR!
CLEAR!
X-RAY SECURE! CLOUD-BREAKER, IT'S ONE OF YOUR GIRLS!

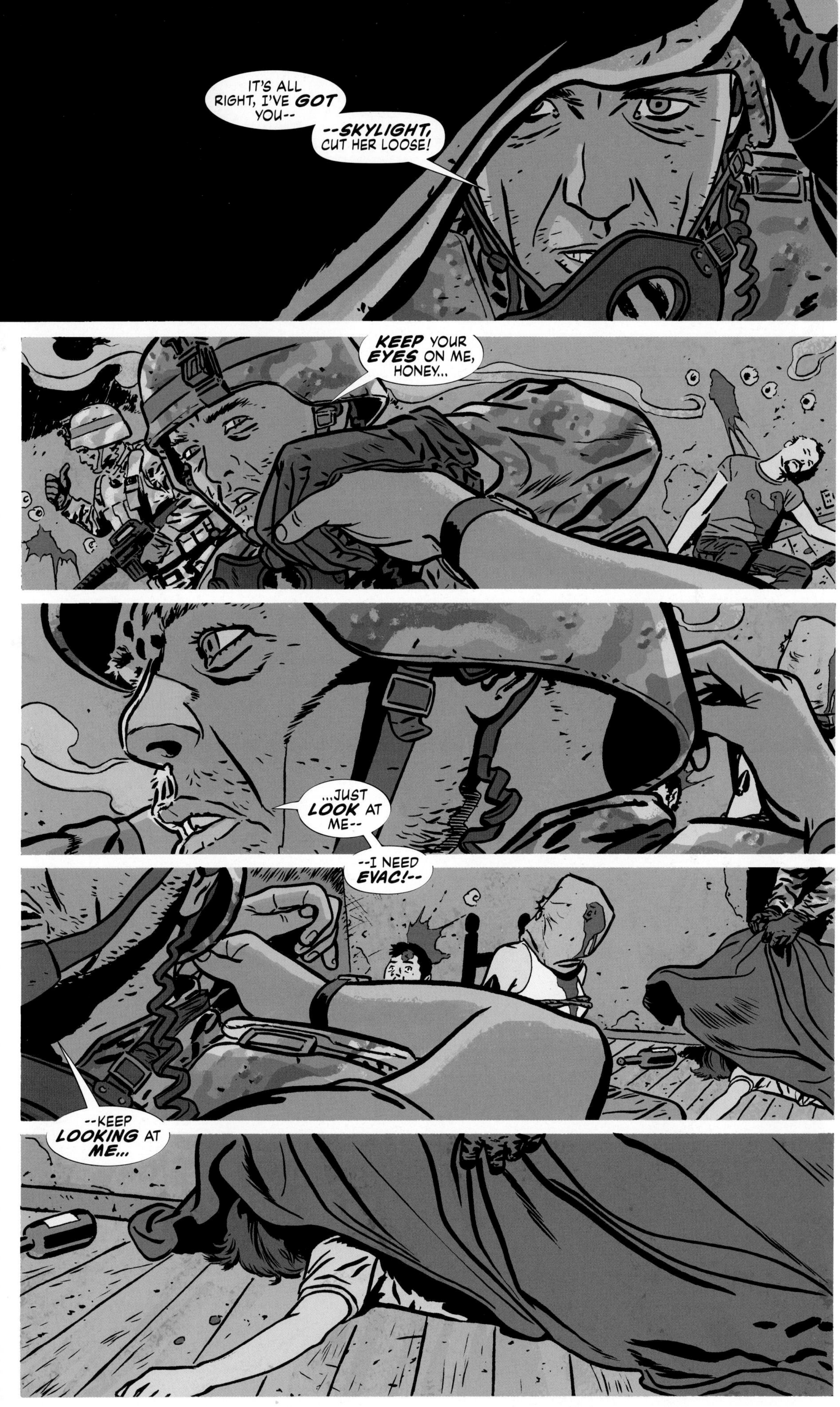
IT'S ALL RIGHT, I'VE GOT YOU--
--SKYLIGHT, CUT HER LOOSE!
KEEP YOUR EYES ON ME, HONEY...
...JUST LOOK AT ME--
--I NEED EVAC!--
--KEEP LOOKING AT ME...

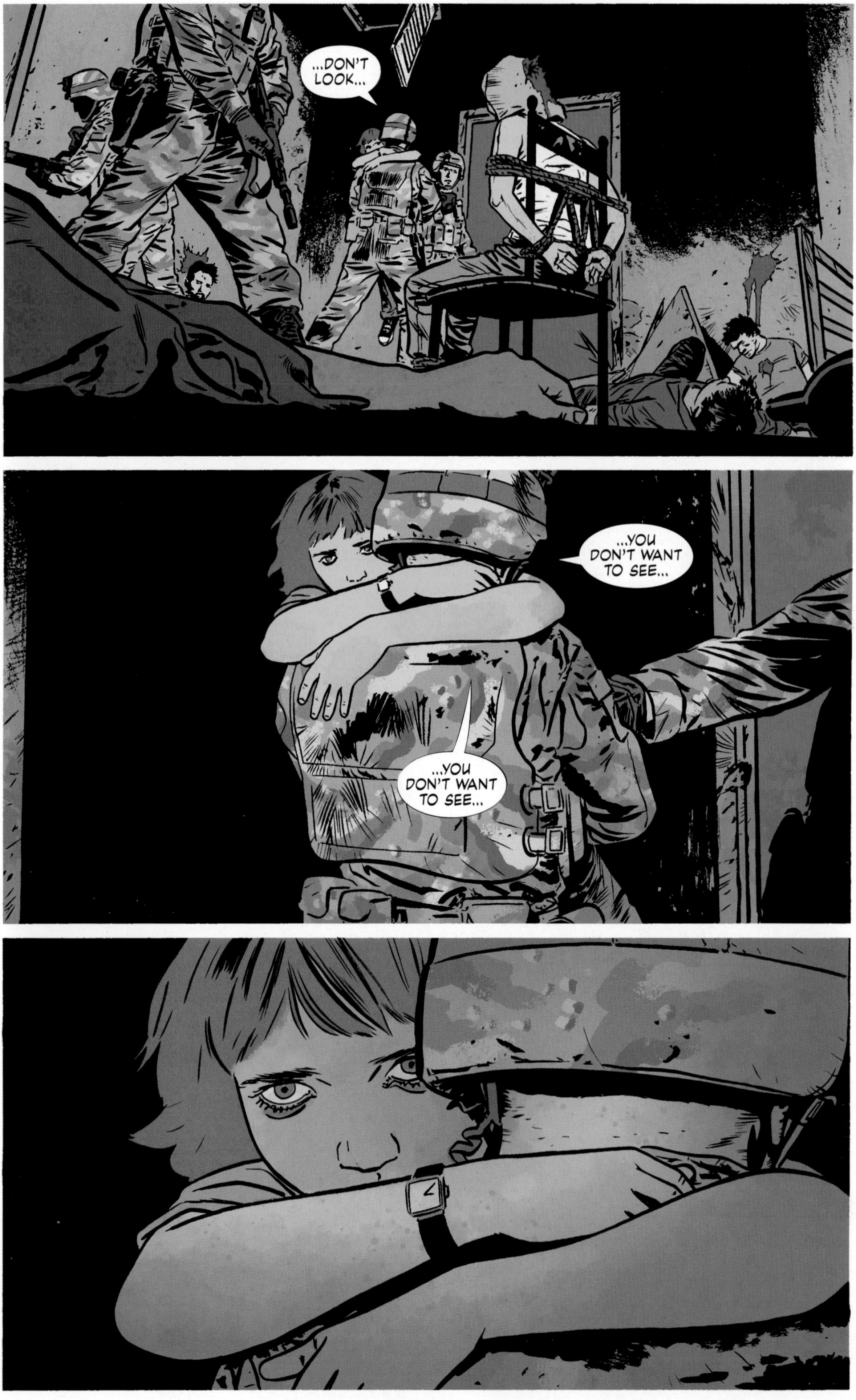
...DON'T LOOK...
...YOU DON'T WANT TO SEE...
...YOU DON'T WANT TO SEE...

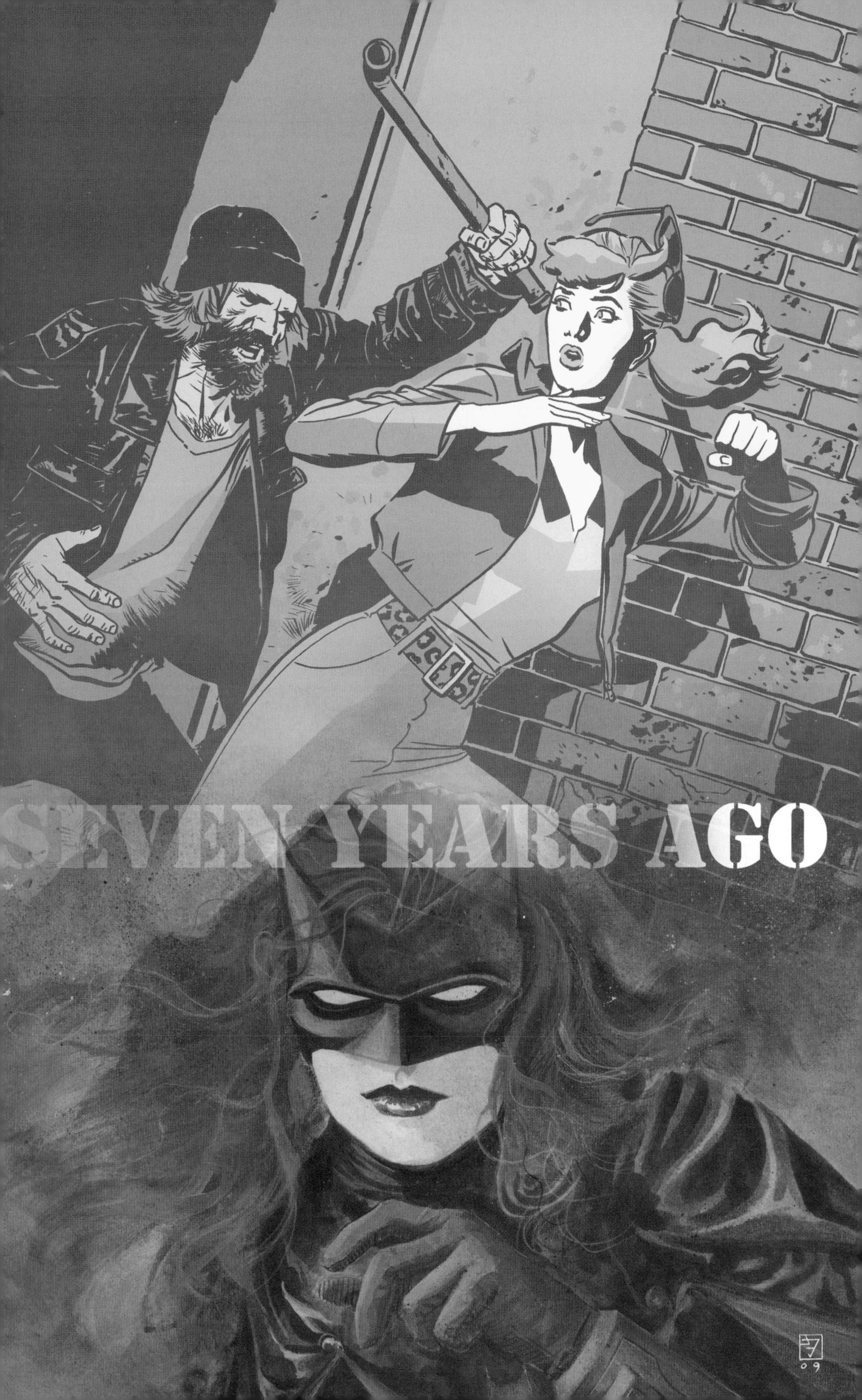
SEVEN YEARS AGO

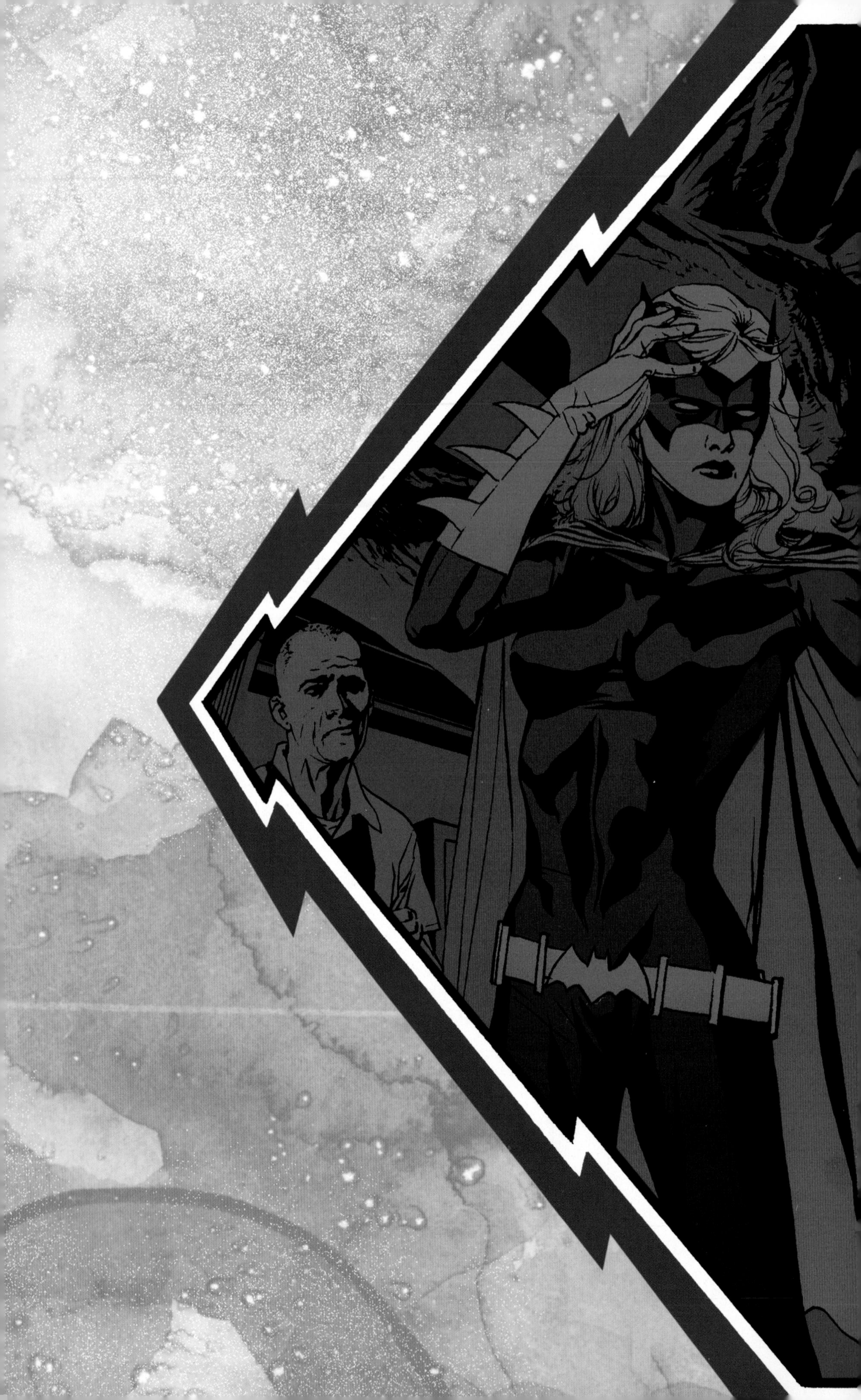

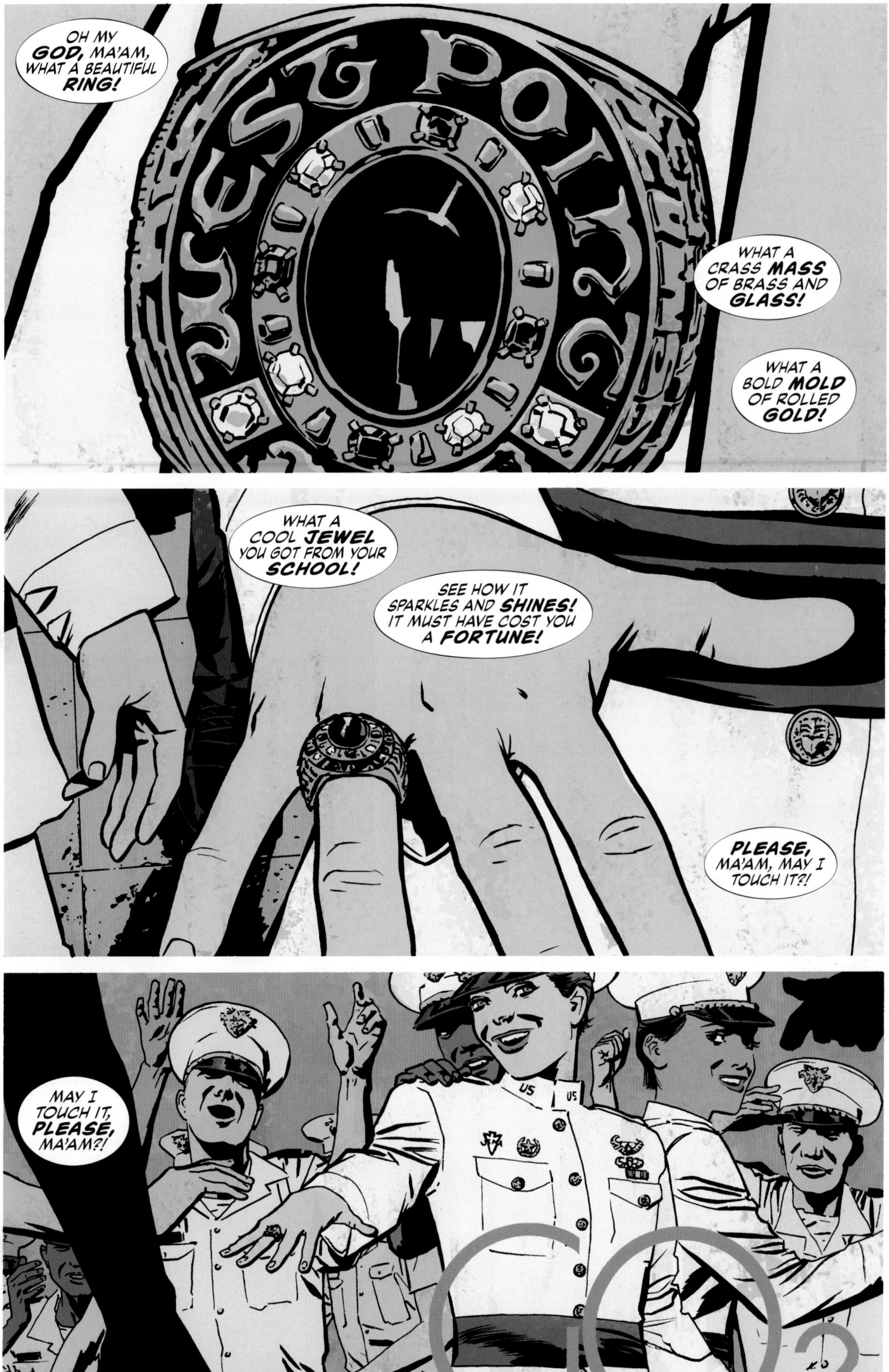
OH MY GOD, MA'AM, WHAT A BEAUTIFUL RING!
WHAT A CRASS MASS OF BRASS AND GLASS!
WHAT A BOLD MOLD OF ROLLED GOLD!
WHAT A COOL JEWEL YOU GOT FROM YOUR SCHOOL!
SEE HOW IT SPARKLES AND SHINES! IT MUST HAVE COST YOU A FORTUNE!
PLEASE, MA'AM, MAY I TOUCH IT?!
MAY I TOUCH IT, PLEASE, MA'AM?!
GO2

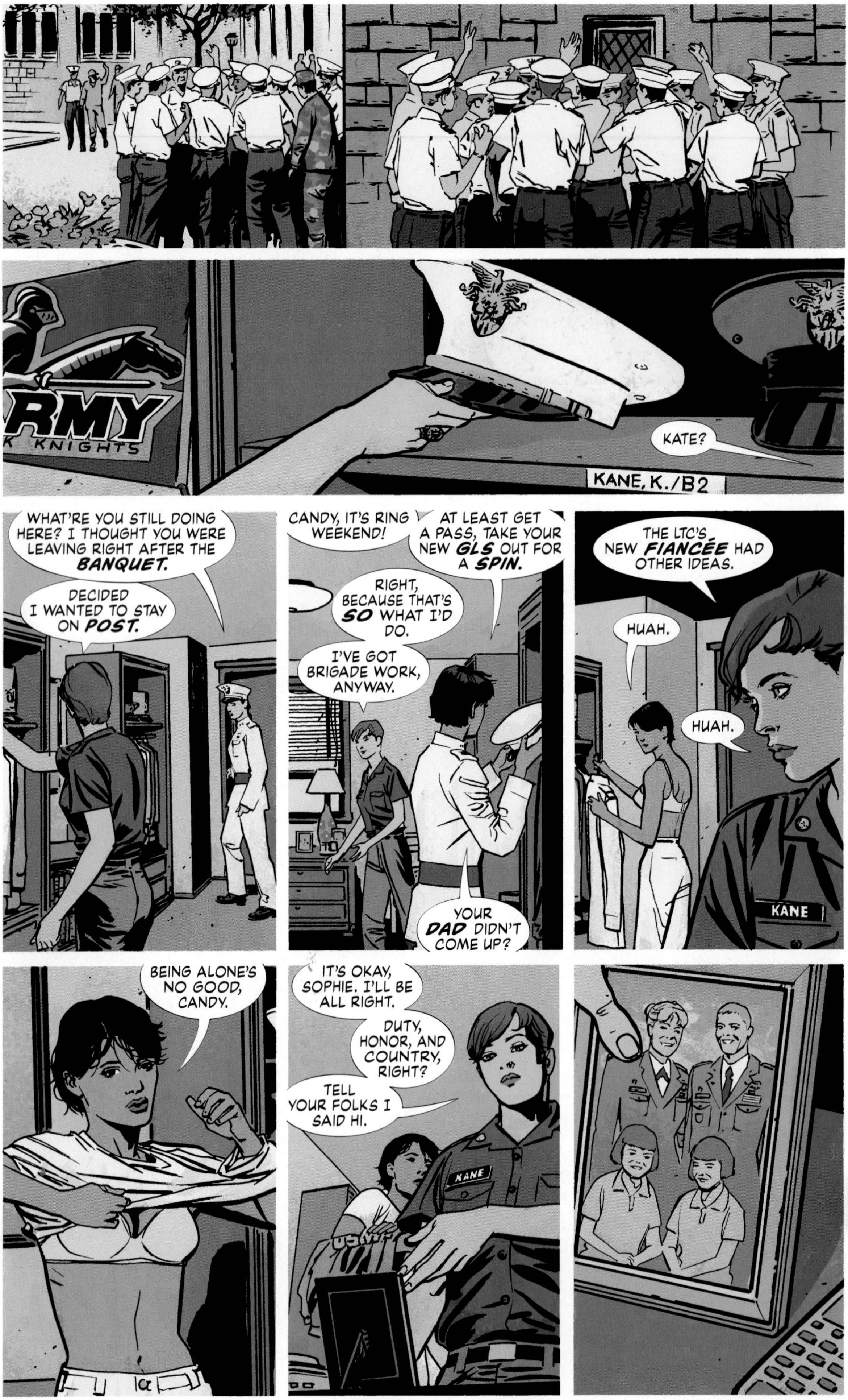
ARMY
KNIGHTS
KATE?
KANE, K./B2
WHAT'RE YOU STILL DOING HERE? I THOUGHT YOU WERE LEAVING RIGHT AFTER THE BANQUET.
DECIDED I WANTED TO STAY ON POST.
CANDY, IT'S RING WEEKEND!
AT LEAST GET A PASS, TAKE YOUR NEW GLS OUT FOR A SPIN.
RIGHT, BECAUSE THAT'S SO WHAT I'D DO.
I'VE GOT BRIGADE WORK, ANYWAY.
YOUR DAD DIDN'T COME UP?
THE LTC'S NEW FIANCÉE HAD OTHER IDEAS.
HUAH.
HUAH.
KANE
BEING ALONE'S NO GOOD, CANDY.
IT'S OKAY, SOPHIE. I'LL BE ALL RIGHT.
DUTY, HONOR, AND COUNTRY, RIGHT?
TELL YOUR FOLKS I SAID HI.
KANE

GREG RUCKA
WRITER

J.H. WILLIAMS III
ARTIST

DAVE STEWART
COLORS

TODD KLEIN
LETTERS

SPECIAL THANKS TO 1LT DANIEL CHOI (USMA 2003) FOR HIS GENEROUS ASSISTANCE IN RESEARCH FOR THIS ISSUE

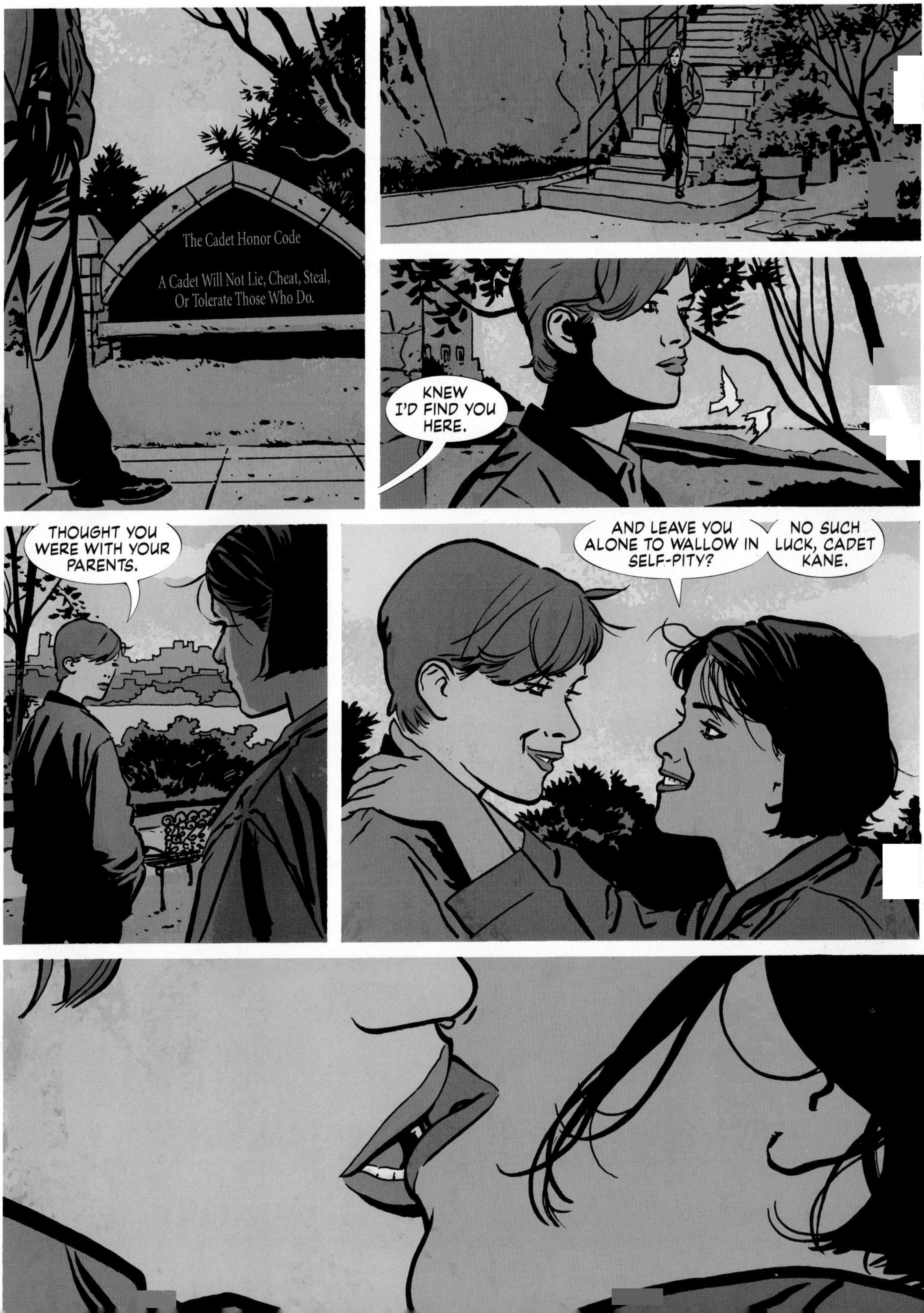
The Cadet Honor Code
A Cadet Will Not Lie, Cheat, Steal, Or Tolerate Those Who Do.
KNEW I'D FIND YOU HERE.
THOUGHT YOU WERE WITH YOUR PARENTS.
AND LEAVE YOU ALONE TO WALLOW IN SELF-PITY?
NO SUCH LUCK, CADET KANE.

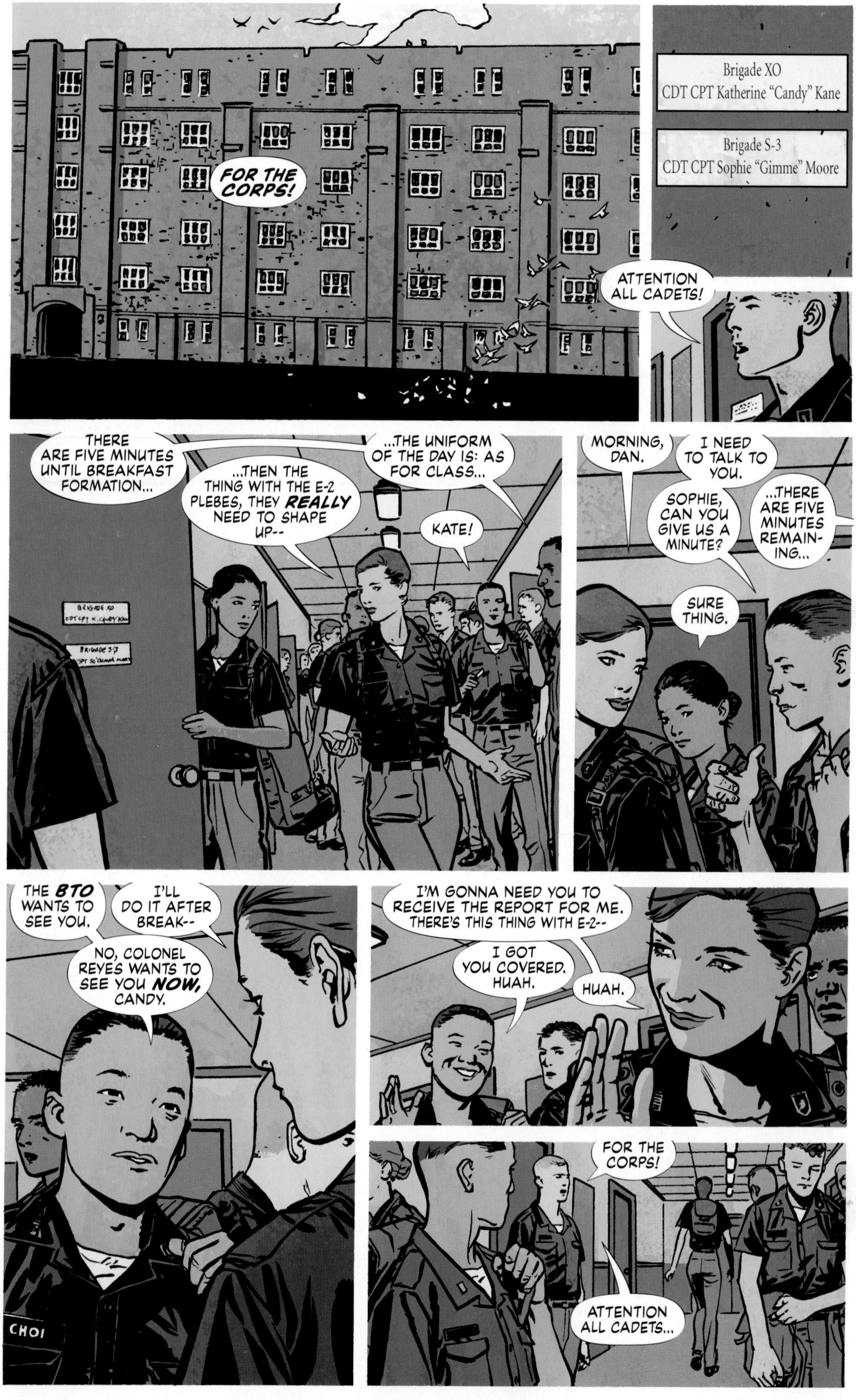
FOR THE CORPS!
Brigade XO
CDT CPT Katherine "Candy" Kane
Brigade S-3
CDT CPT Sophie "Gimme" Moore
ATTENTION ALL CADETS!
THERE ARE FIVE MINUTES UNTIL BREAKFAST FORMATION...
...THE UNIFORM OF THE DAY IS: AS FOR CLASS...
...THEN THE THING WITH THE E-2 PLEBES, THEY **REALLY** NEED TO SHAPE UP--
KATE!
MORNING, DAN.
I NEED TO TALK TO YOU.
SOPHIE, CAN YOU GIVE US A MINUTE?
...THERE ARE FIVE MINUTES REMAINING...
SURE THING.
THE **BTO** WANTS TO SEE YOU.
I'LL DO IT AFTER BREAK--
NO, COLONEL REYES WANTS TO SEE YOU **NOW,** CANDY.
CHOI
I'M GONNA NEED YOU TO RECEIVE THE REPORT FOR ME. THERE'S THIS THING WITH E-2--
I GOT YOU COVERED. HUAH.
HUAH.
FOR THE CORPS!
ATTENTION ALL CADETS...

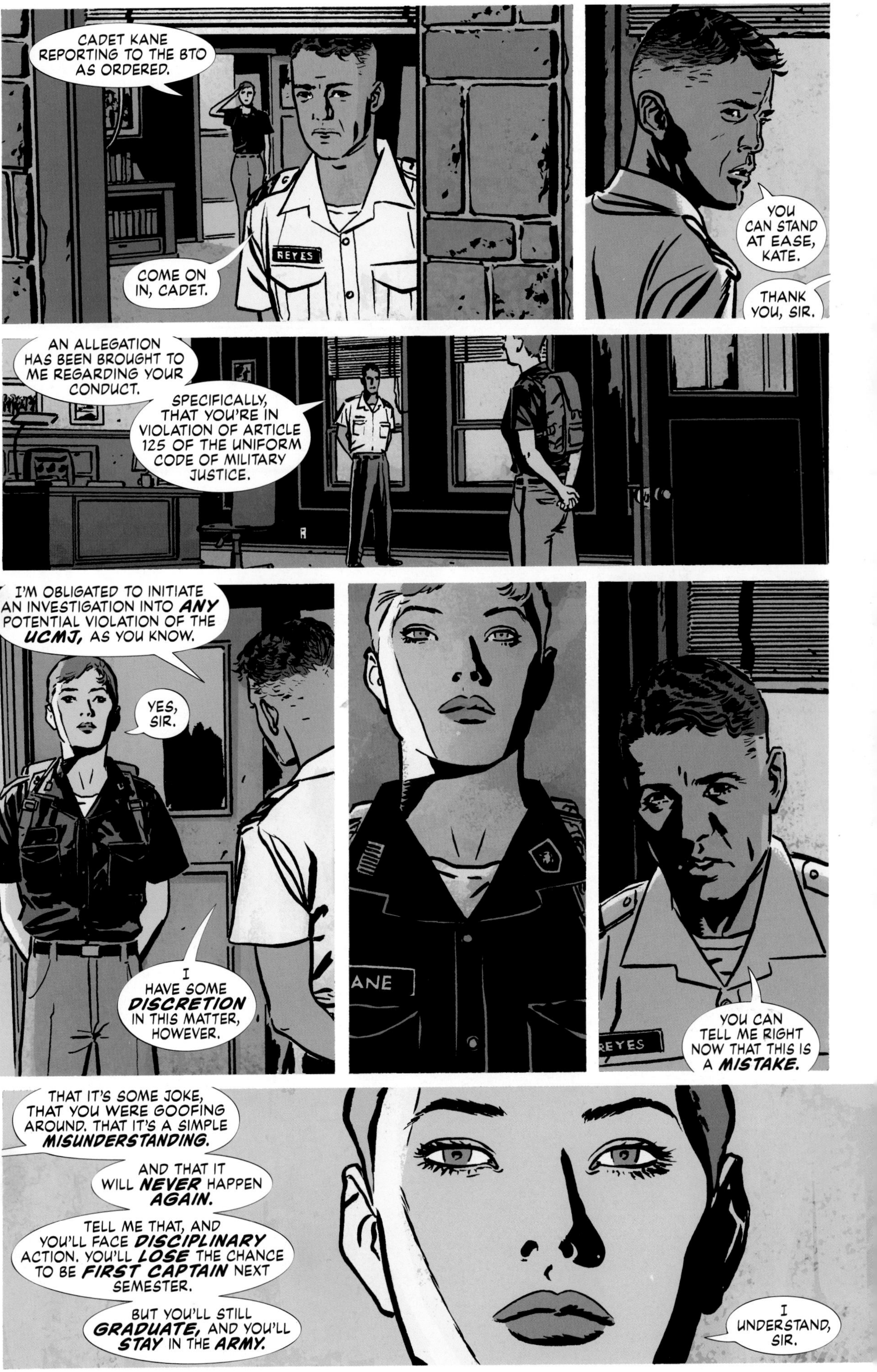
CADET KANE REPORTING TO THE BTO AS ORDERED.
COME ON IN, CADET.
REYES
YOU CAN STAND AT EASE, KATE.
THANK YOU, SIR.
AN ALLEGATION HAS BEEN BROUGHT TO ME REGARDING YOUR CONDUCT.
SPECIFICALLY, THAT YOU'RE IN VIOLATION OF ARTICLE 125 OF THE UNIFORM CODE OF MILITARY JUSTICE.
I'M OBLIGATED TO INITIATE AN INVESTIGATION INTO *ANY* POTENTIAL VIOLATION OF THE *UCMJ,* AS YOU KNOW.
YES, SIR.
I HAVE SOME *DISCRETION* IN THIS MATTER, HOWEVER.
ANE
REYES
YOU CAN TELL ME RIGHT NOW THAT THIS IS A *MISTAKE.*
THAT IT'S SOME JOKE, THAT YOU WERE GOOFING AROUND. THAT IT'S A SIMPLE *MISUNDERSTANDING.*
AND THAT IT WILL *NEVER* HAPPEN *AGAIN.*
TELL ME THAT, AND YOU'LL FACE *DISCIPLINARY* ACTION. YOU'LL *LOSE* THE CHANCE TO BE *FIRST CAPTAIN* NEXT SEMESTER.
BUT YOU'LL STILL *GRADUATE,* AND YOU'LL *STAY* IN THE *ARMY.*
I UNDERSTAND, SIR.

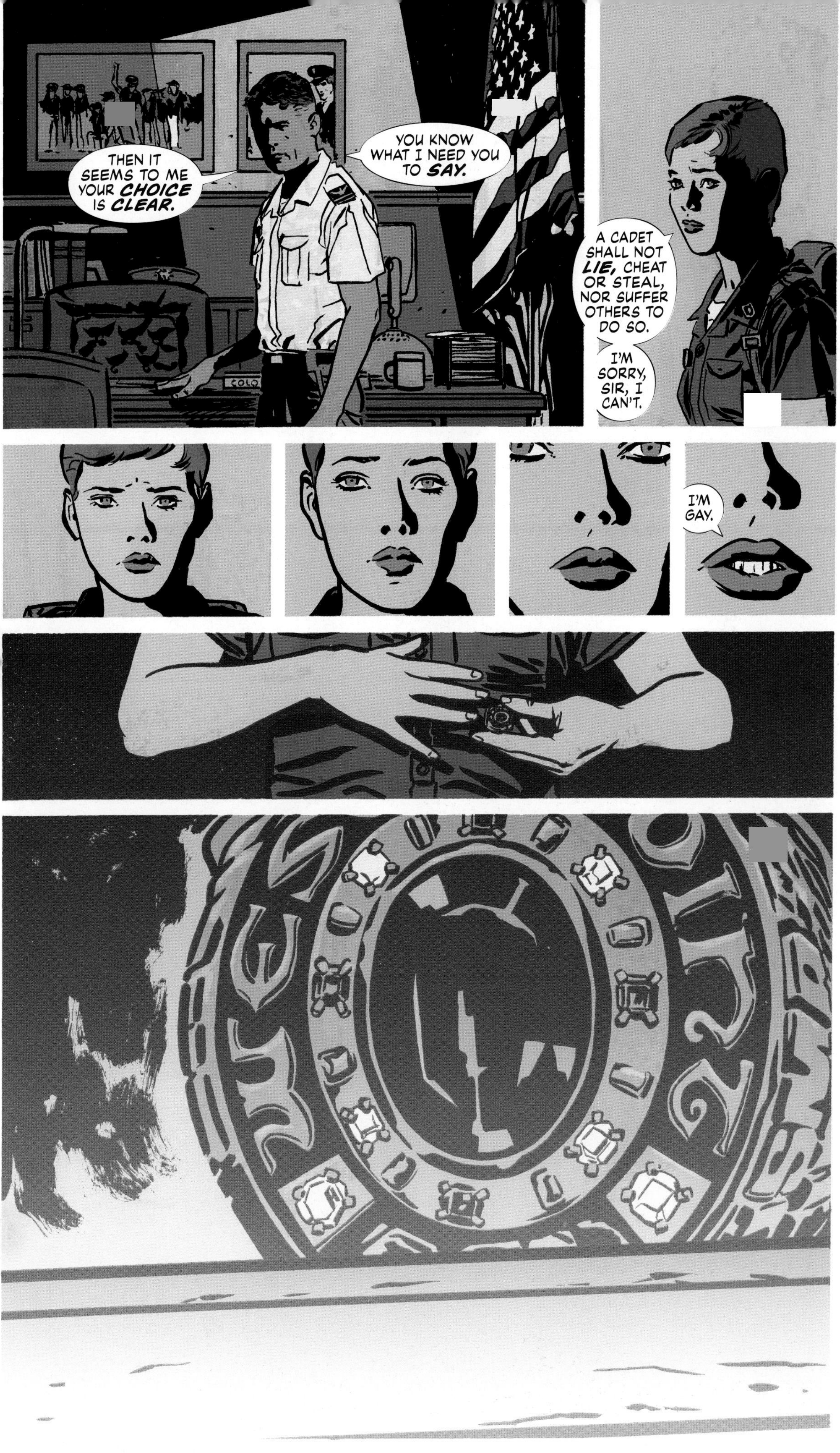
THEN IT SEEMS TO ME YOUR CHOICE IS CLEAR.
YOU KNOW WHAT I NEED YOU TO SAY.
A CADET SHALL NOT LIE, CHEAT OR STEAL, NOR SUFFER OTHERS TO DO SO.
I'M SORRY, SIR, I CAN'T.
I'M GAY.

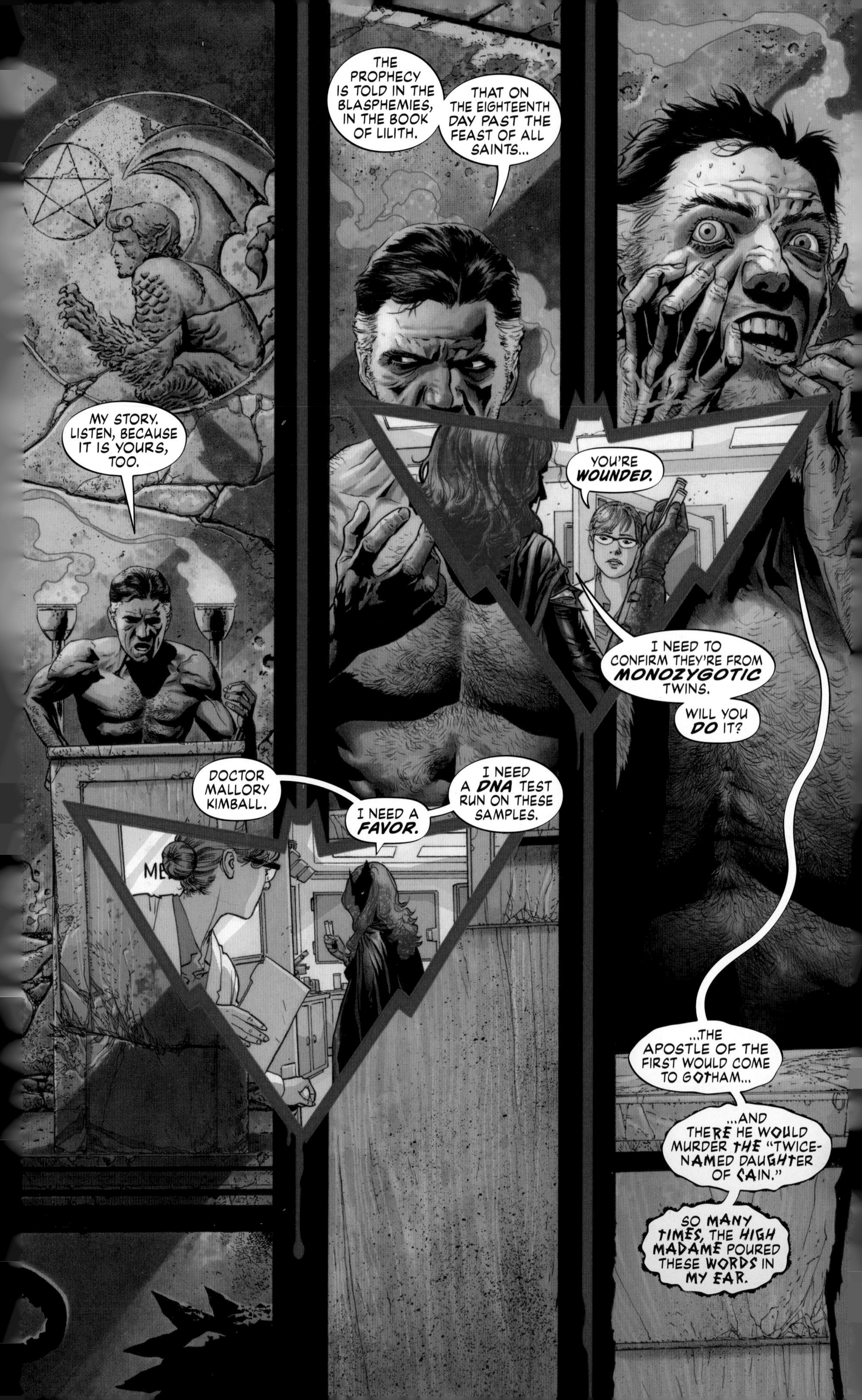
THE PROPHECY IS TOLD IN THE BLASPHEMIES, IN THE BOOK OF LILITH.
THAT ON THE EIGHTEENTH DAY PAST THE FEAST OF ALL SAINTS...
MY STORY. LISTEN, BECAUSE IT IS YOURS, TOO.
YOU'RE WOUNDED.
I NEED TO CONFIRM THEY'RE FROM MONOZYGOTIC TWINS.
WILL YOU DO IT?
DOCTOR MALLORY KIMBALL.
I NEED A FAVOR.
I NEED A DNA TEST RUN ON THESE SAMPLES.
...THE APOSTLE OF THE FIRST WOULD COME TO GOTHAM...
...AND THERE HE WOULD MURDER THE "TWICE-NAMED DAUGHTER OF CAIN."
SO MANY TIMES, THE HIGH MADAME POURED THESE WORDS IN MY EAR.

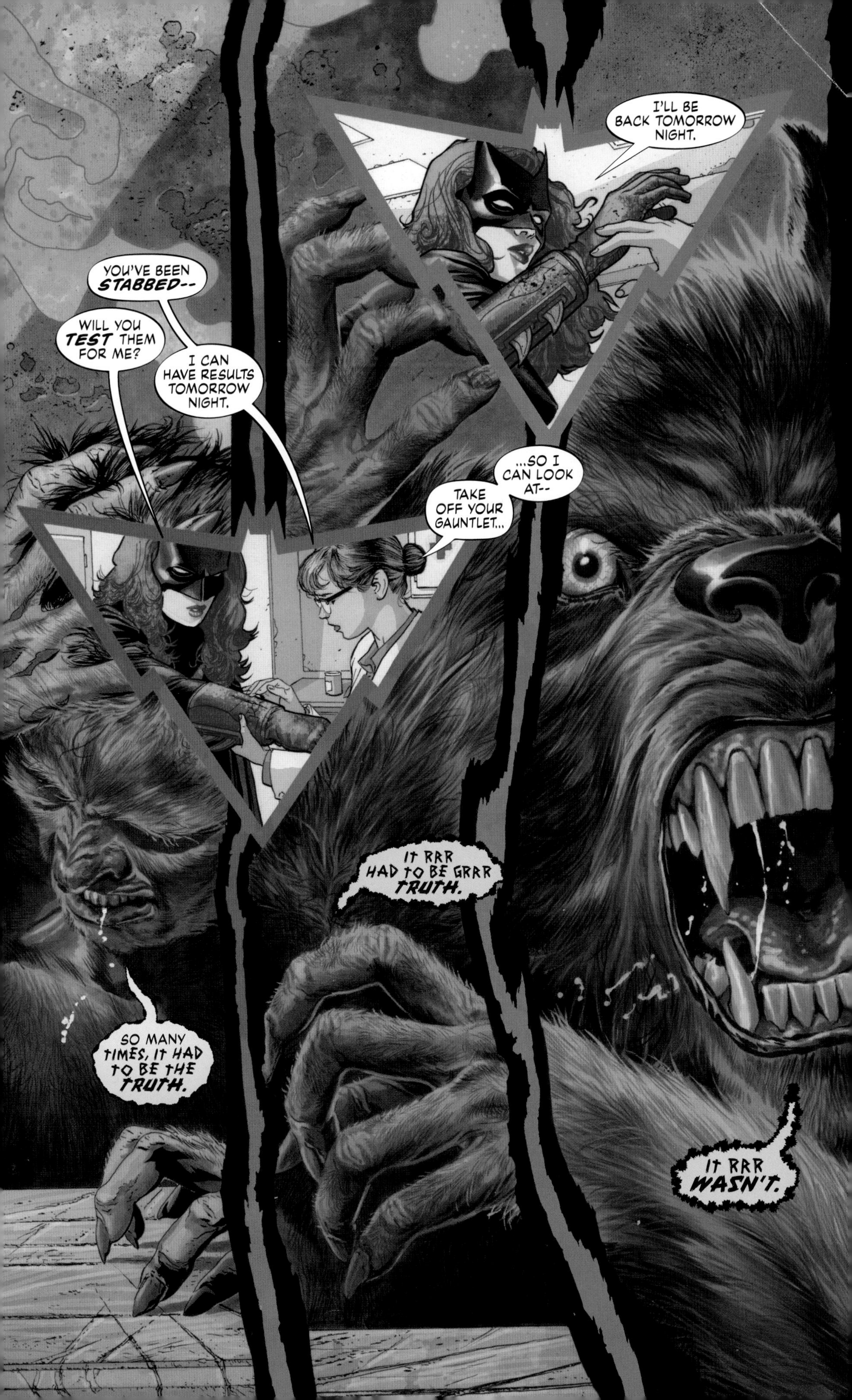
I'LL BE BACK TOMORROW NIGHT.
YOU'VE BEEN STABBED--
WILL YOU TEST THEM FOR ME?
I CAN HAVE RESULTS TOMORROW NIGHT.
TAKE OFF YOUR GAUNTLET...
...SO I CAN LOOK AT--
SO MANY TIMES, IT HAD TO BE THE TRUTH.
IT RRR HAD TO BE GRRR TRUTH.
IT RRR WASN'T.

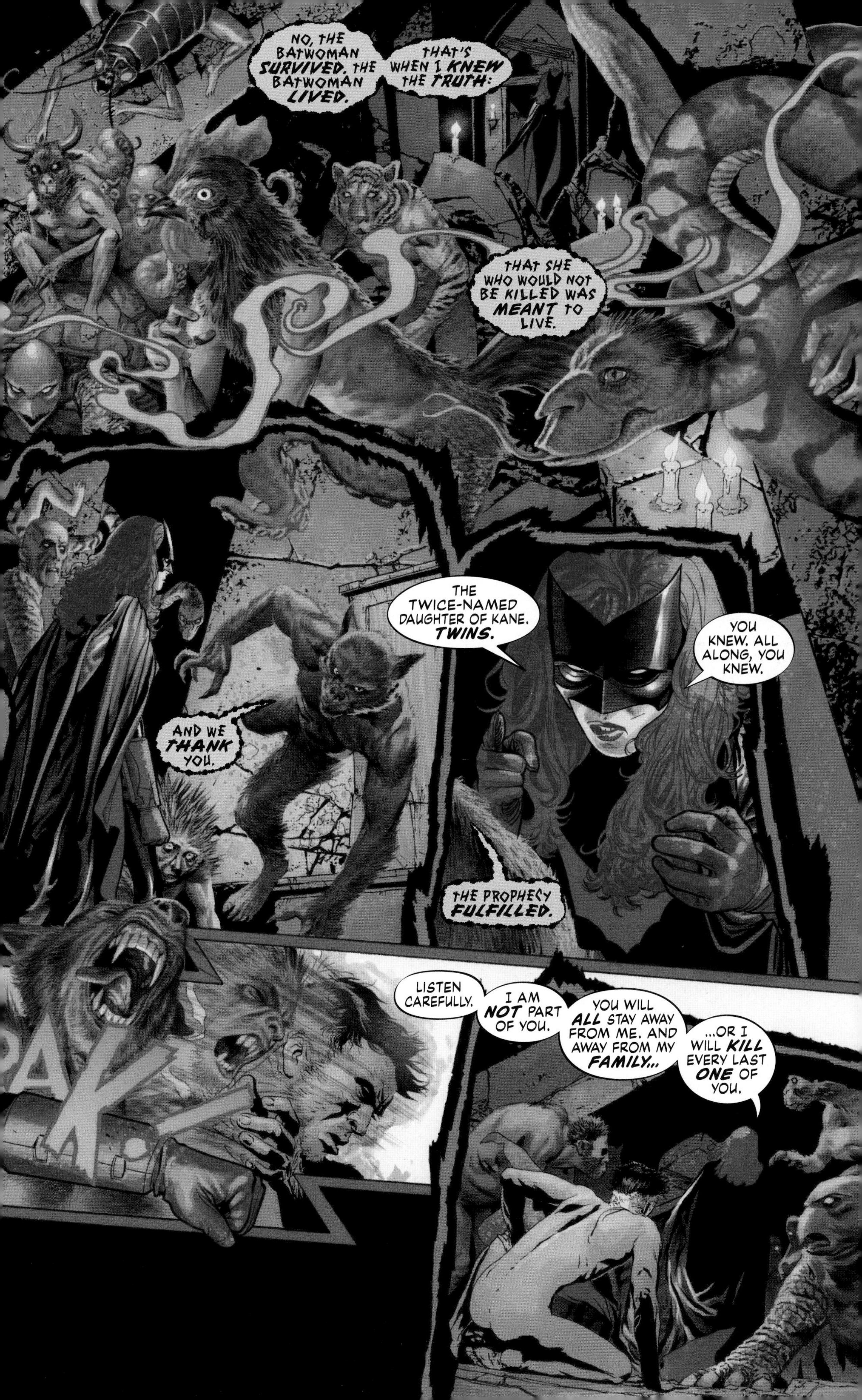

NO, THE BATWOMAN SURVIVED. THE BATWOMAN LIVED.
THAT'S WHEN I KNEW THE TRUTH:
THAT SHE WHO WOULD NOT BE KILLED WAS MEANT TO LIVE.
THE TWICE-NAMED DAUGHTER OF KANE. TWINS.
YOU KNEW. ALL ALONG, YOU KNEW.
AND WE THANK YOU.
THE PROPHECY FULFILLED.
LISTEN CAREFULLY.
I AM NOT PART OF YOU.
YOU WILL ALL STAY AWAY FROM ME. AND AWAY FROM MY FAMILY...
...OR I WILL KILL EVERY LAST ONE OF YOU.

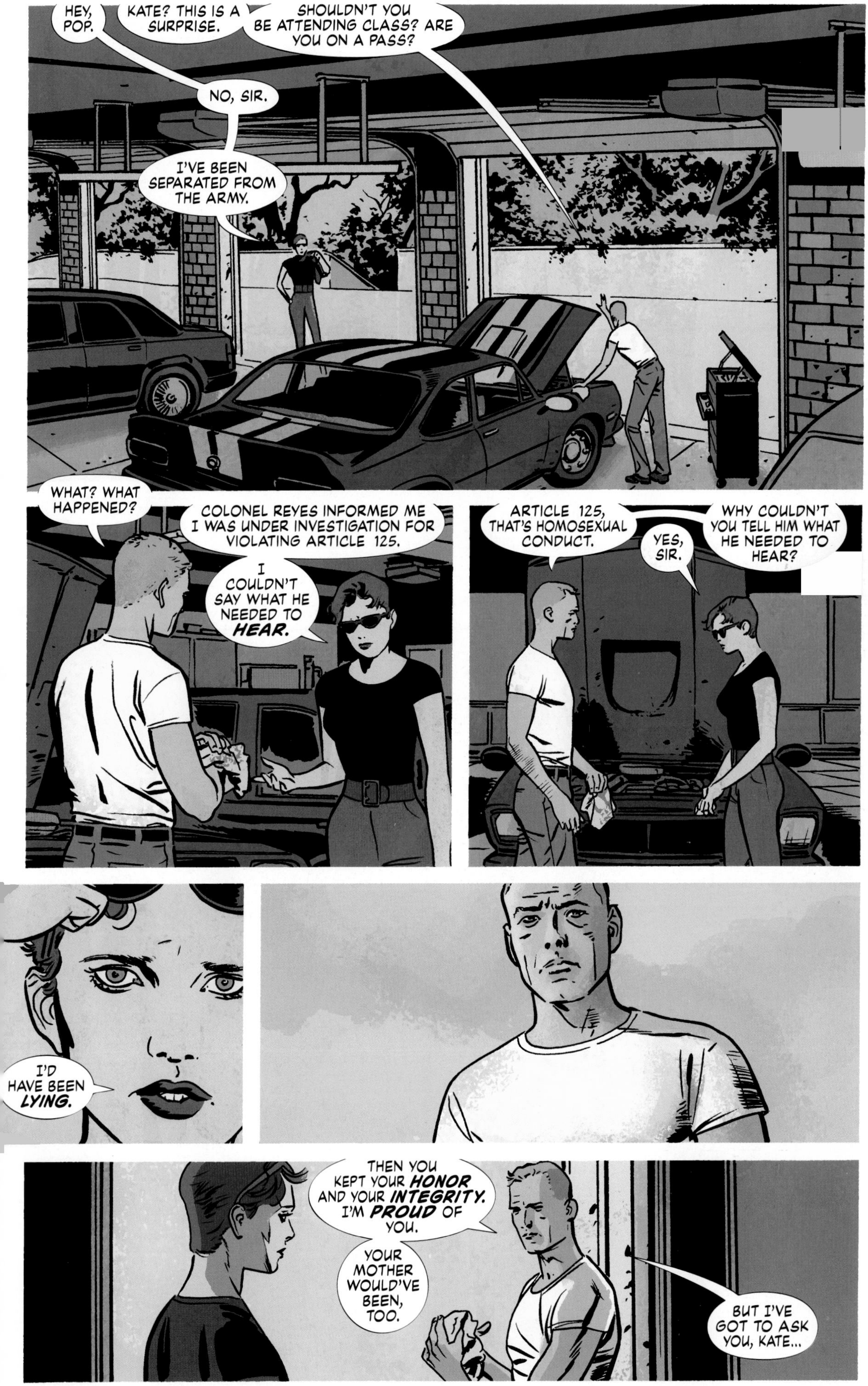
HEY, POP.
KATE? THIS IS A SURPRISE.
SHOULDN'T YOU BE ATTENDING CLASS? ARE YOU ON A PASS?
NO, SIR.
I'VE BEEN SEPARATED FROM THE ARMY.
WHAT? WHAT HAPPENED?
COLONEL REYES INFORMED ME I WAS UNDER INVESTIGATION FOR VIOLATING ARTICLE 125.
I COULDN'T SAY WHAT HE NEEDED TO HEAR.
ARTICLE 125, THAT'S HOMOSEXUAL CONDUCT.
YES, SIR.
WHY COULDN'T YOU TELL HIM WHAT HE NEEDED TO HEAR?
I'D HAVE BEEN LYING.
THEN YOU KEPT YOUR HONOR AND YOUR INTEGRITY. I'M PROUD OF YOU.
YOUR MOTHER WOULD'VE BEEN, TOO.
BUT I'VE GOT TO ASK YOU, KATE...

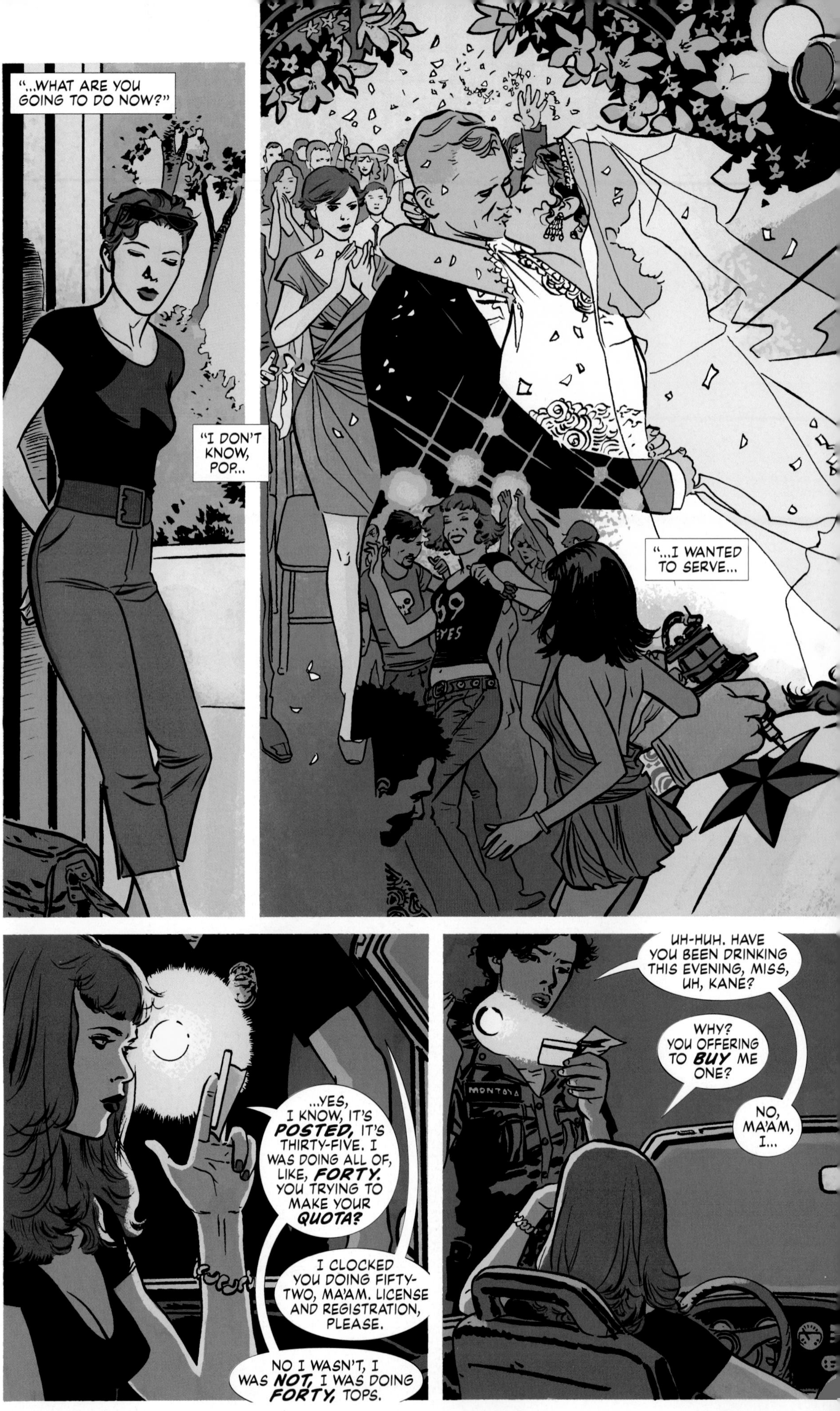
"...WHAT ARE YOU GOING TO DO NOW?"
"I DON'T KNOW, POP...
"...I WANTED TO SERVE...
...YES, I KNOW, IT'S POSTED, IT'S THIRTY-FIVE. I WAS DOING ALL OF, LIKE, FORTY. YOU TRYING TO MAKE YOUR QUOTA?
I CLOCKED YOU DOING FIFTY-TWO, MA'AM. LICENSE AND REGISTRATION, PLEASE.
NO I WASN'T, I WAS NOT, I WAS DOING FORTY, TOPS.
UH-HUH. HAVE YOU BEEN DRINKING THIS EVENING, MISS, UH, KANE?
WHY? YOU OFFERING TO BUY ME ONE?
NO, MA'AM, I...
MONTOYA

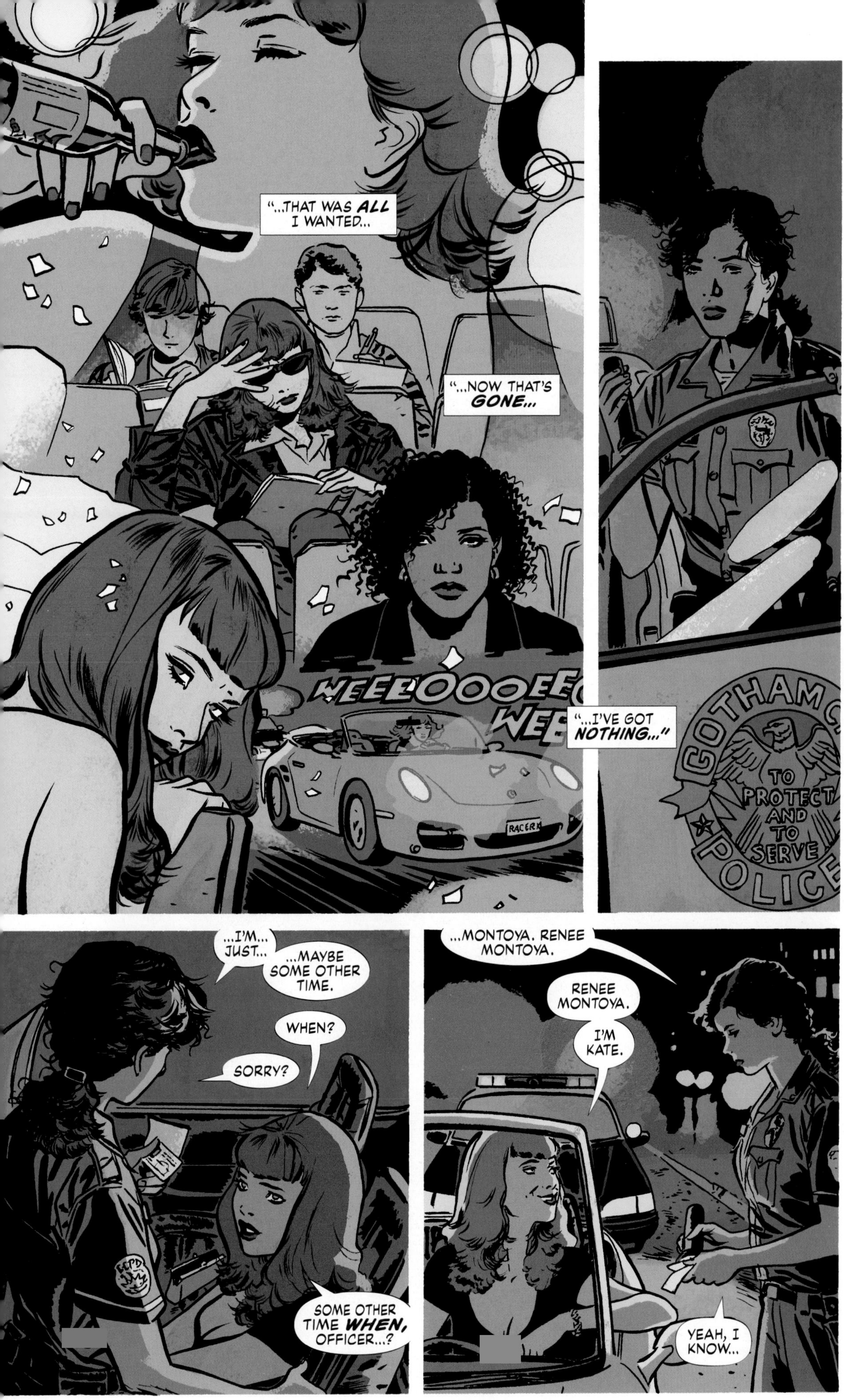

"...THAT WAS ALL I WANTED...
"...NOW THAT'S GONE...
WEEEOOOEE
WEE
"...I'VE GOT NOTHING..."
GOTHAM CITY POLICE
TO PROTECT AND TO SERVE
RACERX
...I'M... JUST...
...MAYBE SOME OTHER TIME.
WHEN?
SORRY?
SOME OTHER TIME WHEN, OFFICER...?
...MONTOYA. RENEE MONTOYA.
RENEE MONTOYA.
I'M KATE.
YEAH, I KNOW...

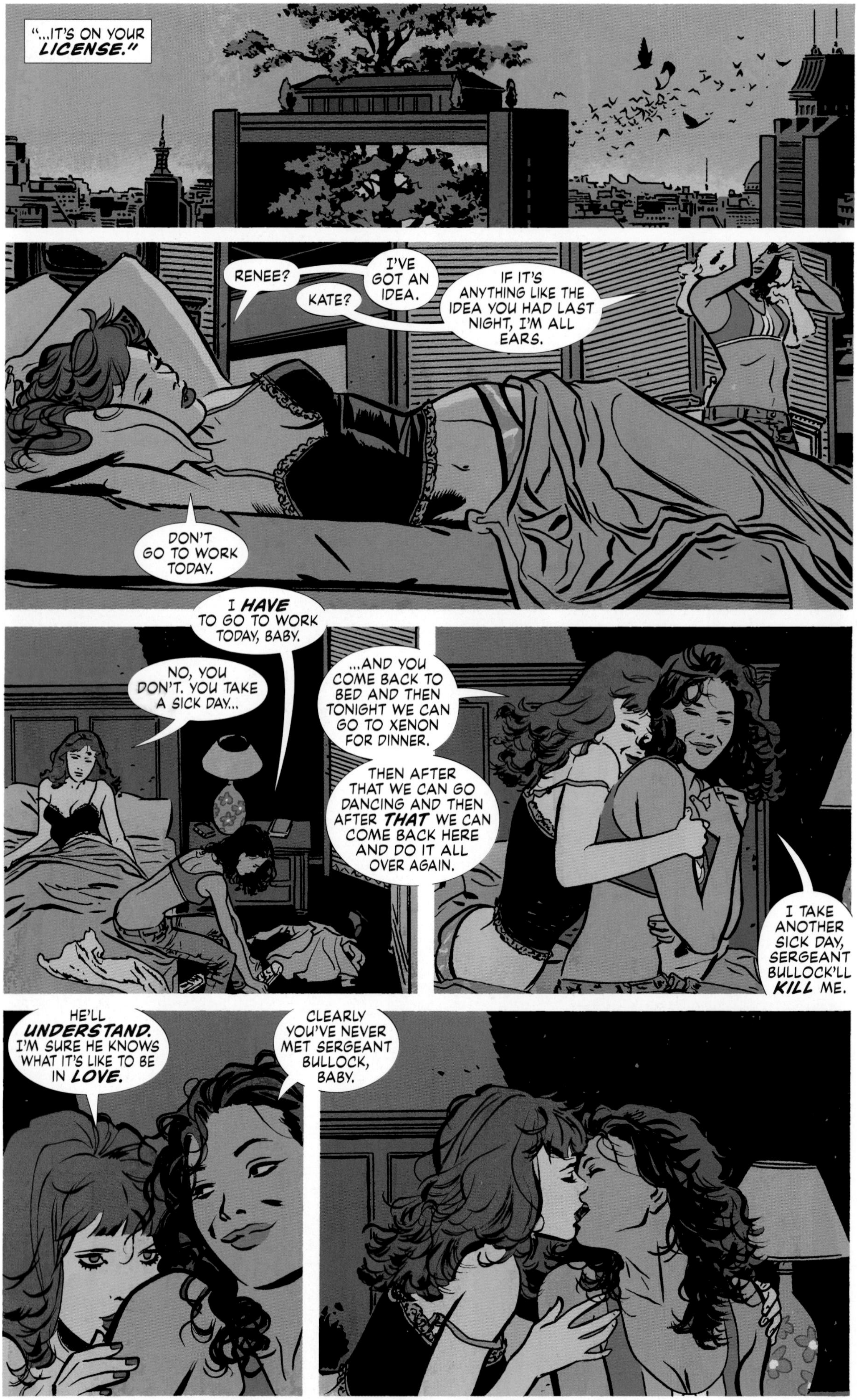
"...IT'S ON YOUR **LICENSE.**"
RENEE?
I'VE GOT AN IDEA.
KATE?
IF IT'S ANYTHING LIKE THE IDEA YOU HAD LAST NIGHT, I'M ALL EARS.
DON'T GO TO WORK TODAY.
I **HAVE** TO GO TO WORK TODAY, BABY.
NO, YOU DON'T. YOU TAKE A SICK DAY...
...AND YOU COME BACK TO BED AND THEN TONIGHT WE CAN GO TO XENON FOR DINNER.
THEN AFTER THAT WE CAN GO DANCING AND THEN AFTER **THAT** WE CAN COME BACK HERE AND DO IT ALL OVER AGAIN.
I TAKE ANOTHER SICK DAY, SERGEANT BULLOCK'LL **KILL** ME.
HE'LL **UNDERSTAND.** I'M SURE HE KNOWS WHAT IT'S LIKE TO BE IN **LOVE.**
CLEARLY YOU'VE NEVER MET SERGEANT BULLOCK, BABY.

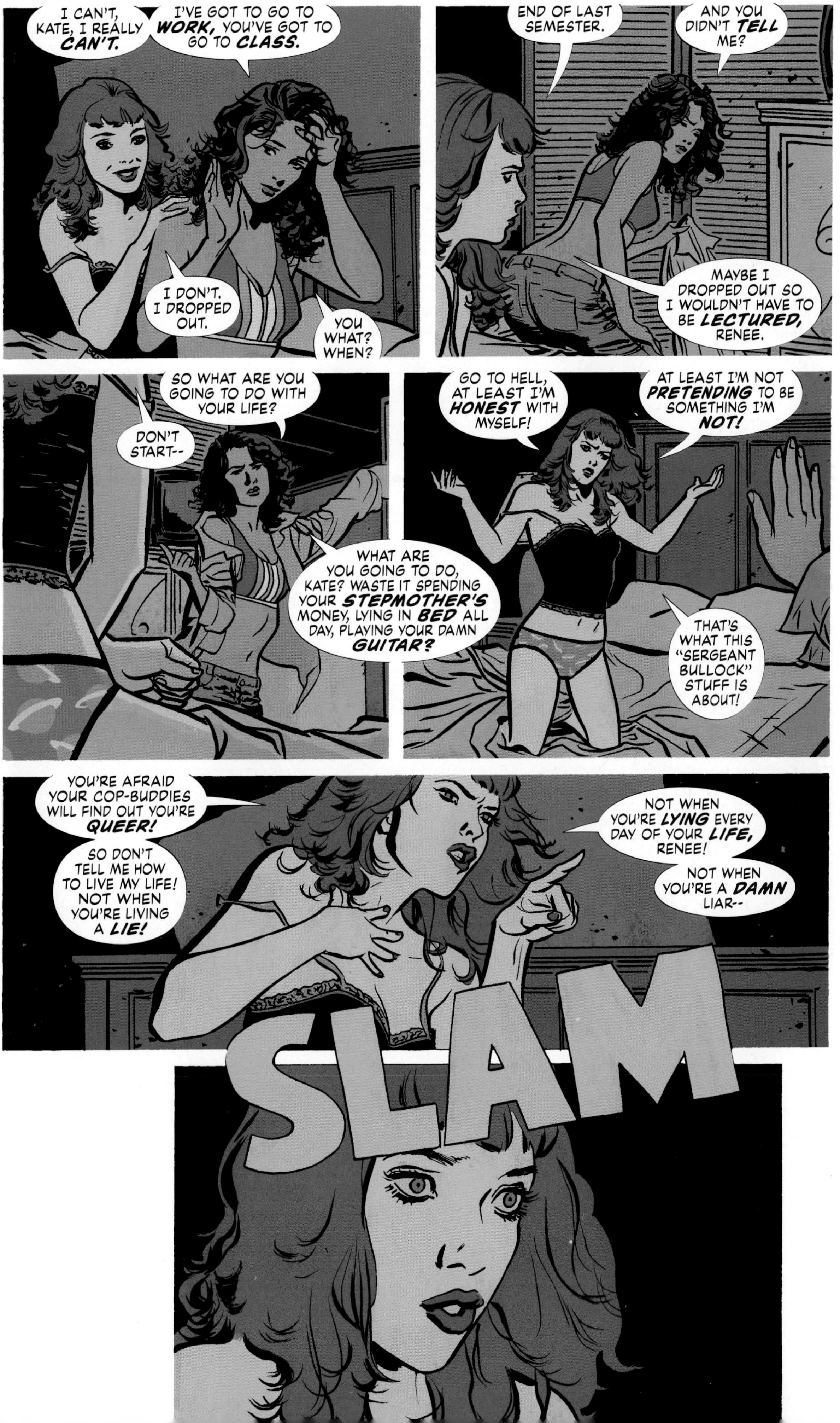
I CAN'T, KATE, I REALLY **CAN'T.**
I'VE GOT TO GO TO **WORK,** YOU'VE GOT TO GO TO **CLASS.**
I DON'T. I DROPPED OUT.
YOU WHAT? WHEN?
END OF LAST SEMESTER.
AND YOU DIDN'T **TELL** ME?
MAYBE I DROPPED OUT SO I WOULDN'T HAVE TO BE **LECTURED,** RENEE.
SO WHAT ARE YOU GOING TO DO WITH YOUR LIFE?
DON'T START--
WHAT ARE YOU GOING TO DO, KATE? WASTE IT SPENDING YOUR **STEPMOTHER'S** MONEY, LYING IN **BED** ALL DAY, PLAYING YOUR DAMN **GUITAR?**
GO TO HELL, AT LEAST I'M **HONEST** WITH MYSELF!
AT LEAST I'M NOT **PRETENDING** TO BE SOMETHING I'M **NOT!**
THAT'S WHAT THIS "SERGEANT BULLOCK" STUFF IS ABOUT!
YOU'RE AFRAID YOUR COP-BUDDIES WILL FIND OUT YOU'RE **QUEER!**
SO DON'T TELL ME HOW TO LIVE MY LIFE! NOT WHEN YOU'RE LIVING A **LIE!**
NOT WHEN YOU'RE **LYING** EVERY DAY OF YOUR **LIFE,** RENEE!
NOT WHEN YOU'RE A **DAMN** LIAR--
SLAM

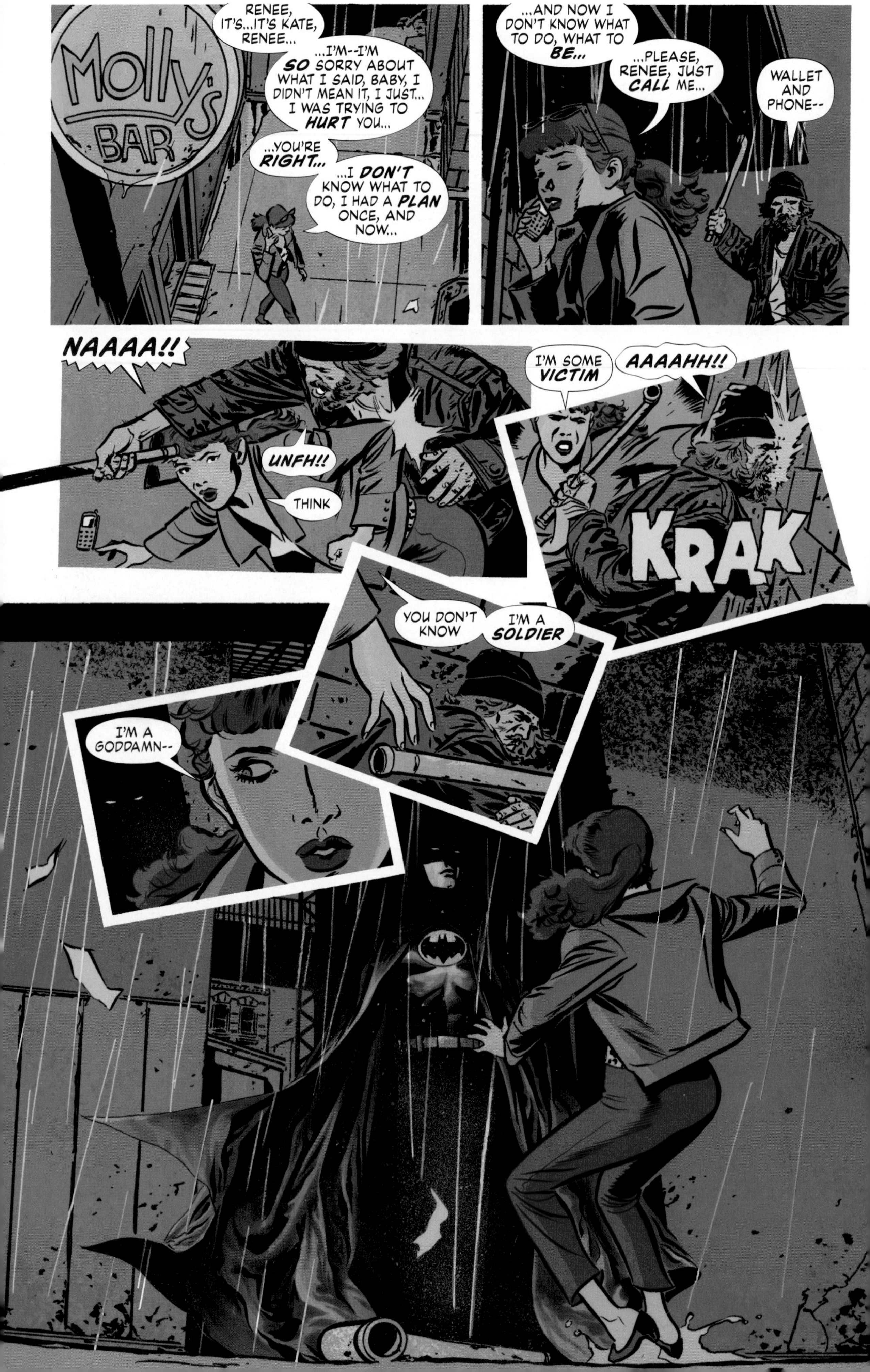

RENEE, IT'S...IT'S KATE, RENEE...
...I'M--I'M SO SORRY ABOUT WHAT I SAID, BABY, I DIDN'T MEAN IT, I JUST... I WAS TRYING TO HURT YOU...
...YOU'RE RIGHT...
...I DON'T KNOW WHAT TO DO, I HAD A PLAN ONCE, AND NOW...
...AND NOW I DON'T KNOW WHAT TO DO, WHAT TO BE...
...PLEASE, RENEE, JUST CALL ME...
WALLET AND PHONE--
NAAAA!!
UNFH!!
THINK
I'M SOME VICTIM
AAAAHH!!
KRAK
YOU DON'T KNOW
I'M A SOLDIER
I'M A GODDAMN--

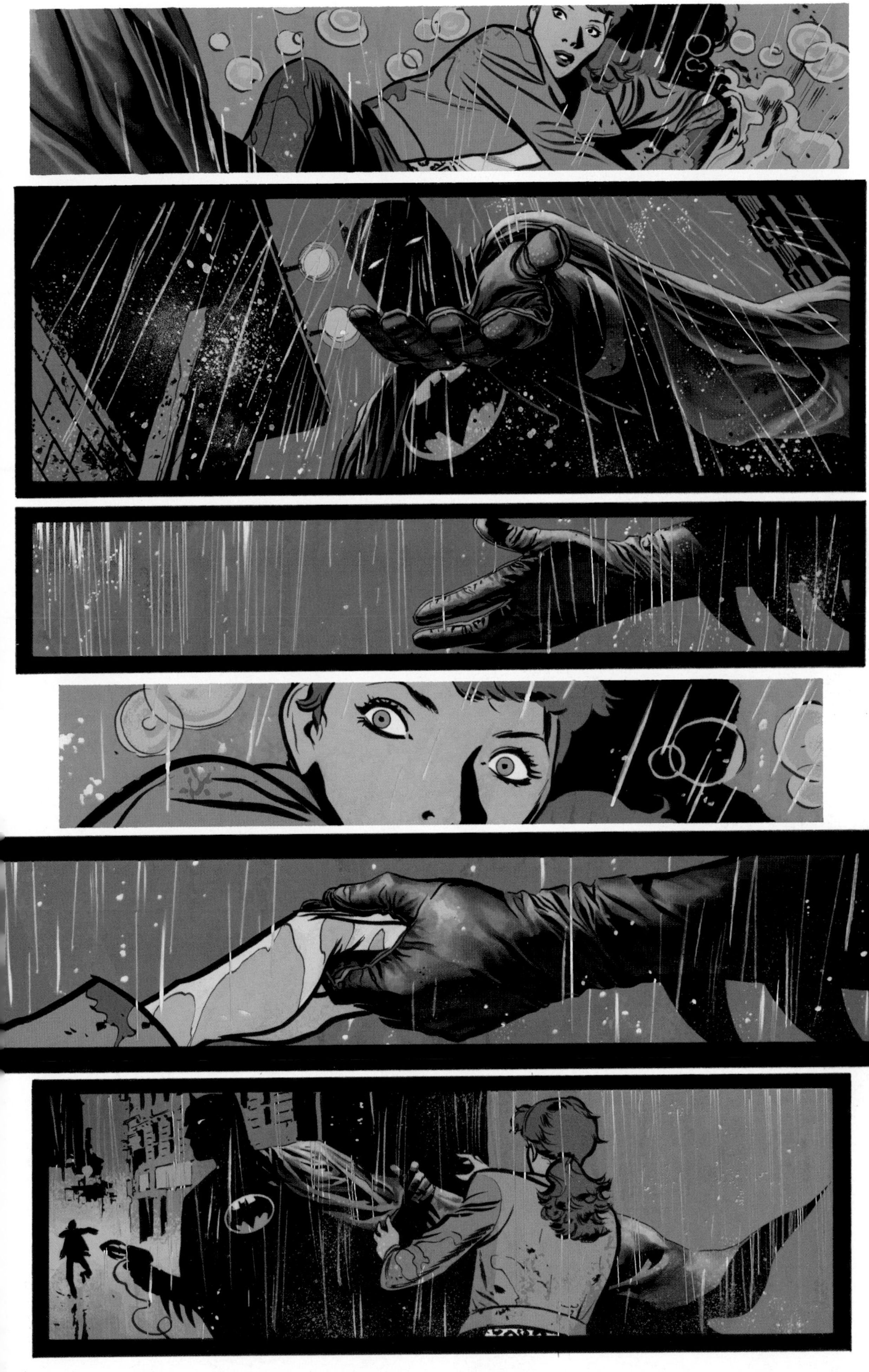

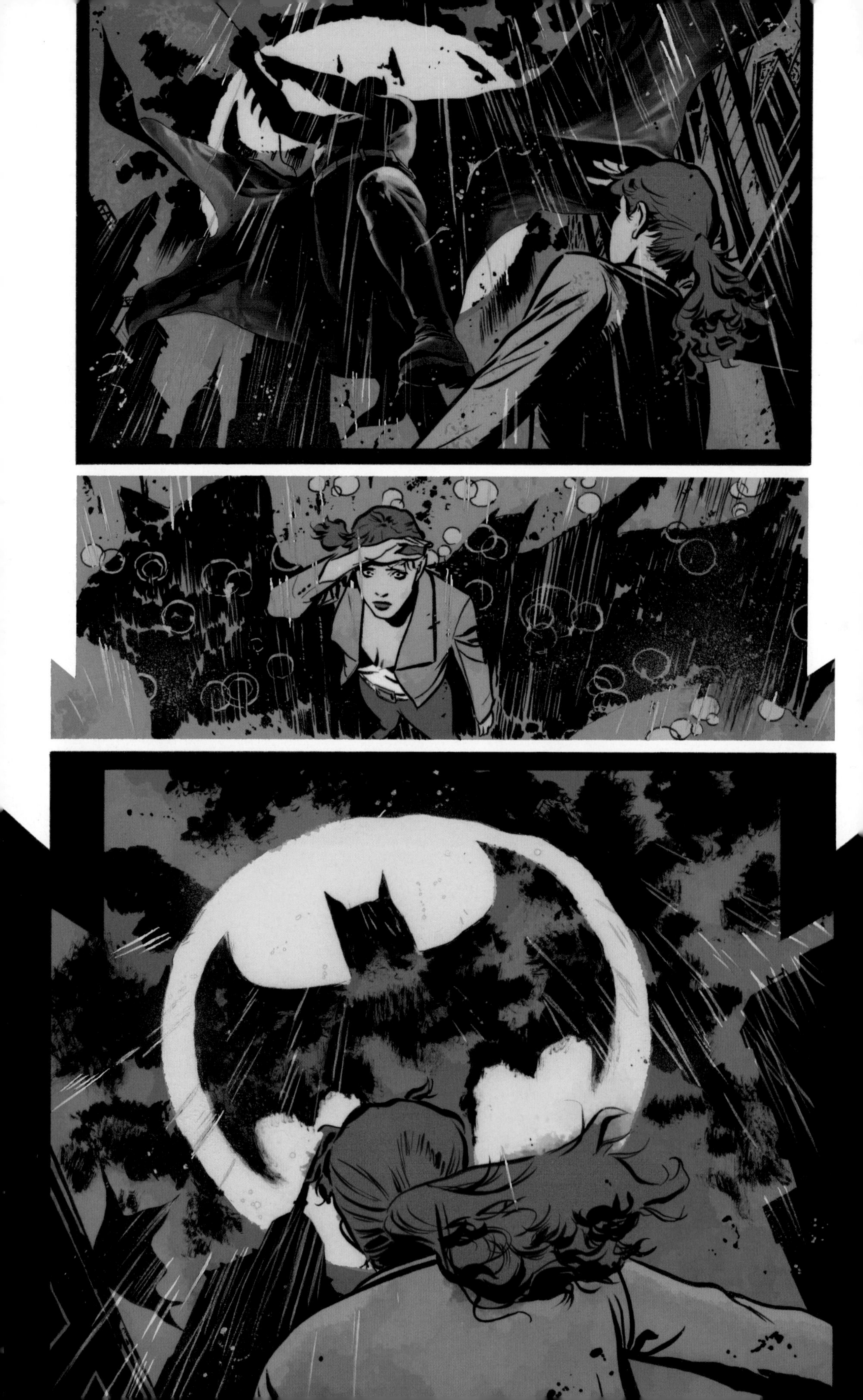

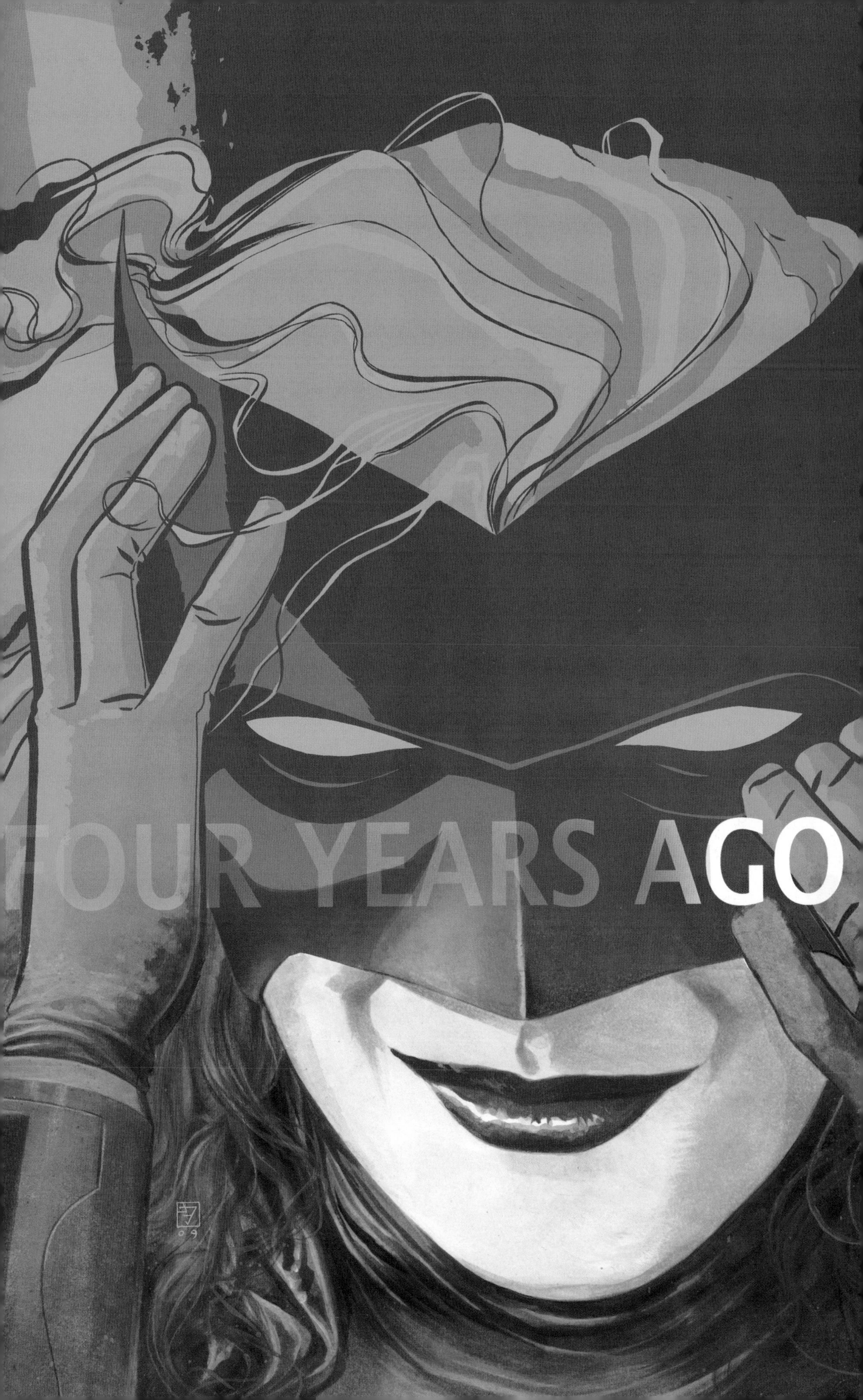
FOUR YEARS AGO

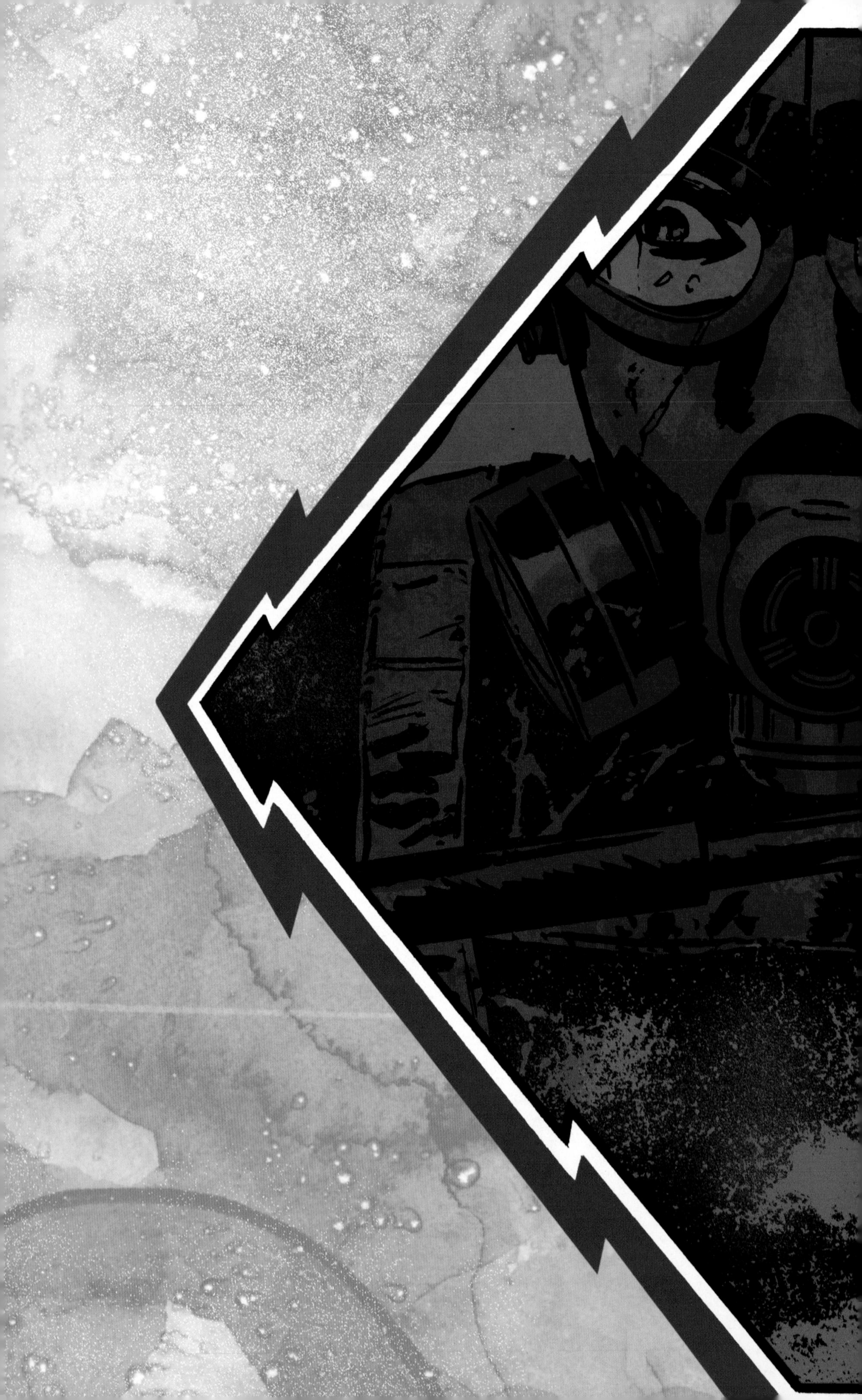

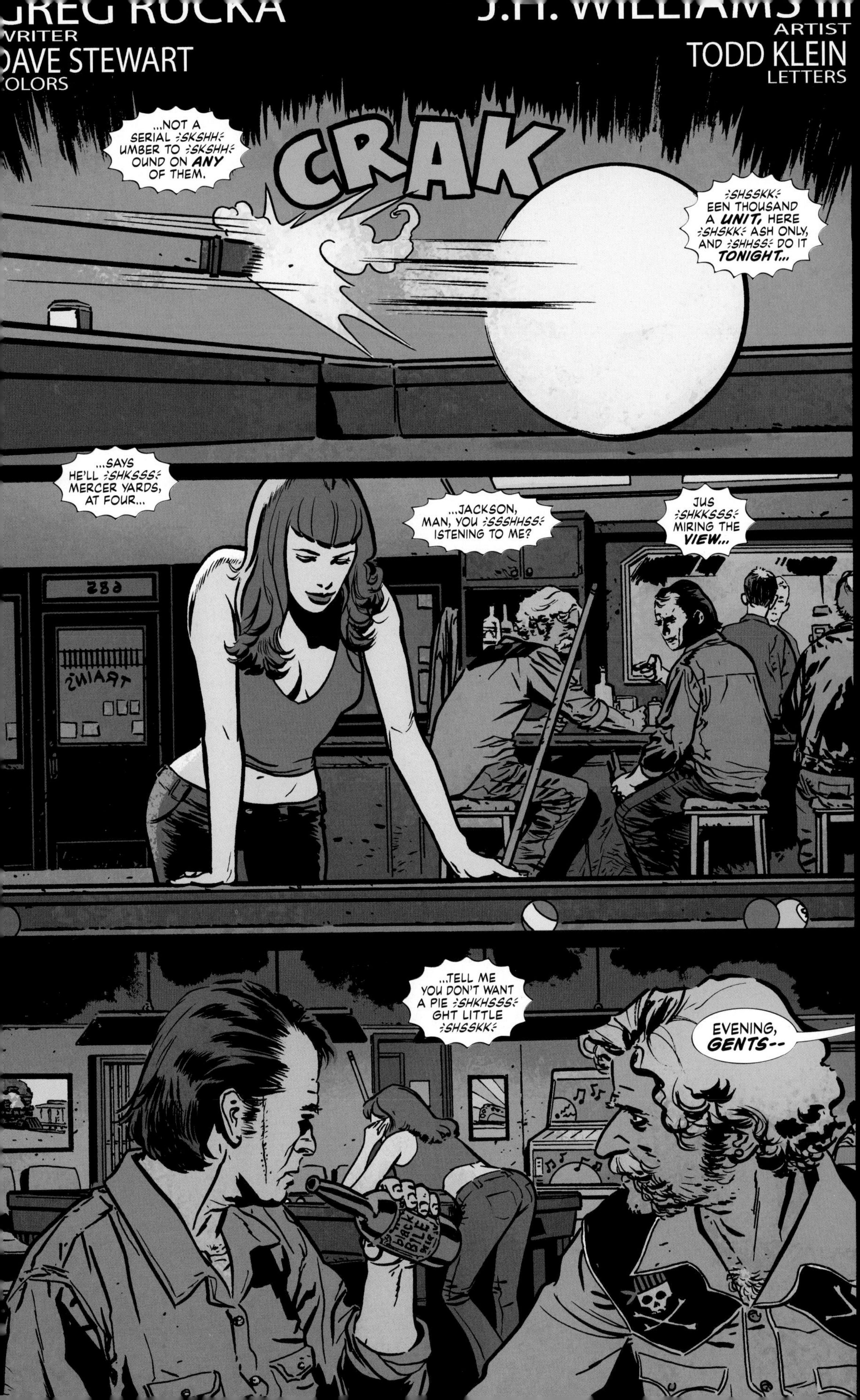
GREG RUCKA
WRITER
DAVE STEWART
COLORS
J.H. WILLIAMS III
ARTIST
TODD KLEIN
LETTERS
...NOT A SERIAL -SKSHH- UMBER TO -SKSHH- OUND ON ANY OF THEM.
CRAK
-SHSSKK- EEN THOUSAND A UNIT, HERE -SHSKK- ASH ONLY, AND -SHHSS- DO IT TONIGHT...
...SAYS HE'LL -SHKSSS- MERCER YARDS, AT FOUR...
...JACKSON, MAN, YOU -SSSHHSS- ISTENING TO ME?
JUS -SHKKSSS- MIRING THE VIEW...
...TELL ME YOU DON'T WANT A PIE -SHKHSSS- GHT LITTLE -SHSSKK-
EVENING, GENTS--

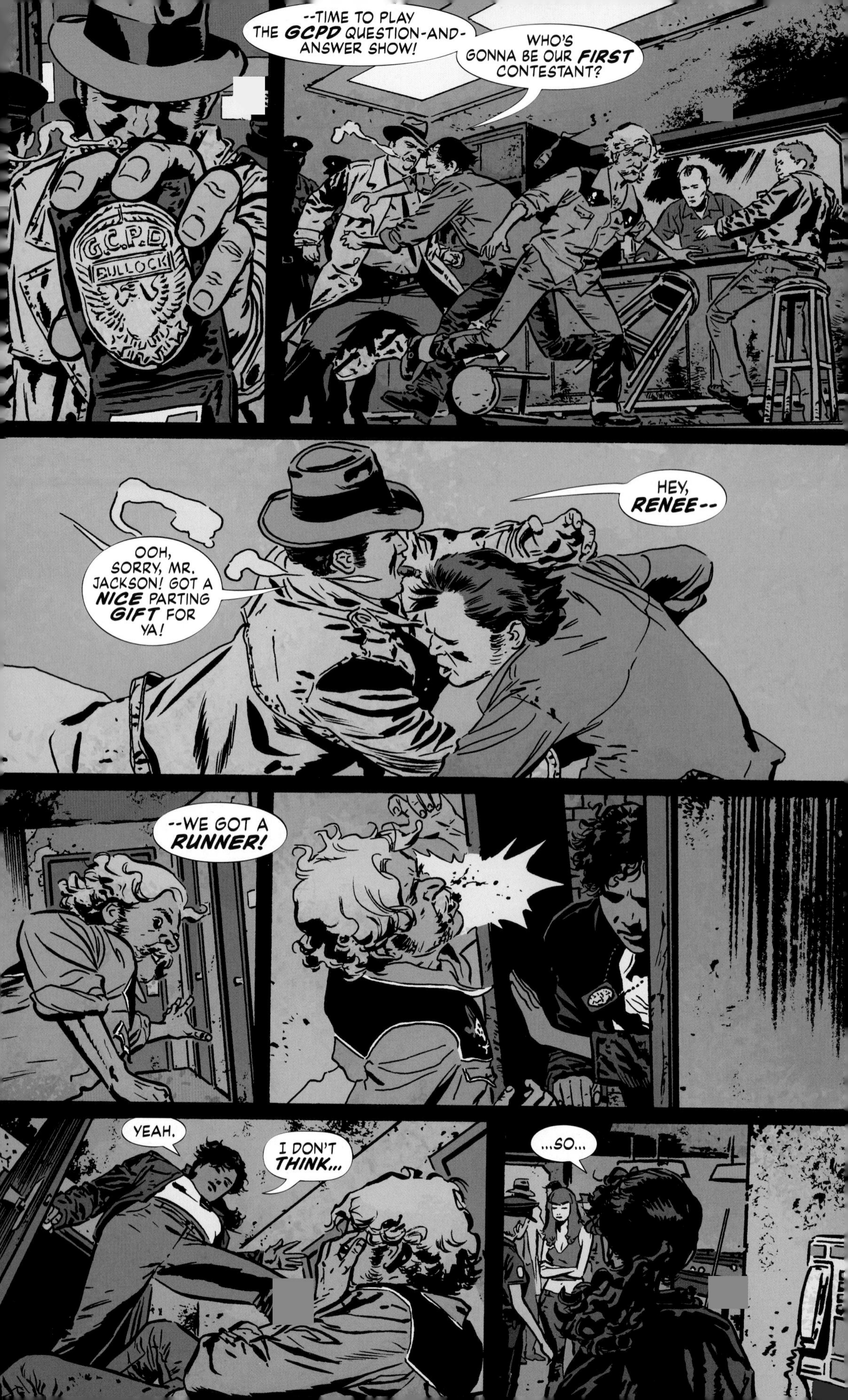
--TIME TO PLAY THE GCPD QUESTION-AND-ANSWER SHOW!
WHO'S GONNA BE OUR FIRST CONTESTANT?
G.C.P.D. BULLOCK
HEY, RENEE--
OOH, SORRY, MR. JACKSON! GOT A NICE PARTING GIFT FOR YA!
--WE GOT A RUNNER!
YEAH.
I DON'T THINK...
...SO...

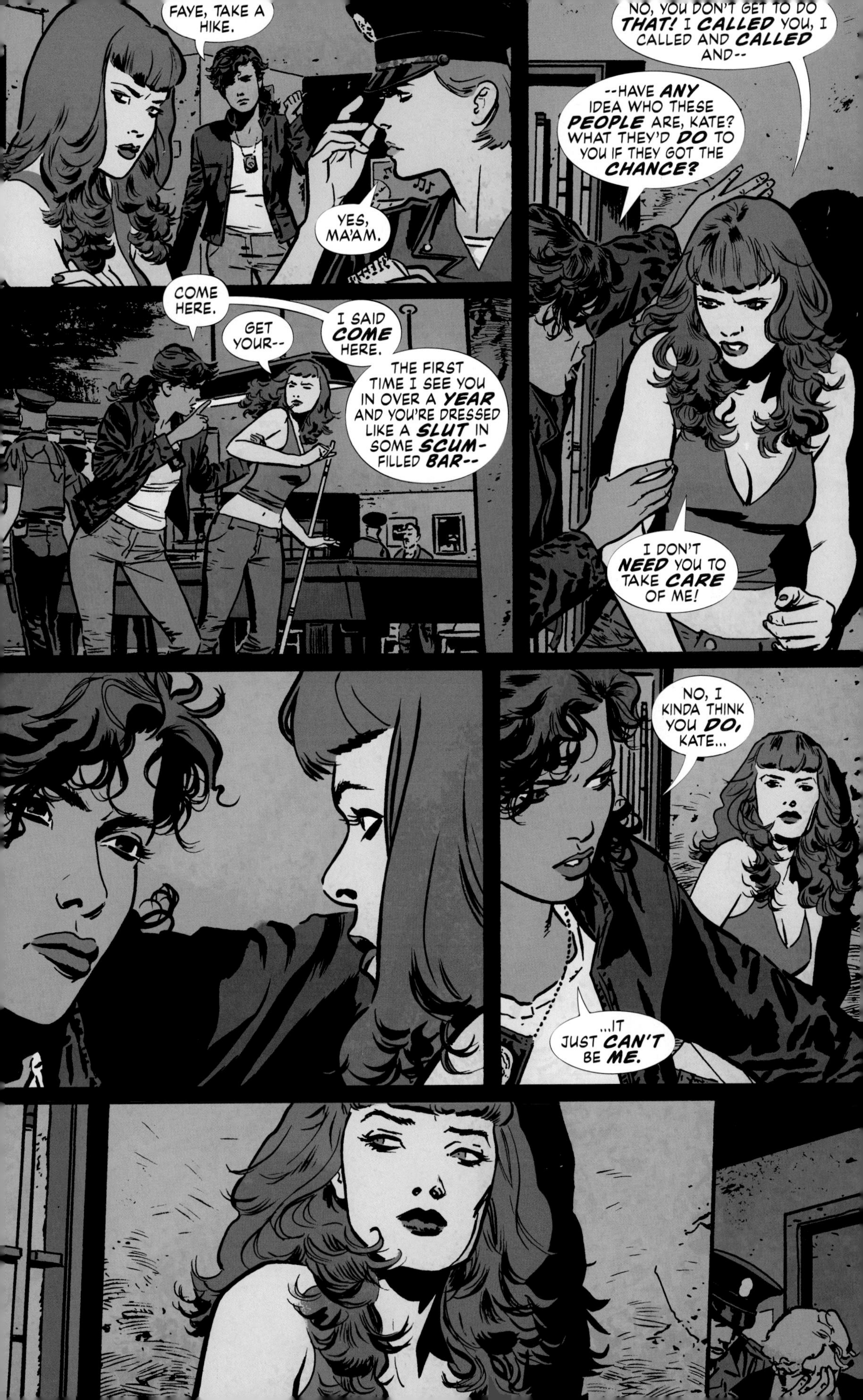
FAYE, TAKE A HIKE.
YES, MA'AM.
NO, YOU DON'T GET TO DO THAT! I CALLED YOU, I CALLED AND CALLED AND--
--HAVE ANY IDEA WHO THESE PEOPLE ARE, KATE? WHAT THEY'D DO TO YOU IF THEY GOT THE CHANCE?
COME HERE.
GET YOUR--
I SAID COME HERE.
THE FIRST TIME I SEE YOU IN OVER A YEAR AND YOU'RE DRESSED LIKE A SLUT IN SOME SCUM-FILLED BAR--
I DON'T NEED YOU TO TAKE CARE OF ME!
NO, I KINDA THINK YOU DO, KATE...
...IT JUST CAN'T BE ME.

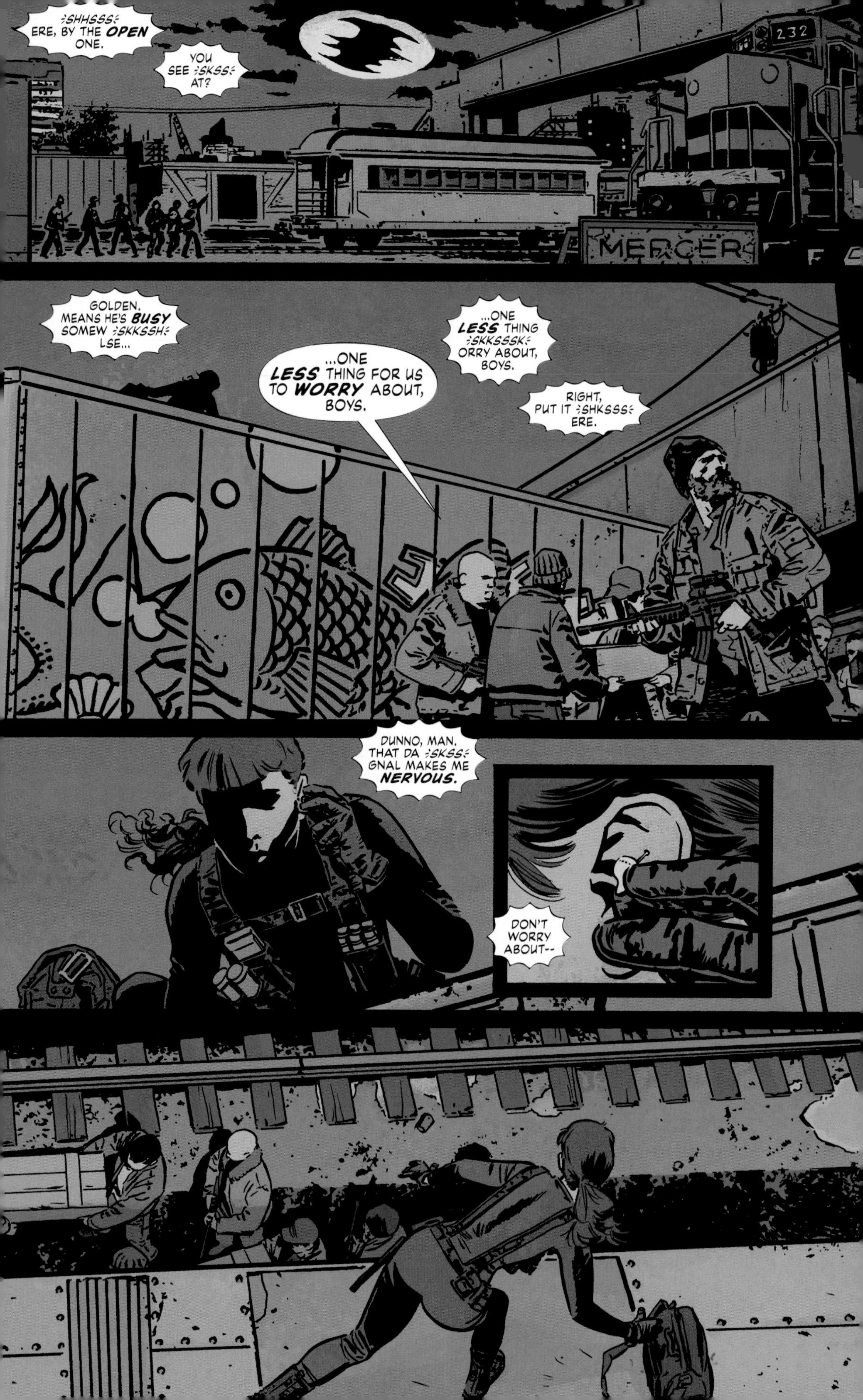

⚡SHHSSS⚡ ERE, BY THE OPEN ONE.
YOU SEE ⚡SKSS⚡ AT?
GOLDEN. MEANS HE'S BUSY SOMEW ⚡SKKSSH⚡ LSE...
...ONE LESS THING FOR US TO WORRY ABOUT, BOYS.
...ONE LESS THING ⚡SKKSSSK⚡ ORRY ABOUT, BOYS.
RIGHT, PUT IT ⚡SHKSSS⚡ ERE.
DUNNO, MAN. THAT DA ⚡SKSS⚡ GNAL MAKES ME NERVOUS.
DON'T WORRY ABOUT--

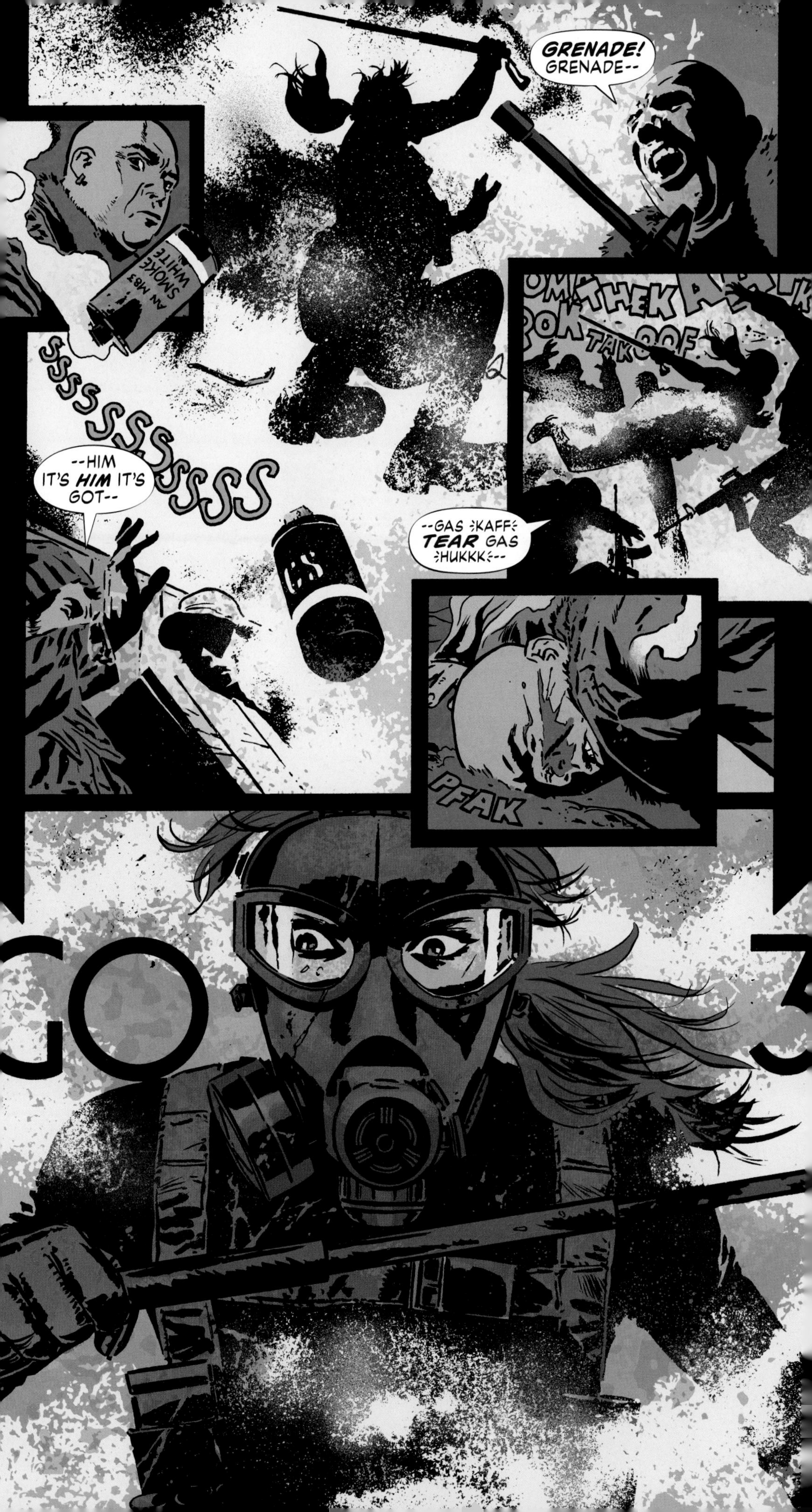

GRENADE! GRENADE--
AN M83 SMOKE WHITE
SSSSSSSSSSSSS
--HIM IT'S HIM IT'S GOT--
CS
THEK
OOF
TAK
--GAS KAFF TEAR GAS HUKKK--
PFAK

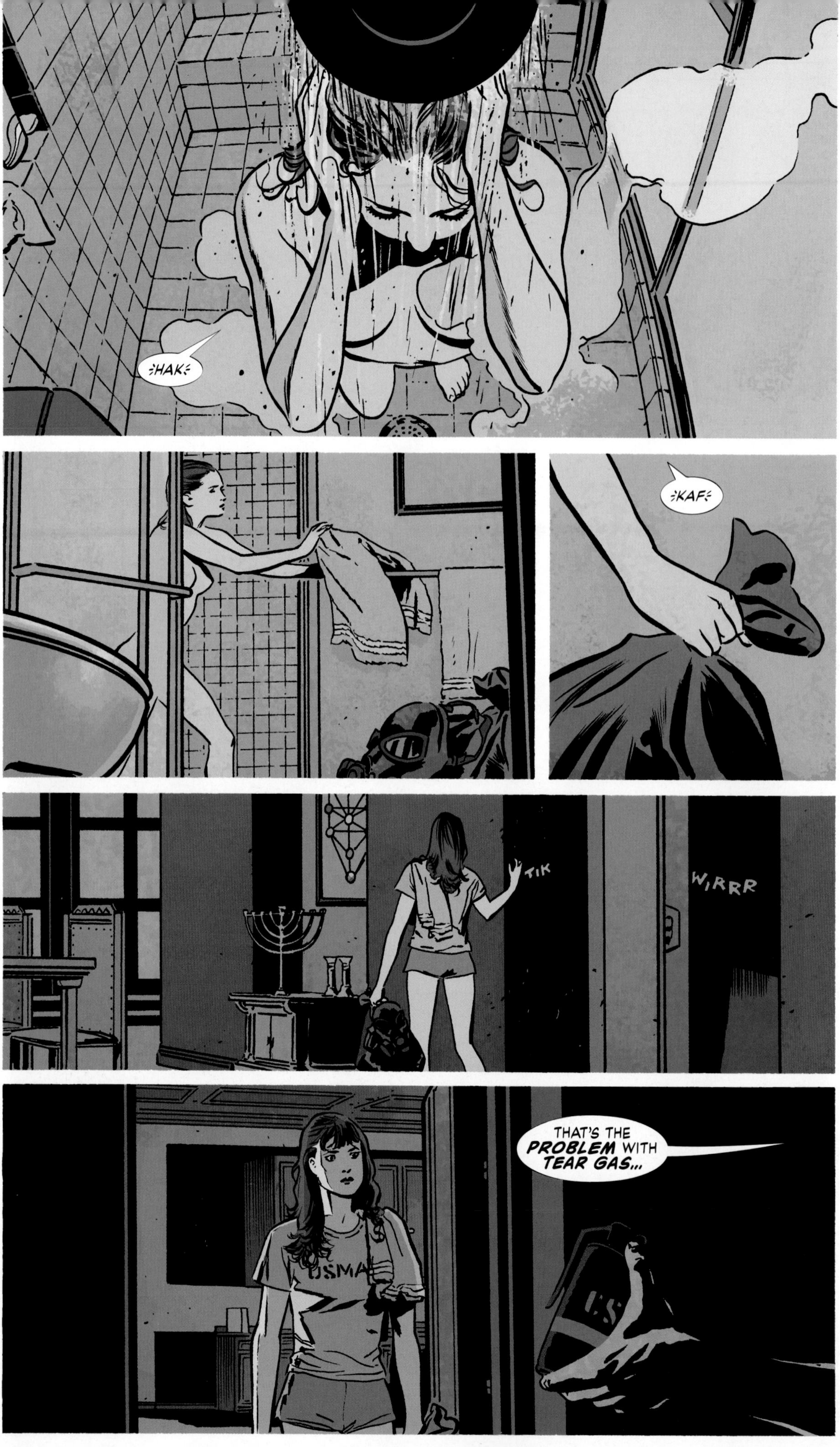
HAK
KAF
TIK
WIRRR
THAT'S THE PROBLEM WITH TEAR GAS...
USMA
CS

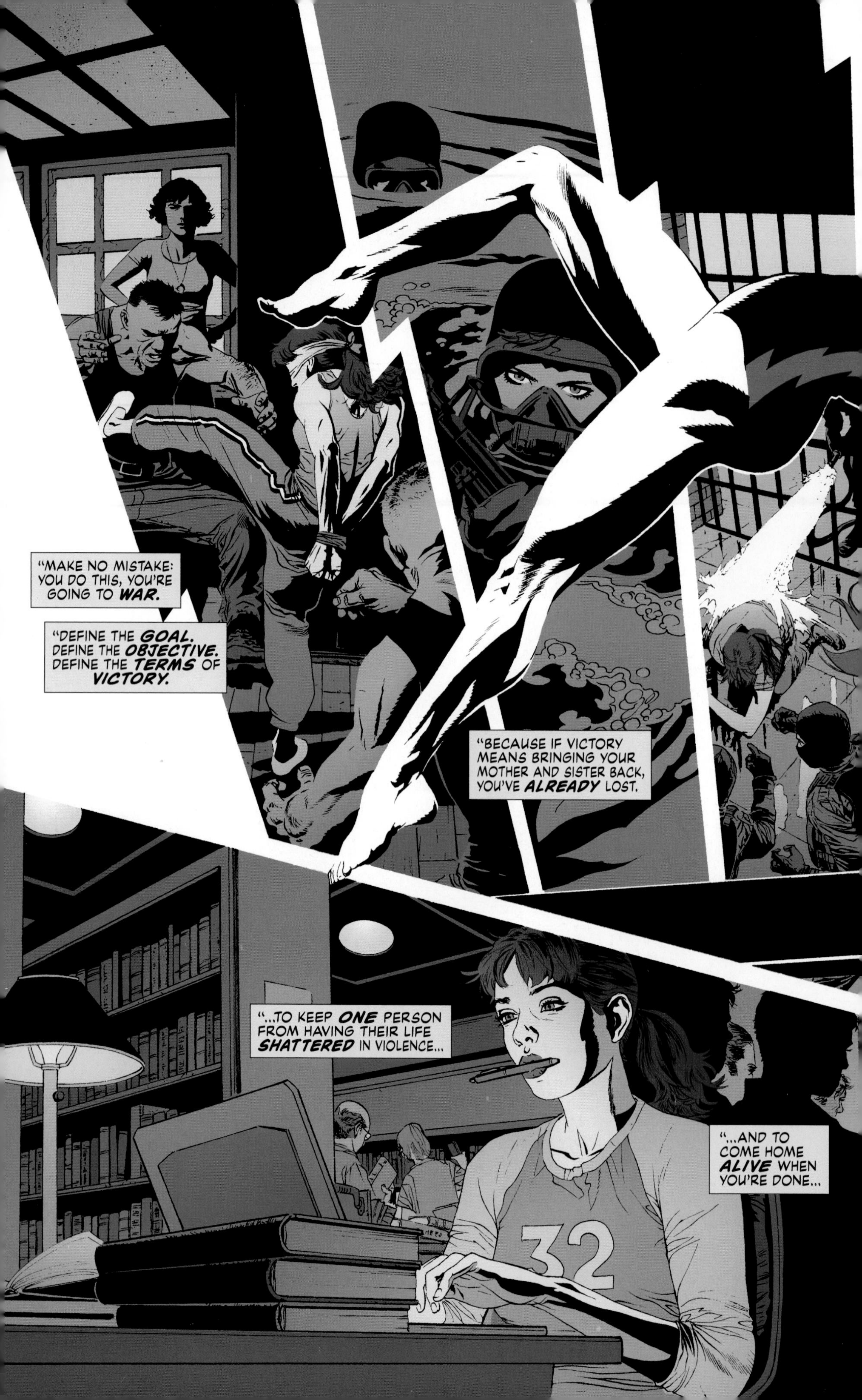
"MAKE NO MISTAKE: YOU DO THIS, YOU'RE GOING TO WAR.
"DEFINE THE GOAL. DEFINE THE OBJECTIVE. DEFINE THE TERMS OF VICTORY.
"BECAUSE IF VICTORY MEANS BRINGING YOUR MOTHER AND SISTER BACK, YOU'VE ALREADY LOST.
"...TO KEEP ONE PERSON FROM HAVING THEIR LIFE SHATTERED IN VIOLENCE...
"...AND TO COME HOME ALIVE WHEN YOU'RE DONE...

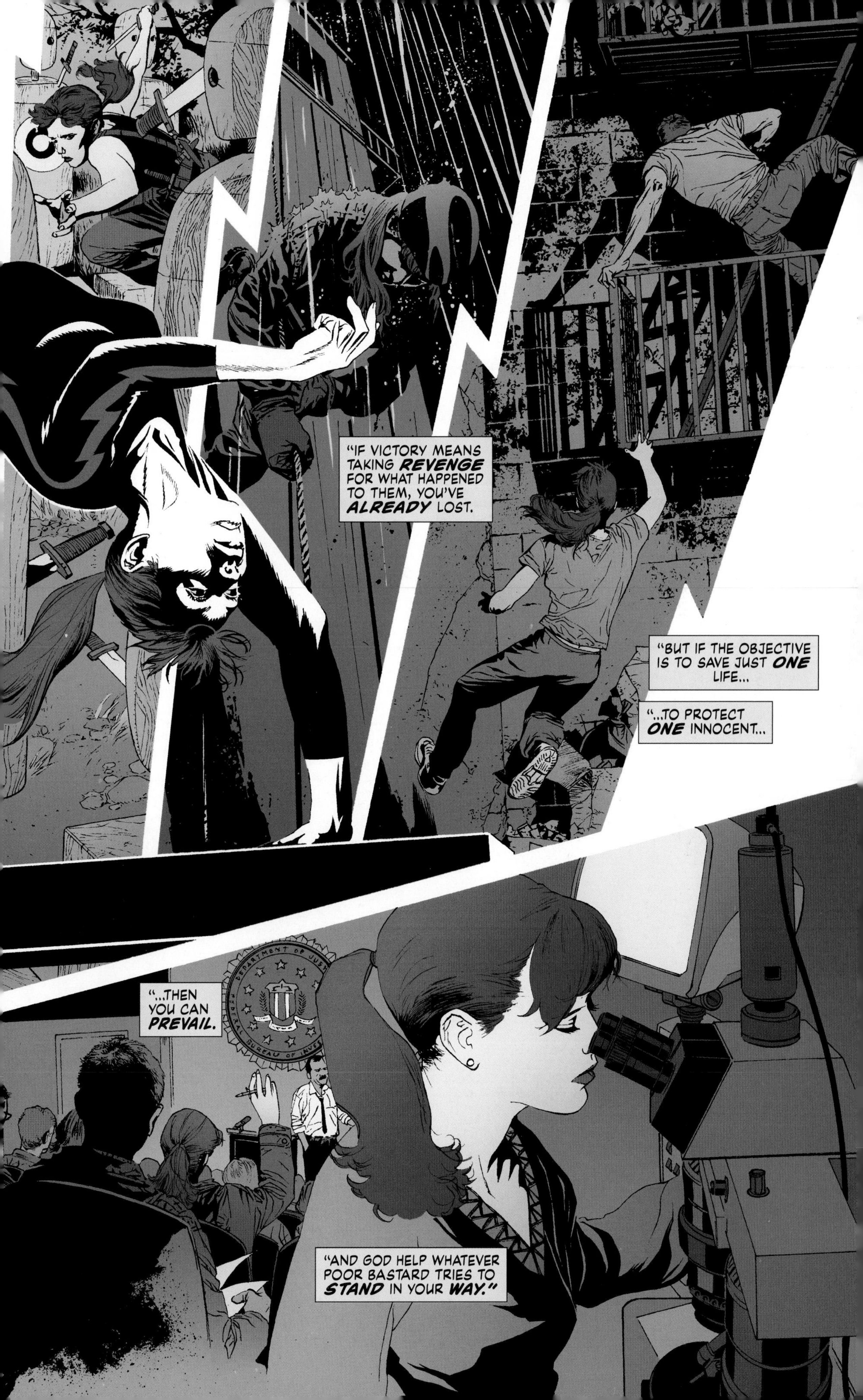
"IF VICTORY MEANS TAKING REVENGE FOR WHAT HAPPENED TO THEM, YOU'VE ALREADY LOST.
"BUT IF THE OBJECTIVE IS TO SAVE JUST ONE LIFE...
"...TO PROTECT ONE INNOCENT...
"...THEN YOU CAN PREVAIL.
"AND GOD HELP WHATEVER POOR BASTARD TRIES TO STAND IN YOUR WAY."

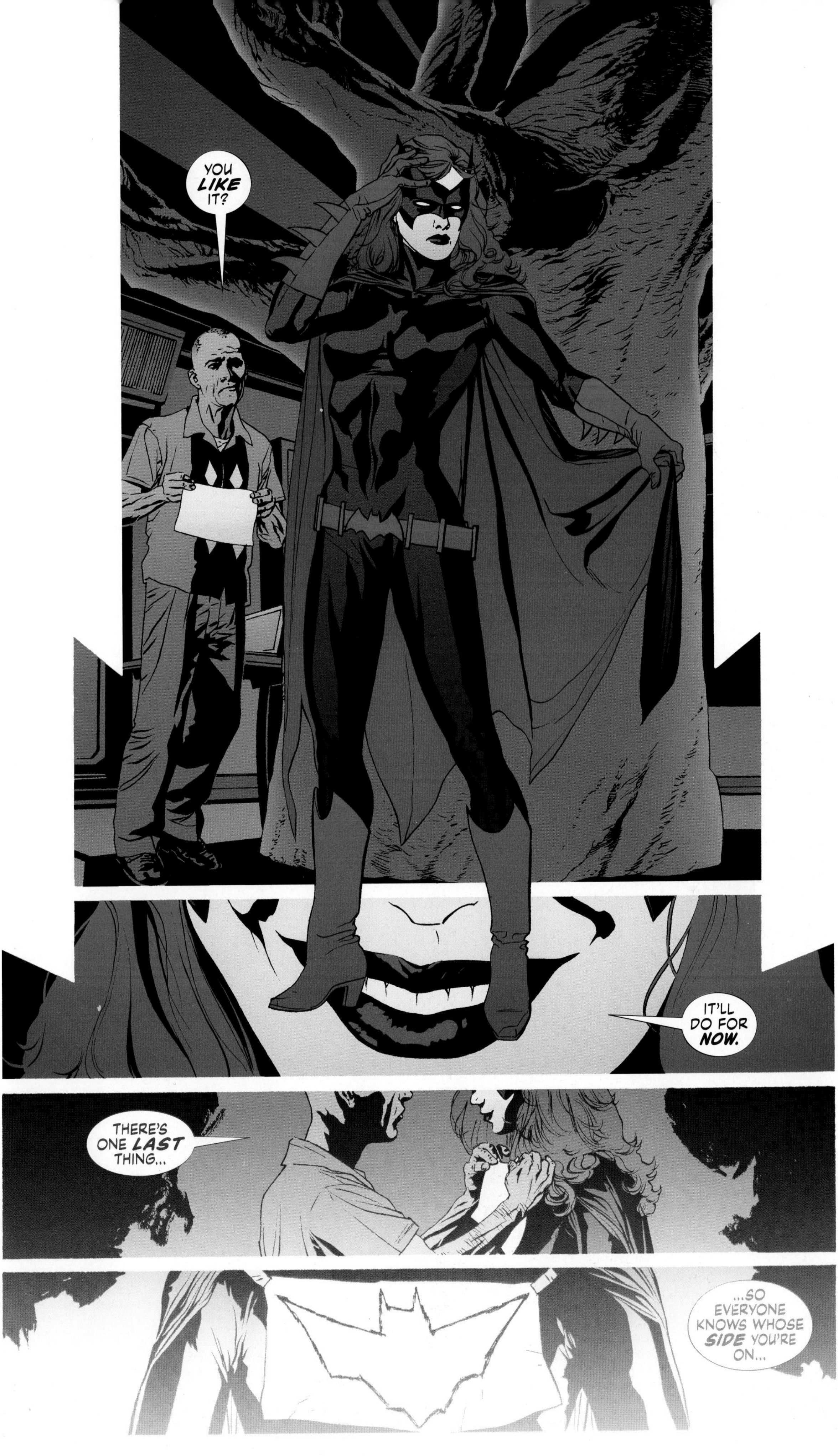
YOU LIKE IT?
IT'LL DO FOR NOW.
THERE'S ONE LAST THING...
...SO EVERYONE KNOWS WHOSE SIDE YOU'RE ON...

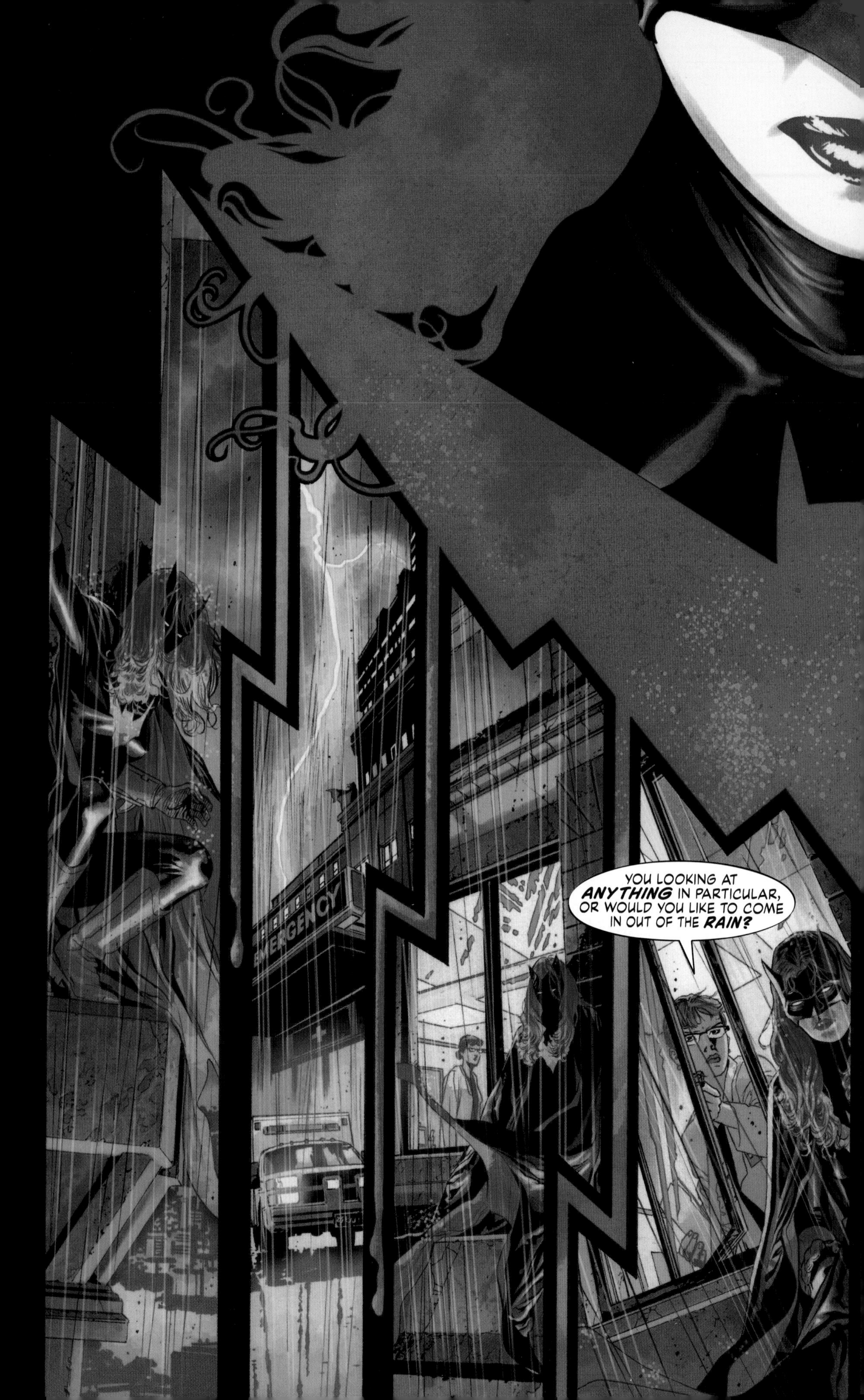
YOU LOOKING AT ANYTHING IN PARTICULAR, OR WOULD YOU LIKE TO COME IN OUT OF THE RAIN?
EMERGENCY

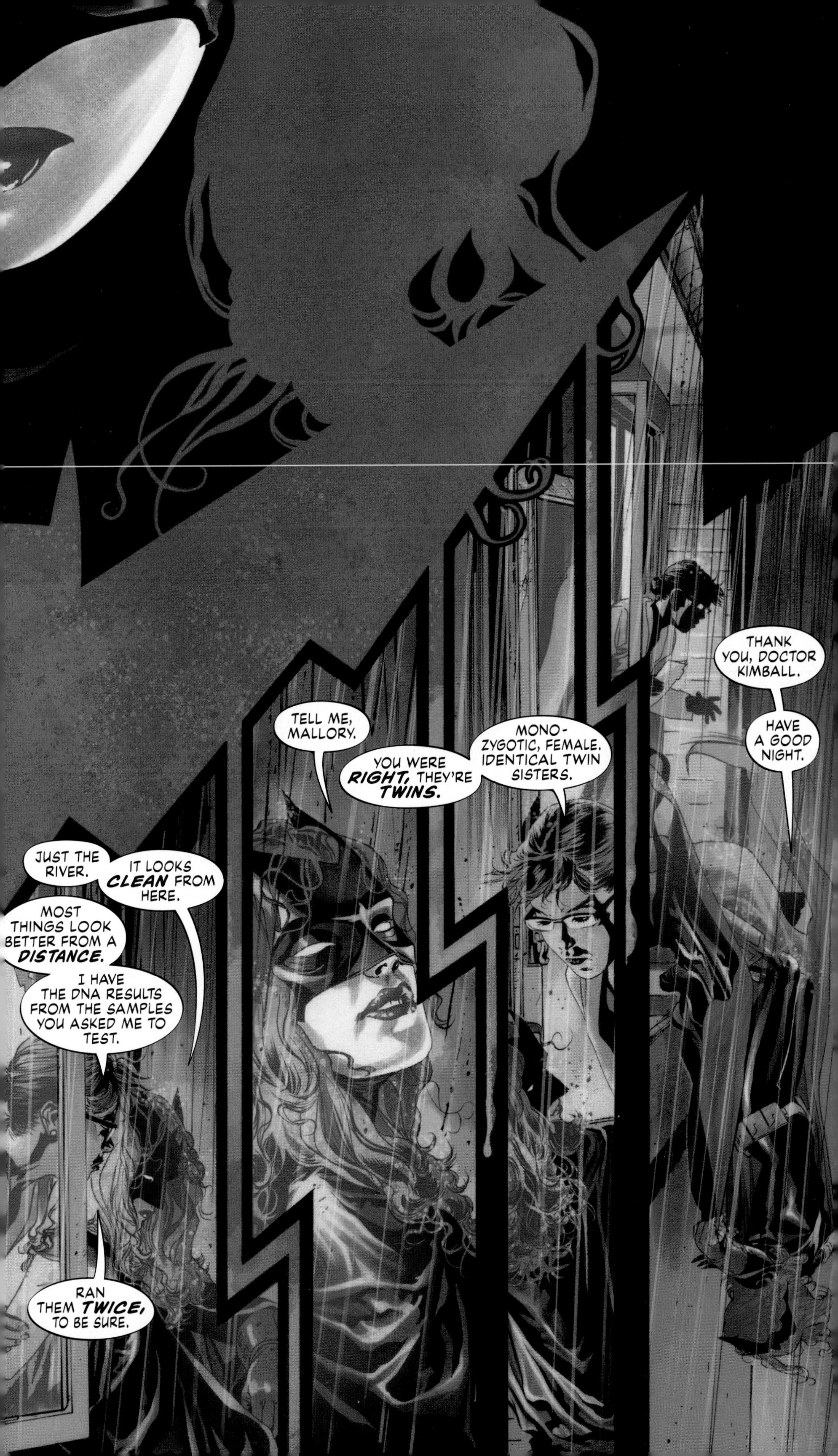
JUST THE RIVER.
IT LOOKS CLEAN FROM HERE.
MOST THINGS LOOK BETTER FROM A DISTANCE.
I HAVE THE DNA RESULTS FROM THE SAMPLES YOU ASKED ME TO TEST.
RAN THEM TWICE, TO BE SURE.
TELL ME, MALLORY.
YOU WERE RIGHT, THEY'RE TWINS.
MONO-ZYGOTIC, FEMALE. IDENTICAL TWIN SISTERS.
THANK YOU, DOCTOR KIMBALL.
HAVE A GOOD NIGHT.

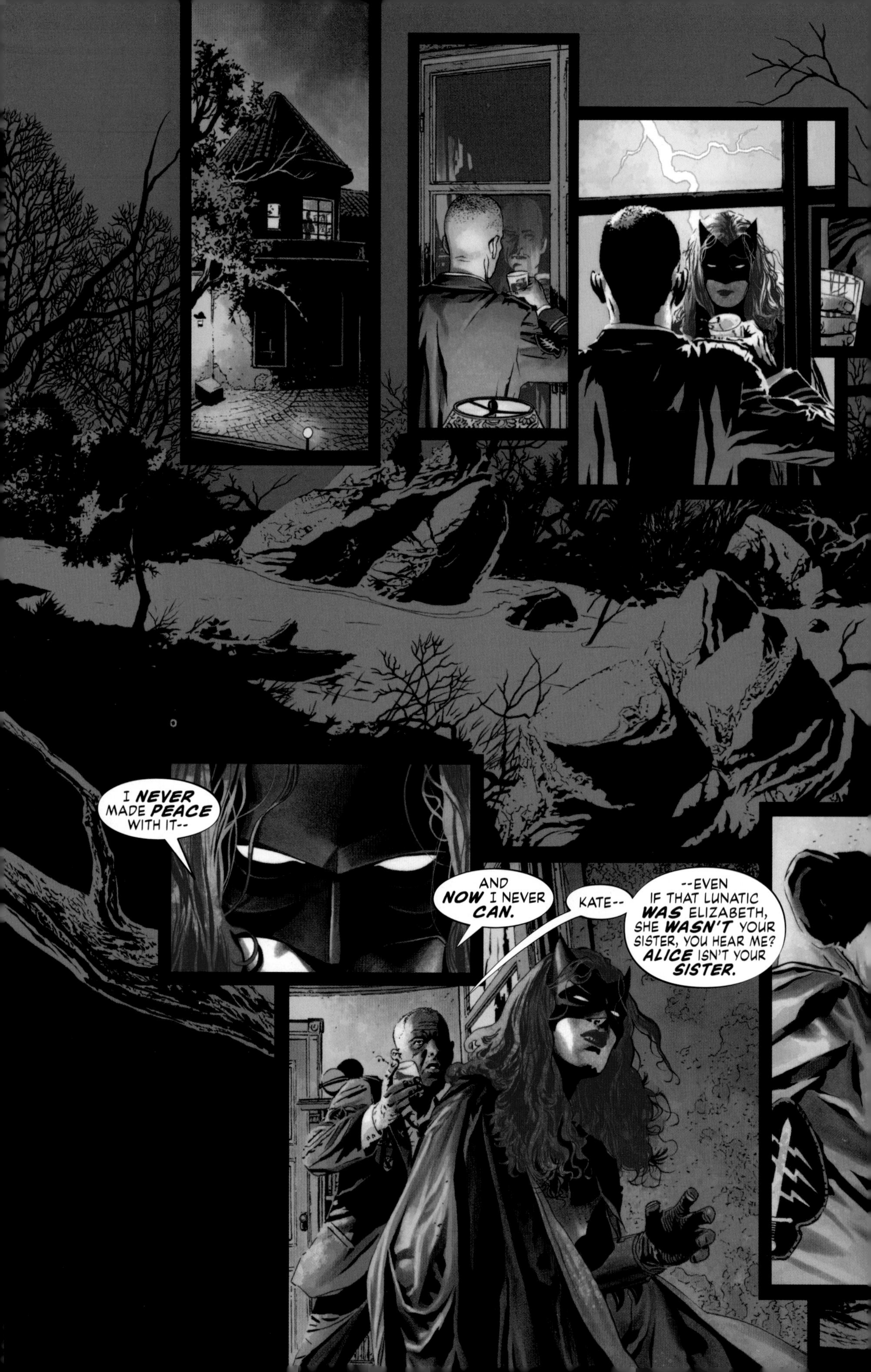
I NEVER MADE PEACE WITH IT--
AND NOW I NEVER CAN.
KATE--
--EVEN IF THAT LUNATIC WAS ELIZABETH, SHE WASN'T YOUR SISTER, YOU HEAR ME? ALICE ISN'T YOUR SISTER.

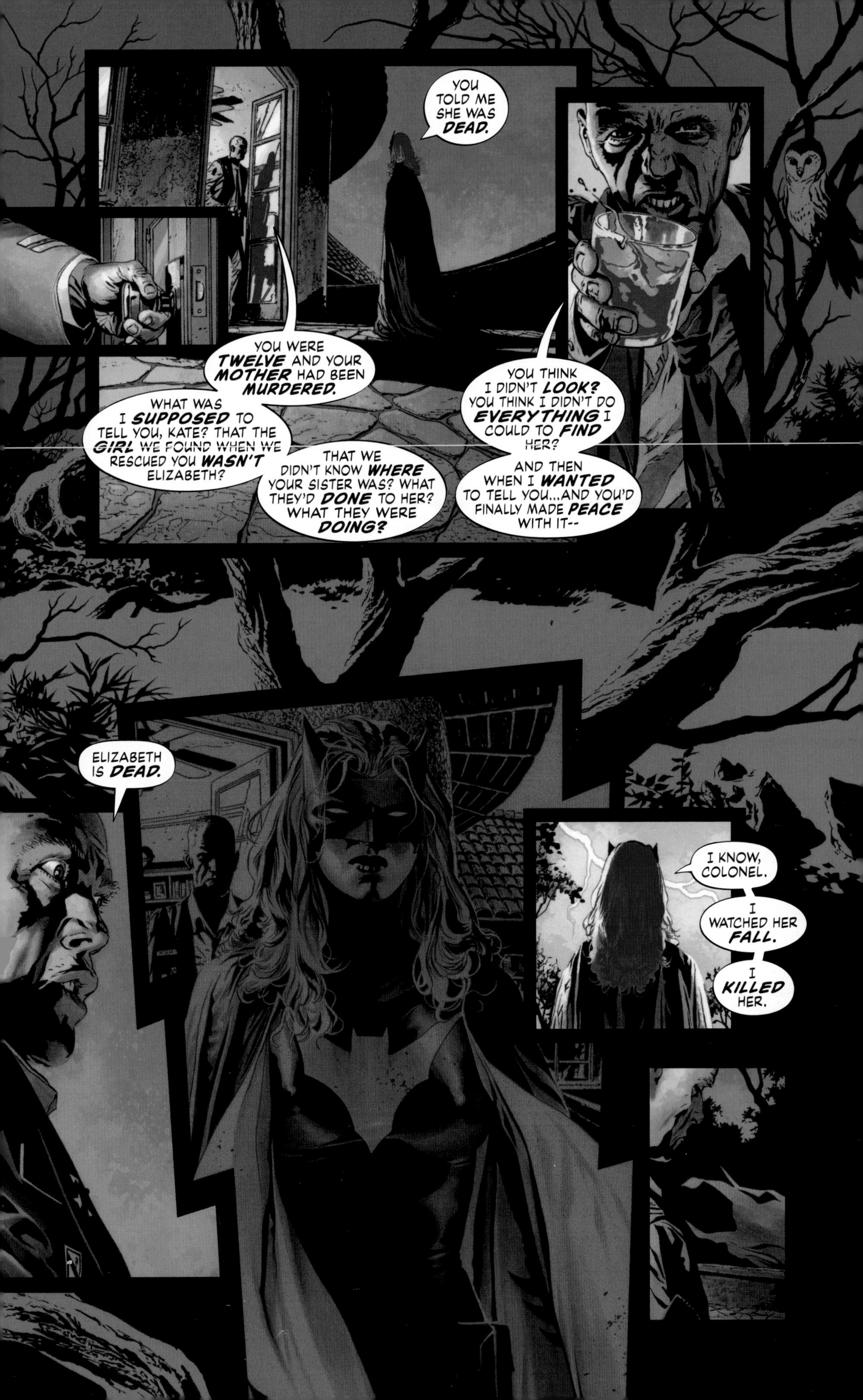
YOU TOLD ME SHE WAS DEAD.
YOU WERE TWELVE AND YOUR MOTHER HAD BEEN MURDERED.
WHAT WAS I SUPPOSED TO TELL YOU, KATE? THAT THE GIRL WE FOUND WHEN WE RESCUED YOU WASN'T ELIZABETH?
THAT WE DIDN'T KNOW WHERE YOUR SISTER WAS? WHAT THEY'D DONE TO HER? WHAT THEY WERE DOING?
YOU THINK I DIDN'T LOOK? YOU THINK I DIDN'T DO EVERYTHING I COULD TO FIND HER?
AND THEN WHEN I WANTED TO TELL YOU...AND YOU'D FINALLY MADE PEACE WITH IT--
ELIZABETH IS DEAD.
I KNOW, COLONEL.
I WATCHED HER FALL.
I KILLED HER.

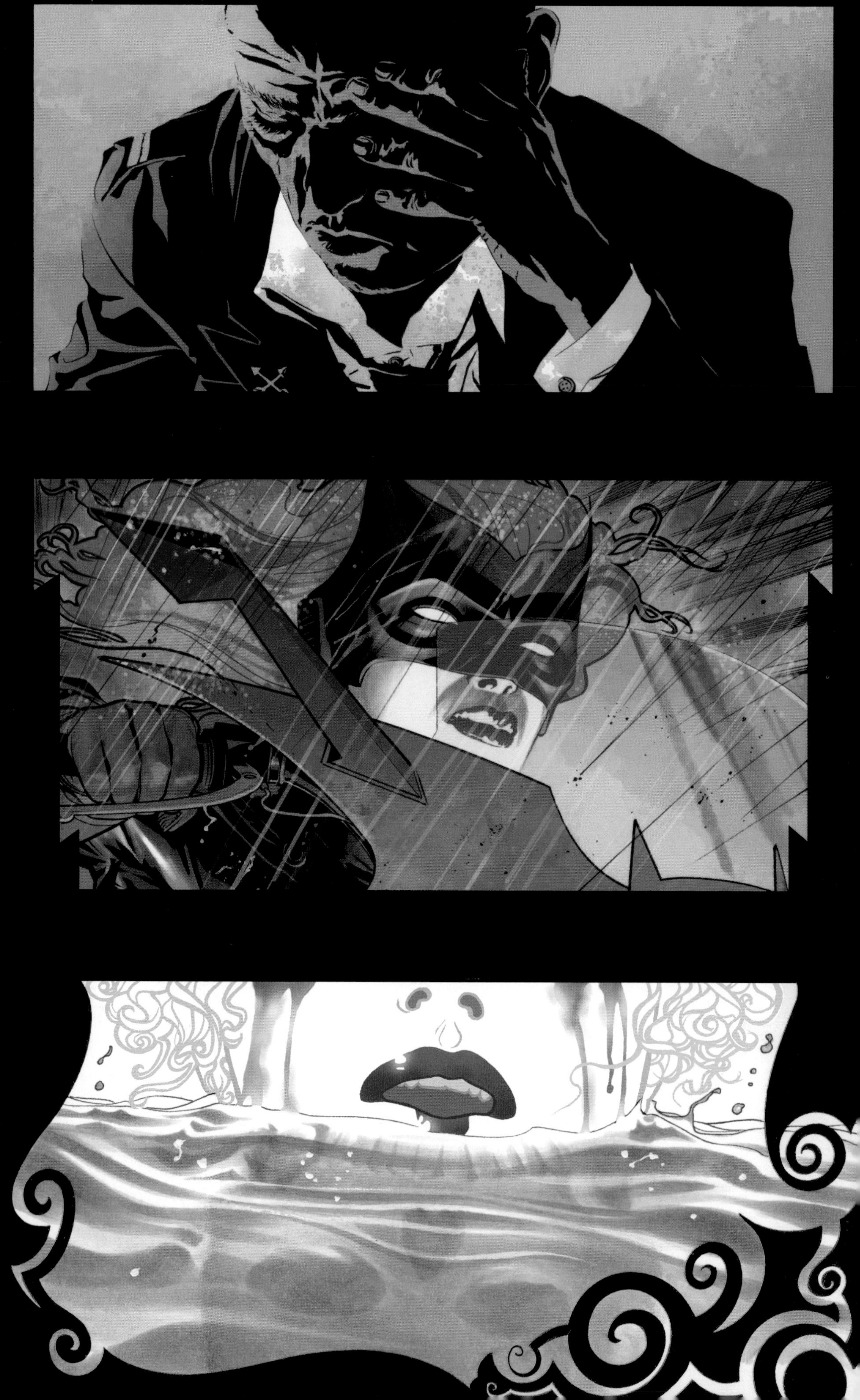

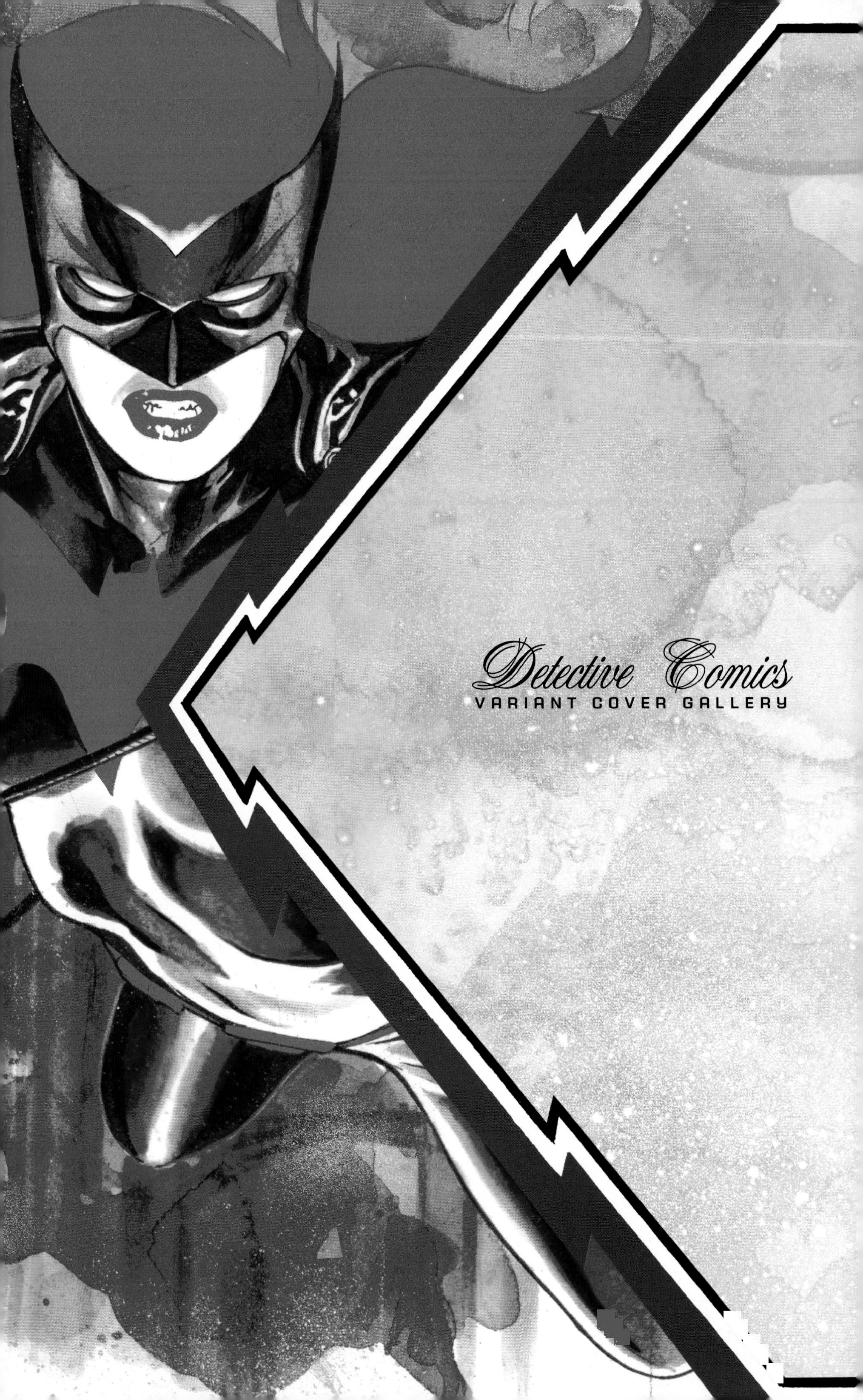

Detective Comics
VARIANT COVER GALLERY

DETECTIVE COMICS #854 VARIANT COVER BY J.G. JONES

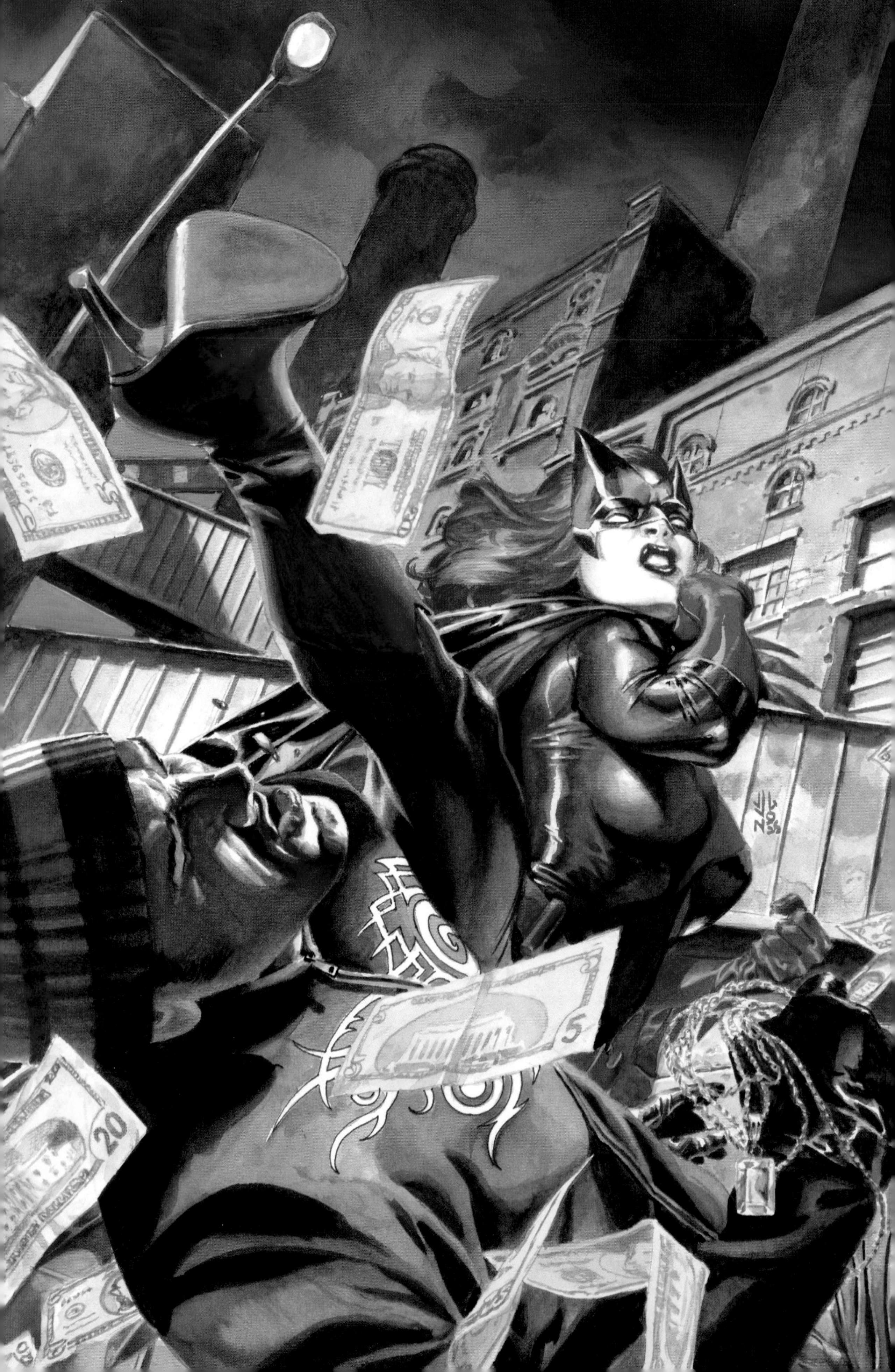

DETECTIVE COMICS #854 2ND PRINTING COVER BY J.H. WILLIAMS III

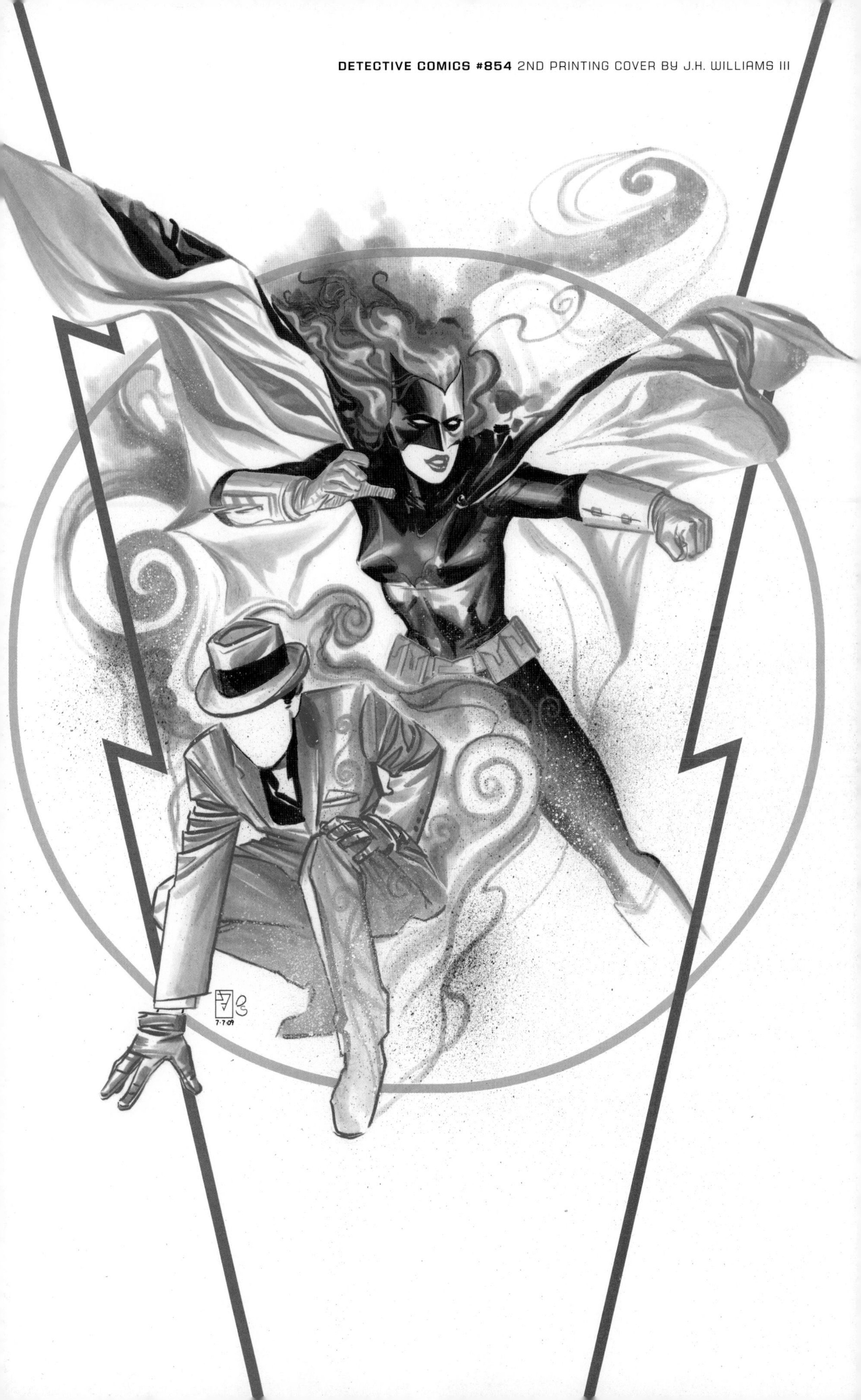

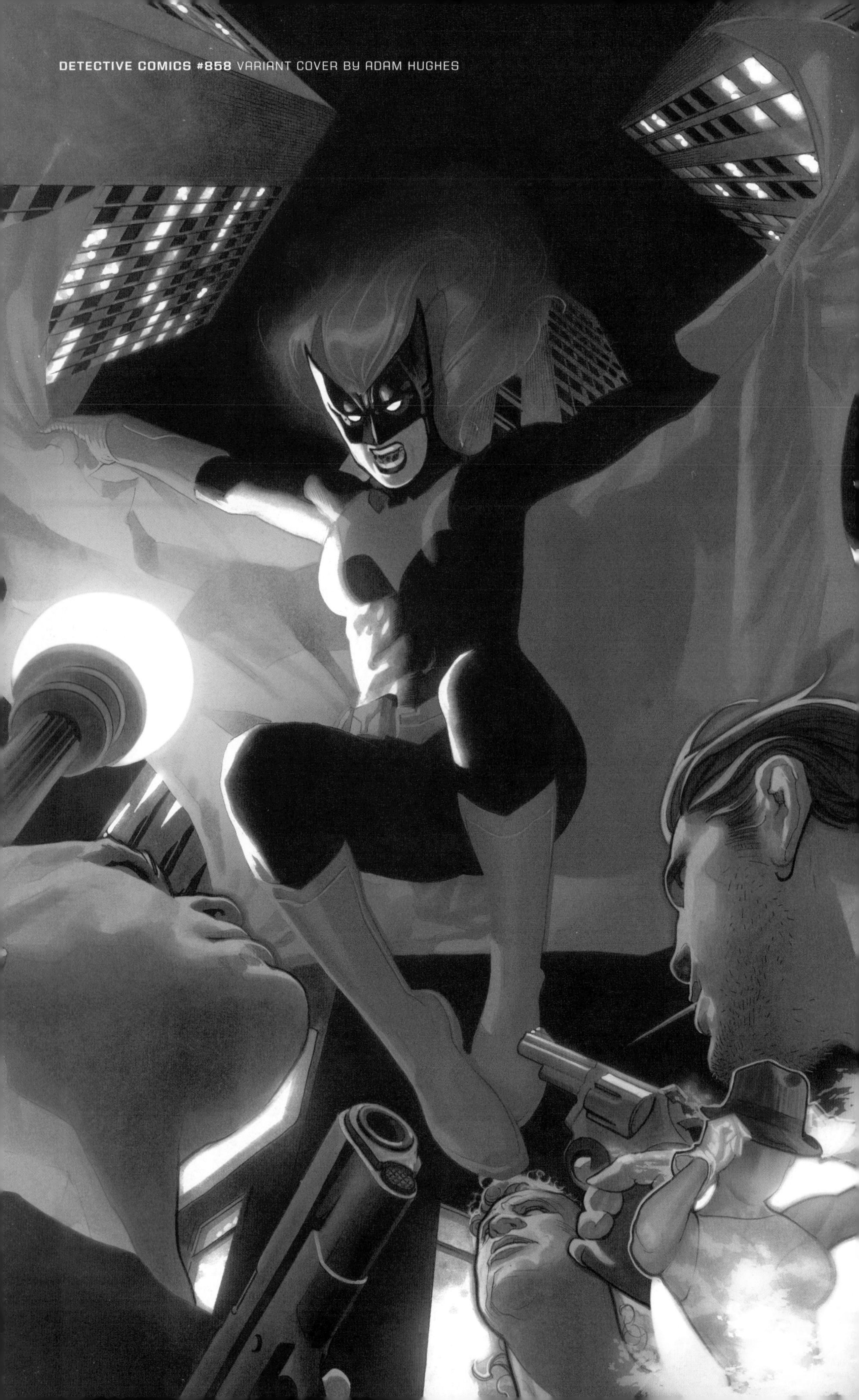
DETECTIVE COMICS #858 VARIANT COVER BY ADAM HUGHES

DETECTIVE COMICS #859 VARIANT COVER BY JOCK

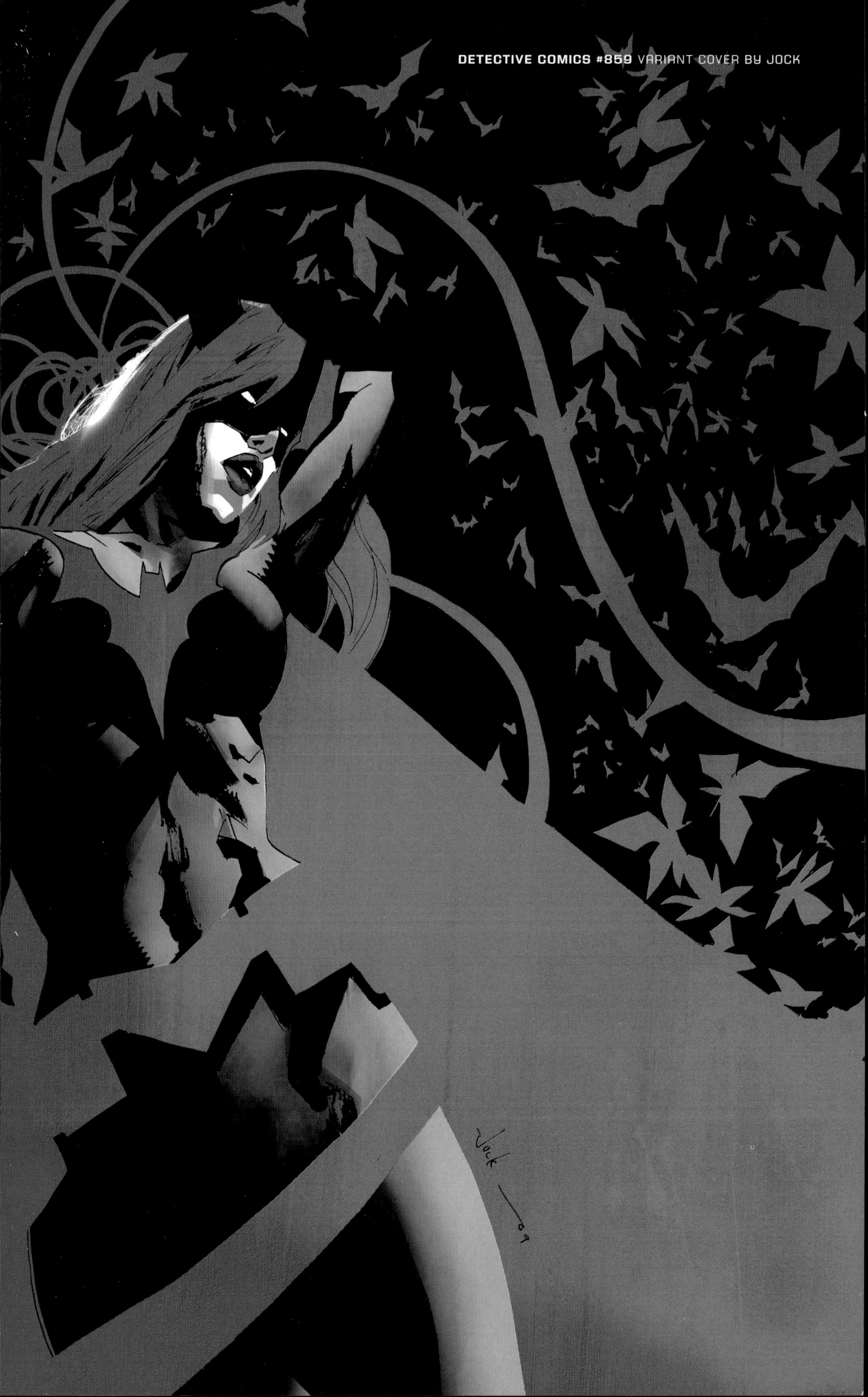
Jock

DETECTIVE COMICS #860 VARIANT COVER BY ALEX ROSS

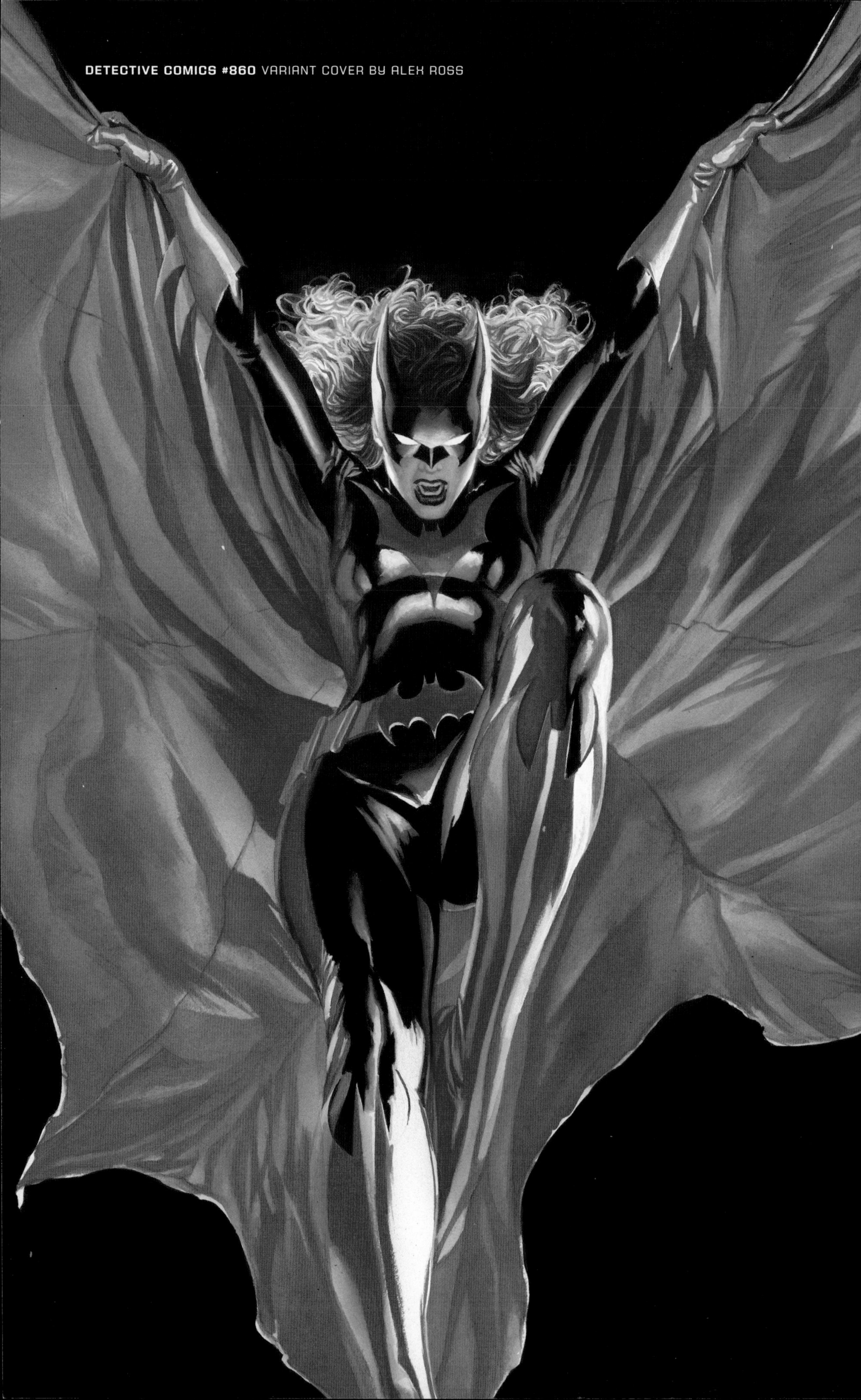

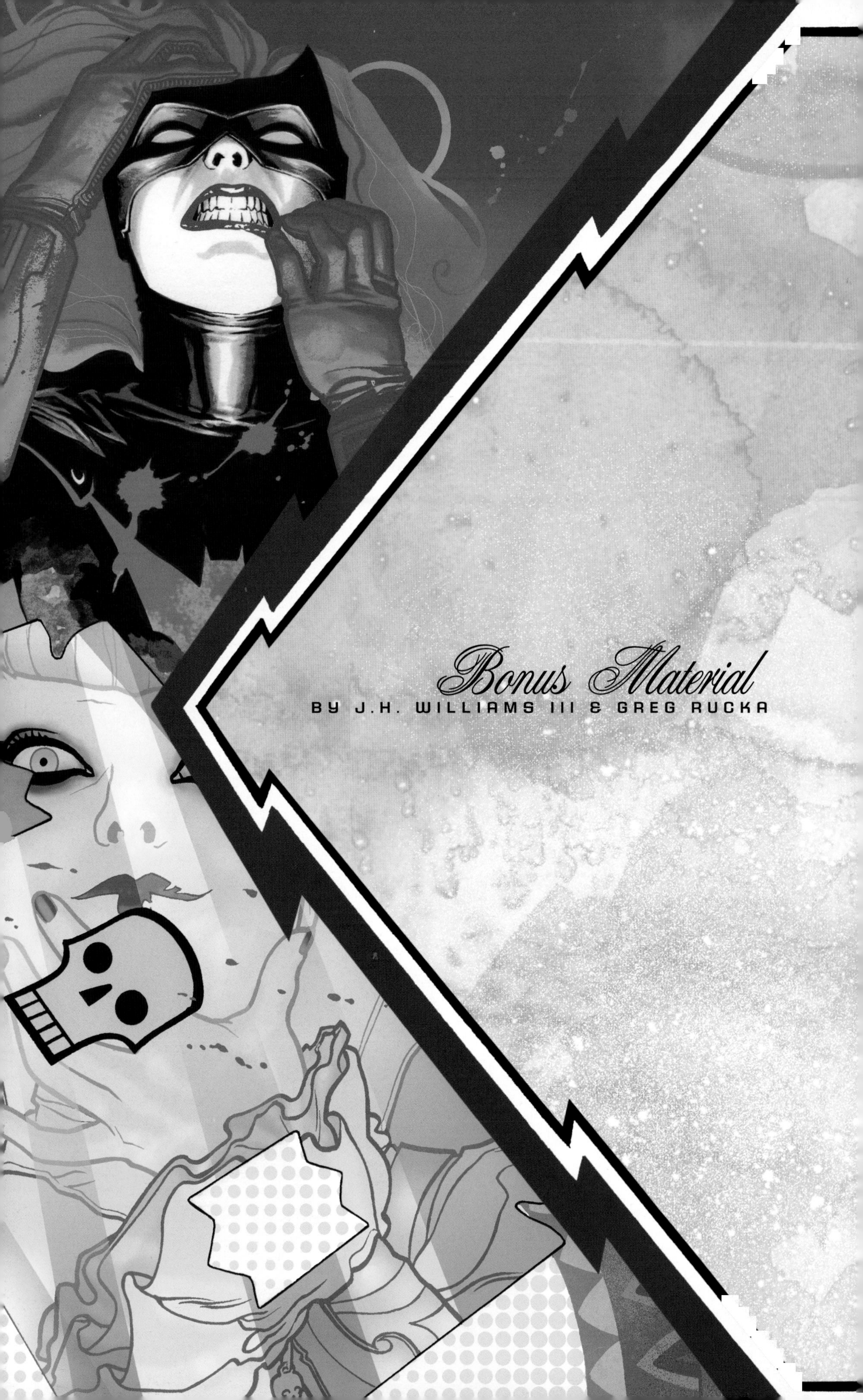

Bonus Material

BY J.H. WILLIAMS III & GREG RUCKA

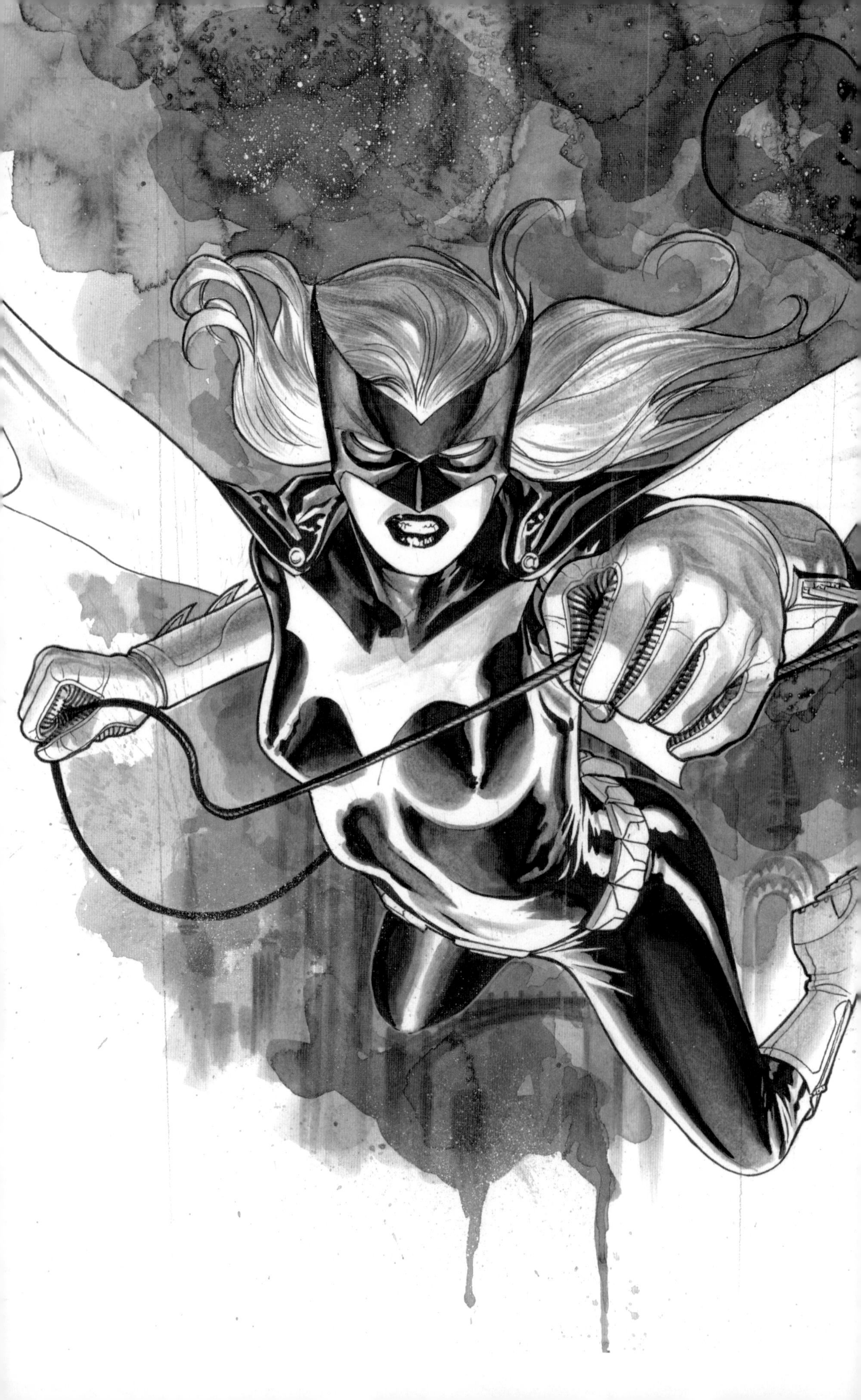

BATWOMAN - CHARACTER SHEET - ROUGHS
THESE CHANGES TO CURRENT COSTUME KEEP THE SAME BASIC LOOK BUT ADD
MORE SENSIBILITY AND FUNCTIONALITY

HAIR WILL BE A DETACHABLE WIG

CAPE FASTENS IN THE
FRONT TO LOWER SHOULDER-
UPPER CHEST AREA

MORE
HEAVY ARMORED
ARM BRACERS THAT
ARE SEPARATE
FROM GLOVES -
GLOVES TUCK
UNDER BRACER AT
WRIST -

BELT IS FASTENED
AND NO LONGER
LOOSE - FITS
TIGHTLY

CAPE IS MUCH
LONGER - DRACULA-
ESQUE

NOTE - THE CAPE
ONLY COMES TO
FIVE POINTS
FORMING A VERY
CLEARLY STYLIZED
GIANT RED BAT
DESIGN WHEN
COMPLETELY
UNFURLED

BOOTS ARE NOW
MORE REALISTIC
TO PURPOSE - NOTE
ON ADDITIONAL
DRAWING THEY ZIP
UP ON THE SIDE

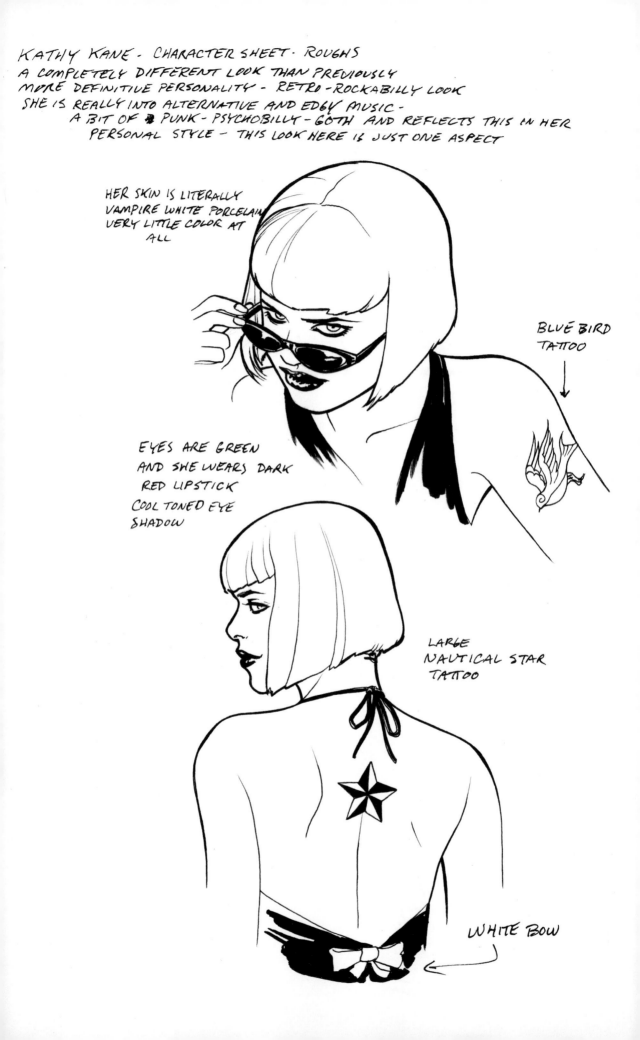

KATHY KANE · CHARACTER SHEET · ROUGHS
A COMPLETELY DIFFERENT LOOK THAN PREVIOUSLY
MORE DEFINITIVE PERSONALITY - RETRO-ROCKABILLY LOOK
SHE IS REALLY INTO ALTERNATIVE AND EDGY MUSIC -
    A BIT OF PUNK-PSYCHOBILLY-GOTH AND REFLECTS THIS IN HER
    PERSONAL STYLE - THIS LOOK HERE IS JUST ONE ASPECT

HER SKIN IS LITERALLY
VAMPIRE WHITE PORCELAIN
VERY LITTLE COLOR AT
ALL

BLUE BIRD
TATTOO

EYES ARE GREEN
AND SHE WEARS DARK
RED LIPSTICK
COOL TONED EYE
SHADOW

LARGE
NAUTICAL STAR
TATTOO

WHITE BOW

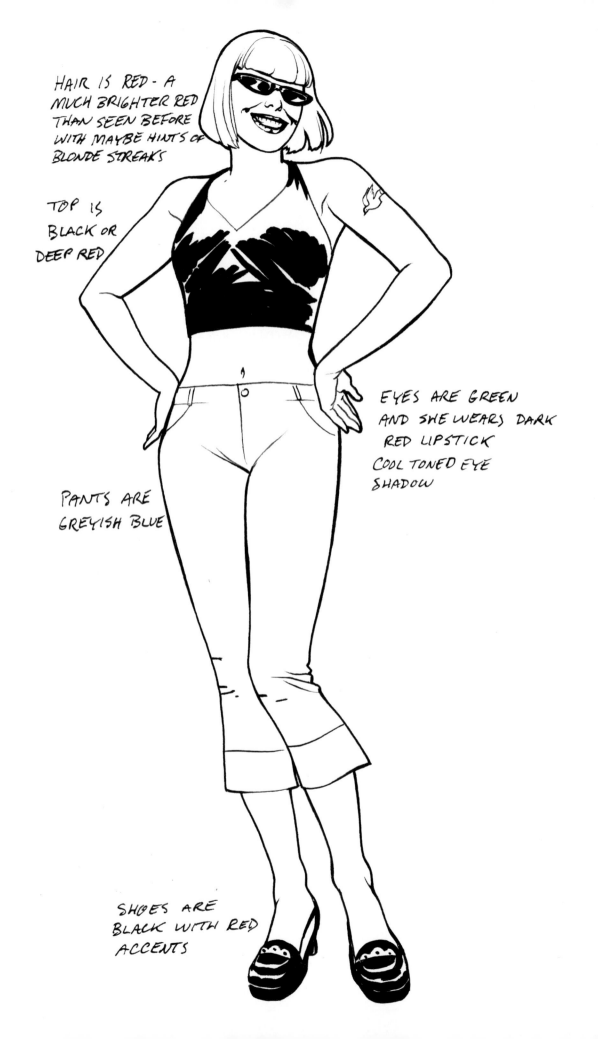

HAIR IS RED - A
MUCH BRIGHTER RED
THAN SEEN BEFORE
WITH MAYBE HINTS OF
BLONDE STREAKS

TOP IS
BLACK OR
DEEP RED

EYES ARE GREEN
AND SHE WEARS DARK
RED LIPSTICK
COOL TONED EYE
SHADOW

PANTS ARE
GREYISH BLUE

SHOES ARE
BLACK WITH RED
ACCENTS

Jim – This is the mirror spread.

ONE:

Full body shot, BATWOMAN. Iconic. More an art element, as discussed, than an actual storytelling panel. This is the mirror to Panel Eight.

NO COPY.

TWO:

Interior of the MAIN COMPARTMENT, as BATWOMAN enters.

ALICE is standing at the PUMP CONTROLS, and she's livid. The fucking thing's broken! This isn't fair! Nothing's fair!! Maybe she's holding one of the BROKEN WHEELS in one hand.

In her OTHER HAND, she's holding a PISTOL, pointed at BATWOMAN.

1 BATWOMAN:	You're done, High Madame.
2 BATWOMAN:	I **disabled** the pump, you're not killing **anyone** today.

3 ALICE:	I ca'n't **stand** this any **longer**!

THREE:

BATWOMAN shielding herself with her CAPE – covering her head with it – as ALICE empties the GUN at her. The BARRAGE of shots is knocking BATWOMAN to a knee.

ALICE is screaming at BATWOMAN as she fires.

4 ALICE:	And as for you!
5 ALICE:	As for you, I'll shake you into a kitten, that I will!!!

6 SFX:	BLAMMBLAMMBLAMMBLAMMBLAMMBLAMMklk
klkklk	

FOUR:

BATWOMAN, on one knee, lowering the CAPE to look.

ALICE has dropped the gun, already going out the ROOF HATCH. Maybe just her legs visible as she climbs out.

7 BATWOMAN:	Dammit, **stop**!

[continued]

FIVE:
Exterior of the plane, ALICE is pulling herself along the wing on hands and knees to reach one of the CANISTERS, determined to succeed. The WIND whips her hair and clothes violently.

BATWOMAN is just emerging from the HATCH behind her, shouting at her. Her GRAPPLING GUN is in her hand.

8 BATWOMAN: It's **over**, Alice!

SIX:
BATWOMAN fires the GRAPPLING GUN, the line catching ALICE around one ANKLE.

ALICE has grabbed the CANNISTER RIG with one hand, holding on to it, and with the other is pointing her REMAINING PISTOL back at BATWOMAN.

She's crying uncontrollably. She doesn't want to lose. She can't lose. If she loses, who is she?

9 SFX: paff

10 ALICE: The **face** is what one **goes** by, generally.

SEVEN:
ALICE SHOOTS, hitting the GRAPPLING GUN in BATWOMAN'S HAND

BATWOMAN is losing the GRAPPLING GUN, obviously.

11 SFX: BLAMMM

12 BATWOMAN: ahg!

13 ALICE: Who am **I**, then?

EIGHT:
Full body shot, ALICE, iconic, the mirror image of Panel One.

NO COPY.

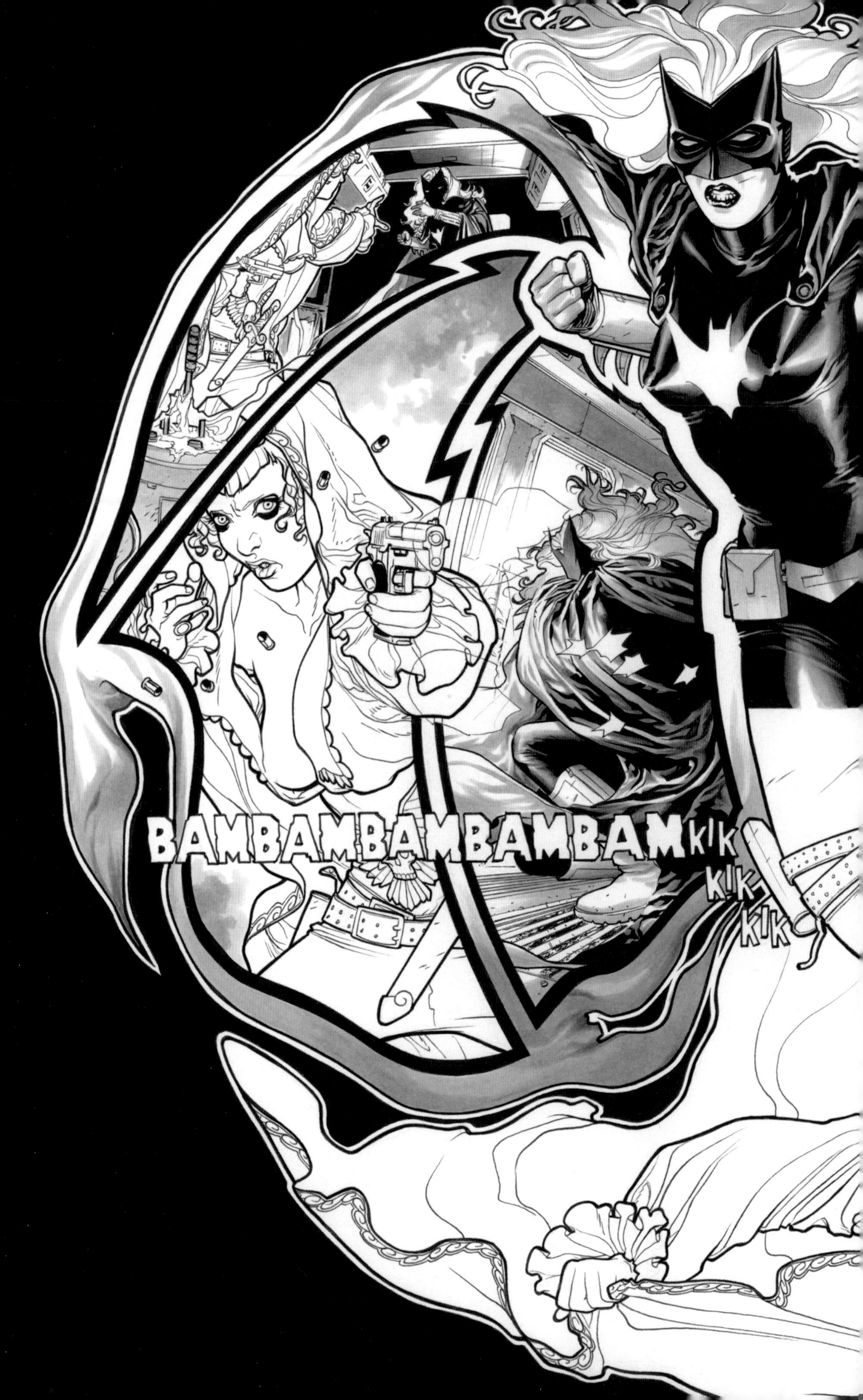
BAMBAMBAMBAMBAM
KIK
KIK
KIK

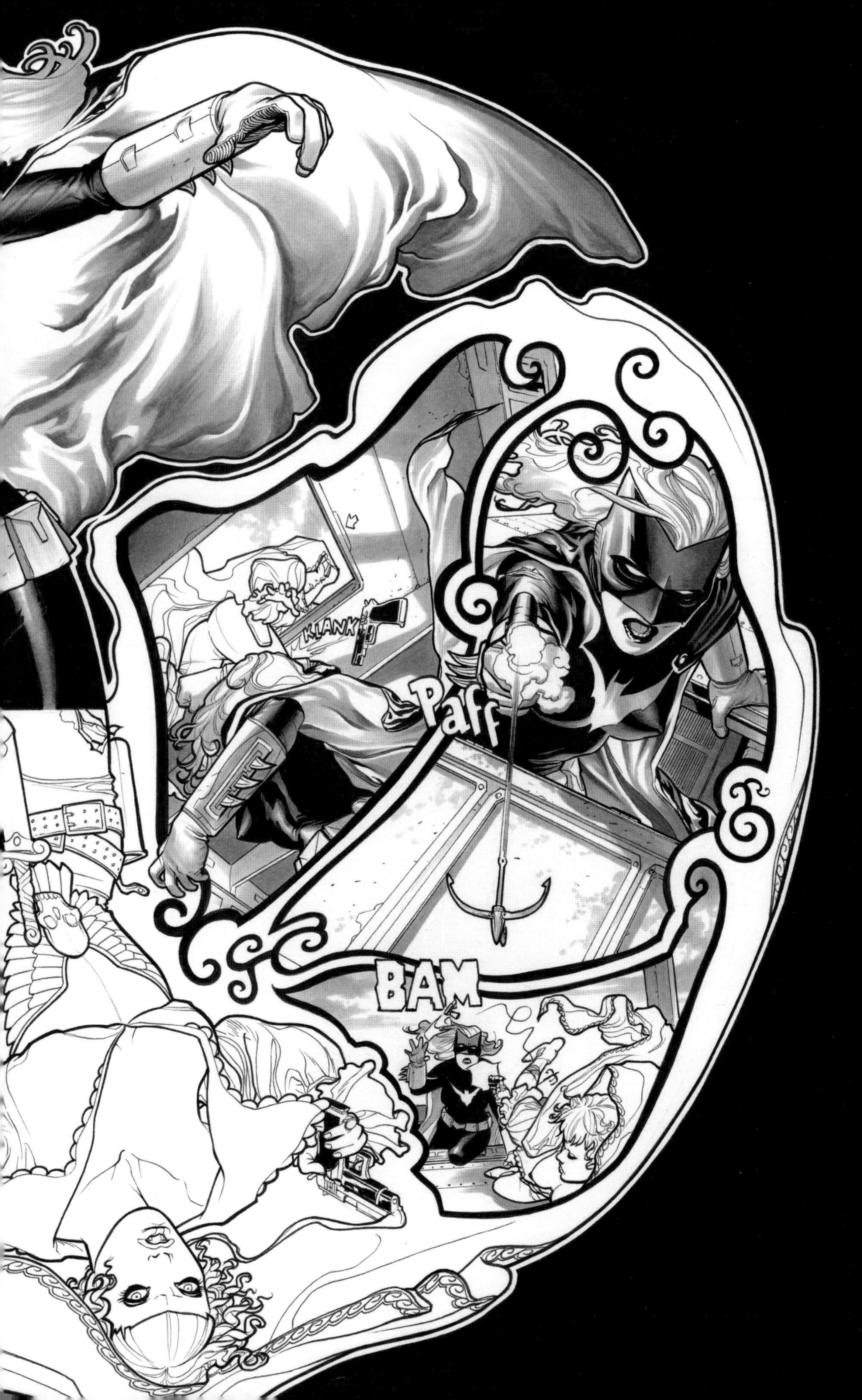
KLANK
Paff
BAM

These two pages reveal the original script by Greg Rucka for DETECTIVE COMICS #859, pages 8 & 9 – followed by the original black and white art for the pages by J.H. Williams III, without coloring or lettering.

ONE:

Wash in on the SYMBOL of the Kane Heresy, the Dark Faith's circle emblem, with a CHALICE on its side, spilling WINE or BLOOD.

We *may* be able to see the top of ABBOT'S HEAD in this panel.

For the record, the Heresy is based in the ruins of pre-No Man's Land Gotham, in what was once a small church before the earthquake. The location serves as a combination place of worship, as well as a dormitory/home for those members of the Heresy unable to control their change, ie, those Monster Men who can't, for whatever reason, revert their forms to "human."

They try to keep it nice, here, but let's face it – it's an old church that was damaged in an earthquake and is buried under ground. How nice can that be? Thing to remember is that Alice's Dark Faith has bucks; Abbot's has nada.

1 ABBOT:	My story. Listen, because it is yours, too.
2 ABBOVE:	The prophesy is told in The Blasphemies, in the Book of Lilith.
3 ABBOT:	That on the eighteenth day past the feast of All Saints…

TWO:

Angle, past Doctor MALLORY KIMBALL, as she enters her office at St. Luke's Hospital, in Gotham.

MALLORY has stopped short, reacting to BATWOMAN standing in her office.

Jim, I'd like to play this differently than in a Batman title, if that makes sense – in a Batman book, Mallory would enter the office, and then we'd see Batman come out of the shadows behind her or something like that. I don't want to do that here with Kate; it's against her character, and frankly we've seen it a million times before.

With that in mind, yes, Batwoman has been waiting for Mallory, but she's not trying to scare her or ninja-tactics her. Not sure where this should put her in the room, or what pose she should be in, but she's been waiting.

BATWOMAN still has the injuries she was carrying last issue – the conceit is that all of the "present" stuff is taking place the same night, which is also the same night as the events of issues 3 and 4.

This means BATWOMAN may still be bleeding from one or two of her various wounds – that stab wound that Alice gave her in the arm is particularly nasty.

4 BATWOMAN:	Doctor Kimball.
5 BATWOMAN:	I need a **favor**.

THREE:

Back to ABBOT, panning down a bit, maybe swinging around to look at him, as if he's speaking directly to us. He's wearing his human form.

6 ABBOT:	…the Apostle of the First would come to Gotham…
7 ABBOT:	…and there he would murder the "Twice-Named Daughter of Cain."

FOUR:
BATWOMAN is holding out the TWO SAMPLE TUBES from last issue, offering them to MAL-LORY. BATWOMAN is doing this with her wounded arm.

MALLORY is reacting to the sight of the STAB WOUND on Batwoman.

8 BATWOMAN:	I need a DNA test run on these samples.
9 BATWOMAN:	I need to confirm they're from **monozygotic** twins.
10 MALLORY:	You're **wounded**.
11 BATWOMAN:	Will you do this for me?

FIVE:
On ABBOT. He's beginning to transform into his WOLFMAN form.

12 ABBOT:	So many times, the High Madame poured these words in my ear.
13 ABBOT:	So many times, it had to be the **truth**.

SIX:
MALLORY has taken the samples in one hand, already setting them aside. With her other hand, she's taken BATWOMAN'S wounded arm by the WRIST. Mallory is clearly concerned about the wound.

BATWOMAN is still in the same place she was last issue, and she's barely feeling the injury, now. Focused entirely on Mallory – the injury doesn't matter, what matters is the DNA test, that's the only thing she cares about right now.

14 MALLORY:	You've been **stabbed**—
15 BATWOMAN:	Doctor Kimball. Mallory. Will you test them for me?
16 MALLORY:	I can have the results by tomorrow night. Now take off your gauntlet, let me take a look at—

SEVEN:
On ABBOT, and he's fully transformed now. Growling out his words.

17 ABBOT:	It rrrr had to be grrr **truth**.

EIGHT:
MALLORY reacting.

BATWOMAN has pulled her hand back, already turning, heading to the window. Business here is done, time to go.

18 BATWOMAN:	I'll be back tomorrow night.

NINE:
Tight on ABBOT, his WEREWOLF EYES.

19 ABBOT:	It rrrr **wasn't**.

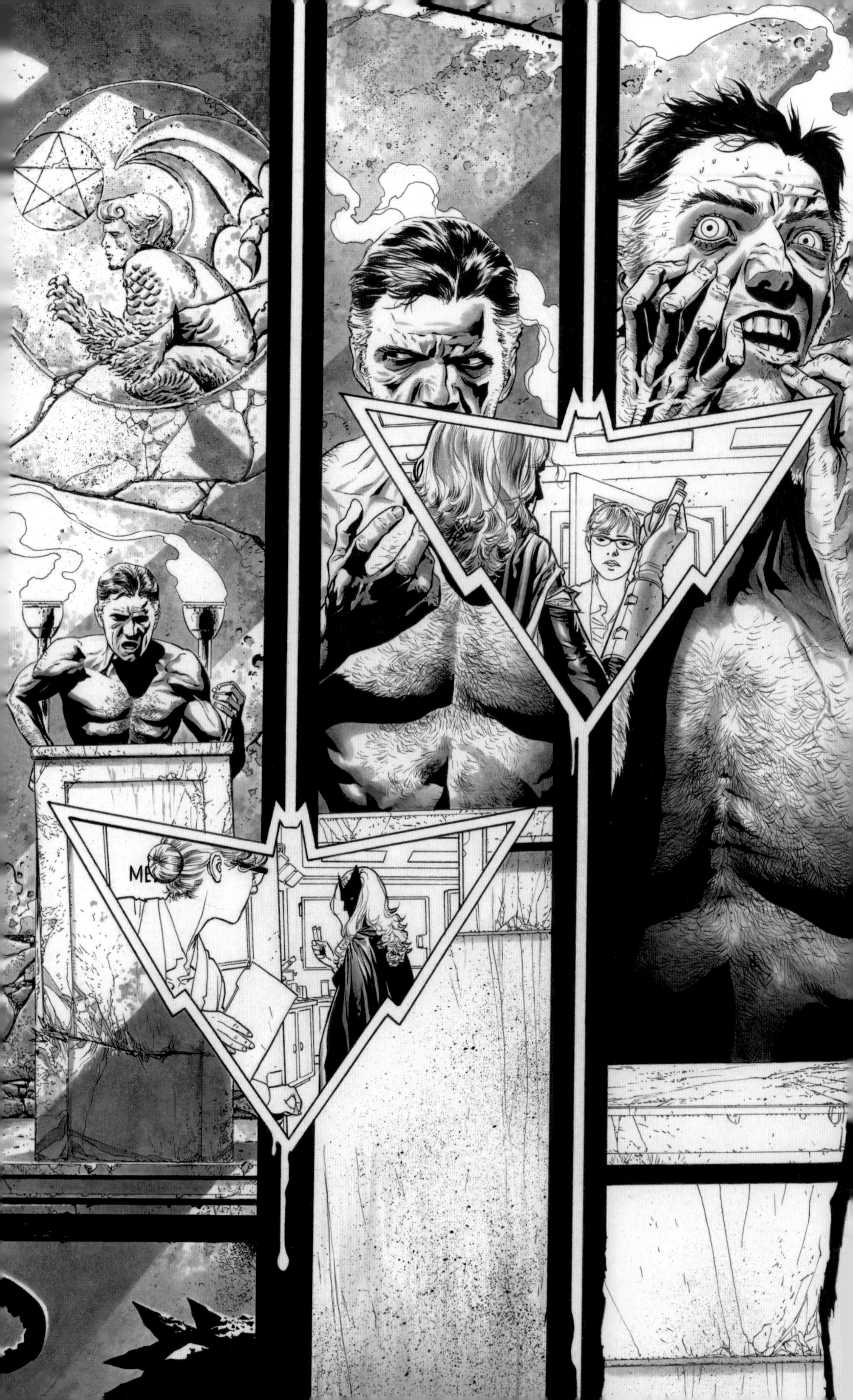

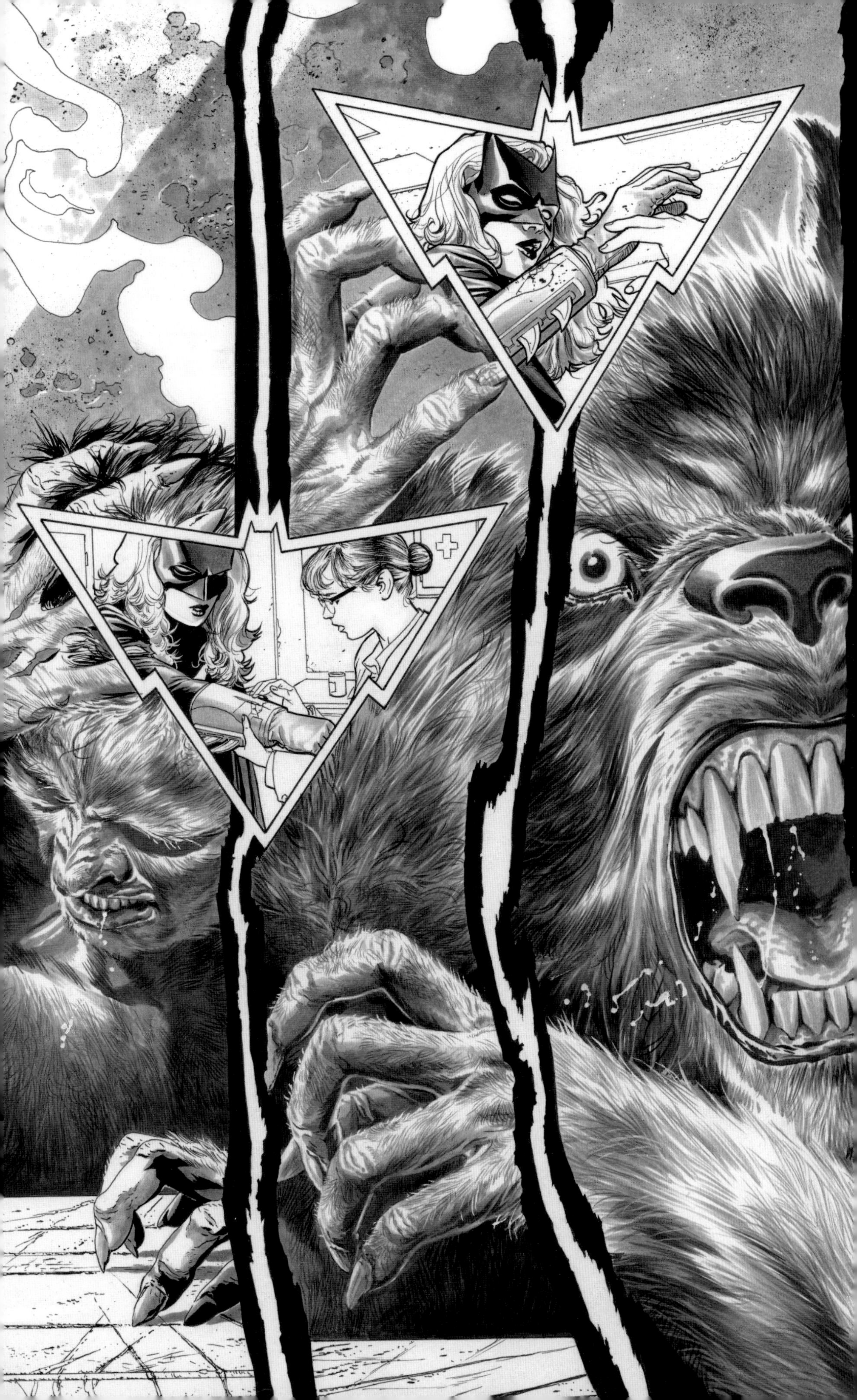

GREG **RUCKA**

is a thriller novelist who became one of the premier writers for
DC Comics in the last decade. His work on BATMAN brought fresh attention
to the character and the inhabitants of Gotham City. Additionally, he won the
Eisner award for best story with GOTHAM CENTRAL's "Half a Life." His other DC credits
include ADVENTURES OF SUPERMAN, CHECKMATE, DETECTIVE COMICS, WONDER WOMAN,
ACTION COMICS and 52. Rucka is married to fellow writer Jen Van Meter and they make
their home in Portland, Oregon.

J.H. **WILLIAMS III**

entered the comics field in 1991 and immediately began getting attention for his finely crafted
work on such titles as BATMAN, STARMAN and his co-creation (with D. Curtis Johnson), CHASE.
His acclaimed artistry was later seen on SON OF SUPERMAN, SEVEN SOLIDERS OF VICTORY and
JONAH HEX, and he has received multiple Eisner nominations for his work on co-creations
DESOLATION JONES (with Warren Ellis), and PROMETHEA (with Alan Moore).
Williams and his wife, Wendy, live in California.

DAVE **STEWART**

began his career as an intern at Dark Horse Comics, and then quickly moved into
coloring comics. His impressive credits include DC: THE NEW FRONTIER, HUMAN TARGET,
SUPERMAN/BATMAN, CATWOMAN: WHEN IN ROME, *Captain America*, *Daredevil*,
Joss Whedon's *Fray*, Mike Mignola's *Hellboy: The Third Wish* and *B.P.R.D.*, Gerard Way's
The Umbrella Academy, and Michael Chabon's *The Amazing Adventures of The Escapist*.
He has won several Eisner Awards for his coloring work, and also colored
Tim Sale's art from the TV series *Heroes*.